GIRLS GROWING UP
ON THE
AUTISM SPECTRUM

What Parents and Professionals Should Know
About the Pre-Teen and Teenage Years

SHANA NICHOLS WITH GINA MARIE MORAVCIK
AND SAMARA PULVER TETENBAUM

Foreword by Liane Holliday Willey, EdD

Jessica Kingsley Publishers
London and Philadelphia

Cover art by Carly Hatton, an award-winning child artist with autism. Carly lives in Ontario, Canada. Carly's whimsical, humorous art is in private collections in Canada, England, Denmark, Israel and the USA. www.CarlysArt.com.

First published in 2009
by Jessica Kingsley Publishers
116 Pentonville Road
London N1 9JB, UK
and
400 Market Street, Suite 400
Philadelphia, PA 19106, USA

www.jkp.com

Library of Congress Cataloging in Publication Data
Nichols, Shana.
Girls growing up on the autism spectrum : what parents and professionals should know about the pre-teen and teenage years /
Shana Nichols, Gina Marie Moravcik, Samara Pulver Tetenbaum.
p. cm.
ISBN 978-1-84310-855-9 (pb : alk. paper)
1. Autism in children. 2. Autism in adolescence. 3. Girls–Mental health.
I. Moravcik, Gina Marie. II. Tetenbaum, Samara Pulver. III. Title.
RJ506.A9.N53 2009
618.92'85882–dc22
2008021126

British Library Cataloguing in Publication Data
A CIP catalogue record for this book is available from the British Library

ISBN 978 1 84310 855 9

Printed and bound in the United States by
Thomson-Shore, 7300 Joy Road, Dexter, MI 48130

To all the girls,
and all the women,
To those who love,
and support them.
Let us see the future,
through your eyes.
It is here
to embrace.

GIRLS GROWING UP
ON THE
AUTISM
SPECTRUM

of related interest

Making Sense of Sex
A Forthright Guide to Puberty, Sex and Relationships
for People with Asperger's Syndrome
Sarah Attwood
Illustrated by Jonathon Powell
ISBN 978 1 84310 374 5

Guiding Your Teenager with Special Needs through
the Transition from School to Adult Life
Tools for Parents
Mary Korpi
ISBN 978 1 84310 874 0

A Self-Determined Future with Asperger Syndrome
Solution Focused Approaches
E. Veronica Bliss and Genevieve Edmonds
Foreword by Bill O'Connell, Director of Training,
Focus on Solutions
ISBN 978 1 84310 513 8

The Complete Guide to Asperger's Syndrome
Tony Attwood
ISBN 978 1 84310 495 7 (hardback)
ISBN 978 1 84310 669 2 (paperback)

MarketPlace: **AUS**	Order Number: **112-8699958-3001845**
Order Date: **2016-09-10**	Email: **rn0gw939m18jn9b@marketplace.amazon.com**

Items : 1

Item		Locator
Girls Growing Up on the Autism Spectrum: What Pare	RY	MUL-7-LG-076-03-4
ISBN : 1843108550		

PrintID: 100004990106

We hope that you are satisfied with your purchase and if so, ask you to leave positive feedback.
If not, please contact us and we will do our best to resolve any issues you may have.

Mulberry House, Woods Way, Goring By Sea, West Sussex, BN12 4QY. Tel:+44(0)1903 507544
Email: international@worldofbooks.com | Twitter: @WorldofBooksltd | Web: www.worldofbooks.com

Contents

Chapter 9 Our Journey: A Mother and her Daughter with Asperger's Syndrome 294

Conclusion: Embracing Change 330

ACKNOWLEDGEMENTS

Ten years ago this book was but a glimmer, a whisper of an idea inspired by a young girl with golden hair and a name to match the spark inside of her. Since then, it has slowly been brought to life by the incredible families I have worked with and spoken to; the girls, the women, young and wise, who live graciously and courageously on the autism spectrum. I have learned immeasurably both from those who embrace who they are, and from those who struggle to make sense of the world and their place in it. Women have a history of sisterhood—of weaving a rich fabric of stories of hope, difficulty, and determination—and passing down their knowledge to others. The story of girls and women with autism spectrum disorders (ASDs) is still young, and I am incredibly grateful to everyone with whom I have worked for enabling me to make this contribution.

Getting well-written ideas that make sense on to the page, and having them come together to create a compelling, readable, and organized narrative is the goal of any writer, and is usually only fully achieved with the assistance of a dedicated and talented editor. For this, I thank my husband, J.P. Grossman, computer engineer by day and gifted amateur editor by night, who not only provided invaluable editorial support, but also understood when silence, an encouraging email, or a trip to the barn was all that was needed.

A special thank you is also owed to Jack Edelson for his untiring assistance with research, resources, references, and all manner of organizational support.

Developing and running our "Girls Growing Up on the Autism Spectrum" groups has been an incredible journey. Working with a team of creative and energetic professionals is so rewarding, and I thank Gina Marie Moravcik, Samara Pulver Tetenbaum, and Halley Ceglia for co-leading this fantastic program. Our peer mentors, undergraduate assistants, and graduate student trainees make our groups an invaluable experience, not only for the participants but also for the lead facilitators.

I believe strongly in empirically supported interventions for individuals with ASDs, and in the integration of clinical practice and applied research.

I owe a great deal of thanks to my supervisors, advisors, and mentors in Toronto, Halifax, Colorado, and New York, especially Isabel Smith at Dalhousie University and the Denver Group, for encouraging and fostering this philosophy which is strongly reflected in this book.

The final chapter in this book was written by Maureen and Maura Petro, a very special mother–daughter partnership. It describes Maura's experiences as a girl growing up with Asperger's Syndrome. We have known Maureen and Maura for many years, and were greatly honoured when they agreed to share their story with us and our readers.

When we started writing this book, we sent out requests asking families of girls with ASDs to share their growing-up experiences with us; the response we received was overwhelming. Thank you to all the families and women who replied, many of whose stories you will read about in this book: your journeys will help guide others along their paths.

Thank you to our families, friends, colleagues, and everyone in our lives who realized the giant undertaking of writing a book. We greatly appreciate your support, how you accepted our rain checks kindly, and understood that we would, eventually, finish.

Finally, to Jessica Kingsley and Liane Holliday Willey for believing in our project and for giving it a home—thank you.

FOREWORD

I met the authors of this book a few years ago when I was speaking for the AHA-NY group. They sat at my table and we casually began discussing the perils of women on the autistic spectrum. We all agreed there was far too little known on the subject. Shana and Gina told me about the clinic they were running that primarily focused on girls with autism. I was amazed that I hadn't heard of it before and thrilled to finally learn of it then. Within minutes, I knew these two experts were women I wanted on my team. They are smart practitioners who have created an environment filled with the possibility of hope and trust. In this book, they bring that environment to a wider audience and all I can say is, hoorah!

Speaking from personal experience, I know all too well how difficult it is to be a female growing up with Asperger Syndrome. And mind you, I was one of the lucky ones. I had a host of supporters. My physicians were tapped into my differences and ready and able to help me find my way. My teachers were caring and generous with their help. Friends and family members stood by me despite my idiosyncrasies and awkwardness. Those in my background came armed with some gift of insight and understanding about Asperger Syndrome long before it became a household name, long before it was even recognized as a developmental disorder. Yet as lucky as I was, I still suffered greatly. Deep depression, an eating disorder, abuse delivered from male acquaintances, low self-esteem, a lack of a will to live...those were the tops of my lows.

I shouldn't look back. I know it is completely unproductive and unhealthy to look back and remember the disturbing things in my life I cannot change. I realize it is a waste of time, not to mention self-defeating. But human nature drives me to remember, to regret, and to despair. I cannot help but think how much better off my early years would have been if *Girls Growing Up on the Autism Spectrum: What Parents Should Know about the Pre-teen and Teenage Years* had sat on my night stand, on my family's library shelf, on my doctor's waiting room table, and in my teachers' lounge.

True. This may not be a comfortable read for some of you. Puberty, sexuality, personal hygiene and all the other adolescent and teen issues go hand-in-hand with awkward discussions and debate, but without frank discussion we do our young women on the spectrum a great disservice. This book hits the real issues head on. There is no ducking out of the way to avoid controversy or discomfort. Authors Nichols, Muscillo and Pulver Tetenbaum, and the very brave women who shared their stories, left no stone unturned in their quest to bring all the conceivable issues surrounding girls and young women with an autistic spectrum disorder out in the open. In so doing, they provide a game plan and solid set of research-backed theories to the spotlight that will pave the way for more resources to be devoted to autism's effect on females.

This is a book with parts as important as its whole. Each chapter stands alone as an important and richly filled chunk of information. While the book is written toward helping females on the autistic spectrum as a whole, it finds a way to address the unique variations of need an affected individual with autism may require. Readers of this book will enjoy a friendly and warm writing style that engages and educates at the same time. The definitions of terms are clearly defined and the often tough-to-understand theoretical concepts are made easy to grasp. Best of all, the recommendations for support are spot on, based as they are on the brave testimonies of women affected with autism, as well as some of the best references our field has to offer.

I invite you to follow Nichols, Muscillo, Pulver Tetenbaum, and the women who contributed their stories, on a journey that will enrich, enlighten and engage you from beginning to end. Then invite everyone you know to take the same journey, because if enough of us take in the wisdom of this book, our females who struggle with autism will struggle far less.

Liane Holliday Willey, EdD
Author of Pretending to be Normal: Living with Asperger Syndrome,
Asperger Syndrome in the Family: Redefining Normal; *and* Asperger
Syndrome and Adolescence: The Ins, the Outs and Things In-Between.

Authors' Notes

Throughout the book we have used the terms "autism spectrum", "autism spectrum disorders", and "ASDs" to mean autism, pervasive developmental disorder (PDD), and Asperger's Syndrome. When referring in particular to individuals with Asperger's Syndrome we may use the abbreviation "AS". For high-functioning individuals with autism we use the abbreviation "HFA". "Aspie" is also used at times in the context of autobiographical descriptions.

The primary audience for this book is parents of girls with ASDs, and so we generally refer to "your daughter" in the text. However, we believe that this book may also be of value to a much wider audience, including teachers, physicians, aides, psychologists, and other family members, so "your daughter" should be read as "your student", "your client", "your niece", and so on, as appropriate.

Girls who are between the ages of 9 and 12 are considered "pre-teens", whereas the term "teen" refers to girls between the ages of 13 and 18 years. The term "young adult" is used to refer to young women between the ages of 19 and 25.

We also use the term "sex" to refer biologically to male and female, not "gender" which is a socialized concept. "Gender" will be used in the context of the development of self.

Many of the strategies discussed in this book are most appropriate for girls and young women with Asperger's or HFA. In most chapters we have included sections that are particularly relevant for youth with limited verbal abilities, or below-average cognitive skills. Books, resources, and curricula are provided for a wide range of abilities.

At the end of each chapter, a "Resources" list is provided, based on the information that appears in that chapter. Academic references that refer to journal articles and scholarly works appear in the References at the end of the book. The authors have read each of the books and scholarly works cited, and have seen or used each curriculum that is recommended.

Some of the chapters in this book will discuss issues that may be sensitive for families from various cultural and religious backgrounds. As professionals, we very much respect families' choices for their children based on belief systems. If you are unsure about any of the information we present or the recommendations that are made, seek guidance from your religious or cultural communities.

CHAPTER 1

What Do We Currently Know about Girls and Women with Autism Spectrum Disorders?

My daughter is 18 and was only diagnosed last year (at 17) with Asperger's Syndrome. I had never even heard of it before last summer. I had shared anecdotes about her with a coworker and he asked me if she had ever been diagnosed with Asperger's. I went online and read up about it—and sat at my computer crying. All of the things we never "got" about her—all of the things we never understood—were finally becoming very clear! I immediately called my sister and she went online and we both read and read and gasped and gasped...over and over. (Mother of a recently diagnosed 18-year-old girl with Asperger's Syndrome)

ASD was not actively pursued as a diagnosis for girls during the early 1990s. I, nor did my family, know that the collective aspects of my personality was in any way related to ASD. My family and I believed that I was just a "unique", if not, "weird" individual. (31-year-old woman with Asperger's Syndrome, depression, and anxiety)

Asking the question...

Until very recently, the question posed in the title of this chapter had received little attention in the academic literature, and yet families of daughters with autism spectrum disorders (ASDs), along with the professionals and educators who work with them, ask it every day. They are looking for answers that will help them to better understand their child, inform educational and treatment approaches, and help them to prepare their daughter for a healthy and safe adolescence and adulthood. In our work with families, we are asked this question often, and in many different ways:

- "Are there going to be *any* other girls in the group?"
- "I can't seem to find any resources geared toward girls with autism."
- "Is there a support group for families of girls on the spectrum?"

- "My daughter is depressed because she doesn't know anyone like her. Can you help?"
- "My daughter is turning 15, and although she's very bright, she can't manage her menstrual cycle. What can we do?"

If you are reading this book, you are probably someone who is looking for answers to similar questions. You are someone who cares about your daughter's future, your student's education, or your client's happiness and wellbeing. You are asking questions, and looking for answers, about girls with ASDs. Though this book is written as a guide for parents, we expect that it will be helpful not only for families but also for others who work closely with girls on the autism spectrum as they face the challenges of entering and navigating adolescence.

Case study: Karen

When Karen came to see us at the clinic, she presented as a shy, anxious adolescent (14 years old) who seemed very unsure of herself. She was soft-spoken, sweet, and would smile and laugh quietly when engaged. She was able to carry conversations, but it often took her a long time to formulate her responses. Karen was very interested in cats and Egypt, and though initially hesitant, she enjoyed sharing these interests with the examiner when prompted to do so. Karen's presence in the room was very unassuming. She often stood with her shoulders slouched and her head down, eyes gazing toward the floor. Her long hair would cover her face, and she tended to wear large, baggy clothing. Karen's mother had been told that she had an anxiety disorder; however, her mother felt that something else was going on. Her difficulties seemed to extend beyond just anxiety.

What families have shared

In our time working and talking with women, families, and daughters, we have asked what they feel are the differences between females and males with ASDs. Some families live in communities so small they know only one or two other children with an ASD. Others have reported that they do not know any other girls like their daughter, and so they are not sure if boys and girls are different. However, many families, and women with an ASD themselves, feel strongly that the difference is there, sometimes subtle, sometimes more obvious. Differences have been hypothesized related to biology, the diagnostic process, communication, behavior, and other clinical symptoms. The following statements summarize quotes from individuals and families, and represent the variety of viewpoints we hear.

- "Girls and women are underdiagnosed, and it takes longer to get a diagnosis."
- "From my experience, it seems like girls have more seizures than boys."
- "Girls fly under the radar, and tend to be more shy."
- "I think boys' symptoms tend to be more classic."
- "Girls' symptoms seem to be more internalized, such as anxiety, which can be overlooked."
- "Girls tend to be less aggressive and intrusive."
- "They seem to have fewer communication deficits."
- "My daughter seems more sensitive, and she cries easier."
- "I have yet to see a marked difference in the boys versus girls at my daughter's preschool."

What we do and don't know about girls with ASDs

In this chapter, we will review what we know today about pervasive developmental disorders in girls. We will discuss issues related to:

- the difference in prevalence between males and females with ASDs
- differences in symptoms and clinical presentation
- diagnostic and treatment issues
- possible causes of sex differences
- sex differences in other disorders and in normal development.

Epidemiology and the puzzle of diagnostic rates

For those of you who did not major in epidemiology, it is the scientific study of the distribution and causes of conditions in human populations. Epidemiologists often examine *prevalence* (the total number of cases in a population at any given time) and *incidence rates* (the number of new occurrences of the condition in the population over a given time period). According to the United States Department of Health and Human Services Centers for Disease Control and Prevention, the prevalence rate for ASDs in February 2007 was 1 in 150, up from the previously published figure of 1 in 166 in January 2004. These figures differ significantly from the earliest estimates of rates of the disorder which were 4 or 5 in 10,000 individuals (Lotter 1966). It remains unclear as to whether the increase in classification of children as having an ASD is caused by a true increase in the disorder, or due to increased awareness of autism and its broad characteristics. Either way, more children are receiving a diagnosis today than ever before.

Even less well-understood than the true prevalence of ASDs is the difference in prevalence rates between boys and girls. Fombonne (1999, 2001) reviewed the literature on epidemiological studies of ASDs and noted that in well-conducted studies, overall sex ratios of the disorder (male:female) ranged from 2:1 to 16:1. The statistic that is most commonly reported in the mainstream literature is that ASDs are four times more common in males than in females (4:1). But does this statistic reflect a true ratio? And have studies been conducted that are designed to answer this question? Parents and some professionals have begun to question the 4:1 ratio, and to wonder whether other factors influence the numbers, such as research studies that include more boys than girls, the ability of current assessment tools to detect the disorder in girls, and different symptom presentations in males versus females. Additionally, the prevalence ratio may be different depending on the severity of the disorder. Attwood (1998) has suggested that whereas the 4:1 sex ratio may apply for individuals with "classic" autism, a 10:1 ratio observed in the clinic may be more accurate for Asperger's Syndrome. Not a single study, however, has examined the sex ratio of individuals diagnosed with Asperger's Syndrome, or as you move along the ASD continuum from "severely impaired" to "mildly affected". The bottom line is that we understand far too little about girls with ASDs, and what may prevent them for being identified early and helped.

Same disorder, different faces?
Sex differences in symptom presentation

Our girls [with ASD] really do seem different than autistic boys we know. For instance, the boys seem to hyperfocus on certain interests like trains, weather, etc. Our girls don't do that at all. In fact, our 18-year-old can't stand to be with her [male] aspie counterparts because they only talk about science and sports, or whatever their thing is. She wants to talk about relationships, art, music, and feelings. I think it all goes back to the typical differences between boys and girls. Since the girls are less likely to have these keen interests I think some doctors don't catch their autism. (Mother of four daughters, oldest 18 with Asperger's Syndrome, youngest 9 with classic autism)

My youngest has autism and although we had her evaluated a number of times... they would say "Well, she is too affectionate to have autism" even though she had so many of the characteristics. We did not get her diagnosis until she was six. I really wish that there was a scale that was more tailored to females for diagnosing autism. Girls are innately more affectionate and compassionate than males whether they have autism or not, and this is what keeps them from being properly diagnosed. (Mother of a 7-year-old girl with autism, diagnosed at age 6)

One of the reasons identifying girls with ASDs is difficult is that, as we are learning, their symptoms may be different from those of boys. Discussions in the published literature of sex differences or issues related to females with ASDs are, for the most part, limited to a small number of topics such as biology (genetics, brain imaging) and differences in symptoms or development (primarily as toddlers or in the preschool years). In the clinical world, therapists, educators, and women with ASDs have begun to speak up and make the autism field in general take notice. Despite the limited research, autobiographical, anecdotal, and clinical reports strongly suggest that observed sex differences are valid and deserve attention; this section summarizes some of the differences that have been observed.

Males with pervasive developmental disorders (PDDs) have generally been found to have higher IQ scores than females (e.g. Tsai and Beisler 1983), and have been considered to be "higher functioning" as a group, but few studies have examined differences in clinical presentation between males and females at the same general level of cognitive functioning. McLennan, Lord, and Schopler (1993) found that males with autism tended to have more serious social and communicative impairments early in life, whereas females displayed more impairments in social interaction during adolescence (after the age of 12). In addition, the play of boys tended to be more restricted in range and more repetitive in content (*see also* Lord, Schopler, and Revicki 1982). In our own work we have noted that girls who present with more subtle ASDs are often eventually able to answer questions about social situations, social communication, and friendships that similarly high-functioning boys would be less able to answer. However, the answers tend not to come naturally or quickly; it often takes these girls longer than normal to process information and then respond. You can imagine the difficulty they would have keeping up in a conversation with a group of chatty teenage girls at school! The answers themselves that the girls provide also seem to reflect a more surface-level understanding rather than the depth of social comprehension, cognition, and awareness observed in typically developing girls.

At the International Meeting for Autism Research (IMFAR) in 2006, two research groups presented unpublished findings from studies that examined sex differences across a range of variables. Hall and colleagues, from the University of South Carolina and Duke University, investigated sex differences in attention deficit hyperactivity disorder (ADHD) symptoms in children with autistic disorder (ages of participants not reported). On a parent report questionnaire of ADHD behaviors (the SNAP-IV), scores on the inattention subscale showed that males with autism had a harder time focusing than females, and were more easily distracted.

Verbalis and colleagues, from the University of Connecticut, examined sex differences on measures of cognitive functioning, adaptive skills, and autism symptoms in toddlers who were diagnosed with either autism or "pervasive developmental disorder-not otherwise specified" (PDD-NOS)—a diagnosis given to individuals with some, but not all, of the characteristics of ASDs. Girls received a lower total score on an autism screening questionnaire (meaning less impairment) and performed better on individual questions such as pointing, pretend play, and following an adult's gaze. Girls received higher (better) scores on the socialization scale of the *Vineland Adaptive Behavior Scales* (a measure of adaptive functioning; Sparrow, Balla, and Cicchetti 1984). On the diagnostic measures of the study, girls scored better on two different measures of communication and play. Girls were also more likely to have a diagnosis of PDD-NOS than autistic disorder.

At the same research meeting the following year (IMFAR 2007), two more presentations looked at sex differences across a number of different variables in children with ASDs. Varley and colleagues, from the University of Washington Autism Center Research Program, examined sex differences in autism in a study of multiplex families (more than one child with an ASD). Females received lower scores than males on a block construction task, and diagnosed males with a female sibling who also had autism performed worse on a number of tasks than diagnosed males with affected male siblings (e.g. more impaired fine motor skills, lower expressive and receptive language skills).

In their presentation on differences in autism symptoms and adaptive functioning in young children with low IQ scores, Penn and colleagues (2007) from York University, Surrey Place Centre, and Children's Hospital of Eastern Ontario, found that girls with ASDs had higher motor skills and overall adaptive functioning than boys (as measured by the *Vineland Adaptive Behavior Scales*). Contrary to what they predicted, girls did not demonstrate higher socialization scores than boys.

A study examining sex differences in young children with ASDs was published in the *Journal of Autism and Developmental Disorders* in 2007. In several areas of functioning, including cognition, language, motor skills, social development, and clinical symptoms, Carter and colleagues (2007) from the University of Massachusetts and Boston University School of Medicine, observed a number of differences between girls and boys. In summary, boys performed better on measures of language, motor skills, and social development. Girls demonstrated stronger visual reception (nonverbal) skills. The authors noted that it was particularly interesting that mothers rated boys as having stronger social skills than girls, which is inconsistent with the findings reviewed above, and with the typical developmental literature. They suggested that mothers may have higher expectations for their daughters' social development compared to that of boys, and therefore rated their skills as lower. The toddlers in this study were all participating in early intervention programs serving youth with developmental delays and ASDs. It is also possible that girls with mild difficulties may not be in programs such as these at a young age, and that their profile of strengths and weaknesses may look very different.

A final study investigated characteristics of disruptive behavior in male and female youth with ASDs. Reese and colleagues (2005) from the University of Kansas and the University of Maryland-Baltimore County, examined what kinds of functions (the purpose of a behavior) disruptive behavior served for young preschool-aged children with autism. The behaviour of 17 boys with autism was compared with that of six girls. Boys with autism tended to engage in disruptive behavior for the purpose of gaining desired objects, escaping demands during repetitive behavior, and escaping undesirable sensory stimulation. The girls with autism, however, engaged in disruptive behaviors for purposes similar to children with global developmental delays. These functions tended to be social in nature, such as gaining caregiver attention, or avoiding nonspecific demands from the caregiver. Despite the small number of children in the study and the use of parent report only, these preliminary findings are quite interesting for helping parents and clinicians to better understand that the behaviors of girls and boys with ASDs may serve very different functions.

Summary of differences in clinical presentation between girls and boys with ASDs

In reviewing these research studies, it is important to note is that the findings differ somewhat depending on the age of the children in the study (e.g. toddlers versus school-aged), intellectual level of the children in the study (e.g. low IQ versus average skills), the type of sample studied (e.g. children referred to a clinic versus children enrolled in an early intervention program), and how behaviors and skills are measured (e.g. parent report versus direct observations). This sometimes leads to conflicting results, making it difficult to draw any definitive conclusions, but there are still a few take-home messages:

- Boys with ASDs tend to have higher IQs overall than girls with ASDs.

- The play of boys with ASDs is more restricted in range and more repetitive. Girls have been noted to have stronger pretend-play skills, and have received better scores on diagnostic instruments that assess play.

- Girls have stronger communication skills as assessed on diagnostic instruments (parent report and direct observation) and score higher on specific communicative behaviors such as pointing and gaze-following.

- Sex-related social difficulties may emerge over time—boys have more impairments early on, whereas for girls social difficulties might appear more in early adolescence.

- Boys are more easily distracted and have a more difficult time focusing than girls.

- Disruptive behavior as observed in boys has a different purpose (e.g. gain objects) than that observed in girls, which is more social in nature (e.g. acquire caregiver attention).

- Parent reports of skills may underestimate girls' abilities as parents may have higher expectations for girls, particularly in the area of communication and social skills.

- Girls with mild difficulties may not be included in research samples with children enrolled in early intervention programs.

- On screening instruments, girls tend to receive lower total scores (less impairment), and with respect to diagnosis, girls are more likely to be given a PDD-NOS diagnosis than autism.

The balance of evidence suggests that sex differences are most definitely real; however, we are nowhere near having a complete picture of what the differences look like, or what they mean. What we do have are intriguing individual pieces to a puzzle that will need much more attention in order to be solved. It is also clear that girls on the autism spectrum face unique challenges not just because they are girls, but because the disorder itself presents differently in them than it does in boys.

Diagnostic implications of sex differences

We had years of difficulty finding out what was going on with [our daughter] and what to do about it. At that time (1998), not many people knew about Asperger's. We certainly had never heard of it. I think because she was very bright there was the feeling nothing was wrong; she just needed to learn some relaxation techniques. When she was finally diagnosed, her psychologist felt that she needed to see a psychiatrist for medication. That psychiatrist didn't believe she had AS because she was so intelligent and expressed herself so well. I knew those were not reasons that disproved AS. (Mother of a bright 16-year-old girl with Asperger's Syndrome and depression)

I knew something was wrong the day my child was born but they kept giving her all these diagnoses when I knew they weren't right so I kept going and fighting till I got a diagnosis that made sense and explained a lot about my daughter. (Mother of a 13-year-old girl with PDD, diagnosed at age 11)

The differences between boys and girls with ASDs have important implications for the assessment and diagnosis of ASDs. Are girls with ASDs being missed or overlooked during an evaluation because their presentation does not fit how professionals currently characterize ASDs (based on a male prototype)? Do girls fly under the radar at school and miss being identified by teachers and school psychologists? From as early as the 1980s, though few people were thinking about sex differences at that time, professionals have suggested that girls may be underdiagnosed, missed, or may express their ASD symptoms differently (Attwood 2007; Ehlers and Gillberg 1993; Kopp and Gillberg 1992; Nyden, Hjelmquist, and Gillberg 2000; Smith 1997; Wing 1981). Unfortunately, there is limited literature to support specific diagnostic guidelines for assessing girls with potential ASDs. It has been suggested that, as a result, there may be significant bias during the diagnostic process (Koenig and Tsatsanis 2005; Volkmar, Szatmari, and Sparrow 1993; Smith 1997).

In their chapter in the *Handbook of Behavioral and Emotional Problems in Girls* (2005), Koenig and Tsatsanis (2005) put forth "assessment suggestions" for those working with girls. These include the following.

- Referral of girls for further assessment even if they come close to but do not meet strict cutoffs on screening tests in all areas.

- Consideration that signs of impairment in girls may manifest more clearly over time, such as during early adolescence.

- Comparison of a girl's social and communicative abilities and behaviors to what is considered normative behavior for *girls* of their age and cognitive ability.

- Developing a solid understanding of typical developmental sex differences in socialization, communication, and behavior, and societal or cultural expectations.

- Avoiding comparison of the presentation of females with what has become the prototypical profile of autism in males.

- Consideration that research shows girls with ASDs may not demonstrate the same level of repetitive behaviors or restricted interested as do affected boys.

- Careful documentation of social and communicative deficits as girls may not present with the same disruptive behaviors that, for boys, become evident in the classroom and often prompt referrals for assessment.

One of the difficulties we have observed with the current diagnostic tools is that they do not explicitly account for the amount of time that it takes individuals to answer questions about social situations, despite the importance of appropriate timing and being able to keep pace with conversations in real-world situations. This is particularly problematic for high-functioning girls on the spectrum who, more often than boys, are better able to answer questions *correctly* in a one-to-one setting, but do so much more *slowly* than typically developing girls. The result is that on today's gold standard assessment instruments such as the *Autism Diagnostic Observation Schedule* (ADOS; Lord *et al.* 1999), a standardized observation of social and communicative behavior in a semistructured context, high-functioning girls with ASDs may receive scores that fall just short of meeting the diagnostic cutoff. Yet on the complementary parent interview—the *Autism Diagnostic Interview-Revised* (ADI-R; Lord, Rutter, and LeCouteur 1994)—parents report past and current difficulties with pragmatic language, understanding others, and making and maintaining friendships. Similarly, when girls join our adolescent social skills program, the difficulties that appeared subtle in a previous face-to-face interview or assessment become much more evident, particularly when observed in direct contrast to the skill set possessed by our typically developing high school peer mentors.

In his book, *The Complete Guide to Asperger's Syndrome*, Attwood (2007) has suggested that girls with Asperger's Syndrome are likely more difficult for clinicians to recognize given the coping mechanisms girls may have developed throughout early childhood. These coping mechanisms may appear as intellectualized, learned approaches to social situations, which are sometimes not evident in a short one-to-one diagnostic assessment. School observations and further assessment reveal the extent of the difficulties experienced by the girls. Alternatively, girls may hide their impairments by watching from the sidelines. Other differences between girls and boys that are also relevant for how well the current diagnostic criteria capture difficulties experienced by girls include qualitative impairments in establishing peer relationships (as opposed to a complete failure to develop friendships), and special interests that may not be as idiosyncratic as those of boys.

Understanding how best to assess and diagnose girls with possible ASDs, in particular girls who may have more cognitive and social strengths, will require international collaboration among research groups and autism centres. In a recent article in the *New York Times* (August 5, 2007), entitled "What Autistic Girls are Made of", Ami Klin, director of Yale University's autism program, described females with autism as "research orphans". Because there are fewer diagnosed females, girls are often excluded from research studies as it is not possible to find a large enough sample size. Sadly, girls are being excluded from important research that could shed light on ASDs in females.

Interventions and supports

With regard to intervention, even less information is available to help guide treatment planning. A single open-label study (the investigators knew whether the child was taking active medication or an inactive placebo) of fluvoxamine (Prozac®) that was designed to treat compulsive behaviors demonstrated that the response of girls with ASDs was better than that of males (Martin *et al.* 2003). After discussions with prominent child psychiatrists who specialize in the assessment and treatment of ASDs,* and a review of research abstracts, we found no further evidence that addresses differential sex responses to medications, or how medication effects may interact with hormones associated with a girl's menstrual cycle. Even in medication studies that report large sample sizes (more than 80 participants), analyses associated with sex have not been conducted.

There are also no findings available to support sex effects of psychosocial or behavioral treatments. Smith (1997) has suggested that outcome studies of early behavioral intervention programs need to examine differences in response to treatment (and in particular specific targeted skills) between girls and boys. It is difficult to work toward the refinement of treatment approaches when little published research has investigated sex differences in interests, preferred leisure activities, preferred types of reinforcement, or social and vocational strengths and weaknesses.

As youth approaches adolescence, in particular, interventions should address sex differences in communication, social behaviors and expectations, self-esteem and mental health, and adaptive skills associated with puberty. With females, parents and professionals need to consider how hormonal changes associated with the menstrual cycle influence behavior, and how best to structure the environment and expectations during the week before menstruation.

What about supports and educational programs for parents? Although there are obvious similarities between the experiences of parents of male and female children with ASDs, the parents of daughters face unique issues (e.g. menstruation, degree of vulnerability, social and cultural expectations for behavior) and often lack a supportive outlet within which to share their concerns and hopes, as well as resources for seeking assistance. Mothers whose daughters participate in our girls' group programming report that not only have their daughters benefited from intervention, but that as parents they have been able to form their own informal group which has been invaluable to them as a source of information, friendship, humour, patience (we *are* talking about teenage girls!), hope, and, above all, support. As parent education

---

*   (Joel Bregman, MD, Medical Director Fay J. Lindner Center for Autism, March 2007, Peter Szatmari, MD, Director Offord Centre for Child Studies, May 2007, personal communication.)

programs are developed and evaluated, sex differences in content, concerns, and models of treatment will need to be considered.

> My daughter enjoys [girls' group] so much and looks forward to it. It's the closest she has to actually having friends. I enjoy speaking with the other mothers in the group! It's nice to be with people who have the same experiences I've had and am having! It's nice to know you're not alone. I was surprised at how similar the other mothers' experiences were to my own. (Mother of a 16-year-old girl with Asperger's Syndrome)

What causes sex differences in ASDs?

We have come a very long way since the days of "refrigerator mothers" (Bettelheim 1967) when it was believed that autism was the result of a mother who didn't love her child enough. From genetics research we know more about the potential causes of ASDs; however, we still know little about the reasons for the sex differences that have been observed. Three general theories have been proposed in an attempt to explain these differences, and these are summarized in (Koenig and Tsatsanis 2005): the Liability/ Threshold Model (LTM); the Greater Variability Model (GVM); and the Brain Differences Model (BDM).

The LTM, one of the earlier models, claims that although males and females are equally likely to have an ASD, the threshold for impairment is higher for females than for males. This model attempts to explain the observations that fewer females present with the disorder, and that when they do, they are affected to a greater degree. Tsai, Stewart, and August (1981) have argued that, based on this model, females with the disorder would have more first-degree family members with ASDs. Though an interesting speculation, this prediction has not been corroborated by epidemiological studies (Pickles *et al.* 1995; Szatmari *et al.* 2000).

The GVM suggests that males display a larger variation in the measurable characteristics of ASDs, so that even minor impairments result in observable symptoms that can lead to diagnosis, whereas females display less variation so that greater impairments are required to produce symptoms meeting diagnostic criteria. This model was originally proposed by Wing (1981); in Constantino *et al.* (2000) it was suggested that the GVM could arise from either external factors (genetic and environmental) or from internal factors (girls may be more socially receptive in general, leading to reduced expression of an ASD).

The BDM is at once the broadest and most straightforward model, suggesting that the sex differences in ASDs are simply the result of differences between male and female brains, including hormones, brain structure, circuitry, and patterns of activation of brain areas. For example, one could reason that if male brains are "hard-wired" for understanding and building systems, and female brains are "hard-wired" for empathy, then females are less susceptible to ASDs because of the more sophisticated social competencies of their sex. This model was originally proposed in 1997 (Baron-Cohen and Hammer 1997) and is further discussed as the "extreme male brain" theory in Baron-Cohen's (2003) book, *The Essential Difference: Male and Female Brains and the Truth about Autism*.

Although interesting ideas, none of the above theories has much of a solid basis in the empirical literature, nor are they currently able to provide an adequate explanation for observed sex differences (though the "extreme male brain" theory has been the subject of the most scientific inquiry). It is not surprising then that much more research is needed to better understand why a sex difference exists in ASDs, and how much of that difference is biological, social, or influenced by diagnostic bias.

More recent work suggests that sex differences are caused by both genetic and neurological differences between males and females with ASDs. In 2006, Schellenberg and colleagues published a study that made popular press headlines about genetic linkages that included families with only male-affected children or at least one female child. Their main finding was that different genes may be responsible for causing autism in boys than in girls. Given that there are likely many genes contributing to autism (studies indicate possibly up to 30 minor and major genes!), the authors also suggest that it may take more "risk genes" for a girl to be affected—a possible cause of the high ratio of males to females with ASDs.

Publications about brain differences between males and females also have significant implications for understanding autism and observed (or not) sex differences. For years the mass media has been fascinated by what is more often called "gender differences", and in a light-hearted way has taken advantage of human interest in the much debated topic. Books related to gender differences fly off of bookstore shelves, as women and men try to "understand" each other. For example, the book *Men Are From Mars, Women Are From Venus* by John Gray (1992) was a *New York Times* bestseller for years. Whether you are more of a "gender similarities" or "gender differences" believer, society as a whole tends to favor the flashier, competitively spirited idea that men and women, as well as girls and boys, differ in critical ways. Apparently this helps us to understand or explain how we communicate, and how we get along—or don't—in the sandbox/marriage together! Despite the fact that the topic is somewhat politically loaded, interest in gender differences, and in particular *brain* differences, has led to important scientific work which it is hoped will help us to better understand females with ASDs.

Research in neuroscience has provided compelling evidence for brain differences between males and females in structure, chemistry, genetics, hormones, and function. Louann Brizendine, MD, neuropsychiatrist and founder of the Women's and Teen Girls Mood and Hormones Clinic in San Francisco, has written an intriguing and comprehensive book, *The Female Brain* (2006), about females' unique biology, and in particular how our brains make us women. In reading her book, we were struck by how many exciting and important questions can be raised about the directions of the field of autism research! Do females with ASDs have higher levels of testosterone? Do young girls with ASDs demonstrate different play behaviors than typically developing girls? Is the chemistry of the hypothalamic-pituitary-ovarian system different in females with ASDs? Her chapter "Teen Girl Brain" is an essential read for any parent of a teenage daughter (with a diagnosis of ASD or not!) who is trying to ride the monthly mood swings without being pummelled by the waves. Are there sex-related brain differences in structures thought to be associated with autism (e.g. amygdala, anterior cingulated cortex, prefrontal cortex)? For example, do females with ASDs show differences compared with males with ASDs, and, more importantly, do they show differences when compared with typically developing females (matched on important variables such as age and IQ)? Dr Brizendine's account of the female brain is not only well-written but is also an enjoyable engaging read.

Two studies have compared the brain anatomy of girls and boys with ASDs, one of which has also made the important comparison between typically developing girls and girls with autism. In 1997, Lainhart, of the University of Utah's Brain Institute, and colleagues published a paper in which they reported a larger brain size (macrocephaly) in females with ASDs than males: this was established by measuring the average head circumference of a community-sample of participants with ASDs (children and adults). More recently, Bloss and Courchesne (2007) set out to compare the pattern of neuroanatomical abnormalities in girls and boys with autism; their study involved magnetic resonance imaging (MRI) of girls and boys both with and without autism. They found that all size-related abnormalities observed in boys were also present in girls, and, in addition, girls with autism exhibited enlargements in the temporal lobe and a reduction in volume of the cerebellum. There was also a positive relationship between age and white matter volume for girls (older girls, greater volume), but not for boys.

What does this all mean? With so few studies it is hard to say, but there are a few hypotheses that may be made. Bloss and Courchesne (2007) suggest that the observed pattern of neuroanatomical abnormalities in girls indicates a possible earlier onset of the disorder, which may be related to the level of severity of autism often seen in girls. More research of this kind, which includes both sexes, will be important in shedding light on the neurological and genetic roots of autism.

Sex differences in other developmental disorders

We understand far too little about girls with ASDs and what has prevented them from being identified and helped. Daughters, students, and clients are paying the price for delayed or inaccurate diagnoses, and they follow in the footsteps of girls and women with other developmental disorders, such as attention-deficit/hyperactivity disorder (ADHD) and oppositional defiant disorder (ODD), who have experienced similar situations.

Our appreciation of how ADHD and ODD is expressed in females has come a long way—much farther than our understanding of sex differences in ASDs. In 1994, the National Institutes of Health (NIH) held a meeting about sex differences in ADHD and a conference summary was published in 1996. By 1997, enough research studies had been conducted on sex differences in ADHD to perform a meta-analysis, which combines results of many studies into one large study (Gaub and Carlson 1997). In 2006, Waschbusch, King, and the Northern Partners in Action for Children and Youth published a research paper in the *Journal of Consulting and Clinical Psychology* in which they asked whether sex-specific norms should be used to assess ADHD and ODD. Their hypothesis was that "biased diagnostic criteria" have contributed in part to the observed sex differences in ADHD and ODD. For the authors, biased diagnostic criteria refers to the *content* of the criteria (types of symptoms), and/or the *number* of symptoms necessary to meet criteria. They found that a number of elementary school girls received elevated scores on their parent and teacher report measures, but did not meet full *Diagnostic and Statistical Manual of Mental Disorders* fourth edition (DSM—IV) (APA 1994) criteria for ADHD or ODD. However, when sex-specific norms were used, this group of girls had significantly more severe impairments than the other female participants. This finding is echoed by recent suggestions in the autism literature that sex-specific norms and lower thresholds for diagnosis may be critical for identifying an important subset of girls with ASDs.

It has taken a long time for the autism field to arrive at its current awareness of sex differences, and few studies have been conducted to address such important issues as diagnostic norms. To truly understand girls with ASDs, and to help them achieve their full potential, we need to follow the direction of ADHD and ODD researchers, placing much more of a spotlight on the differences between boys and girls with ASDs.

The importance of understanding typical developmental sex differences

In considering sex differences in ASDs, it is important to characterize girls within the context of typical development—how do *neurotypical same-aged females* act, think, feel, and develop? What are the societal and cultural expectations that have shaped perceptions of males and females? Fortunately for us, decades of developmental research have been conducted that can help with this comparison. Across all ages it has been found that females are more skilled than males in face and affect recognition (McClure 2000), the decoding of nonverbal communicative cues (interpreting gestures), empathic responsiveness, the expression of emotions, and perspective-taking or "theory of mind" (Baron-Cohen, Tager-Flusberg, and Cohen 2000). In 1998, Bacon and colleagues published a study in the *Journal of Autism and Developmental Disorders* in which they investigated empathic responses of typically developing preschool children, children with autism, and children with language disorders. Across all diagnostic groups, including the autism group, girls were more likely to respond with prosocial behavior to the distress of another child. The authors highlighted the persistence of sex differences in empathic responding despite all children in the autism group having impaired social skills and understanding. In addition, neurotypical girls tend to interact and play with a greater emphasis on cooperation and comradeship, and less emphasis on competition.

The unique social challenges faced by girls may also influence the manner in which the dysfunction associated with autism is expressed. For example, during adolescence, social interactions and relationships are generally more complex and intricate for females than for males, explaining reports suggesting greater socialization difficulties during this developmental period experienced by females with autism than their male counterparts. If teenage girls' relationships are based primarily on "talking" and intimate social communication, and boys more so on "doing", girls with ASDs are going to have a much harder time with the level of communicative skill and social understanding required to fit in with female social groups.

It is now well-known that girls and boys also fight differently. Nicki Crick, Director of the Institute of Child Development at the University of Minnesota, and colleagues began to study female aggression in the mid-1990s (Crick and Grotpeter 1995) and found that gender differences in aggression emerge in the preschool period. Unlike the overt aggression observed in boys, girls aggress in more subtle indirect ways. Termed "relational aggression," girls will act in ways to manipulate third-party relationships in order to be hurtful toward another girl. Examples of relational aggression include spreading rumors, gossiping, exclusion, "the silent treatment", and other nonverbal behaviors such as giggling and eye-rolling. As parents, professionals, and educators, it is essential to develop a better understanding of the nature of girl fights and bullying in order to be able to help our daughters, clients, and students respond to situations that might arise at school and in the community. In Chapter 6 we will return to the topic of friendships and social interactions, and how you can learn more about relational aggression and the culture of pre-teen and teenage girls.

Clinical programs: are they out there?

For the past two years we have been running a highly successful "Girls Growing Up with ASDs" program at our centre (originally begun by Shana Nichols at the JFK Partners Center for Autism and Developmental Disabilities, University of Colorado at Denver and Health Sciences Center), which includes group therapy and friendship skills development for teen girls with ASDs, community outings, parent support and networking, individual sessions for girls who need more individualized work, and consultation and training about growing-up issues such as puberty and menstruation. When girls have participated in these same-sex groups and are aged 18 years and older, they can participate in our young adult program which gives them the opportunity to practice skills they have learned in mixed company. Participation in this group is often a significant goal for these girls! When we began writing this book we were very interested to learn whether programs such as ours were happening at other clinics in other parts of the country. How is the community of professionals and educators supporting girls and women with ASDs?

An extensive internet search revealed only a handful of (English-speaking) programs. If you are looking for an intervention or educational program for your daughter in your area that either addresses issues specific to girls with ASDs, or will likely have more than one girl in the program, contact your local autism society. Currently, few programs are widely advertised.

A window of knowledge: personal stories by women with ASDs

Even less has been published in the academic literature about the experiences of adult women with ASDs. We are fortunate that a number of women with ASDs have written about their experiences in both published autobiographies and online articles and blogs. Personal accounts provide important insights into the unique challenges and experiences faced by females with ASDs. They also suggest avenues for potentially important research studies related to sex-differences. Some of the more well-known books written by women with ASDs include works by Temple Grandin and Donna Williams; Liane Holiday-Willey's story *Pretending to be Normal*, and the edited book *Women from Another Planet* (*see* Resources). Though each woman's experiences are clearly her own, common themes arise throughout their accounts, including:

- facing expectations from family members and from society about how females are "supposed" to behave, think, and feel
- issues with gender and not connecting with female roles
- struggles with identity issues and self-esteem
- difficulties playing with and establishing friendships with other girls
- feeling confused about social situations and often being misunderstood
- hypersensitive emotionality
- fears related to growing up
- diversity in socio-sexual relationships

- naiveté, vulnerability, and experiences of being taken advantage of, exploited, or abused
- feelings of anxiety, being overwhelmed, and experiencing sensory overload
- mental health concerns, including depression, anxiety, and feeling isolated
- intense interest and connection with animals
- a history of misdiagnoses and hospital stays.

In her book, *Build Your Own Life. A Self-Help Guide For Individuals with Asperger's Syndrome*, Wendy Lawson (2003, p.81) writes about her experiences of autism and her gender:

Autism: My Gender

My gender and I are a package.
We come as part of the deal.
"But autism shows far more damage".
"Look at the things that you feel".

I cannot account for these feelings.
Emotions intense and extreme.
But my issues with everyday dealings,
Can cause me to rant, shout and scream.

I don't desire the "make-up"
Fashion and high-heels don't appeal.
I don't like perfume or my hair cut,
But my need for "understanding", is real.

The expectations placed upon me,
Being female and all,
Push me further into pain and grief,
With my back against the wall.

"I cannot multi-task", I say.
"But you must, You're a woman. You can".
You must cook, clean, organise and play
The role that supports your man.

Your children and men depend on you,
You must be strong, in control and sure.
"What if these things I cannot do?"
"What if my timing is poor?"

"You must work harder, try harder to be,
What society says and dictates".
"But both my autism and gender are me, you see
They both influence my states".

As a woman I function differently.
As a woman I think, see and feel.
As a woman I value all that is me.
My autism is part of the deal.

Routes to a diagnosis for females and their families

Over the years, we have worked and communicated with hundreds of families of girls and women with ASDs about their diagnostic journey—how did they receive an official diagnosis for their daughter, or for themselves? What has become clear is that there are many different routes to a diagnosis that families have experienced. For some girls, the journey was short—they demonstrated classic symptoms of autism at a young age and were diagnosed before the age of five. For other girls and women, the path has been circuitous, labyrinthine and roundabout, with many red herrings in the way. These experiences have left families feeling confused, puzzled, frustrated, discouraged, and disillusioned with a system that is supposed to help them better understand their daughter, not further muddy the waters. Some of the roads to an eventual diagnosis for a girl and her family include the following.

- Previous diagnosis (or diagnoses) of another disorder, including ADD/ADHD, anxiety, depression or mood lability, obsessive compulsive disorder, a language disorder, or an eating disorder. Often, the older the girl, the more diagnoses that fill the metaphorical suitcase she carries around with her.

- A diagnosis of social anxiety, or general concerns about social difficulties and seeming lost in social situations.

- Women with ASDs who were diagnosed at a late age often report previous diagnoses of schizophrenia or psychotic disorder.
- A sibling or other family member has a diagnosis on the autism spectrum and the family begins to question whether their undiagnosed daughter might in fact be on the spectrum as well.

My youngest is 7 years old and was not properly diagnosed until she was 6. She was globally delayed from birth and is also mentally retarded, but most of her problems can be explained from her autism and her sensory problems. Unfortunately, we are also in the process of having our 10-year-old evaluated for possible Asperger's in a couple of weeks. She has always had tendencies toward autism all her life, but she does well in school and she has friends, so I never felt like she would be diagnosed because it would be too mild, but as I have learned more about girls with autism and how they differ from males, we are wondering if she does in fact have Asperger's? It is to the point where she is asking me why she is different and thinks in a way that is not like other girls her age. She "wants" to know what is wrong. I just think it will be hard to get her diagnosed because of those same "girl" things with autism...good behavior at school, friends, etc. We will see. (Mother of a daughter officially diagnosed with autism, and another daughter with possible Asperger's)

- For girls with more mild symptoms, seeing deterioration in academic skills and social competencies as both worlds become more complex (grades three and four, during middle school, and during adolescence). Girls often present with anxiety and depression and a drop in self-esteem, which may be recognized by a teacher or a counselor at school.
- As girls approach adolescence, they may demonstrate difficulties with coping with puberty, or may not demonstrate what are considered to be typical adolescent interests for females (e.g. fashion, interest in dating).
- Increased national media attention to issues facing girls with ASDs (e.g. national news broadcasts, a contestant with Asperger's Syndrome on the television program *America's Next Top Model*). In our clinic this has prompted periods during which we received many phone calls and emails from concerned parents, other relatives, and individuals themselves.

I'm still not sure what her diagnosis is...

Maybe you are reading this book because you think your daughter has an ASD but has not been diagnosed, or you have been told she has other diagnoses (e.g. anxiety, depression) but they just don't quite seem to capture her behavior the way you and your family experience it. While it is helpful to receive an accurate diagnosis as early as possible, it is never too late. If your daughter is in elementary, middle, or high school, or even in college or employed, and does not have a diagnosis, or you feel she has been misdiagnosed, it will be important for you to have her seen for a comprehensive evaluation at a specialized autism center in your state, province, or country. Even for professionals who have chosen to specialize in autism (e.g. psychologists, psychiatrists, developmental pediatricians), and who see hundreds of youth and adults a year, making a diagnosis can sometimes be quite difficult; a lot of information needs to be considered about your daughter's current functioning, and integrated with information that you can provide about what she was like when she was young. Perhaps she really does have depression, and she is demonstrating flat affect and avoidance of eye contact, or perhaps she has an ASD, alone, or with a co-occurring mood disorder. It is very important to see a professional who is capable of making that distinction because many of the treatment approaches will be different depending on the condition.

Resources

General books on girls' issues

Attwood *et al.* (2006) *Aspergers and Girls.* Arlington, TX: Future Horizons Inc.

Ernsperger, L. and Wendel, D. (2007) *Girls Under the Umbrella of Autism Spectrum Disorders. Practical Solutions for Addressing Everyday Challenges.* Shawnee Mission, KS: Autism Asperger Publishing Company.

Articles on girls' and women's issues

Faherty, C. (2002) 'Asperger's syndrome in women: A different set of challenges?' *Autism Asperger's Digest.* July–August 2002. Arlington, TX: Future Horizons Publications, Inc. Available at www.autismtoday.com/articles/Aspergers_in_Women.htm

Flora, C. (2006) 'The Kiriana conundrum: Plumbing the contradictions that define Asperger's Syndrome.' *Psychology Today 39,* 96–100.

New York Times. (2007) 'What autistic girls are made of.' August 5. Available at www.pai-ca.org/news/NYT2007Aug05AutisticGirls.htm

Mothers' accounts

Claiborne Park, C. (2002) *Exiting Nirvana: A Daughter's Life with Autism.* Boston, MA: Little, Brown & Company.

Cutler, E. (2004) *A Thorn in my Pocket: Temple Grandin's Mother Tells the Family Story.* Arlington, TX: Future Horizons Inc.

Downey, M.K. and Downey, K.N. (2002) *The People in a Girl's Life. How to Find Them, Better Understand Them and Keep Them.* London: Jessica Kingsley Publishers.

Summers, L. (2006) *Autism is Not a Life Sentence. How One Family Took on Autism and Won.* Shawnee Mission, KS: Autism Asperger Publishing Company.

Personal accounts by women

Birch, J. (2003) *Congratulations! It's Asperger Syndrome.* London: Jessica Kingsley Publishers.

Blackman, L. and Attwood, T. (2001) *Lucy's Story: Autism and Other Adventures.* London: Jessica Kingsley Publishers.

Grandin, T. (1995) *Thinking in Pictures: My Life with Autism.* New York, NY: Knopf Publishing Group.

Grandin, T. (1996) *Emergence: Labeled autistic.* New York, NY: Warner Books, Inc.

Lawson, W. (2000) *Life Behind Glass. A Personal Account of Autism Spectrum Disorder.* London: Jessica Kingsley Publishers.

Miller, J.K. (ed.) (2003) *Women From Another Planet?* Bloomington, IN: 1st Books Library.

Prince-Hughes, D. (2004) *Songs of the Gorilla Nation. My Journey Through Autism.* New York, NY: Harmony Books.

Purkis, J. (2006) *Finding a Different Kind of Normal.* London: Jessica Kingsley Publishers.

Willey, L.H. (1999) *Pretending to be Normal.* London: Jessica Kingsley Publishers.

Williams, D. (1992) *Nobody Nowhere: The Remarkable Autobiography of an Autistic Girl.* New York, NY: Harper Collins Publishers.

Williams, S. (2005) *Reflections of Self.* Arlington, TX: Future Horizons Inc.

Personal accounts by girls and young adults

Brosen, S.K. (2006) *Do You Understand Me? My Life, My Thoughts, My Autism Spectrum Disorder.* London: Jessica Kingsley Publishers.

Jackson, N. (2002) *Standing Down, Falling Up.* Bristol: Lucky Duck Publishing Ltd.

Peers, J. (2003) *Asparagus Dreams.* London: Jessica Kingsley Publishers.

Other resources

'Autism_in_Girls' Yahoo!® email group, started in July 1999.

Centers for Disease Control and Prevention (Information on the epidemiology of autism.) Available at www.cdc.gov/ncbddd/autism/overview.htm

The Center on Human Policy, Law and Disability Studies, Syracuse University, Autism and Gender Resources (An online resource section that addresses gender issues and ASDs. They provide short synopses of books, news media and web articles, film, and scientific journal publications that are relevant for understanding sex differences and the experiences of women with ASDs.) Available at http://disabilitystudies.syr.edu/resources/autism.aspx

Neurodiversity.com Autism and Gender (links to other websites, articles, and programs). Available at www.neurodiversity.com/gender.html

Autism is a World (2004), Academy Award-nominated autobiographical film of Sue Rubin, a young woman with autism.

CHAPTER 2

Approaching Adolescence: Anticipation, Anxiety, Adaptation and...Acceptance?

This is the hardest time we've had since she was diagnosed as a preschooler. I often don't know whether her behavior and moods are due to autism, adolescence, or both! How do we tease these apart? (Summary experience of families)

Adolescence: the wild ride

Navigating adolescence is one of the most important challenges in your daughter's life—so much happens just before, during, and just after the teen years. Adolescence marks the transition from being a child, dependent on one's parents, to an adult, independent and responsible for one's own behavior. Additionally, during adolescence teens learn more about their own strengths and weaknesses, and how to work with them. Success in adolescence is marked by progress toward independence and responsibility while answering the questions of "Who am I?" and "What is my place in the world?" The answers to these questions will differ based on the teen, as will the definitions of independence and personal responsibility.

The transition from childhood to young adulthood is a time of marked rapid change. Many theorists describe adolescence as a difficult transitional period which is of utmost importance for a successful transition to adulthood. Hall (1904) pioneered the scientific study of adolescence and coined the period as one of "Storm and Stress" (or "Sturm und Drang"). The changes that occur throughout adolescence can indeed be stressful, and the fact that they are perfectly normal is often of little comfort to teens and their parents. All adolescents undergo these developmental changes, regardless of diagnosis or cognitive level. Moreover, individual differences in rate of development make these changes unpredictable, and therefore more challenging.

Although the changes and experiences of adolescence are sometimes scary, they can also be positive and exciting. We want your daughter to overcome the challenges of adolescence to the best of her capabilities so you can both enjoy this exciting time of her life. In this chapter we will review the developmental changes that occur throughout adolescence, integrating the views of many of the prominent theorists in the field of adolescent development. We will describe some of the difficulties experienced by girls with ASDs during adolescence, and some specific approaches that have been successful in addressing these problems. Finally, we will introduce some general teaching guidelines and techniques that can help your daughter throughout adolescence: these will become your "teaching toolkit", which we will refer to throughout this book, and that you can use for all aspects of your daughter's education. By the end of the chapter, we hope that you will have a better understanding of what the combination of adolescence and autism looks like, and that you will feel prepared to face the challenges that lie ahead.

Developmental tasks

Developmental theorists have described several sets of *developmental tasks* that adolescents complete between the ages of 9 and 21 years (e.g. Cobb 1996; Havinghurst 1971; Perkins 2001). These tasks are accomplished at various ages dependent on individual differences. They are critical to adolescent development: success in accomplishing them leads to personal satisfaction and encourages further development, whereas difficulties in accomplishing the tasks lead to dissatisfaction and discouragement, and provide obstacles to future development. Developmental tasks fall into several broad areas that teens with ASDs may find complex and problematic: physical development, social development, personal identity, cognitive development, and independence or autonomy.

Physical development

Scary as it may seem, little girls will grow into young women. So what physical changes are in store for your daughter? First is the growth spurt. At an average age of 9 years, girls begin to grow rapidly in height, with the peak of growth occurring at about 11½ years (Santrock 2007), and with a peak growth rate of 3½ inches (8.5 cm) per year. Of note, this occurs approximately two years earlier for girls than for boys. This change in height is accompanied by an increase in weight. At the peak of weight gain (at approximately 12 years) girls will gain an average of 18 pounds per year!

The other major physical change—sexual maturation—tends to coincide with this growth spurt. Sexual maturation can produce dramatic differences in appearance between children and teenagers. The specific timing of sexual development can vary significantly among girls: if you think back to your teens, you might remember how different each girl looked in terms of physical maturity. However, there does tend to be a set order to sexual development. First, breasts will begin to enlarge and pubic hair will appear. Then, armpit hair develops, and a widening of the hips occurs. We will talk more about these pubertal changes in Chapter 3. Finally, *menarche* (the first menstruation) usually occurs toward the end of these changes. Menstruation is covered in greater detail in Chapter 4.

Accepting the changes in body shape and size is a difficult task for most adolescent females, and even more so for girls with ASDs who often dislike change of any sort. By the age of 9 or 10, 40% of American girls express concern about their weight (Smolak 2006). When girls commence puberty, their body esteem tends to drop even further as their bodies move from the culturally perceived ideal of thinness. Research has shown that pubertal development in girls is associated with the development of a negative body image (Piran and Ross 2006), and that 60% of adolescent girls are dissatisfied with their body weight or shape (Field *et al.* 1999). Body dissatisfaction is often associated with disordered eating, low self-esteem, and depression. Adolescents may need extra support during this time to understand and accept the changes in their bodies and their new figures. Although no research has been conducted on body image in girls with ASDs, we may assume they will also need this support as girls with ASDs often react poorly to change in general. More information on this topic can be found in Chapter 5.

The *timing* of physical maturation is also relevant to how teenage girls view their bodies; early maturation, in particular, can cause problems. On average, girls develop two years earlier than their male counterparts. Girls who develop even earlier are likely to be taller and more sexually developed than their friends, which also often implies that they will weigh more. These girls are at increased risk for disordered eating, depression, poor academic performance, teasing, early sexual behavior, early substance use, long-term substance abuse, and delinquency (Ge, Conger, and Elder 1996; Mendle, Turkheimer, and Emery 2007).

Learning how to manage one's new body in public requires social insight, understanding, and awareness—difficult skills for girls with ASDs. When a 7- or 8-year-old sits in a skirt with her legs open, it might be overlooked.

However, once she is older and is developing into a young woman, sitting in a skirt with open legs becomes much less appropriate. One mother with whom we worked praised the "skort" (a skirt with attached shorts) as the saviour for her 14-year-old daughter with autism.

As they develop, young women are also introduced to a whole new department of clothing: lingerie. Because individuals with ASDs often have sensory issues related to the feel of their clothing, it may be necessary to spend some time helping your daughter grow accustomed to wearing a bra. Many mothers of daughters with ASDs choose to have their daughter practice by wearing a sports bra before progressing to fasteners, adjustable straps, and underwire. As with everything else, it helps if you and your daughter prepare yourselves. There is also the matter of figuring out appropriate clothes, bras, and undergarments, which is a complicated process when you are suddenly growing breasts, hips, and body hair. Tank tops from last year might not fit over this year's bra. That cute strapless dress might suddenly need the support of a strapless bra. Learning how to match appropriate underwear with low pants, light-colored or sheer items, or even tight pants and tops is complicated, and it may take your daughter a long time to learn all of the subtle rules that are involved. In Chapter 5 we will return to this topic in the broader context of fashion and style.

Social development

As a teenage girl moves through adolescence, her dependence on her parents decreases, and her social circle expands beyond the family. At this point in a girl's life, friendships become increasingly important (Sullivan 1953). During childhood, friendships center on playing—children who are "good" at being friends are those who know how to play cooperatively. The friendship relationship and the skills required enter a new level of complexity in adolescence. Friendships become, in part, about intimacy or the sharing of private thoughts (especially for girls). This type of friendship requires the skills of sharing information about oneself appropriately, providing emotional support to others, and managing disagreements without hurting one another. In particular, social problem-solving becomes increasingly important.

The development of new and more mature relationships with same-sex peers is clearly not an easy task; the increased demands of friendships are both difficult and stressful. This can be especially true for girls with ASDs, who may have problems with the required social skills. However, these early social relationships are important as they prepare teens for future relationships, including romantic relationships and work-related relationships. Additionally, studies have found that, for teenagers, high-quality friendships are correlated with higher self-esteem, an increase in coping skills, and increased independence (Berndt 2002).

Also important is the development of relationships with members of the opposite sex. Between the ages of approximately 8 and 12, children tend to be homosocial. That is, they prefer to play with others of the same sex, and friendships tend only to exist with members of the same sex. This is often referred to as the "cootie" stage, where children view members of the opposite sex as "gross" and "icky". Heterosociality begins around ages 13–14. This is the stage when adolescents begin to enjoy the company of peers of both sexes; these friendships may lay the groundwork for romantic relationships. It is unclear to what extent this transition applies to girls with ASDs, particularly since they may have been surrounded by boys throughout their childhood because of the sex ratio of their disorder and their participation in male-dominated social skills and therapy groups.

In summary, friendships in adolescence become more intimate, involve more social problem solving, begin to include members of the opposite sex, and become more important. We will return to the topic of friendships in Chapter 6. All of these changes are challenging to any female adolescent; when we add the social skills deficits seen in girls with ASDs, social development becomes even more daunting.

Personal identity

Erik Erikson, the first developmental theorist to write about the importance of identity development, described development as a series of psychosocial stages encompassing the entire lifespan (Erikson 1950, 1968). He characterized adolescence in particular as a period when individuals develop a sense of identity: they are faced with deciding who they are and what roles define them. Identity development is not a simple short-term process. In fact, Erikson proposed that events prior to adolescence influence identity development and that identity is further altered as time progresses throughout adulthood.

Identity encompasses all of the answers to the question "Who am I?", including:

- vocational or career identity
- political identity
- religious identity, including spiritual beliefs

- relationship identity (single versus married versus cohabiting)
- extent of motivation to achieve
- sexual identity (heterosexual versus homosexual versus bisexual)
- cultural identity—how intensely one identifies with cultural heritage
- interests, such as sports, music, and other hobbies
- personality characteristics such as introversion, conscientiousness, and agreeableness
- physical identity (body image).

That's quite a lot to swallow! In the context of identity exploration, Erikson (1950, 1968) viewed adolescence as a period of psychosocial moratorium, or the gap between childhood security and adult independence. Because a stable sense of self has not yet been developed, adolescents will experiment with many different roles, styles, and overall identities. This may be the point in a girl's life when she wants a different hairstyle each month, dresses in a different style each week, and has a new best friend or crush every day. This role-exploration is sure to cause anxiety for the teen (and the parents)! To complicate matters, an individual's role can change depending on context (for example, with one's family as compared to with one's friends), making an integrated identity very difficult to achieve. James Marcia (1980, 1994) referred to this period of identity development, where the adolescent chooses among alternatives, as a *crisis*; not knowing who you are and where you are going can be extremely anxiety-provoking.

The thought and process of exploring our identity is stressful, but it is very important. Identity *foreclosure* occurs when adolescents do not explore their identity options but instead find an identity forced upon them. Foreclosed individuals cannot tolerate change and tend to perform poorly under stressful conditions (Rice and Dolgin 2005). Their security lies in avoiding all changes, decisions or stressors, and relying on others to handle these conflicts for them. Identity foreclosure is often the result of well-intentioned parents who feel that they know what is best for their teen and force these decisions on their child. This is not to say that every child who obeys their parents is unhappy; it simply stresses the importance of presenting a child with choices rather than directives. This is especially true for parents of teens with ASDs, as they may tend to impose on their child what they perceive to be the *only* choice, even though there may be more options that they are not aware of. Although there is little knowledge of how identity develops in girls with ASDs specifically, *self-determination* may assist in positive identity development. Self-determination means engaging in self-regulated goal-directed behavior; it will be discussed further in Chapter 5.

For girls with ASDs, their diagnosis will likely form a part of their identity. An understanding of their own strengths and weaknesses will become increasingly important as they enter adulthood. Depending on cognitive ability, different amounts of information about ASDs may be helpful in explaining the diagnosis. Understanding that their identity is not *solely* based on their diagnosis may be difficult for some girls; additional support, in the form of counseling with a therapist who has experience in the area, may be helpful. Several authors have written extensively on the topic of being a teen with autism and what it has meant to their identity (*see* Resources at the end of the chapter).

Cognitive development

With the transition to adolescence, several changes occur in a girl's cognitive processes, or thinking abilities. The stage of cognitive development achieved in adolescence has been referred to as *formal operational thought* (Santrock 2007). In this stage abstract thought is developed. Teens should be able to reason logically about hypothetical situations and develop a conceptual understanding of things that are not concrete (such as tranquillity, hostility, being nice). Rule-based reasoning is less likely to form the basis of problem-solving in adolescence—gray areas, differing perspectives, opinions, and independent ideas are more important. Additionally, another area of abstract thought, *metacognition* (thinking about your own thoughts; awareness of what influences how you think; monitoring of your thoughts), is further developed during adolescence. Abstract thought is an area of difficulty for many teens with ASDs who tend to think in literal and concrete terms.

In later adolescence, future planning and decision-making are two cognitive tasks that become important for all teens, and which require abstract thought and reasoning about hypothetical scenarios. At this point in their lives, adolescents are expected to be able to think ahead and plan for their futures. They are also expected to begin to make their own decisions and understand the logical consequences and future implications of their behavior. These may be areas of difficulty for teens with ASDs, who frequently have impairments in *executive function* (which comprises planning and directing activities, initiating tasks, working memory, sustaining attention, monitoring performance, and inhibiting impulses). Future planning and decision-making can be anxiety-provoking for any teen, but particularly so for teens with ASDs because of their cognitive style and the changes that are implied by consideration of the future.

Independence and autonomy

Teens are faced with the task of gradually moving toward emotional, psychological, and financial independence from their parents. All of the other tasks of adolescence lead to this goal of independence. In fact, one could argue that *all* developmental tasks, beginning in early childhood, have this ultimate goal in common. Independence and autonomy can be difficult for teens with ASDs who are most often more reliant on their parents than their neurotypical peers. The degree of independence that a girl with an ASD will be able to achieve depends on her cognitive abilities and level of impairments, but the goal should still be for her to learn to function with the least support from her parents to the best of her capability.

Adolescence × Autism = A^2?

The quote at the beginning of this chapter represents a summary experience, as conveyed by numerous families of youth with ASDs who have entered adolescence. When we show families the equation we have used to start this section we often hear a resounding "YES!" in response. Adolescence and autism each present their own set of challenges; the combination of the two can be confusing and unpredictable. Many families can relate to the experience of not knowing from one day to the next whether their child's behavior is best accounted for by autism, adolescence, or both. In one case, a mother came to us seeking help for her 14-year-old daughter's new behaviors. The daughter was suddenly taking a long time getting ready in the bathroom in the morning and was talking back to her parents. She had even accused her mom of being "not cool". After evaluating the situation, we informed the mother that no, this was not a new problem behavior related to her daughters diagnosis of PDD-NOS; it was simply the behavior of a typical 14-year-old. The mother didn't know whether to be relieved or upset that her daughter was finally acting "typical". This is just one example of the most common question asked by parents of teens with ASDs: Is it autism or adolescence? In most cases it is a combination of the two. Is a 14-year-old taking too long to get ready because her perseverative and repetitive behaviors are increasing, or it is because she's experimenting with her mom's make-up and other beauty products? In this particular situation, it was the latter combined with poor fine motor skills, but this could only be determined by having the parent periodically check in on her daughter in the bathroom, and by interviewing both the mother and the daughter. The behavior of adolescents with ASDs should be monitored closely, and all analysis should keep in mind both the function of behavior, and its developmental appropriateness.

Specific challenges of adolescence

Adolescence introduces a whole new set of difficulties related to being a teenage girl. For example, the rate of depression in male and female children is the same; however, beginning at age 13 the rate of depressive symptoms in females becomes significantly higher (Twenge and Nolen-Hoeksema 2002). The following is a summary of many of these difficulties, but it is by no means a comprehensive list. It is always important to take note of any changes in your daughter's behavior which may be indicative of a larger problem.

Precocious puberty

Pubertal development in US children has a typical onset between 8½ and 13 years of age (Murphy and Elias 2006). In girls, *precocious puberty* is when pubertal development begins prior to age 7. Precocious puberty may be more common in children with ASDs than in their typically developing peers (Sicile-Kira 2006), and it can have serious medical and psychological complications. Precocious puberty often results in short stature: the body stops growing after puberty is completed, so although the child may be taller than their peers at first, they will stop growing too soon. Children who begin puberty early may feel different and excluded from their peers. This can lead to low self-esteem and depression.

- *What to look for*: If your daughter exhibits breast growth, menstruation, pubic or underarm hair growth, adult body odor or acne before age 8, she may be experiencing precocious puberty.
- *What to do*: If you think your daughter may be entering puberty earlier than normal, it is important to speak with a physician about the possibility of precocious puberty. This condition is diagnosed by using blood tests to check hormone levels, and can be treated using prescription medications which delay puberty.

Seizures

Approximately 25% of all individuals with ASDs experience seizures (Cantino 2007), though it is not known whether the prevalence of seizures is sex-related. A recent study of 60 individuals with ASDs aged 12–29 years found that 38.3% of the sample experienced seizures (Rossi, Posar, and Parmaggiani 2006). Some 66.7% of the sample reported that their seizures had begun after 12 years of age, and the mean reported age of seizure onset was 11 years and 11 months. This study indicates that adolescence is a crucial time in the development of seizures. Although the majority of teens with ASDs do not experience seizures, parents need to be aware of the signs and symptoms of seizure disorders.

- *What to look for*: Some seizure activity is obvious, such as when individuals lose consciousness and have violent convulsions. However, some seizure activity is less obvious. There may be short periods of time (sometimes only seconds) during which the individual is unresponsive and may stare off into space or display unusual motor behavior. Some signs that adolescents may be experiencing undetected seizures are:
  - sudden lack of academic progress
  - loss of behavioral or cognitive gains
  - sudden appearance of behavior problems, such as aggression and self injury.
- *What to do*: If your daughter shows any signs of seizure activity, an appointment with a neurologist is necessary. They may recommend an electroencephalogram (EEG), which measures the electrical currents in the brain, to assess for seizure activity. If they find evidence of seizure activity, medication will be prescribed to help regulate and prevent seizures.

Depression

By age 13, adolescent females have significantly more depressive symptoms than males, and by age 15 the rate of depression in adolescent females is twice that of males (Santrock 2007; Twenge and Nolen-Hoeksema 2002). It has also been noted that a large number of individuals with Asperger's Syndrome and high-functioning autism have a comorbid (meaning co-occurring) diagnosis of depression during their teen years (Ghazziudin 2002; Ghazziudin, Ghazziudin and Greden 2002)—we will discuss this further in Chapter 5. What does this mean for girls with ASDs? Are they doubly at risk for depression? Unfortunately, we do not have an answer. However, it is important for anyone working with a teenage girl with an ASD to be aware of the high risk as well as the signs and symptoms of depression (*see* Chapter 5).

When individuals with ASDs reach adolescence, they often begin to realize that they are different from their peers and experience difficulty fitting in. As previously discussed, the nature of friendships changes during adolescence. Friendship moves from a playmate relationship to a more complex relationship involving trust, sharing, and support. This can make social situations more difficult for individuals with ASDs, who in turn may feel excluded and different. Constant feelings of exclusion, and lowered self-esteem associated with feeling different, often lead to depression.

- *What to look for*: Depression in adolescence is characterized by sad moods, withdrawn or irritable behavior, and hopelessness. Further symptoms include loss of interest in activities, significant weight loss or gain, changes in sleeping patterns, and fatigue.

- *What to do*: Cognitive behavioral therapy (CBT) can be effective for less cognitively impaired teens with ASDs; we will describe this therapy and its uses in detail in Chapter 5. Additionally, a psychiatrist with experience working with ASDs can diagnose depression and provide medication to reduce depressive symptoms.

Anxiety

Temple Grandin described her adolescence as "the worst years of my life" (Grandin 2006, p.xiii). For her, puberty brought extreme anxiety and panic. She describes living in a "constant state of stage fright" (Grandin 1995, p.111). This type of report is common: adolescence and growing up brings many changes that are particularly anxiety-provoking for teens with ASDs. Friendships become more complex and require an extensive knowledge of social problem-solving which is typically impaired in teens with ASDs. As teens become more independent they are expected to rely more on their own organizational skills—a challenge for teens with deficits in executive function. Academic work in high school becomes less concrete and more abstract: students must read Shakespeare and other literature that requires an understanding of character-based plot and perspective-taking, which is again extremely difficult for a teen with an ASD.

Not only is adolescence a period of intense change, it is also a period of time with increased levels of uncertainty. Table 2.1 highlights some aspects of adolescence that have been reported by parents and youth with ASDs as anxiety-provoking at various times. Early sources of anxiety are predominantly related to changes in the body, which are scary but also predictable—little decision-making is required. In contrast, the sources of anxiety that appear later in adolescence are not as clear and require decision-making as multiple options are present. Whereas a 12-year-old may be facing the obstacles of menstruation and bras, a 17-year-old typically has already come

---

Table 2.1 Parent and youth report of "growing up" anxiety at different ages

Pre-teen "growing up" anxiety: ages 8–12

- Start of puberty:
  - menstruation
  - breast development, bras
  - hormonal changes
- Becoming a "teenager", a "grown-up"
- Social world becomes more complex
- Academic expectations increase; curriculum becomes more abstract

Early to mid-teen "growing up" anxiety: ages 13–15

- Personal hygiene expectations increase
- Hair growth, shaving
- Wearing deodorant
- Acne
- Menstruation management
- Emotion dysregulation and mood swings
- Loss of friendships as peers' interests change
- Peers' interests in having a girlfriend or boyfriend
- Fear of "letting go" of immature interests, toys, games, activities

Mid to late-teen "growing up" anxiety: ages 16–19

- Learning to drive (multitasking, organization, motor coordination)
- Thinking about life after high school (college, job preparation)
- Possibility of moving out of parents' house
- Responsibility
- Getting around in the community
- Desire for a relationship, or lack of interest in relationships
- Maintaining friendships

to terms with these changes, and instead faces anxiety related to relationships, jobs or college, and where they will live following high school.

- *What to look for*: Anxiety in adolescence may manifest in a number of ways, including withdrawal, anger, agitation, and physical arousal (e.g. increased perspiration, flushed face, muscle tension, faster breathing). Teens with ASDs may show increased perseverative behaviors, rigidity and inflexibility, and psychomotor agitation in anxiety-provoking situations, or they may withdraw from interactions. Changes in eating habits and sleep patterns may also be indicative of anxiety.

- *What to do*: Preparing your daughter for the changes associated with adolescence may reduce her anxiety. Deep breathing, yoga, and other relaxation strategies can also be used to alleviate anxiety. As with depression, CBT is effective for less cognitively impaired teens, and a psychiatrist with experience working with ASDs can help diagnose anxiety and provide medication to reduce anxiety symptoms. Chapter 5 will talk more about ways to help your daughter with anxiety.

Body image and disordered eating

As previously discussed, negative body image is common in adolescent girls: about 60% of adolescent girls are dissatisfied with their body weight and shape (Field *et al.* 1999). Additionally, disordered eating* occurs in more than one-half of adolescent girls, although most do not meet the full criteria for eating disorders (Smolak 2006). Body dissatisfaction and disordered eating have negative consequences, such as increasing the risk of developing a full-fledged eating disorder, and in some cases preventing participation in athletic activities.

Eating disorders are the third most common illness among adolescent girls (Rosen 2003). Two well-known disorders are *anorexia nervosa* and *bulimia nervosa*. Anorexia nervosa is defined as having an intense fear of gaining weight and weighing less than 85% of what is considered normal for one's age and height. It has been described as 'the relentless pursuit of thinness through starvation' (Santrock 2007). Bulimia, another eating disorder, is

---

* *Disordered eating* is not the same as an *eating disorder*. An eating disorder implies a *DSM-IV* diagnosis; disordered eating is less severe and is more prevalent in the general population.

defined as engaging in an eating pattern of *binging* (eating excessively) and *purging* (self-induced vomiting, use of laxatives, excessive exercise, etc.). Both anorexia and bulimia are about ten times more common in females than in males (Santrock 2007). Unlike individuals with anorexia, those with bulimia do not appear underweight and are likely to be of average or slightly above-average weight. Both disorders are extremely dangerous, and if left untreated may lead to death.

There is little research on the prevalence or trajectory of eating disorders in individuals with ASDs; we will return to this topic in more depth in Chapter 5. A recent epidemiological study highlights social cognition deficits in anorexia suggestive of a genetic link between anorexia and autism (Zucker *et al.* 2007). *Food selectivity*, a refusal to eat all but a select group of foods, has been documented to occur more frequently in individuals with ASDs (Schreck and Williams 2006). As parents, it is important to differentiate between food *selectivity* caused by textures and other sensory concerns, and food *refusal* because of a desire for thinness. Two key distinctions are that food selectivity is likely to follow a long history of selective eating, and that the foods being avoided in food selectivity are not correlated with caloric value.

- *What to look for*: Keep an eye out for major changes in your daughter's eating habits. Additionally, pay attention to any substantial weight loss or gain. Take note of any comments your daughter might make about her own body image and the bodies of those around her, both in real life and in the media.

- *What to do*: Before your daughter exhibits any disordered eating or body dissatisfaction, the best thing any mother can do is model both healthy eating and a healthy body image. Genetics play a large role in body type, so daughters are likely to have some of the same physical characteristics as their mothers. A mother who is constantly complaining about her thighs might be sending a strong message of body dissatisfaction to her daughter! If body dissatisfaction is a concern for your child, a cognitive behavioral therapist can be a helpful resource.

If your daughter is exhibiting any disordered eating patterns, a visit to her physician is necessary. There are a number of interventions for disordered eating which include CBT, family therapy, nutritional counseling, and sometimes antidepressants.

Hygiene problems

For a variety of reasons, teens with ASDs frequently have difficulty with hygiene and self-care. One reason is pubertal changes, which may require new or modified hygiene tasks (e.g. frequency of showering, putting on deodorant, using maxipads, what do about body hair). Those who dislike change in general may try to avoid these tasks. Pubertal and menstrual hygiene will be discussed further in Chapters 3 and 4.

A second reason that teens with ASDs may have hygiene difficulties is fine-motor deficits and problems with motor coordination. Adaptations of self-care equipment may be necessary. We worked with one family whose 16-year-old daughter was having difficulty grasping a bar of soap, and was therefore was not washing herself in the shower. We set her up with a wash-cloth mitt and body wash in a pump, and she was suddenly capable of washing most of her body independently. Be sure to talk with your daughter's occupational therapist to see if they can work on hygiene goals as part of her occupational therapy program.

A third potential cause of difficulties with hygiene is sensory issues, which are common in individuals with ASDs. The smells and textures of soaps, shampoos, and deodorants may be aversive to these teens. Finding products that are less scented and then desensitizing your daughter to the feel of these products may help. Some teens have particularly sensitive areas of their body, such as their gums or their scalp. If this is a problem for your daughter, consider working with a behavioral therapist to develop a plan which allows her to become more accustomed to pressure on these areas.

Behavior problems

Many teens with ASDs exhibit problem behaviors such as aggression, property destruction, self-injury, and tantrums. Such behaviors have the potential to affect quality of life negatively by limiting opportunities in the community for education, socialization, and employment (Koegel, Koegel, and Dunlap 1996). In addition, problem behaviors may increase stress on family members and other caregivers (Lucyshyn et al. 2002). One common cause of problem behaviors is that, similar to younger children with ASDs, teens with ASDs may not be able to properly express their wants, needs, or other more complex emotions, particularly when they are feeling overwhelmed. This may lead to rages, tantrums, or meltdowns.

Behavior problems are often seen as a "male" issue. Society expects boys to be rambunctious by nature, and people may not be as surprised when boys act in a loud or aggressive manner. When a teenage boy gets into a fight, people may just chalk it up to "boys will be boys." Girls, however, are expected to be polite and well-behaved, the "good girl." When a girl displays problem behaviors she is being "un-lady-like;" this makes problem behaviors displayed by girls more conspicuous. Additionally, girls with ASDs may have difficulty fitting the societal mold for what a "young woman" should be.

Not all problems stem from having an ASD; teens with ASDs can also display "typical" teenage issues. Parents of teens with or without ASDs often describe their teens using terms such as *noncompliant, lazy, rude, rebellious,* and *obnoxious.* Adolescents may not want to follow their parents' rules (such as curfews) because they want more autonomy, even though they are not yet ready to be economically and emotionally independent from their parents. This leads to the so-called "problem behaviors" of adolescence, which include rule-breaking. Additionally, the anxiety of adolescence associated with socialization and decision-making is often a precipitating factor in problematic behavior. An additional factor in adolescent problem behavior is the influence of hormones and, for girls in particular, the emotional and physical side-effects of menstruation. These will have varying effects depending on a girl's ability to understand and cope with her hormonal and physical changes.

We often see parents of girls with ASDs who have struggled with severe problem behaviors for years. Sometimes, parents do not seek assistance until their child reaches adolescence. When your daughter is younger, behavior problems seem easier to deal with; for example, a small child who is throwing a tantrum can be picked up and taken out of a store. However, once her size increases and she become more "adult-like", this strategy no longer works. Unfortunately, when a behavioral problem has existed for many years it becomes much harder to correct. It is therefore extremely important to address the problem properly as soon as it emerges; don't wait for behaviors to become unmanageable before getting help!

For all problem behaviors, a functional analysis should be conducted to determine the function of the behavior. These functions may include gaining attention from others (Durand *et al.* 1989), avoiding or escaping an aversive situation (Carr, Newsom, and Binkoff 1980), and obtaining tangible items (Durand and Crimmins 1988). Several meta-analyses have found that interventions based on function are twice as likely to succeed as those which are not based on an assessment of function (Carr *et al.* 1999; Didden, Duker, and Korzelius 1997; Didden *et al.* 2006). Once the function of the behavior is determined, an appropriate intervention plan can be developed.

For additional help with problem behaviors, it is advisable to work with a behavioral therapist. Problem behaviors can often be decreased by using visual supports and implementing strategies such as *token economies*, a technique where positive behavior earns "tokens" (e.g. pennies, poker chips) that may be used to "purchase" a reward. For those individuals with ASDs and milder cognitive impairments, working with a cognitive behavioral therapist on anger management and emotional regulation can also be helpful.

Sexuality and masturbation

Most parents find sexuality to be a difficult topic to talk about with their child. It is, however, extremely important for parents of youth with ASDs to discuss sexuality, including masturbation, with their children. Keep in mind that although girls with ASDs may be delayed in emotional or social development, it is likely that their biological development will occur at a typical rate.

Sexuality is more than just sex. It also includes relationships, gender identification, morals, body image, and the emotional components of being a sexual person. Although much of sexuality is driven by biological influences, there are rules which we have been taught that govern our sexual behaviors. We learn these rules from parents, school, peers, religious institutions, and the media, and they guide our overall sexual development. There are a lot of rules to learn when it comes to sexuality—many of which are unwritten and rely on social understanding and nuances. Girls with ASDs need this information to be taught to them explicitly, and parents are the best source of this information. Without parental involvement, girls are likely to rely on other sources of information, which may not always be accurate or reflect your family's beliefs. Chapter 7 will talk more about sexuality and how to broach this topic with your daughter.

Masturbation is a way of exploring one's own sexuality, and is a normal part of sexual development. However, there are societal stigmas regarding masturbation, and some religions teach against the practice of masturbation. Consider your own views on the topic, and those of your family, when you discuss masturbation with your child. It is extremely important to teach your child specific rules as to where and when masturbation is appropriate. Although masturbation itself is normal, it can become problematic when it is done in public or when it becomes an obsession.

Your "teaching toolkit:" guidelines and techniques

There is a lot of material that your daughter will need to be taught as she reaches adolescence. We have reviewed a number of topics, each of which is complex and most of which will be discussed in further detail throughout the book. Although many of the issues and skills related to adolescence are new, the techniques used to teach them are not: the same therapeutic and educational concepts that have worked with your child in the past can be used to teach these new skills. Believe it or not, there is not much difference between teaching your child how to write her name and how to wear a maxipad! The biggest difference will be in your own comfort level. The subject matter of adolescence tends to be more sensitive, embarrassing, and less enjoyable to discuss. The following is a review of teaching guidelines, many of which will be familiar to you.

- *Be proactive*: As much as possible, teach skills *before* there is a problem. Certain events in your daughter's life are predictable (e.g. menstruation): plan ahead for these events and teach ahead of time so that your daughter will be ready. Also, try not to underestimate how long it will take for your daughter to learn a new skill. Keep in mind your daughter's areas of difficulties (e.g. sensory issues, resistance to change, motor difficulties). Plan for extra teaching time when a new skill will involve an area of difficulty.

- *Be concrete*: Individuals with ASDs often have difficulty with abstract or temporal information, so present material as concretely as possible. For example, a teen with an ASD may not understand that she has to change her pad when it "needs changing" or "in a few hours." Instead, establish an explicit schedule for changing her pad at set times throughout the day.

- *Be consistent*: Be consistent with your expectations and demands on your teen. If you are teaching a new skill, consistency is essential. For instance, when teaching privacy, a rule should be established that your daughter can only change her clothes in her bedroom or the bathroom. Do not make an exception if you are in a rush one day and tell her that it is okay to change in the kitchen. This is likely to confuse your daughter and undo your teaching efforts.

- *Be specific*: Similar to consistency and concreteness, specificity in your expectations and demands for your teen is essential. For example, instead of asking your daughter to clean her room, make a specific list of what that entails (e.g. make the bed, put books on shelf, take dirty clothes off floor and put in laundry basket).

- *Keep things simple*: Simple teaching helps your child learn more effectively. Determine what you want your daughter to understand at a basic level—you can always add more information later. There is also no need to complicate reinforcement (reward) systems. We have seen several parents create reinforcement systems so complex that they can barely follow them, their child does not understand them, and it becomes too labor-intensive to implement them. Simplicity helps everyone!

- *Repeat often*: When working with teens with ASDs, keep in mind that information and skills are often not learned the first time: multiple repetitions are needed. Plan on teaching things several times, and do not be discouraged by slow progress. It is also important to teach in multiple settings so that your daughter can generalize her skills. For example, she may know what to do if a stranger rings the doorbell, but not what to do if a stranger approaches her in a mall or at the movie theatre. It may seem obvious to you, but it might not be to her. When something is this important, risk being boring and repetitive!

- *Provide opportunities for practice*: You wouldn't teach a child to ride a bicycle if they did not have access to a bicycle. Similarly, you shouldn't teach any other skills without providing opportunities for practice. This may include staging situations where a coworker pretends to be a stranger, or making field trips to the convenience store to make small purchases. Remember, although it may be easier to wash your daughter's hair yourself, this does not teach her how to do it on her own. Take the time to let her practice the skills you have been working on.

- *Teach to multiple senses*: Many individuals with ASDs have difficulties with auditory processing. Does this mean you should not speak to your daughter? Of course not. However, it does mean you shouldn't rely on verbal instruction alone. The use of visual supports is essential across the full range of cognitive abilities seen in ASDs. Depending on the child, this may take the form of pictures or written words. Some individuals with ASDs learn better by physically manipulating materials. For these teens, practice with props will be essential.

- *Divide tasks into small components*: Many tasks that we do on a regular basis, such as washing hair or doing laundry, are a lot more complex than we think. Use a *task analysis* to break these activities down into simplified steps. For example, instead of instructing your daughter to put shaving cream on, it is better to say first wet your legs, then put a golf ball-sized amount of shaving cream in your hand, then rub the shaving cream on the front of your leg, then the sides of your leg, etc.

- *Provide adequate reinforcement*: Do not assume that an activity will be naturally reinforcing for your daughter. Things that may seem pleasant to you (e.g. going to a party, taking a long shower), may be anxiety-provoking, aversive, or uninteresting to your daughter. Find out what *is* reinforcing for your daughter (e.g. books, video rentals, edibles), and provide more reinforcement for more aversive tasks.

- *Incorporate social goals*: Explain the social reason for any new tasks that you are teaching to your daughter (e.g. if you don't brush your teeth, you will smell bad and no one will want to go near you). Teens with ASDs may not understand the social implications of behaviors without being taught them explicitly. Additionally, whenever you are with your daughter, be on the lookout for *teachable moments*: situations that arise naturally in your daughter's environment and which provide valuable lessons and examples.

- *Be calm, supportive, and serious*: Clearly this will be easier for some topics than for others. However, it is essential to realize that your child will respond to topics based on how you present them. If talking about something embarrasses you, your daughter will likely learn that it is a topic to be embarrassed about. Always present yourself as a calm and objective source of information. Be supportive, not judgmental. Most importantly, don't panic! This will only cause your daughter to panic too. You *can* teach your child!

The following is a set of teaching techniques that we have found useful in helping adolescent girls with ASDs to learn the skills necessary for adolescence and accept their changing role as a young woman. Each teen will be different; what works for one may not work for another. It is important to know what works best for your daughter. Has video modeling been successful in the past? If so then continue to use it; if not then you may want to try something else. Unfortunately, there is no set protocol to determine which techniques will work best. Use methods that play to your daughter's strengths, which may involve using multiple techniques for one topic. Take note of the strategies that work best and keep those in mind when you approach a particularly difficult topic. Remember that you already have years of experience teaching your daughter how to navigate the world; now is the time to take advantage of that experience!

- *Visual supports*: Visual supports can take many forms and are appropriate for a large range of ability levels. They may be used for teaching and as reminders to maintain a routine. Some visual supports include calendars, activity schedules, pictures, reminder cards, checklists, and picture schedules.

- *Routines and schedules*: Routines and schedules help make life predictable, which is important for girls with ASDs. They can be written out and displayed for your daughter to look at while doing something. For example, a shower schedule that details the steps to showering may be laminated and placed in the shower. Additionally, schedules of what activities your daughter has for the day may be helpful. Some girls choose to carry those schedules with them throughout the day.

- *Modeling*: Parents, peers, and siblings can all serve as models of behavior that you want your daughter to learn. Explain to her very specifically what the model is doing that you want her to learn to do.

- *Video modeling*: Another effective modeling strategy is to videotape the behavior that you want your daughter to learn. You can then replay, rewind, and pause to highlight specific portions of the skill that you want your daughter to master.

- *Role-playing*: Some teens learn best by doing. You may want your daughter to practice what to do in role-play scenarios. This may be particularly useful for social situations, dangerous situations, and situations which are unlikely to arise naturally.

- *Narratives about social situations*: Write short narratives about social situations with your daughter as the protagonist. Include in the narrative some of the things that might happen in a given situation, how your daughter is supposed to act, and *why* she should act in a certain way.

- *Social scripts*: Social scripts are written prompts of what to do or say in specific social situations. Examples of social scripts include what to say when you answer the phone, or how to buy tickets to a movie.

- *Power cards*: A power card is a visual support that uses a child's special interest to teach appropriate social interactions, including routines and behavior expectations. A power card consists of two parts: the first explains how the child's favorite character handles a problem or behaves in a certain scenario; the second encourages the child to act in the same manner when in a similar scenario or faced with the same problem.

- *Television and movies*: Television and movies often provide excellent demonstrations of typical social situations your teen may encounter, and are accessible as teens find it easy to identify with their favorite characters. When watching a television show or movie with your daughter, if something interesting or applicable comes up then talk to her about it. Make use of the teachable moment.

- *Books and the internet*: Many teens with ASDs like to read— particularly those with relatively unimpaired cognitive skills. These teens may prefer reading about a topic as opposed to discussing it with their parent. This may be especially true for more personal topics such as menstruation or masturbation. You may want to give your daughter material to read and discuss it with her afterwards. Additionally, there are many excellent websites listed in the Resources sections throughout this book that have material you can print out for your daughter. Some websites have videos of some difficult to understand topics (e.g. tampon placement), which are excellent teaching tools.

Lessons from Nemo

After spending so many years nurturing and protecting your daughter, watching her grow up can be a bit scary at times. The world within the four walls of a family home is safe, but we cannot keep girls enclosed in those walls forever. One mother compared the feeling of her daughter growing up to what Marlin felt in the animated Disney movie about fish, *Finding Nemo*. Marlin, an overprotective single father, was extremely anxious about his son, Nemo, leaving for school. Nemo was born with a misformed fin after a predator attacked both Nemo's mother and all her eggs. Marlin was used to doing everything for his son. Despite his father's constant warnings about many of the ocean's dangers, Nemo was abducted by a boat and had to fend for himself far away from his father (which he did successfully). Yes, the story was about fish, but it does teach us a lot about the anxiety felt by both parent and child when we must let our children grow up and leave. It also teaches us that although it may be scary to see our children go out and handle their problems on their own, they might actually surprise us and handle them well, even with a misformed fin or, in the non-animated version, with an ASD.

Resources
General books on adolescence and ASDs

Bolick, T. (2001) *Asperger Syndrome and Adolescence: Helping Preteens & Teens Get Ready for the Real World*. Gloucester: Fair Winds Press.

Boushéy, A. (2007) *Talking Teenagers. Information and Inspiration for Parents of Teenagers with Autism or Asperger's Syndrome*. London: Jessica Kingsley Publishers.

Gabriels, R.L. and Hill, D.E. (eds) (2007) *Growing Up with Autism. Working with School-Age Children and Adolescents*. New York, NY: Guilford Press.

Korpi, M. (2007) *Guiding Your Teenager with Special Needs through the Transition from School to Adult Life: Tools for Parents*. London: Jessica Kingsley Publishers.

Molloy, H. and Vasil, L. (2004) *Asperger Syndrome, Adolescence, and Identity: Looking Beyond the Label*. London: Jessica Kingsley Publishers.

Sicile-Kira, C. (2006) *Adolescents on the Autism Spectrum: A Parent's Guide to the Cognitive, Social, Physical, and Transition Needs of Teenagers with Autism Spectrum Disorders*. New York, NY: Perigree Trade.

Smith Myles, B. and Adreon, D. (2001) *Asperger Syndrome and Adolescence: Practical Solutions for School Success*. London: Jessica Kingsley Publishers.

Willey, L.H. (2003) *Asperger Syndrome in Adolescence: Living with the Ups, the Downs and Things in Between*. London: Jessica Kingsley Publishers.

Yoshida, Y. (2006) *How To Be Yourself in a World That's Different: An Asperger's Syndrome Study Guide for Adolescents*. London: Jessica Kingsley Publishers.

Personal accounts by teens

Brosen, S.K. (2006) *Do You Understand Me? My Life, My Thoughts, My Autism Spectrum Disorder*. London: Jessica Kingsley Publishers.

Jackson, L. (2002) *Freaks, Geeks & Asperger Syndrome: A User Guide to Adolescence*. London: Jessica Kingsley Publishers. (Winner of the NASEN & TES Special Educational Needs Children's Book Award 2003.)

Jackson, N. (2002) *Standing Down, Falling Up*. Bristol: Lucky Duck Publishing Ltd.

Peers, J. (2003) *Asparagus Dreams*. London: Jessica Kingsley Publishers.

Books for parents about stress, anxiety, and coping

Cautela, J.R. and Groden, J. (1978) *Relaxation: A Comprehensive Manual for Adults, Children, and Children with Special Needs.* Champaign, IL: Research Press.

Dunn, K.B. and Curtis, M. (2004) *Incredible 5-Point Scale—Assisting Students with Autism Spectrum Disorders in Understanding Social Interactions and Controlling Their Emotional Responses.* Shawnee Mission: Autism Asperger Publishing Company.

Gagnon, E. and Chiles, P. (2001) *Power Cards: Using Special Interests to Motivate Children and Youth with Asperger Syndrome and Autism.* Shawnee Mission: Autism Asperger Publishing Company.

Groden, J., LeVasseur, P., Diller, A. and Cautela, J. (2001) *Coping with Stress through Picture Rehearsal: A How-to Manual for Working with Individuals with Autism and Developmental Disabilities.* Providence: The Groden Center, Inc.

Lipsitt, L.P., Groden, G., Baron, M.G. and Groden, J (2006) *Stress and Coping in Autism.* Providence: The Groden Center, Inc.

Smith Myles, B. and Southwick J. (2005) *Asperger Syndrome and Difficult Moments. Practical Solutions for Tantrums, Rage, and Meltdowns.* Shawnee Mission: Autism Asperger Publishing Company.

Books for youth about anxiety and coping

American Girl Publishers. (2002) *The Feelings Book. The Care and Keeping of Your Emotions.*

Buron, K.D. (2006) *When My Worries Get Too Big: A Relaxation Book for Children Who Live with Anxiety.* Shawnee Mission: Autism Asperger Publishing Company.

Jaffe, A. and Gardner, L. (2006) *My Book Full of Feelings: How to Control and React to the Size of Your Emotions.* Shawnee Mission: Autism Asperger Publishing Company.

Romain, T. and Verdick, E. (2000) *Stress Can Really Get on Your Nerves!* Minneapolis, MN: Free Spirit Publishing.

Other resources

The Groden Center: Based in Rhode Island, USA, the Groden Center is recognized internationally for its work with individuals with autism, and most recently, innovative programming in relaxation, stress reduction, and using visual supports to develop coping skills. Available at www.grodencenter.org

Off to the movies! Using video for teaching

We have spent hours watching television shows and movies to find examples of the social concepts we try to teach to girls with ASDs. The following shows and movies are the best of the bunch, and we use many of them in our girls' groups. Because they come from different movie eras, and are based around different sports and activities, we hope there is enough variety for you to find something that you and your daughter will enjoy. What's nice about some of the teen movies is that even though they might not be Oscar-worthy, they often contain exaggerated of facial expressions, tones of voice and behaviors that you will want your daughter to notice.

If your daughter is not interested in watching movies, then think about possible rewards and reinforcements. What could she earn for having a "movie night" with you? Could you reciprocate by watching a *Yu-Gi-Oh* episode with her? The learning opportunity for your daughter might be well worth it! Remember the different activities you can do with television and film:

- watch short segments
- pause and have discussions
- turn off the volume and watch the nonverbal cues; decipher the message
- listen to tone of voice to determine a character's message; does the tone of voice match what is spoken?
- follow story lines, developing understanding of character's perspectives
- talk to your daughter about decision-making; what should the character do?
- show examples of appropriate and inappropriate behavior; use rating cards for her to determine *how* inappropriate a particular behavior is—make it interactive!

1980s/1990s

Can't Buy Me Love

Some Kind of Wonderful

Pretty in Pink

Say Anything

10 Things I Hate About You

She's All That

Can't Hardly Wait

2000s Romantic

The Prince and Me

A Cinderella Story

A Walk to Remember

Love Actually

Girl cliques
Mean Girls

Clueless

Young teen
High School Musical

Older teen/young adult
Napoleon Dynamite (young man with unidentified Asperger's)

Hitch

How to Lose a Guy in 10 Days

50 First Dates

Never Been Kissed

Skating
The Cutting Edge

Ice Princess

Dancing
Center Stage

Save the Last Dance

Step Up

Sports
Fever Pitch (baseball)

Summer Catch (baseball)

Friday Night Lights (football)

For Love and Basketball (basketball)

Wimbledon (tennis)

TV shows
My So Called Life (very realistic; off the air)

Dawson's Creek (tame; re-runs)

Degrassi Junior High (tame; re-runs)

One Tree Hill (racy)

The OC (racy)

Gossip Girl (racy)

CHAPTER 3

Puberty *or* "Do my Parents Know You're Here?"

Are you ready?

Receiving the news that your daughter has an ASD is a difficult and painful experience. Regardless of when families learn this truth, a parent's hopes and dreams for the future change forever. Thoughts of best friends, sleepovers, sweet-sixteen parties, first kisses, prom dates, walking your daughter down the aisle, and having grandchildren become uncertain, and other thoughts begin to intrude. Worries surface about bullying and loneliness, self-esteem, vulnerability to abuse, handling puberty and menstruation, the possibility of unwanted pregnancy, being loved, and having a trusting intimate relationship. Parents frequently doubt themselves and begin to ask, "Will we be able to protect our daughter and keep her healthy, safe, and happy?" Sometimes it can be easier to look away and try to believe that your daughter will stay a little girl forever: to pretend that she is not really growing up. Fears can reach a pinnacle as a daughter approaches adolescence, when her mind and body will begin to transform into those of a woman.

In 2005, Advocates for Youth* published an educational campaign entitled "Parents: It's Time to Talk", promoting the importance of talking with your children about sex and sexuality. One of their multimedia materials is a cartoon that we use in almost every talk we give on growing up with a developmental disability. In fact, we find the message so important that we've quoted the cartoon in the title of this chapter. The cartoon shows a young girl, about eight or nine years of age, holding a doll and looking up with puzzlement at a bizarre pink polka-dotted elephant-like creature with "puberty" emblazoned on its chest. The little girl asks hesitantly, "Do my parents know you're here?" The creature replies, in a delightful Grinch-like manner with a smile, "Not likely."

Uncertainties about when puberty will begin—or even whether or not it has already begun—worsen the fear and anxiety associated with adolescence. At times, the worry can become consuming, resulting in well-

---

* Available at www.advocatesforyouth.org (accessed on March 27, 2008)

meaning but misguided overprotection. Dave Hingsburger, a Canadian sexologist, talks about "the prison of protection" (Hingsburger 1995) and the balance between wanting to meet the learning needs of your child while keeping them safe. This is not an easy line to walk. In fact, we feel strongly that overprotection is a completely understandable response, and far preferable to underprotection. However, when parents are able to find a balance, the thought of adolescence becomes less overwhelming and frightening. Adolescence can then include positive and exciting learning experiences for both yourself and your daughter.

Mixed feelings about the start of puberty

In our clinic we have worked with families whose responses to their daughter growing up have ranged from denial, apprehension, and fear to

Case study: Caitlin

Caitlin is a 14-year-old young woman with high-functioning autism. Though Caitlin is extremely bright in many ways and does well in school, she experiences seizures and can take a long time to process information. During conversations, her responses are often delayed, and it is unclear whether she understands everything that is being discussed. Caitlin's mother was nervous about adolescence, and in particular what the future would hold for her daughter. Caitlin had difficulties with personal hygiene and her discomfort with having her hair washed made it hard for her to be clean every day. Caitlin's mother was also disappointed that her daughter showed little interest in personal appearance, style, or clothing; she chose to wear only comfortable loose clothing and at times looked unkempt. Though she had not yet expressed an interest in boys or dating, Caitlin's mother was concerned that she would eventually desire a relationship but would not be able to find someone who would want to be with her. At the beginning of our parent group, Caitlin's mother was quite unsure about her ability as a mother to help Caitlin achieve her full potential. By the end of the group, that viewpoint had shifted. The future was no longer a menacing unknown, and she felt supported in her optimism for her daughter's future. On her course evaluation she wrote: "I have learned that my child has a future—a positive future—with regard to a sexual relationship and marriage. I was much more fearful of the prospects before the class. Now I look forward with hope and excitement, watching my daughter grow up. This, I hope, will translate to a more helpful support for her from me."

acceptance and excitement. As part of the "Growing Up with ASD" program at our clinic, we offer a 10-week parent psychoeducation and support class that is aimed toward helping parents navigate puberty and better understand their child's emerging sexuality. One of the primary goals of the course is for parents to become more comfortable and accepting of the journey into adolescence, and to feel that they can provide the learning opportunities and experiences necessary for their child's healthy development. Though many families wish it could be otherwise, growing up does not come with an "opt-out" ticket—adolescence will happen, whether you are ready or not! As a parent, the best thing you can do is to be prepared and informed about the changes that are about to occur.

Taking the plunge

In this chapter we are going to discuss how to prepare for puberty and how to acquire the skills and knowledge that are necessary for parents and daughters to enter adolescence successfully. We know that being ready for puberty is not easy for any parent. If you are a parent of a girl with autism or another developmental disability, the transition to adolescence can be even more overwhelming and difficult to accept, let alone embrace! For girls with a developmental disability, puberty can often "sneak up" unawares. We have worked with many families who have called us in a panic because their daughter started her period and they were unprepared, or they received a telephone call from school about their daughter being teased in the changing room because she was not yet wearing a bra. Maybe you are a parent who has experienced something similar, or perhaps you have been very prepared and are surprised that this might happen to anyone. How does it happen that well-meaning and caring families are caught off-guard by puberty? They have handled the transition to preschool and elementary school, and have been on top of their daughter's educational and intervention needs. So what happens? It's actually not too surprising when you consider two things: the disparity between mental and physical development for girls with ASDs as they approach adolescence, and a family's desire to protect their child and keep them from harm. The "prison of protection", mentioned earlier, is often quickly built, and then difficult to dismantle.

ASDs and adjusting to puberty

It is important to understand how your daughter's autism will play a role in puberty, growing up, and her changing body and feelings. For example, does she have sensory sensitivities? Does she tend to have difficulties when things in her life change? This understanding, combined with your aware-ness of what teaching approaches work best with your daughter, will enable you to develop an effective plan for the transition to adolescence. If your daughter is already in the midst of pubertal changes, think about how she is doing: Is there anything you can approach from a different perspective that would be helpful for her? As you read through the remainder of this chapter, keep in mind your teaching toolkit, and the particular strategies that you have found to be most effective so far. Remember, every young woman will have her own unique experience of adolescence; no two girls go through puberty in exactly the same way. There are, however, some common char-acteristics associated with ASDs that can present challenges during adoles-cence. Which of those listed below are most relevant to your daughter?

- Difficulties with novelty and change.
- General anxiety.
- Sensory challenges.
- Difficulties regulating emotions and communicating feelings.
- Executive function impairments (organization, planning, time management).
- Problems with manual dexterity and motor coordination.
- Delayed social maturity.

When does puberty start?

Most girls (approximately 95%) enter puberty between the ages of 8 and 13 years, depending on ethnicity. Although some preliminary work is being conducted on the age of menarche for girls with ASDs, it is currently thought that the physical development of girls with ASDs mostly corresponds to that of their neurotypical peers. If girls with ASDs mature physically within an age-appropriate range, what is happening with their cognitive, emotional, social, and psychological development? We know that for many girls with ASDs cognitive skills can be delayed. Even girls whose overall intellectual abilities fall within the average to above-average range often have diffi-culties with higher-level cognitive skills and abstract conceptual thought.

Overall, the physical development of girls with ASDs may closely match their chronological age, yet their mental, emotional, or social age is often delayed by between two and ten years. If your daughter is 14 years old, but she plays with dolls and watches *Blues Clues*, it may be difficult to think of her as a "14-year-old" who needs the knowledge and skills to manage pubertal changes such as onset of menstruation. Some parents we have worked with have thought that physical development and emotional or cognitive development occur together, so that if their daughter has a mental age of seven years then, despite being 14 chronological years old, her physical development should also be comparable with that of a seven-year-old. Because of this, they are not expecting puberty and are unprepared when it arrives.

Since girls usually start puberty between the ages of 8 and 13, parents should be observant of their daughter's growth and bodily changes beginning around the age of seven. We recommend an appointment with her physician when you begin to notice the earliest signs of physical maturation. If this occurs when your daughter is younger than seven years of age, she may be experiencing precocious puberty and it will be important for her to see a physician immediately. Your daughter's physician will be able to determine what stage of psychosexual development she has reached, and approximately when you might expect her to begin to grow pubic hair or start menstruation. If you have an idea of when specific developmental changes will likely occur, you can create your teaching plan and begin preparing your daughter (and yourself!) for the new experiences to come. Take a deep breath and practice your own coping skills… you will be as ready as you can be.

Teaching tips: visiting the doctor

Visiting the doctor can be a challenging experience for girls with ASDs for a number of reasons, including sensory issues and anxiety about novel, uncertain experiences. Help your daughter prepare for her appointment ahead of time so that she can be as informed and relaxed as possible.

- Book the appointment at least a week in advance so you have time to prepare.
- Write the appointment on a calendar so that you can refer to it together.
- If possible, visit the clinic before the appointment. Take pictures of the building and staff, if permitted.

- Use pictures or written stories to describe the visit to the doctor and what will happen there. Include in the story what she can do if she begins to feel nervous or uncomfortable (e.g. deep breathing, listen to music, ask for a break).

- Practice relaxation strategies before the appointment.

- Use visual supports such as flow charts and diagrams to explain to your daughter the purpose of the visit. Be positive about the experience. Even if you feel uncomfortable going to the doctor yourself, do not convey these feelings to your daughter. Your daughter needs to feel as comfortable and positive as possible.

- If you have access to a toy doctor's kit, practice using the stethoscope, the blood pressure cuff, and looking in her ears and throat. Role-play together and let your daughter be the doctor also. Have fun with it!

- Try to book either the first or last appointment during the day, or find out when the office tends to be less busy. Booking a double appointment may be necessary if your daughter will need time to get used to the setting and having a physical examination.

- Bring something your daughter likes to do while in the waiting room. Listening to music can sometimes be relaxing and can block out the sounds of a noisy reception area.

- If your daughter is easily overwhelmed in novel, busy situations, see if the doctor's office has a quiet area where you can sit before your appointment.

- Make sure her doctor and the other staff at the clinic are aware that your daughter has an ASD. Encourage the doctor and nurses to show or tell your daughter what is going to happen next during the examination. Bring your story book into the appointment with you.

- Reward your daughter for being able to cope with and participate in the appointment. Decide on what the reward will be ahead of time, and what is expected of her in order for her to earn it. Allow her to play an active role in the decision-making.

Foundational skills

By age eight, parents should begin to establish their daughter's *foundational skills*, which comprise four skill sets:

- Following guidelines for public versus private places (e.g. clothing, topics, behavior).
- Participating in hygiene routines.
- Respecting others' privacy.
- Understanding rules for personal space and touching.

Foundational skills are essential for every girl growing up, regardless of diagnosis, verbal skill, or cognitive ability level. They are universal skills, achievable for everyone with the appropriate teaching and behavior management strategies. We have found this to be true in our own work, as have others, including the professionals at TEACCH, in North Carolina. In 1982, Gary Mesibov wrote a paper about matching skills to the ability levels of individuals when teaching about sexuality (Mesibov 1982). Mesibov reported that these skills can be taught using *discriminative learning*, which teaches a child to discriminate between two alternatives (e.g. okay to be naked versus clothing required). We use discriminative learning in our own practice, and have also found it to be effective. Whatever teaching approach works best for your daughter, it is important for her to learn these foundational skills as a first step toward preparing for adolescence.

In the following sections we will take a closer look at the first three foundational skill sets—public versus private places, hygiene, and respecting privacy—which are particularly relevant to puberty. The rules for personal space and touching will be discussed in Chapter 7.

Wearing clothes in public places

When we think about wearing clothes, it is important to remember that this is a learned, social concept. Covering one's body with articles of clothing in particular situations is not something that children spontaneously begin to do on their own as they grow up. Think about how cultural and social expectations influence society's guidelines regarding privacy. One may walk topless, and even bottomless, on many beaches in Europe, but you would not likely do so on a beach in Florida! How did you learn this? For those of us who do not have an ASD, this occurs gradually through early learning experiences such as incidental teaching, naturalistic teaching, modeling, and imitation. When you were young you learned when and where you could be naked from your parents, older siblings, other family members, and peers, and those guidelines changed depending on how old you were. For example, while it was okay for you to have bathtub photographs taken when you were a toddler, that changed as you got older. For youth with ASDs wearing clothing in public can be challenging from a very young age. They have difficulty learning from naturalistic social experiences, and sensory issues can also cause an aversion to clothing. Many parents report that it is difficult for them to keep their young child from disrobing.

We might think that wearing clothes in public should be straightforward once the concept is taught. The difficulty is that when two or more rules interact, prioritizing them appropriately can be challenging for girls with ASDs.

Case study: Jessica

Jessica is a 14-year-old bright young woman with Asperger's Syndrome. She generally learns concepts quickly and is doing quite well at school—she even leads her own individualized education plan (IEP) meetings! Jessica's mother thought that she would have no difficulties with understanding privacy concepts and when to be clothed. For the most part, she was right. Jessica had been doing fine following the rules ever since she was seven years old. One day, Jessica's family was running behind schedule; her mother and father were finishing packing up the car to go on a family trip. Jessica was still getting ready. Her father, frazzled about being late, went into the house and yelled up the stairs "Jessica, we have to go now! Come on!" Jessica, not wanting to disobey her father, came out on to the landing and shouted "I'm not dressed yet!" And she wasn't... Though Jessica had demonstrated that she understood the rules about being clothed, when presented with a scenario in which there was a conflict (I'm not dressed, but my dad is asking me to go now) Jessica chose immediately to listen to her father and leave her room without clothing. Needless to say, her father wasn't expecting that, and Jessica and her mother needed to review more scenarios about being naked and clothed. This time she practiced opening her bedroom door and saying "I'm not dressed yet. I'll be out in a minute."

What Jessica and her family experienced with the complexity of a seemingly simple concept is not uncommon. Many youth with ASDs have difficulties with concepts that are learned from observing and interacting with others, and are based on underlying social rules. If it wasn't for other people and social guidelines for behavior, privacy wouldn't be an issue! If your daughter is having difficulty with understanding or following privacy/naked/clothed rules, you are not alone, and we recommend the use of visuals and models to help your daughter's learning in this area.

Whenever concrete concepts need to be explained, use *simple visuals* to support your daughter's learning. For example:

- Use a sorting activity to identify pictures of public and private places (e.g. bathroom, kitchen, backyard, bedroom, classroom, doctor's office). Pair public places with a picture of a child that is clothed and private places with two pictures of a child: one clothed and one naked (or in underwear).

- If your daughter needs visual cues at home to remind her where she can be undressed, place pictures of red Xs and green checkmarks at the entrances to various rooms in your house. Use additional written supports if this is an effective strategy for your daughter (e.g. "Wear clothing please").

Teach by example; *model* appropriate behavior within the family. For example, require your family members to wear a bathrobe when walking between the bedroom and bathroom. If your daughter finds wearing a full bathrobe to be uncomfortable, consider having her use a Velcro towel. This will be easier than trying to coordinate tucking the towel ends under her armpits and will reduce the chance of the towel falling to the floor on the trip back to the bedroom! If everyone in the family gets into the habit of wearing a bathrobe or towel, you will have naturalistic teaching at work every day.

Proper attire

The next step after learning *when* to wear clothes is learning *what* clothes to wear. Different settings call for different attire: casual clothes (e.g. jeans, T-shirt, sneakers) are appropriate for school; formal clothes (e.g. dresses, slacks, blouses) should be worn at special events, nice dinners or religious services; and beachwear (e.g. bathing suit, flip-flops) should be reserved for beaches, showers, and other water-related activities. Again, these rules probably seem obvious to you, but they are social in nature and are not always intuitive for girls with ASDs. There are, of course, many additional and more subtle rules regarding clothing and style (hence the entire fashion industry!)—we will return to this in Chapter 5 when we discuss fashion and developing a sense of style.

There are a number of effective techniques you can use to teach your daughter the different types of attire and where they are appropriate. Think about your daughter's learning style and which approaches might work best with her.

- Use picture-pairing activities, with pictures of girls wearing different types of clothes and pictures of different venues.

- Read illustrated storybooks, and explicitly point out the type of clothing that people are wearing in different locations.

- Use a doll with a variety of outfits; tell your daughter where the doll is going (e.g. to the swimming pool, to a birthday party) and have her dress the doll appropriately.

- If your daughter likes to draw, replace the doll with the outline of a girl and have your daughter draw the clothing.

Part of being dressed properly is making sure that your undergarments (bra, underwear, slip, etc.) are not showing. Teach your daughter that wearing

Case studies: Madison and Caitlin

Two mothers in one of our growing-up parent groups had daughters who struggled with keeping their legs closed while sitting. Madison, a bright girl with Asperger's Syndrome, was 13 at the time and her mother lamented that they had finally decided that she could no longer wear skirts. Despite having attempted many different strategies for teaching, and despite Madison being very bright, she was an active girl who was completely unaware of needing to keep her legs closed or her feet on the ground while sitting when wearing a skirt. Caitlin's situation was similar: despite being bright, Caitlin liked to wear short shorts in the summer and would often sit cross-legged or with her heels up on a chair, exposing both her underwear and, every month, her maxipad. Both Madison and Caitlin knew the social rule, but they had difficulties translating that rule into day-to-day life, and they also struggled with understanding the social meaning behind the rule. Without being fully aware of why there was a problem, they were unable to self-monitor and therefore self-correct their behavior.

underwear does *not* mean that she is dressed. When she puts on clothes she should make sure that her underwear is not visible (which includes not wearing dark underwear underneath light clothing). She should also learn to keep her legs closed when she sits down while wearing short shorts, a skirt or a dress; this rule is particularly important for your daughter to learn as she enters puberty to avoid uncomfortable situations for those around her.

Private topics

In addition to learning rules for wearing clothes, your daughter needs to understand that some topics of conversation are personal and are only discussed with certain people (e.g. her mother) and at the appropriate time (e.g. when no one else is around). Private topics may include bodily symptoms and physical health (e.g. the difference between sharing "I have a cold" versus "My vagina is itchy"), menstruation, mental health, and family difficulties. Teach your daughter the difference between public and private topics using picture stories, and by pairing pictures of people, places, and topics of conversation. Always reward her when she demonstrates good judgment and decision-making.

Although having a period is a natural and healthy part of a woman's growth and development, Western society continues to be uncomfortable with that information being shared broadly with others. Hence the advertisements for tampon packaging that looks like a lipstick dispenser! Your

Case study: Karen

Karen is a 14-year-old girl with high-functioning autism. She has had her period for less than a year and has been working very hard at becoming more independent with her menstrual routine. One night, she was at home with her parents, and family friends were sitting in the living room having a visit after dinner. Karen had excused herself to use the washroom and upon her return proudly stated loudly to everyone that she had changed her pad herself and threw it in the correct garbage. While her parents were thrilled that she was beginning to follow her menstrual routine independently, they were less than thrilled that she chose the public forum to share her great news! With some additional teaching, and "private talk time" with mom (10 minutes before bed each night), Karen was able to save her news until the appropriate time and place to share it.

daughter will need to learn to carry hygiene products at school discreetly, and store them in a special private place at home. Even before your daughter begins her menstrual cycle, have her get used to carrying a small purse or pocketbook while at school. The bag should be small and have a long strap that can go over her head so that she can carry it across her body. This will reduce the risk of it getting lost or left behind somewhere. Things to carry in her purse include maxipads, tampons, tissues, lip gloss, hair brush or comb, and deodorant. Many girls are now carrying purses at school in addition to their book bag or knapsack. Enlist the assistance of school staff if your daughter needs reminders to carry her purse with her, or to bring it with her to the bathroom.

Private behaviors

A final important distinction between public and private locations is the set of behaviors that are appropriate in each. Examples of inappropriate public behaviors include clipping nails, scratching private parts, nose-picking, making distracting noises, and commenting loudly on the appearance of others. Socially expected public behaviors include covering one's mouth when yawning, saying "excuse me" after burping, and saying "bless you" when someone nearby sneezes (and not "Wow, that was loud!"). These social rules can (and should) be taught well before puberty; as your daughter approaches puberty it becomes important for her to also learn that touching her private parts and self-pleasuring are private behaviors, and are not allowed in public places. In Chapter 7 we will discuss self-pleasuring in more detail.

Personal hygiene and grooming

My daughter Amanda is a fourth-generation scout. She loves scouting, and her troop definitely increases her opportunities to socialize. I was so completely amazed when Amanda came to me and asked to go to resident summer camp the very first time. She was only a Brownie, but she knew what she wanted— enough to get her hair cut short and learn to wash it all by herself in order to earn the trip! She made a number of personal strides that spring to reach a level of self-help competence that would let her make it at camp! (Mother of a 12-year-old girl in sixth grade with diagnoses of PDD-NOS, OCD, and ADHD)

One of the areas in which families often report difficulties is helping their daughter establish independence in personal hygiene and grooming routines. Although not all girls will be able to perform these routines fully independently, as a foundational skill it is important for your daughter to learn to participate in hygiene routines to the best of her ability. Before puberty, the necessary skills include:

- toileting
- bathing or showering, including hair washing
- face- and hand-washing
- teeth-brushing and flossing
- hair-brushing and combing
- cleaning eyeglasses or contacts
- trimming fingernails
- foot care
- dressing independently and neatly in clean, appropriate clothing.

Once puberty begins, other hygiene and grooming tasks become important, such as:

- applying deodorant
- skin care
- shaving
- menstrual hygiene
- wearing a properly fitted bra
- applying makeup (optional).

One mother described feeling as if she was "losing the battle" when her daughter entered puberty. Her daughter was still struggling with being able to brush her teeth properly, let alone figuring out shaving! Other mothers have also described challenges in teaching tasks such as hair-brushing and completing a nighttime routine without reminders. If you have had difficulty in this area, you are not alone.

So where do you begin? First, think about how your daughter's autism affects her skill development and her understanding in this area. Table 3.1 provides a general overview of how your daughter's cognitive, language, and motor skills will influence what she will be able to accomplish during puberty. One girl with whom we worked had sensory issues that interfered with being able to shower and wash her own hair—she didn't like the feel of fingers on her head or of shampoo foaming up. These issues were addressed with a gradual desensitization program paired with rewards, and although she still has occasional difficulties, she is now able to wash her hair independently. There are many other reasons that having an ASD can affect your daughter's grooming and hygiene; another issue was particularly relevant for Christie and her mother.

Case study: Christie

Christie is a 15-year-old young woman with high-functioning autism. Since she was young, she has had low muscle tone and motor weaknesses. Christie has long dark hair which, when brushed, looks beautiful. Unfortunately, her hair tends to form knots, and it quickly becomes messy and challenging to brush. Christie is able to begin brushing her hair, but after a few strokes, and a few particularly stubborn knots, her arms become tired. Christie's mother has lamented that her daughter's gorgeous hair can turn into a rat's nest in the blink of an eye! (How many of you remember your mother calling your hair a rat's nest?) In the mornings before school, Christie and her mother usually end up in a frantic rush to get her hair brushed before heading out the door to catch the bus. If the bus arrives in the middle of the morning hair drama, Christie will pull her mother behind the front door so that "the other kids don't see you brushing my hair." Despite wanting to be able to brush her hair, Christie has had limited success and is beginning to feel frustrated and down on herself. It's time for Christie and her mother to develop a plan that will involve occupational therapy, adjusting her schedule to get up earlier in the morning, and perhaps some changes to her hairstyle.

Table 3.1 Puberty: What your daughter *can* learn

Moderate to severe cognitive and motor impairments
- Cooperate with personal hygiene routine provided by caretakers
- Participate (assist) in steps of personal hygiene routines with supports (e.g. rubs wash cloth on arms and legs)
- Discrimination learning (e.g. where and when to be naked, where and when to engage in self-pleasuring)

Mild cognitive and motor impairments
- Management of most steps in a hygiene routine
- May need reminders in the form of verbal, visual or written cues
- May need assistance with steps involving some motor skills (e.g. reaching all teeth when brushing)
- Concrete understanding of puberty and the process of growing up

Average and above-average intelligence and motor skills

- Independent management of hygiene routines

- May need visual/written reminders (e.g. daily routine checklist)

- Full understanding of the "how" and "why" of personal hygiene and grooming

- Deeper understanding of puberty and the process of growing up from biological, emotional, and psychological perspectives

---

Visuals, visuals, visuals: supporting your daughter's hygiene and grooming skills

Families with whom we have worked have often reported that using visual supports (including modeling) is the most effective strategy when teaching about hygiene and grooming. Visual supports can take the form of pictures, symbols, or written words. Given the nature of autism, difficulties are often observed in organization, planning, and sequencing of activities. It can be very challenging for girls with ASDs to complete a daily routine involving multiple tasks with multiple steps under tight time constraints such as a bus departure time! Think about what your family's morning and evening schedule looks like. With your daughter's help (if possible), decide on which tasks can be completed in the evening before bed (e.g. taking a bath or shower) and which need to be done in the morning (e.g. hair-brushing). Some daily activities, such as teeth-brushing, will need to happen both in the evening and in the morning. For some families, showering before bed will be easier than trying to fit it in during the morning rush. When you have decided on the schedule, evaluate how well your daughter is able to complete each activity on her own. Perhaps she does an excellent job washing her face but has a lot more difficulty with showering. What kinds of visuals you will need to use will be determined by two factors: your daughter's skill level in the tasks she must complete and her overall ability to independently organize her time and activities. If she is able to complete individual tasks then you will not need detailed visuals outlining how to perform these tasks, but you might need to provide her with extra support in completing all the tasks together as part of an efficient morning or evening routine. In that case, the kinds of visuals you will need and the level of support will be different (e.g. a "bathroom basics" list, or a "got everything?" list).

Detailed visual supports include everything from laminated shower schedules that are hung in the shower and may be used with a washable crayon, to picture schedules of steps for shaving legs. Remember, if you want to teach the steps of a particular skill, you will need to do a *task analysis* first. A task analysis involves breaking down an activity into its smallest components parts, including steps such as turning on the water and wetting the razor. Your list of steps for any given activity might be very long at the beginning of teaching: one of the mothers with whom we worked developed a task analysis for shaving legs that initially included 56 steps! As her daughter mastered each step along the way, she was able to remove them from her list or combine them with other steps. Eventually, she had 10 steps on a laminated card that was attached to the bathtub. In italics were reminders for her daughter that included steps she sometimes forgot, such as doing the back of her legs in addition to the front, and remembering not to push too hard with the razor. Her daughter also wanted to include a little humour about what would happen if she forgot to moisturize. By participating in choosing the text, her daughter became much more engaged in the learning process. Her final steps for shaving her legs were:

1. Do I have what I need? (razor, shaving gel, towel)
2. Wet legs and razor.
3. Lather legs *front and back.*
4. *Lightly* smooth razor up my legs.
5. *Rinse razor* after each stroke.
6. Be careful around my ankles!
7. Did I remember all areas? *Front and back?*
8. *Rinse my razor* when done.
9. Dry my legs.
10. Moisturize—no crocodile legs!

This mother's daughter was an active swimmer and needed to shave her legs once a week. As a reward for shaving, she earned $3 for each successful shave without reminders. By the end of the month, she had earned enough money to go to a movie with her friend. Remember, teach with visuals, and then reward success.

Other examples of using visuals to teach hygiene and grooming include:

- video modeling (Charlop-Christy, Le & Freeman, in press)
- picture and written stories
- calendars (daily, weekly, monthly)
- picture exchange communication system (PECS), developed by Lori Frost and Andrew Bondy

- ISPEEK visual aids (*see* Resources)
- cue cards.

For additional suggestions regarding using visuals to support teaching, we recommend *Visual Strategies for Improving Communication: Practical Supports for School and Home*, by Linda Hodgson, and *Taking Care of Myself* by Mary Wrobel (*see* Resources). Being creative in using visual supports can take you and your daughter a long way.

Teaching your daughter the "why" behind personal hygiene

Just as important as learning *how* to take care of oneself is learning *why* we do so. What is the *motivation* to brush your hair when it's early in the morning, you're tired, and your arm is going to end up aching after only a minute? Good personal hygiene and grooming is essential for health-related reasons, but even more importantly, it is an expected social norm. While teaching your daughter *how* to develop appropriate hygiene skills, also think about teaching her *why* she should care about being clean and well-groomed. Depending on your daughter's age and ability level, "why" can be explained in many different ways. You might present simple pictures portraying a girl who has not showered standing by herself, and the same girl clean and neat standing with a group of other girls. For older girls who may be interested in dating, or who want a part-time job, it will be important to convey the message that potential dates and employers are interested in people who are

Case study: Bethany

Bethany's mother had been trying for years to get her to brush her teeth every morning before school without needing to be reminded. Bethany is 15 years old and is capable of completing this task independently, but does not like actually doing it. It became such a battle at home that Bethany started telling her mother that she had brushed her teeth, even when she hadn't. Bethany's mother knew that there was a boy at school whom Bethany liked. One morning, in exasperation, Bethany's mother said to her "Matthew sure isn't going to want to be around a girl who doesn't brush her teeth." Without a word, and with only a slight pause as if considering the importance of what her mother has just said, Bethany marched back upstairs and brushed her teeth. She did so the next day, and the day after that. Score one for social motivation!

presentable and who take care of themselves. You will want to talk with your daughter (including the use of visuals and written scripts as needed) about bad breath, body odor, oily hair, and their impact on first impressions. Social motivation is something that may never be very important for your daughter, or it may develop over time. If social motivation is not going to be effective, you will need to come up with other rewards for her to feel motivated to work on hygiene skills. What motivators have worked in the past? Maybe she can earn an allowance, earn extra time on the computer, or go out to her favorite restaurant. Be creative in thinking of rewards, and make them comparable with the effort required to complete the task. If brushing her hair is very difficult, the reward your daughter earns should reflect that.

Pat Crissey has written a fun book for youth and teens entitled *Personal Hygiene? What's That Got to Do with Me?* which tackles this issue head on—youth with ASDs often do not understand the social importance of maintaining appropriate hygiene. Incorporating quizzes and activities, the book covers topics such as having a clean hand that others would like to shake, and the implications of having bad breath. Working with your daughter to help her recognize the importance of good hygiene and grooming for her relationships with others may take a lot of time, but the end result will be well worth your effort.

Respecting privacy

As girls enter puberty, issues related to personal boundaries and touching become increasingly important. We will revisit this in more detail in Chapter 7 in the context of sexuality, but the first step is to ensure that your daughter understands the rules for respecting other people's privacy. This is a foundational skill that should be taught starting at an early age; teach your daughter to knock on closed doors and not to disturb people during "private activities" (e.g. changing, using the bathroom). Use repetition and visual aids to help her master this skill. For example, if she has difficulties remembering to knock, then post a written checklist outside bathroom and bedroom doors to outline the appropriate procedure:

- Is the door closed?
- Knock.
- Wait for an answer.
- Go in if invited.

Sometimes it is necessary to apparently violate a privacy rule for the purpose of teaching your daughter, for example many mothers will have their daughter watch them change a maxipad as part of their daughter's menstrual hygiene education. Make sure your daughter understands the difference between these teaching scenarios and the general rules for respecting privacy. It's okay to come into the bathroom with mom when invited, but it's not okay to ask Aunt Mabel if you can watch her change her maxipad!

Teaching tips: a foundational skills checklist

Foundational skills become increasingly relevant as youth enter puberty. Throughout adolescence, pay close attention to your daughter's skill development in these areas. Are there any concepts that need further attention? The following checklist should help guide you in determining your daughter's learning needs. If she is doing well in all areas, wonderful!

My daughter has demonstrated competence in the following skills:

- distinguishing public and private places
- knows how to dress appropriately in public
- distinguishing public and private topics
- distinguishing public and private behaviors
- participates in personal hygiene routines
- carries personal hygiene items discreetly at school and in the community
- knocks on closed doors and respects the privacy of others.

Navigating pubertal change

Although puberty affects everyone differently, nearly all girls progress through the same five basic stages as they develop. Thank you puberty goddess for being at least somewhat predictable! Learning these stages will help you be prepared for what will likely occur next in your daughter's development. They also provide a structure for teaching your daughter about what will be happening to her body and her feelings. How long puberty lasts depends on many factors. For your daughter, it could take between one and five years for her to progress through each of the stages. Whether it is one year or five, you will want to be as ready as you can. Table 3.2 outlines the five stages of puberty. Remember, your daughter may demonstrate uneven progress; for example, her breasts may develop more quickly than other areas of her physique. What's most important is that you have an overall sense of the developmental progression.

Table 3.2 Stages of normal pubertal changes in girls

Stage 1: 8–11 years
- Ovaries enlarge; hormone production begins; no outward signs of development

Stage 2: 8–14 years
- Growth spurt in height and weight; hip and thigh development; "breast buds" emerge; first pubic hairs develop (fine and straight "peach fuzz"); hormone production continues, mood changes

Stage 3: 9–15 years
- Breasts continue to grow; first armpit hairs develop; pubic hair becomes darker and coarser; darkening and growth of leg hair; menstruation may occur

Stage 4: 10–16 years
- Pubic hair begins to take a triangular shape; underarm hair continues to grow; sweating and body odor occur; pimples develop; menstruation; ovulation may occur

Stage 5: 12–19 years
- Breast and pubic hair growth are complete; full height is reached; girl is physically an adult; menstrual periods are regular and ovulation occurs monthly; sexual and romantic feelings develop

---

Note: includes information from the Tanner Stages (Marshall and Tanner 1969).

In Chapter 2 we discussed the anxiety that many youth with ASDs feel about growing up. For some, the idea of becoming a grown-up is scary, as is being "responsible", having a job, and possibly living independently. Others become anxious about the physical changes themselves, and what they represent (becoming a teenager). Given that puberty is known as "the time of change", and that change in general tends to be more anxiety-provoking for youth with ASDs, it is not surprising that entering adolescence comes with its own set of fears and uncertainty for many girls.

What should you be doing as a parent to prepare your daughter for upcoming changes in her body? First step, brush up on your biology! When was the last time you thought about a woman's internal reproductive anatomy, or the phases of the menstrual cycle? For dads, you may have never learned about these topics when you were growing up. Take a look at some books for girls about puberty. You can also find some good websites with information about the physical changes that occur in puberty (*see* Resources at the end of the chapter).

Next, think again about your teaching toolkit. How does your daughter learn best? What approaches will be most effective in teaching your daughter about the physical changes that occur during puberty? Remember, the amount and complexity of information you will want to share with your daughter will depend to a large extent on your daughter's cognitive skills and verbal abilities. For girls who are less verbal and have more cognitive impairments, pictures of pubertal changes (e.g. breast development) paired with positive emotions (e.g. happy faces, celebrations) and a personalized connection (e.g. a picture of your daughter paired with the stage of development which she is at) may be the most effective teaching approach. Used as picture stories, you can communicate with your daughter that she is becoming a woman as she gets older. Be creative with how you use visuals to support your daughter's learning. We have worked with families who develop "I'm Growing Up" books that mothers use during pre-planned "mother–daughter talk time". These books include photos of daughters participating in important growing-up events such as starting middle school or high school, or getting her first purse or pocketbook. They also include illustrations of expected physical changes. Linda Hodgson's book, *Visual Strategies for Improving Communication: Practical Supports for School and Home*, provides excellent ideas for using visual strategies as part of teaching and communication. The resources list at the end of this chapter includes websites and books on growing up where you can find clear illustrations of pubertal changes to share with your daughter.

Talking about change

An important part of teaching your daughter about the changes she faces is being able to talk to her about them. A direct approach, however, may not be effective; your daughter may feel uncomfortable participating in specific "growing up" discussions. She may want to read a book independently, or look at some websites and come to you with questions if there is something she does not understand. You can also check her understanding during naturalistic teaching opportunities that arise (e.g. while shopping at the drug store). Respecting how she would like to learn is important; forcing conversations if she is not ready may lead her to withdraw, even if there is something she would like to discuss with you

Case study: Paula

Paula is a 13-year-old adolescent girl with high-functioning autism and mild verbal cognitive difficulties. Puberty began early for her, when she was only nine years old, and she was not ready to accept her body's changes. When she began to grow underarm and pubic hair, she wanted to shave it all off. She refused to wear deodorant or a bra because she was "a little girl" and "little girls don't wear deodorant or bras." When Paula's mother tried to talk to her about growing up, she became very upset and would leave the room or start screaming and crying. After almost a year of trying to talk with Paula and convince her that growing up was okay, her mother began to look through books and copy pages she thought might be interesting for Paula. She would write a sentence or two about the pictures and how they applied to Paula. A few weeks later, Paula asked her mother a question about breast size (why are they sometimes not the same size). Paula's mother answered her question and held her breath, waiting for the inevitable meltdown. It didn't happen. Paula answered "okay" and walked away. Their mother–daughter dialogue had finally begun.

Teaching tips: talking to your daughter

- Be available to talk.
- Normalize her experiences and feelings.
- Reflect and validate her fears and concerns.
- Provide concrete information—verbally and with visual supports.
- Be calm, reassuring, and positive.
- Talk at her speed; provide enough time for her to process information.

Normalizing change

During early adolescence, most girls question, "Am I normal?" It is natural for a girl to have questions about what is happening to her body, and to wonder if what she is experiencing is normal. Your daughter likely has these questions, but if she has few friends then she is missing out on a peer group who can normalize her experiences for her. She isn't hearing "Oh yeah, that happens to me too!" from her friends and classmates. Living in a "peer void" prevents girls with ASDs from receiving an important source of support, understanding, and shared experience—the same-sex peer group. Who in your family or among your circle of friends can work with you to normalize the experiences of puberty for your daughter? Does your daughter have older siblings or cousins? Is she close to an aunt or one of your family friends? Do your friends have girls who would be able to spend time with your daughter? With changes that can be anxiety-provoking, or contribute to feelings of embarrassment, it often helps to know that you are not the only one experiencing them and that they are a natural part of growing up.

Finding teaching materials

We have found that girls who are able to read and enjoy learning about factual information often benefit from having books to read about puberty, or websites to look at. If your daughter is a reader and likes nonfiction, take advantage. When you go to the bookstore or library, you will find hundreds of books for girls about puberty and growing up. The selection can be a little overwhelming, and not all books are appropriate for girls with developmental or social learning disabilities. Sometimes the information is too complex, sometimes there are not enough visuals to support the text, or the way the book is organized may not be very clear. Many of our families have shared that their daughters really enjoy the *American Girl* book series, and in particular the titles under the "Body and Mind" section on their website (*see* Resources). In the resource list, we have included titles that we recommend for girls of all ages based on our own and parents' experiences. Again, be creative when using books to support your teaching. The following are some suggestions for how to read books about growing up.

- Use the illustrations only.
- Photocopy a page or two of the book for you and your daughter to read.
- Photocopy pages of illustrations and have your daughter color the parts of her body that have already begun to change.
- Read and discuss the book together, one section at a time.
- Read a topic and then look for additional information on the internet.
- Read a topic and then add it to her "I'm Growing Up" book.

- Have your daughter read a section or chapter independently, then discuss it with her during talk time.

There are also many websites for girls and their parents about growing up and sexuality. We have included some of the most informative and appropriate websites in the Resources section at the end of the chapter. As with books, you can use websites to support your daughter's learning in a number of different ways. You can look at websites together, or independently. You can print information to read later, or review it online. Many of the websites also have quizzes to complete. It might be fun for both of you to learn "Do you eat too much junk?", "Are you fashion-focused?", "What's your secret talent?", or "Do you mind your manners?" Taking a quiz together is an example of a casual, low-key way to think about a particular topic, without having to come at it head-on.

What about magazines for girls? Today, many neurotypical pre-teen and teen girls have subscriptions to magazines that they devour from cover to cover when they arrive in the mail. These magazines include topics from friendships and dating, to fitness, fashion and beauty, self-esteem and safety, parties and crafts, celebrities, current events, and inspirational stories. Given that your daughter has an ASD, she might not be as interested in some of the articles. Choose articles, quizzes, or advice columns that have information related to puberty and growing up. Read them together or separately and then have a discussion. Using magazines will come up again in later chapters when we discuss safety and self-esteem; they're a great way to get your daughter engaged.

The Resources section contains a more comprehensive list of magazines, but a few examples are worth mentioning to give you an idea of what is available. *Discovery Girls* is a pre-teen magazine created "by girls, for girls" ages 7–12 years. The magazine features girls from different US states and Canadian provinces and focuses on issues faced by real girls at school, at home, and out in the world. It encourages girls to challenge themselves to be their best. Another popular magazine for pre-teens is *American Girl*. Some of the major women's fashion magazines now publish teen versions, such as *Cosmo Girl*, and *Teen Vogue*. Other magazines for teens have a celebrity and music focus, such as *Teen* and *Twist*. Use your own judgment as to what is appropriate for your daughter given her interests, her reading and language skills, and her maturity level. See what kinds of articles and topics are most interesting for her, and in what ways is it easiest for you to get her involved. Have fun with it!

Managing the locker room

Anxiety about a changing body as puberty begins can come to a head in the middle-school locker room, where girls change and shower in plain view of one another. The experience is made even more difficult by accompanying social changes: what used to be merely a room in which you quickly and uneventfully changed your clothes for gym has become a chaotic scene fraught with emotions, activity, and enough drama to compete with the most sensational soap opera on daytime television. Girls will gossip, swap clothing, comment on each other's outfits (both outer and inner garments), gripe about their bodies, put on deodorant, makeup, hairspray, perfume, talk on their cell phones, make plans for the weekend, and catch up on all the events that happened within the past hour at school. The room is often full of different aromas, from perfumes and deodorants to sweaty clothes and dirty shoes. Sounds of laughter and shouting echo from the reverberating concrete walls; bad fluorescent lighting, which more often than not flickers and hums, spotlights the cloudy haze that develops as girls spray various products in their efforts to beautify before continuing their day. Add this sensory overload to a discomfort with changing clothing or showering in front of others and you have a situation that creates a lot of anxiety for many girls with ASDs.

Some of the women with ASDs whom we have interviewed have shared with us memories of feeling ashamed of their bodies or being overwhelmed by the locker room noise:

> I personally found the locker room in high school a humiliating experience. I found P.E. a humiliating experience as well. I hid as much as I could whenever I changed so as not to be seen by other people—I was extremely ashamed of how I looked. (30-year-old woman with Asperger's Syndrome)

> Ugh. Locker rooms. I can share mine, but nothing I did helped because *gym class* was so overwhelming I ended up crying after no matter what we did! And I'm in good shape too so everyone thought it was ridiculous but it was the *noise*, not the exercise. (25-year-old woman with high-functioning autism)

One of the girls with whom we have worked began to refuse to go to school on Wednesdays. After careful assessment of her schedule, it became evident that Wednesday was PE day and she had been having significant difficulty changing in front of the other girls in her class. She was too embarrassed to tell anyone, and thought it would be better to just avoid going. This is not uncommon for many young women with ASDs, but fortunately there are some solutions. The first step is to call a meeting with your daughter's school team. Everyone will need to be on board with whatever plan is created, including your daughter's gym teacher, classroom teacher, autism consultant, and school psychologist. Options that some of our families have chosen include:

- leaving gym class 10–15 minutes early to have time to start changing before the others

- staying later to help clean up and changing after most of the other girls are finished

- wearing an athletic outfit to school and not having to change

- creating a schedule with PE during the last period of the day so that showering can occur at home

- developing a behavior plan (with strong motivators) that includes desensitization (exposure combined with relaxation) and gradual practice spending time in the locker room.

Success in managing locker rooms is possible. This mother's story illustrates how she planned ahead, addressing her daughter's specific issues, and was able to help her daughter transition fairly smoothly to the middle school locker room.

My daughter Amanda just started sixth-grade and middle school this fall. She is diagnosed with PDD/NOS. At the school book fair last spring she chose an *American Girl* book, *A Smart Girl's Guide to Starting Middle School*. The *Smart Girl's Guide* brought up the subject of group showers. Amanda had several months to prepare and get used to the idea. We worked out a plan for getting gym clothes back and forth between school and home every week without forgetting, talked about how she and the other girls would feel about changing in front of others, and asked a seventh-grade friend how it was going for her. No children changed out for PE the first week of school, so we also had time to contact Amanda's tracking teacher to liaise with the gym teachers (there are seven of them; we have big middle schools down here in Houston).

Amanda has some difficulties with sensory defensiveness, especially noise. We knew that the PE teachers had made arrangements for Amanda's friend (diagnosis, AS) to shower in the women's coach's shower, and we could have asked for the same. But, Amanda also has profound anxiety issues. At home, she has to take showers with a waterproof radio or she imagines sounds outside and panics that "something scary" is on the other side of the shower curtain. With some help to visualize the differences, she chose to take showers with the other girls. It was her personal choice that the noise and smells of the locker room and showers were not as unpleasant as taking her shower down a frighteningly quiet corridor all alone.

A big issue for Amanda is also getting ready quickly enough. She finds it very upsetting if she is yelled at to hurry, but she also gets upset if she isn't ready when others are. Her fine-motor skills are poor, so she ties shoestrings very slowly. We went to some trouble to find Velcro-closure gym shoes in a size big enough for Amanda, which would greatly speed her dress-out time. We also made it a point to buy school clothes for this year which are easy to change in and out of since, unlike elementary school, PE would be every day. (Mother of a 12-year-old girl with PDD-NOS, OCD, and ADHD)

Hormones and emotions

Not only are a lot of changes happening to the outside of your daughter's body during puberty, but she is also going to be experiencing many ups and downs with her feelings and thoughts during this time. Are you ready? Hormonal changes can create mood swings and stress that appear without warning out of nowhere. This can feel very scary for your daughter, as if she is out of control. One of the girls with whom we have worked said that she feels like an "unpredictable beast". For reasons that are not yet known, parents of girls with ASDs report even more extreme mood swings during puberty than have been observed in their typically developing siblings, or their friends' daughters. If youth with ASDs have difficulty in general with self-regulation, we may imagine that additional hormone changes may compound the problem.

So what can you do as a parent? Helping your daughter to understand the different feelings she is experiencing is a very important step. Use your teaching toolkit to select the best instructional approaches for your daughter. Along with understanding emotions come coping skills. What can your daughter do when she is feeling overwhelmed, stressed, sad, or angry? Chapter 5 will review mental health and stress management in more detail. However, if you feel that your daughter is really unable to manage without assistance, speak with your doctor or someone at your daughter's school. She may need to see a counselor or therapist for more intensive support during this time. Otherwise, general strategies for self-regulation and coping include relaxation and breathing, positive self-talk (changing negative statements into positive ones), writing things down and keeping a diary, talking with a trusted friend or adult, regular exercise, doing things she loves, and taking her own time out. As a parent, try to model healthy coping strategies for your daughter. The more she can learn about managing her feelings and life difficulties now, the better able she will be to handle stressors as an adult.

Resources

Books on personal self-care and puberty (autism and learning disabilities)

Crissey, P. (2005) *Personal Hygiene? What's That Got to Do with Me?* London: Jessica Kingsley Publishers.

Wrobel, M. (2003) *Taking Care of Myself: A Hygiene, Puberty, and Personal Curriculum for Young People with Autism.* Arlington, TX: Future Horizons, Incorporated.

Books on personal self-care and puberty (typical development)

American Medical Association and Gruenwald, K. (2006) *Girl's Guide to Becoming a Teen. Getting Used to Life in Your Changing Body.* (Amy B. Middleman, ed.). San Francisco, CA: Jossey-Bass.

Bourgeois, P. and Martyn, K. (2005) *Changes in You and Me. A Book About Puberty Mostly for Girls.* Toronto, ON: Key Porter Books.

Crump, M. (2002) *Don't Sweat It! Every Body's Answers to Questions You Don't Want to Ask.* Minneapolis, MN: Free Spirit Publishing.

Harris, R.H. (1994) *It's Perfectly Normal. Changing Bodies, Growing Up, Sex and Sexual Health.* Cambridge, MA: Candlewick Press.

Jukes, M. and Knopf, A.A. (1998) *Growing Up It's a Girl Thing. Straight Talk about First Bras, First Periods, and Your Changing Body.* New York, NY: Knopf.

Madaras, L. (2000) *The "What's Happening to My Body?" Book for Girls. A Growing-Up Guide for Preteens and Teens Including a Special Introduction for Parents.* New York, NY: Newmarket Press.

Madaras, L. (2003) *Ready, Set, Grow! A "What's Happening to My Body?" Book for Younger Girls.* New York, NY: Newmarket Press.

McCoy, K. and Wibbelsman, C. (2003) *Growing and Changing: A Handbook for Preteens.* New York, NY: Perigree.

Schaefer, V. (1998) *The Care and Keeping of You. The Body Book for Girls.* Middleton, WC: Pleasant Company Publications.

Resources to assist with teaching

Dixon, J. (2007a) *ISPEEK at Home* (CD-ROM). London: Jessica Kingsley Publishers.

Dixon, J. (2007b) *ISPEEK at School* (CD-ROM). London: Jessica Kingsley Publishers.

Frost, L. and Bondy, A. (2002) *The Picture Exchange Communication System Training Manual* (2nd edition). Available at www.pecs.com

Hodgdon, L. (2005) *Visual Strategies for Improving Communication: Practical Supports for School and Home.* Troy, MI: Quirk Roberts Publishing.

Nikopoulos, C. and Keenan, M. (2006) *Video Modelling and Behaviour Analysis. A Guide to Teaching Social Skills to Children with Autism.* London: Jessica Kingsley Publishers.

Personal accounts by girls and young adults

Peers, J. (2003) *Asparagus Dreams.* London: Jessica Kingsley Publishers.

Girls magazines

For pre-teens

Discovery Girls: a magazine created for and by girls geared toward pre-teens aged 7–12. *Discovery Girls* is a magazine where girls can express their ideas about life. Addresses topics such as middle school, fashion, friendships, and inspiring stories.

American Girl: for girls aged eight and up, *American Girl* is considered an alternative to typical teen magazines. Features include stories and advice, contests and games.

New Moon: *New Moon* magazine is both written and edited by and for girls aged 8–14. It is a six-time winner of the Parents Choice Gold Award. Considered to be groundbreaking and imaginative, *New Moon* magazine promotes healthy female role models through self-expression in writing and artwork.

For teens

Justine: a magazine for teen girls that focuses on a healthy lifestyle. With a positive voice for girls, *Justine* magazine addresses topics such as fashion, beauty, and entertainment.

Girl's Life Magazine: for girls aged 10 and up, *Girl's Life Magazine* is a five-time Parents Choice Award Winner. Topics include ideas and advice, self-esteem and friendships, and fashion and celebrities.

Cosmo Girl: a magazine for older teen girls with features on beauty, fashion, and celebrities.

Seventeen: on the scene since 1944, *Seventeen* magazine covers both light and heavy inspiring stories and articles in addition to emphasizing lifestyle, fashion, and beauty.

Teen Vogue: follows in the footsteps of its adult-focused predecessor—*Vogue*—and presents high fashion and down-to-earth trends for teens.

Websites for girls and their parents

Advocates for Youth: an excellent source of accurate information on issues related to youth sexual health for professionals, parents, and teens. Available at www.advocatesforyouth.org

American Girl ("Fun for Girls" has articles, quizzes, and fun activities for girls to complete). Available at www.americangirl.com/fun

Birds and Bees Project, The: provides comprehensive reproductive health information to youth, teens, and adults. Available at www.birdsandbees.org

Girl Power!: the homepage for the national public education campaign sponsored by the US Department of Health and Human Services targeting physical and emotional health for pre-teens aged 9–13. Available at www.girlpower.gov

Girl's Health: developed by the Office on Women's Health in the Department of Health and Human Services, the Girl's Health website was developed to promote healthy, positive behaviors in girls aged 10–16 years. Reliable and useful information health information is provided, as are tips on handling relationships with family and friends. Available at www.girlshealth.gov

Girl's Incorporated: award-winning website associated with the girls' rights movement (roots dating to 1864), Girl's Incorporated is a national nonprofit youth organization dedicated to inspiring girls to lead successful and fulfilling lives. Available at www.girlsinc.org

Go Ask Alice!: offered through Columbia University's Health Services, Go Ask Alice! is a website for young women to access reliable information about emotional and physical health, sexuality, and relationships. Available at www.goaskalice.columbia.edu

iEmily.com: a health and wellness site for girls. Your daughter can look up information, watch videos, and take quizzes. Available at iemily.com

KidsHealth: KidsHealth is the award-winning, most-visited website that provides doctor-approved health information about children from before birth through adolescence. Created by the Nemours Foundation's Center for Children's Health Media, KidsHealth provides families, youth and teens with accurate, up to date, and jargon-free health information, including articles, games, and animations for youth. Available at www.kidshealth.org

Planned Parenthood: Planned Parenthood Federation of America (PPFA) is the United States' leading women's healthcare provider, educator, and advocate, whose mission is to improve health and safety, advance rights and abilities to make informed choices, and provide medically accurate information on sexual health and reproduction. Available at www.plannedparenthood.org

Teenwire: an award-winning sexual health website for teens. Teenwire.com is the Planned Parenthood Federation of America website for teens. Available at www.teenwire.com

CHAPTER 4

The Red Spot: Periods, Pads, and Pelvic Exams

Those of you whose girls haven't gotten their periods yet and are stressing over it (I was there once)...you'd be very surprised at how your daughter might handle it. I tried to model it and show my daughter that it wasn't a scary thing as she used to get so upset with a bloody nose. I couldn't imagine her handling a period every month. She finally got her period at 12½ and surprised me in how well she took the whole thing in her stride. Her teachers put together a whole task analysis for her at school and the step-by-step process really helped her. I'd suggest that if you think your daughter is getting close to that time, start having her wear a pantiliner every day so she gets used to something being in her underpants. I'm so thankful that our pads today are so thin and more comfortable than those thick ones we used to wear when we first started out. (Mother of a 19-year-old young woman with autism)

Out of all the challenges posed by the onset of puberty, menstruation can be singularly difficult for both parents and daughters alike. Perhaps your daughter has already begun her menstrual cycle and it isn't going very well, or perhaps her period is due any day now but you are not feeling very prepared. If so, you are not alone. Menstruation is hard enough for typically developing adolescents and their parents; when exacerbated by a developmental disability it can seem overwhelming.

The good news is that there are many steps you can take to prepare your daughter for her period and ensure that her experience (and yours) is as positive as possible. You can work together toward the goal of having your daughter independently manage her period. When we work with families during the "pre-period preparation phase", we focus on four important goals that will be reviewed in the following sections.

- Keeping a positive outlook.
- Providing accurate and appropriate information.
- Practicing skills.
- Planning for the first and subsequent periods.

Goal 1: Finding your positive tone

> I will tell her it's something all women go through and she is going through it just like everyone else. A party, no, I will not celebrate. I hope that she is able to handle this on her own, but since she can't wash her own hair properly, I will most likely have to change her pads, etc. That is not a reason to celebrate. But, on the other hand, if she is able to handle it on her own, then maybe a party is in order! (Mother of a 12-year-old daughter with autism)

Few women are thrilled when their period arrives—the possible exception being women who have written books on celebrating menstruation (*see* Resources). Most women would probably consider themselves to fall somewhere on the continuum between vague annoyance and absolute dread; nowhere near having a celebratory attitude. As such, being positive about menstruation may not come naturally, but it is an important first step in preparing for your daughter's period.

For your daughter with an ASD, *any* change is often stressful—even a positive one. If you approach her first period with dread, or even visible trepidation, she is going to have all the more reason to fear the start of her menstrual cycle, which will ultimately make the process more difficult for both of you. Many mothers of girls with developmental disabilities have shared with us that the two things they worry about most about their daughter growing up are the potential for abuse, and managing her menstrual cycle. You might very well be feeling as if your daughter's period arriving is right up there with life's most terrible experiences. That's okay, and perfectly understandable. Sit with that feeling for a little while because you are absolutely allowed to feel that way, and then get ready to move on. If you are going to make this transition a smooth one for you and your daughter, you will need to get beyond your fear and anxiety.

Overcoming the cultural taboo

Unfortunately, society does not make it easy to think about menstruation in an open, positive way. From secretive code names like "Aunt Flo is visiting", to a general negative attitude that aims to keep menstruation hidden, modern industrial cultural continues to portray menstruation as something to be embarrassed about, or at the very least something you do not discuss openly. In contrast, many other cultures, such as hunter-gatherers, consider menstruation to be a sacred time in a woman's life when a woman is most powerful. In India, a young woman's first period is a joyful event that is celebrated by her entire community and marks the day that she can begin wearing a sari, the traditional female garment. Can you imagine having celebrated the start of your period with your entire family and community?

Think about the role that your own cultural or religious background plays in menstruation. Did your background contribute to what your early menstruation experiences were like? Will it affect how you approach menstruation with your daughter? If your daughter is able to read and is interested in different cultures, you might want to do some research with her online to learn more about different cultures and religions and how they approach a woman's monthly cycle. What about advertisements on television and in magazines? You might also explore with your daughter how modern society portrays menstruation in the media.

A happy period

However you begin to explain menstruation to your daughter, whether visually or with verbal and written support, you will want to communicate with a positive affect—a positive tone of voice, positive phrases in writing, and pictures of happy young girls. Remember the Always® slogan, "Have a happy period"? This campaign has antagonized many women who feel strongly that there is nothing happy about having your period. While you may feel the same way, try not to communicate this to your daughter. This is not to say that you want her to have misconceptions about her period and believe that menstruation will be a warm and fuzzy experience. She will need to understand that there may be physical discomforts and emotional difficulties associated with getting her period each month; however, the overall message you want to convey is that it is exciting that she is becoming a young woman, and that there are solutions to dealing with some of the physical and emotional experiences she will be having.

Some mothers share with their daughters that this is a time when women can go shopping, eat chocolate, or have a nice relaxing bath. They take time during the week their daughter is menstruating to do something fun together. Maybe your daughter would like to go to her favorite restaurant? Or have extra time to play her favorite video game? What can you do with your daughter to help her have a "happier period"?

How to throw a period party

If you have decided that you want to celebrate your daughter's first period, there are a number of fun ways to mark the occasion. By having other family members involved such as aunts, grandmothers, cousins, and even male relatives, your daughter will feel more comfortable with this important change in her life. Families celebrate with favorite home-cooked meals or a trip out to a restaurant. Pot-lucks or parties where other girls and women are invited are also common. Natural celebrations, such as planting trees or hiking or going camping, teach girls about the connection between women and the world around them. Get creative—share a poem, a picture, or make a book about your daughter becoming a woman. Think about your daughter's interests and skill level; pairing a first period with a fun family dinner might be the perfect celebration.

Case study: Allison

Allison, a 12-year-old girl with Asperger's Syndrome, was due to get her first period within the next few months according to her pediatrician. She was quite anxious in general, and always had a hard time waiting for stressful events, such as upcoming exams and visits to her cousin's house. Allison had recently joined a social skills group and had made a few friends in the class. She was also starting to spend some time during lunch with a couple girls she had met at school. Allison really wanted to make friends, but her anxiety often got in the way and she wasn't always sure what to say to the other girls. Allison's aunt thought that it might be fun to have a small get-together to celebrate Allison's first period, and that she might enjoy having her new friends come to her party. Allison's mother wasn't so sure, but agreed to give it a try. They talked to Allison about celebrating her period by having a "Red Party". Allison's favorite colour was red and she was excited about getting to wear red clothing and eat red foods. Allison chose to invite four friends to her party; her mother contacted their parents to explain what a red party was all about. Three of the other girls had already started their periods, and all of the families were excited about the idea. The day after Allison started her period, her mother sent out very cool red invitations. That weekend, Allison, her mom, her aunt, and her four new friends went at dusk to have a firelight picnic in the park. Everyone wore red—hats, scarves, shirts, jewellery; and each brought a different red food—strawberries, tomatoes, pizza with red sauce! Though the ceremony was interspersed with off-tangent discussions of anime and Game Boy, the girls had a great time and Allison was very proud of herself. Two months later, Allison received an invitation in the mail—a "red party" for the fourth friend who had just started her period.

A period party can be a lot of fun for your daughter. Involve her in planning activities and deciding who to invite, and make the party as elaborate or as simple as you and your daughter would like. In our experience, parents of girls who have had "red parties" report that their daughters are less negative about subsequent periods and are more open to asking questions and discussing their experiences with menstruation each month. A positive outlook and open communication—what more could you want?

Goal 2: Providing accurate information

When I experienced my first period, it was timed around a few days that I would be spending with my aunt and uncle. It turns out that I was not completely informed about the female anatomy (or I believed differently of what went where). For the life of me, I was convinced that a tampon would block the flow of urine if I tried to urinate. The trick worked because I unwittingly held it in for a day until I changed my tampon. This is one of the many things I had to figure out on my own because it was assumed I knew differently. (31-year-old woman with Asperger's Syndrome, depression, and anxiety)

Do you remember what you were told about your first period? Think back... were you told everything you needed to know before your menstrual cycle began? How about even a fraction of what you wanted to know? When asked about their first period, many women today share that they felt ill-informed, which contributed greatly to being unsure and nervous about getting their period. One of the most important things you can do for your daughter during this time is to provide her with accurate and relevant information appropriate for her age about menstruation. The following information-gathering activities will be important for you to complete as a parent as you begin to provide your daughter with information about menstruation:

- Think about how your daughter will feel when you begin to talk to her about getting her period. Will she be curious, excited, embarrassed, nervous, frightened? Understanding how your daughter is feeling will tell you a lot about how best to teach her. If she is curious, she may enjoy reading books about menstruation. If she is nervous, gentle and gradual discussion may be the best approach.

- Think about how your daughter's ASD will affect her learning, skill development, behavior, and preferences related to menstruation and menstrual management.

- Find out what your daughter already knows about menstruation. Has she taken a health class at school? Does she spend time with female cousins who are a few years older than her? Make a list of the information you think she already knows.

- When you begin to share information with your daughter, find out if what you think she knows is in fact accurate. At the beginning of this section we quoted a woman who shared that her family overestimated the amount she knew, making her first period more difficult.

- Finally, gather information for yourself. Do you know your reproductive anatomy? Are you knowledgeable about the biology of the menstrual cycle? Brush up on your biological facts if you need to. You will feel more comfortable if you have answers to your daughter's questions and if you have a clear idea of what you want to be able to teach her. Don't worry if you don't know everything. In fact, it might be fun for you and your daughter to do some research together.

Teaching tips: what to teach your daughter about periods

- Periods are an important part of growing up.
- When you get your period, blood comes out of your vagina.
- You will put a pad in your underwear to absorb the blood.
- Your period could start at any time of day or night.
- Your period will probably last four to seven days.
- Your back, tummy, and head might hurt when you have your period.
- You might feel more angry or sad than usual when you have your period.

Many parents have asked us two important questions about period discussions: At what age is it okay to start teaching about periods? And, what should I be teaching first? It is generally accepted that by age eight you can begin to share with your daughter basic information about her body (including her reproductive organs) and how a girl becomes a woman. For all girls, regardless of skill level, the use of visuals is essential. Many books have excellent drawings of external and internal reproductive anatomy. Even if your daughter will not be able to understand menstruation at a conceptual level, it will be important for her to identify which of her body parts are involved in menstruation if she is going to be able to maintain an independent menstrual hygiene routine.

Learning about body parts

We recommend that families begin by teaching the *name* and *function* of the three major body parts that are most important for hygiene and menstrual health: the urethra, the anus, and the vagina. Your daughter may have already learned about the urethra and anus when you worked on toileting. Teach your daughter the role of these three body parts.

- *Urethra*: urination (urine comes out of your urethra when you go to the bathroom after you drink liquids).
- *Anus*: bowel movements (stool comes out of your anus when you go to the bathroom after eating).
- *Vagina*: menstruation (blood comes out of a woman's vagina when she has her period once a month).

When you are ready to address menstrual hygiene, you can teach your daughter that a tampon may be inserted into the vagina to absorb the flow of blood and prevent leaking on her clothing. You will also be able to teach

Teaching tips: menstruation basics—What does your daughter know?

- Can identify urethra, vagina, and anus in a picture (pointing).
- Can identify urethra, vagina, and anus on her own body (pointing).
- Can identify the basic *functions* of each of these body parts.
- Is aware that menstrual blood is okay (natural) and is not the same as bleeding from being injured, or having blood in urine or stool.
- Can provide a simple definition of menstruation and the menstrual cycle.

her when (and if) she is ready that a man's penis is inserted into a woman's vagina when they engage in sexual intercourse, and that a baby comes out of a woman's vagina when it is being born. For now, all your daughter needs to know is that something specific comes out of each of these three parts of her body: urine, stool, and menstrual blood.

Families have reported to us that their daughters often have difficulties understanding their anatomy, especially when body parts are difficult to observe, are internal, or require some awareness of bodily sensations. Start slowly, and start early with teaching. Your daughter will need time to process the information, and repeated presentation of the material (in different ways) will likely be necessary. Use visual supports as much as you can when teaching. Most of the books on puberty and menstruation that are available for young women have chapters dedicated to understanding your body, and suggest taking a look down below with the assistance of a mirror. If you are a woman and you haven't taken a look at your own body, now might be the time! Remember, we are all working on feeling more comfortable with our bodies. A mirror can be very helpful if your daughter is having difficulty understanding the functions of her body parts, or if she wants to use tampons some day. We recommend that parents assist their daughters with this exercise; however, we understand that not everyone is comfortable with this approach. Talk to your daughter's doctor if you are unsure how to proceed or how best to help her with learning in this area.

Explaining menstruation

In addition to learning the name and function of genital body parts, some girls will also be able to understand and describe what actually happens during menstruation. Think about your daughter's skill level and cognitive abilities. Is she able to understand an in-depth explanation of menstruation and hormones? If she is, do you think she will be interested in knowing the details of how her body operates? Some girls with ASDs are very interested in science and facts, and will love to know all they can about what is happening inside them. Others girls are less interested in things to do with people, even themselves and their own bodies.

Below is a simple explanation of menstruation in the context of puberty, to be used with visual supports, appropriate for girls who might have trouble understanding (or who would not be interested in) a detailed explanation.

Teaching tips: simple explanation of menstruation (to be used with visual supports)

- Our bodies change on the outside as we grow up.
- Girls grow taller and bigger.
- Girls develop breasts and their hips get bigger.
- Girls grow pubic hair between their legs and hair under their arms.
- Our bodies also change on the inside.
- Girls have an important body part on the inside that boys do not. It is called the uterus.
- A girl's vagina connects her uterus to the outside of her body.
- Your vagina is between your legs. It is one of your private body parts.
- When a girl's body is ready, she will have her first period.
- A period is when blood comes from a girl's uterus and down her vagina.
- Periods are special because they are part of a girl growing up and becoming a woman.

More detailed explanations of menstruation, including hormonal changes and the journey of the egg from the ovary down the Fallopian tubes, may be found in books for young women about growing up, and also in curricula for youth with learning disabilities. Based on your daughter's cognitive and verbal skills, and her interest, decide how much information is appropriate for her to know about menstruation. If you are interested in teaching her more than the basics, there are a number of excellent books in the resources at the end of this chapter. One book in particular, *Becoming a Woman* by Elaine Cooper, has a wonderful teaching curriculum for individuals with learning disabilities which uses concrete visual supports and includes lessons on menstruation, menstrual management, and associated emotional changes.

"Advanced" menstruation knowledge involves everything from defining internal body parts to being able to describe what happens during a woman's monthly cycle. What does your daughter know from the list below (see teaching tips box on p.106)? What would you like to teach her?

Teaching tips: advanced menstruation knowledge— What does your daughter know?

- Can identify the following internal body parts in a picture: vagina, uterus, cervix, ovaries, Fallopian tube, egg.
- Can identify the basic *functions* of each of these body parts (by matching pictures or stating the function).
- Can define ovulation—the body's preparation for a potential pregnancy each month.
- Can describe the natural physical process of a woman's monthly cycle.
- Can describe the role of hormones in a woman's menstrual cycle.
- Knows menstrual cycle facts: how long a menstrual cycle is, how long periods last for, and what occurs on the different days of the menstrual cycle.

Hints about menstruation

After deciding what you want your daughter to learn, it's time to go back to your teaching toolkit. How will your daughter learn best? The following is a list of some of the teaching approaches that we have used and that families have shared with us.

- Create a set of picture cards for matching body parts with functions.
- Using both side- and front-view drawings of reproductive body parts, label the parts with names and what comes out of each part (i.e. urine, stool, menstrual blood).
- Using a mirror, assist your daughter in exploring her private body parts. If she can do so independently, encourage her to spend time on her own. If you need assistance, talk to your daughter's physician.
- Use large brown craft paper to draw a life-sized outline of your daughter's body. Work with her to identify major body parts and physical sensations and feelings.
- On her body outline, draw your daughter's internal reproductive organs (practice beforehand if you are not an artist!). Using red

crayons or markers, show how the lining of the uterus is shed and comes down the vagina as a "period". Draw a picture of her underwear and, using a red or brown crayon, colour a spot in the underwear to demonstrate that she will see blood in her pants when she starts her period.

- Create an "*I'm Becoming a Young Woman*" picture story with your daughter. Use photographs of her from when she was a baby, toddler, preschooler, in elementary school, and now. If she is nervous about becoming an adult, you may want to use different words or phrases that might be less intimidating for her, such as "I'm Growing Up", or "My Body is Changing".

- Using a drawing of her internal reproductive system, illustrate for your daughter how an egg is released from the ovary, travels down the Fallopian tube, and eventually sits in the wall of the uterus. You can use a red crayon to demonstrate how the uterine lining becomes thicker as the egg gets closer to the uterus.

- Use a 28-day round calendar drawing to represent your daughter's menstrual cycle. Each period represents the start of a new cycle so color days one to five in red to illustrate menstrual bleeding. You can also indicate when she might ovulate (on average, day 14 of her cycle), which is when the egg begins its journey to the uterus.

While teaching, continue to reassure your daughter that:
- having a period is a natural positive sign that she is becoming a young woman
- she has not done anything wrong
- having a period is *not* the same as wetting yourself
- menstrual blood is different from having a cut
- menstrual blood is not harmful and it will not hurt her
- all young women have periods
- no two periods are exactly the same: they vary from person to person and even from month to month.

Goal 3: Practicing skills ahead of time

We prepared Kayla by introducing wearing pads slowly. We started with panti-liners, putting it on then immediately taking it off and gradually increasing the time. Then we upgraded to thicker pads in the same manner, until she was wearing it all day. When she did start her period, it had been a long time since her practice session, but she had no problems wearing it. I had talked to her on and off about blood in her panties, kept it very simple, and mentioned it every once in a while, not knowing how much she understood or retained. When she did start, she very matter of factly said "blood in panties", and that was that. We got her on pads and she's been fine with that ever since. It's the PMS-ing that she has more troubles with and I have trouble explaining to her about emotions because that's not concrete like bleeding. (Mother of a 16-year-old girl with autism who was diagnosed at 3 years with PDD-NOS and then with autism at 3½ years)

Like any other life experience, you don't want your daughter to be unprepared when she has her first period. In addition to providing her with information about menstruation, you will want to show her what having a period will be like, and that includes practicing the skills she will need to master ahead of time. Start at the beginning. What is a maxipad and how do you use one? We'll talk about tampons later in this chapter.

Make a field trip to the pharmacy by yourself first. Take a look at the shelves with menstrual hygiene products and imagine you are seeing this aisle for the first time. All those boxes and bags and pastel colours can be overwhelming! Where do you begin? There are so many different brands and types of maxipads that vary in length, width, thickness, material, absorbency level, wings, curve, and deodorant. Some of the websites for maxipad brands have "product selector" tools that enable you to consider activity level, the heaviness of your flow, and whether it is for daytime or nighttime wear. Most teens report preferring to wear thin pads because they are more comfortable and more discreet. Given the sensory issues that some girls with ASDs have, thickness and bulk might be highly relevant factors in pad selection. You will also want to consider your daughter's fine-motor skills when deciding between maxipads with and without wings. Can she manage the added adhesive strips and flaps that come with wings? Bring home a variety of brands and sizes of maxipads for your daughter to experiment with. We recommend doing the following activities with your daughter so that she has practice with maxipad selection, use, and disposal.

- Open up the packages together and spend some time exploring the pads, including how they fasten in her underwear. Explain that girls and women wear a maxipad to absorb the menstrual blood that occurs for a few days each month.

- Let your daughter decide between scented and unscented maxipads. You might like perfumed pads, but she might find the smell aversive.

- Have your daughter wear a maxipad while fully clothed for a few minutes. Is she bothered by having the pad in her underwear? If so, you will want to start a gradual *desensitization program* during which she wears a pad for increasing periods of time, after which she is rewarded for her progress. First, try out a number of different pads and have her communicate with you (with words or pictures) which ones are most comfortable for her.

- When you have settled on which maxipads are most comfortable and are appropriate for daytime and nighttime use, bring your daughter to the store with you and teach her how to find the correct aisle and identify the boxes or bags on the shelves. Use this as an opportunity for working on independent living skills as well!

- While your daughter watches, fill a clear container with three to eight tablespoons of water and red food coloring. This represents the average amount of blood a woman discharges during her period. Using a medicine dropper, have your daughter experiment with how the maxipad absorbs liquid (you will be able to do the same activity with a tampon). Demonstrate what happens if the maxipad is not placed appropriately in her underwear (e.g. is off to one side) or is left in her underwear for too long.

- Have your daughter practice carrying a maxipad in her purse or pocketbook while at school.

Your daughter might need a lot of preparation time before getting her first period, or she might need only a short introduction. Some girls with whom we have worked have needed five to nine months of preparation because of anxiety and sensory issues. One 12-year-old, by contrast, after being taught how to place a maxipad and practicing for an hour, said to us, "That's it? That was easy. What's next?"

Being attuned to her body

My daughter often seems unaware of sensations like cramping, wetness, leakage. She wets her pants sometimes, too, and seems unaware this has occurred. And despite many attempts at anatomy lessons she still says the blood comes from her tushy. She is uninterested in all this stuff, too, so that is surely a big part of her lack of understanding of her anatomy. (Mother of a 14-year-old daughter on the autism spectrum with OCD and anxiety)

One basic skill that many of us take for granted is being aware of sensations in our own bodies. This skill is crucial to successfully navigating

Case study: Paula

When Paula first got her period it came as a huge surprise to her mother, and Paula herself wasn't even aware that something had happened until she went to get changed into her pyjamas that night. For months, Paula would get her period and it would be hours before she, her mother, and her teachers realized she had started menstruating. Paula has always had difficulties being able to notice and describe her own physiological states and bodily symptoms (e.g. feeling cold, feeling anxious). For most women who are attuned to the physiological states of their bodies, getting their period is preceded by a specific set of symptoms, such as cramping or back aches. When menstruation begins, many women report being aware of a sensation of light fluid seepage, which is a sign to make a trip to the bathroom. Knowing that your period has begun without having to constantly check your underwear is important. Paula was not able to do this, and given that she used the bathroom infrequently during the day, this became a problem when her period arrived and she was unaware of it. In working with Paula and her mother we developed a specific program to target body awareness. Additionally, Paula and her mother began tracking her menstrual cycle so that Paula could start wearing a pad before her period started. At school, Paula was prompted to go to the bathroom each morning and afternoon during the week before she was expected to start menstruating to check whether her cycle had began. After a number of embarrassing incidents in the classroom, Paula was more motivated to pay attention to her body and to track her cycle. She still has difficulties with body awareness, but is now more able to detect changes in physiological states than she was before.

menstruation, but many girls with ASDs have poor self-awareness and require extra support in this area. Before your daughter gets her period for the first time, try to prepare her for some of the physical sensations that she may experience when she begins menstruating. If your daughter has limited verbal skills, plan to use pictures to support teaching in this area. Think about your own premenstrual symptoms, or those of your family members. Many physiological symptoms are common in families and will give you a clue as to what your daughter might experience. Do you tend to get headaches, backaches, cramps, bloating, or breast tenderness? What are the signs every month that your period is about to begin? Create picture cards representing possible premenstrual and menstrual symptoms that you can use within the context of a "becoming a woman" picture story. Even if your daughter has strong verbal skills, we have found that it can be very helpful to use pictures to supplement discussion about bodily sensations. One activity we have found to be successful with girls is using craft paper to draw a life-sized outline of their body. The girls then identify various feelings they experience by coloring the appropriate parts of their bodies. For example, when we teach about anxiety, girls might color their heart red for "heart beating faster", or their head for "headaches".

Goal 4: Preparing for the first period

I received a call from Natalie's teacher and she asked me if I knew that Natalie had started her period. Somewhat embarrassed, I replied "No..." She had had her period for three days and hadn't told me. I had begun preparing Natalie for getting her period a number of months prior. She was reading books about how to manage her first period, and she was carrying maxipads in her school bag. The school reported that there were no problems, and that she was doing well. When I asked Natalie about why she hadn't told me, she stated in a matter-of-fact manner, "It didn't say in the book to tell your mom." (Mother of a 12-year-old girl with high-functioning autism)

The final goal is to prepare your daughter—and the professionals who work with her—for the onset of her very first period. From her doctor, you should have a rough idea of when to expect her first cycle to begin. Talk to your daughter's educational team at school about preparing for her first period. Her teachers and the school nurse will need to be on board with your plan. Have your daughter carry a maxipad in her pocketbook or school bag, or have a supply in the nurse's office just for her. Remember, if your daughter has sensory issues she will likely not feel comfortable using an unfamiliar maxipad from the nurse's office. If your daughter uses the bathroom with assistance, make sure her school team knows when you are expecting her to begin menstruating. If she uses the bathroom independently, tell her, with visual supports as needed, what to expect for her first period. First periods are usually light. Tell her that she will see a red or brownish-red spot or stain in her underwear when she goes to the bathroom. Communicate with her about staying calm and being able to follow her plan. If she is at school and does not have a maxipad with her, have her ask to go to the nurse's office immediately. If she is at an event in public and you are not there, have her tell a female adult who is part of her group.

Preparing for your daughter's first period is like preparing for any other new event, with perhaps a bit more associated anxiety. If you have taken the time to make sure your daughter, her educational and therapeutic team, and yourself are ready, things will go as smoothly as they can.

Successful management of menstrual hygiene

Now that you have gotten a handle on the *start* of her period, it's time to discuss menstrual hygiene and the regular monthly management that comes with being a young woman. In talking to grown women with ASDs, we have found that many women have had very difficult or traumatic experiences with their menstrual cycles when they were younger. Often this was related to not having enough information, planning, or skills to handle their periods successfully. We are going to review three important components of monthly menstruation management: being aware of your daughter's cycle, regular menstrual hygiene, and addressing PMS.

Cycle awareness

Cycle awareness is a critical part of knowing when your daughter's next period is due. And as we know, girls with ASDs tend to handle situations much better when they are prepared. So, having a rough idea of when you can expect your daughter's next period is going to be helpful for both her and yourself. Some women are fortunate in that their menstrual cycles run like clockwork—exactly 28 days long. For other women, if they are not taking a birth-control pill, the length of their cycle can vary from month to month. The most accurate way to determine when your daughter's period will begin is to chart her primary fertility signs: daily waking temperature and changes in cervical fluid. If your daughter is cooperative and motivated, you might be able to work on this as a project together. Remember, any activity your daughter does to increase her body awareness is going to be beneficial for her as she grows up. Learn more about how to chart waking temperature and cervical fluid by looking up information online (*see* Resources at the end of this chapter), or by visiting your daughter's physician. *Cycle Savvy*, by Toni Weschler, is also a great book for teenage girls (and their parents) to understand more about their bodies and menstrual cycles.

It is also important to be aware of secondary fertility signs as ovulation approaches, such as lower abdominal pain, water retention, breast tenderness, and bloating. The more familiar you and your daughter are with her natural cycle, the more you will be able to:

- predict when her period will begin, preventing stained clothing and embarrassing moments
- detect any unusual vaginal symptoms and secretions that might suggest an infection
- determine whether her period that month is "normal", or unusual in its length, type of bleeding, amount of pain, etc.

We are strong proponents of being "body aware"! If your daughter is able to chart her primary and secondary fertility signs on her own, she will learn a lot about her body, and will be prepared each month for her period. If you are able to keep track of your daughter's cycle for her, you will be able to help your daughter stay healthy and be prepared for her menstrual cycle each month. It may seem like a lot of work, but in the end, the positive outcomes can really outweigh the effort involved.

Regular menstrual hygiene

Depending on your daughter's cognitive and motor abilities, she will be able to deal with her period each month with varying levels of independence. Your goal as a parent is to promote the greatest independence possible within the limits of her skill set. Table 4.1 outlines what you can expect her to be able to accomplish. Regular menstrual hygiene each month should be just

---

Table 4.1 Her menstrual cycle: what your daughter can learn

Moderate to severe cognitive and motor impairments
- Cooperate with menstrual hygiene routine provided by caretakers
- Participate (assist) in steps of menstrual hygiene routine with supports (e.g. pulls down clothing, discards used pad)

Mild cognitive and motor impairments
- Management of most steps in menstrual hygiene routine
- May need reminders in the form of verbal or visual/written cues
- May need assistance with steps involving some motor skills (e.g. proper placement of pad in underwear)
- May not be able to use tampons

Average and above-average intelligence and motor skills
- Independent management of menstrual hygiene routine including use of tampons
- May need visual/written reminders (e.g. menstruation calendar)

that—regular, and routine. Your daughter should have a routine that she follows each time she has her period, and this routine should carry her from the onset to the end of her period. At first, when your daughter has only been getting her period for a year or two, she will likely need more assistance with and reminders about her routine. Remember, it can take girls with ASDs much longer than their neurotypical peers to establish a functional menstrual hygiene routine. This doesn't necessarily mean that it won't happen, it just means that it may take your daughter longer to get there. So pull out your teaching toolkit again, and be prepared to take the time that you and your daughter need. In this section we are going to discuss the steps and skills involved in menstrual hygiene in the context of maxipads; we will review the use of tampons later in this chapter. Take a look at the list below and make a note of which steps your daughter can currently do independently.

Checking for stains

- checks to see if her underwear has been stained
- recognizes menstrual blood in her underwear
- places soiled underwear in the laundry basket and gets a clean pair of underwear.

Changing her pad

- goes to the bathroom to check her maxipad; knows how frequently to go to the bathroom depending on how heavy her cycle is
- if the maxipad has blood on it, she removes it, rolls it up in toilet paper, and throws it out in the appropriate disposal bin (does *not* flush it!)
- selects an appropriate maxi pad (e.g. thickness, width) for the current day of her cycle
- unwraps the package
- removes the strip from the back of the maxipad and places the maxipad in her underwear
- throws the empty package and the strip in the garbage
- when dressed, washes her hands with soap before leaving the bathroom.

Nighttime routine

- at night, has a bath or shower to clean her private areas with soap and wash away any menstrual blood

- dries herself after her bath
- puts on fresh underwear and a new maxipad for night time
- puts on her pyjamas
- knows how long a period lasts and is aware of how many more days she will have her period.

These steps can be broken down into even smaller steps after completing a *task analysis* (determining the smallest individual steps in a larger, more complex skill). If your daughter is having difficulty with some of the steps, work with a behavioral psychologist and perhaps an occupational therapist to determine how to break the task down into smaller components that will be easier for her to learn. Practice some of the trickier motor skills and motor sequences (e.g. remove maxipad from underwear, fold it in half, roll it up in toilet paper, throw it out in the appropriate disposal bin) when she does not have her period. Choose one step at a time to work on. Your psychologist can help you decide which step will be the best one to start with, and which teaching approaches will be most helpful. They will also be able to help you determine which steps your daughter will ultimately be able to do independently, and which she will need more support with. You might want to look up behavioral teaching methodologies such as *backward chaining*, *forward chaining*, or *behavioral momentum*, which are very useful techniques when teaching skills that come together in a series of steps (e.g. bathing, menstrual hygiene).

Teaching tip: behavioral teaching techniques

- *Backward chaining*: the strategy of teaching a multistep task in *reverse order* (e.g. starting with throwing out the maxipad in the disposal bin).
- *Forward chaining*: the strategy of teaching a multi-step task in *chronological order*, starting with the first step (e.g. unwrapping the maxipad).
- *Behavioral momentum*: the strategy of teaching easy tasks first followed by tasks that are not liked or that are found to be frustrating. Behavioral momentum is meant to "get the ball rolling" with easier tasks before moving on to the harder ones.

Take another look at the list of menstrual hygiene steps. With your knowledge of your daughter's learning style, what approaches will you want to use as part of teaching? We have found the following strategies (combined with positive reinforcement and rewards) to be the most successful.

- *Recognizing menstrual blood*: practice, practice, practice looking at underwear that is clean, and underwear that has been colored to simulate menstrual blood. Using visual supports (check-marks, Xs), have your daughter identify which underwear has blood on it. Practice having your daughter let you know when she sees that her underwear has blood on it. As she becomes more independent with her menstrual hygiene routine, she will not need to let you know any longer when she starts her period.

- *Using the laundry basket*: use visuals to encourage your daughter to place her clothing in the laundry basket. Use a picture story, with photos of your daughter successfully completing the various steps. Practice placing dirty clothing in the laundry basket.

- *Selecting a maxipad*: until your daughter is able to select appropriate maxipads on her own, use containers or drawers that are labeled according to which day of her period it is, and whether she is selecting a maxipad for daytime or nighttime wear. You will need to know what your daughter's flow is like on each day of her cycle in order to select the correct thickness of pad. Remember to have your daughter keep track of which day of her cycle it is with her period calendar. If your daughter is carrying maxipads in her pocketbook or bag at school, help her to choose the correct maxipads to put in her bag in the morning before she leaves the house.

- *Changing her maxipad*: outline each of the steps for changing her maxipad on a card that can be placed on the wall beside the toilet in the bathroom, or laminated in her purse. As she becomes more independent, use fewer words or pictures as needed. Practice the motor skills involved.

- *Checking her maxipad*: most girls with ASDs will need some form of reminder system to cue them to go to the bathroom to check their maxipad. We have worked with families on experimenting with different kinds of cues for their daughter (auditory, visual, written). Do the same! Try out different kinds of reminders to see what works best. We recommend that girls go the bathroom on a preplanned schedule that is connected to specific events in her daily schedule, such as right before breakfast, right before lunch, before leaving school for home, before dinner, before bed (after showering/bathing). You will need to see which intervals are most appropriate given your daughter's daily schedule and the heaviness of her period. She may need to go to the bathroom more often if she has a very heavy flow. For tech-savvy daughters who don't want to stand out, use a PDA alarm reminder—a buzzer or a visual cue that pops up on the screen. Other visuals include checklists that can be placed on her desk at school, or a picture of a clock. Teachers or classroom aides can play a role in reminding your daughter to look at her schedule or the clock to see what time she needs to go to the bathroom.

- *Hand-washing and bathing*: follow the suggestions outlined in the hygiene section of Chapter 3. Take a look at some of the books related to teaching adaptive living skills (*see* Resources at the end of Chapter 3). The most effective strategies for developing hygiene skills are breaking tasks down into smaller steps, using visual and written supports and reminders, and practicing the steps. Remember, use rewards when your daughter is successful!

- *Overall menstrual hygiene routine*: one of the difficulties that even bright girls with ASDs may face is the organizational and sequencing challenges that come with managing a menstrual hygiene routine. As a result of deficits in executive functioning (higher-order cognitive skills), it can be quite difficult for girls to keep track of all the tasks involved in successfully taking care of their menstrual hygiene for an entire week each month. We have found that most girls will need some kind of support to help them keep track of their periods. Work with your daughter to find the most effective reminder for her.

Prepare yourself, and your daughter for (sigh) PMS

Yep. PMS monster two weeks before it hits. Mean, bloated, grumpy, sleepy, and aggressive. (Mother of a 16-year-old profoundly autistic daughter with cognitive impairments)

Parents of girls with ASDs—whether the girls are nonverbal, somewhat communicative, or highly talkative and verbally sophisticated—have reported to us that their daughters frequently experience symptoms of pre-menstrual syndrome (PMS) each month which, in the words of one mother with whom we work, "can really rock your world upside down". And not in a good way! We know of no research that has documented whether, as a group, girls with ASDs tend to experience more significant PMS than their neurotypical peers; however, our clinical experience suggests that this might in fact be the case. Why would that be? Are the neurotransmitter systems that are involved in some of the symptoms of PMS also involved in autism? Do girls' hormones interact with some other systems affected by autism in a way that triggers extreme PMS symptoms? Do existing difficul-ties with emotion regulation become exacerbated each month, contributing to significant dysregulation? Do sensory sensitivities heighten the emotional response to physical PMS symptoms? Right now, we just don't know. Later in this chapter we will review the gynecological examination, and discuss a research study which may shed some light on the issue. It is our hope that further research will illuminate the causes of severe PMS for young women with ASDs, and help families alleviate some of the "demon", "devil", "flip child", "tiger", and "monster" experiences that we have heard about over the last few years. Let's talk now a little about PMS, and what you can do to try to help your daughter.

PMS is a group of symptoms linked to the menstrual cycle that can be different for every woman. Some of the girls with whom we have worked have not experienced much difficulty with PMS, whereas others have had significant difficulties with regulating their emotions and behavior each month. Girls with severe PMS may have what is called premenstrual dys-phoric disorder (PMDD). Talk with your daughter's doctor if you are con-cerned about the severity of her PMS symptoms. PMS often includes both physical and emotional symptoms. Common reported symptoms of PMS fall into four different categories:

- *Type A—Anxiety*: tension, irritability, mood swings, angry outbursts.
- *Type B—Bloating*: breast tenderness, swelling, upset stomach, constipation or diarrhoea, weight gain, swollen hands or feet.
- *Type C—Cravings*: appetite changes, cravings for certain foods, overeating, feeling tired.
- *Type D—Depression*: moodiness, memory loss, sadness, crying spells.

Other potential symptoms include a worsening of acne, insomnia, headaches or backaches, joint and muscle pain, difficulties concentrating, and feeling overwhelmed or out of control. Not fun for anyone, but imagine how it must feel for a young woman with an ASD who thrives on stability. The following is a list of recommended strategies for managing PMS each month. Remember, if your daughter has significant symptoms, we strongly recommend that you consult with her physician.

Diet

- Eat a balanced diet rich in whole foods, non-starchy vegetables, and healthy proteins and fats.
- Eat fruit daily as a healthy alternative to sweets.
- Be sure to eat regular meals and snacks during the day to facilitate balanced blood sugar, which can help with mood stability.
- Lower sugar, salt and caffeine intake.
- Take a daily multivitamin.

Managing a healthy diet can be difficult for restricted or picky eaters. You may want to get a referral to see a dietician who has experience working with girls with ASDs.

Exercise

- Engage in regular aerobic exercise: at least 30 minutes of exercise, three times a week.

Many youth with ASDs tend to be sedentary. Difficulties with motor coordination and clumsiness contribute to a lack of interest in physical activity. Contact your local autism society or community recreation centre to find programming specific for youth with ASDs.

Sleep

- Get eight hours of sleep a night.

Many youth with ASDs have difficulty sleeping. Work with your daughter's doctor and a behavioral psychologist to establish good sleep hygiene and a regular nighttime routine.

Coping skills and relaxation

- Don't overschedule your daughter around her period. Plan specific times for rest and relaxation, and if there are stressful events to put on the calendar, schedule them for *after* her period is over.

Developing healthy coping skills and stress management strategies should be a life goal for girls with ASDs. Work with a psychologist for parent training and individual therapy for your daughter to develop relaxation skills and healthy coping.

Some families with whom we have worked have decided with their daughters' physicians to complete a trial of a birth control pill or a selective serotonin reuptake inhibitor (SSRI) as a means to regulate the emotional ups and downs associated with her menstrual cycle. A birth control pill can help to "even out" hormone levels throughout your daughter's cycle. An SSRI can help with anxiety, irritability, and depressive symptoms. For some girls, we have seen dramatic improvements in mood and behavior, whereas for others there has been limited change. The girls in our groups for whom improvement was significant talk about the effect as being "life-changing". Another reason given by families for using a birth control pill is that it makes their daughter's periods more predictable, and therefore more manageable:

> It took us about two years to get her to the point that she would remember to change her pad, and then we put her on birth control at age 11 to help regulate her periods in order for her to be able to keep track of them and know better when they should be showing up. (Mother of a 13-year-old girl diagnosed at age 11 with PDD-NOS, bipolar disorder, ADHD, and OCD who also has temporal lobe seizures)

Choosing to try the birth control pill or an antidepressant for mood management or period regulation is a very personal decision that is often influenced by cultural and religious factors. Talk to your daughter's doctor if this is a strategy you might be interested in trying.

The great debate: pads, tampons, or both?

> Unfortunately, I had abnormal uterine bleeding which meant I would bleed for days and even weeks on end. I could not stand the feeling of Kotex—they were too scratchy, fat and sticky. This left me with the reality of having to use two extra-large tampons at one time. Not a safe thing to do. In fact, on more than one occasion, I discovered I had left a tampon in, after taking only one out. Toxic shock could have been my partner on any given month. Scary stuff. Only the odor reminded me of what was going on! Nasty stuff. During my periods it did not dawn on me to wear dark clothing and at least a dozen times I had to literally run from school to get myself home to change my light-colored pants, which were stained a deep red by then. Luckily, my school nurse always helped

me get back into school understanding why I had run from school without going through the appropriate protocol. These days, I doubt a child would be given the freedom I was given. If I had had a peer helper or counselor who could have taken me under their wing in a healthy and non-interfering way, perhaps they could have reminded me to bring extra clothing, wear dark clothing, put a mark on a calendar to remind me to take out the tampons, etc. What an easier and healthier life I'd have led! (40-year-old woman with Asperger's Syndrome)

One of the most frequently asked questions we hear related to menstruation management is: "Do you think my daughter can handle using tampons?" The dangers of mismanagement of tampons are certainly higher than with maxipads given the possibility of developing toxic shock syndrome—the quote above illustrates some of the problems that can arise. Nevertheless, tampons are a viable option for many girls with ASDs, and have many potential benefits. Two things to consider when deciding whether tampons are in your daughter's menstrual future are: her motor skills and motor coordination, and her ability to manage her period while using maxipads. We recommend that girls start developing menstrual hygiene routines with maxipads, then gradually move toward using tampons as appropriate.

Why would you want your daughter to be able to use tampons? If your daughter swims or enjoys any activities that require wearing a body suit or shorter shorts (e.g. gymnastics or dance), she will need to either wear a tampon or refrain from engaging in these activities when she has her period; disrupting your daughter's recreational schedule may not be very desirable. Comfort is another issue; like many women who choose to use tampons, your daughter may be very sensitive to wearing a pad, however thin, for an entire week. Finally, women who use tampons report that they find it easier to stay clean during their period because the menstrual blood is absorbed by the tampon. Some parents with whom we have worked have expressed concerns about the use of tampons, sexual activity, and virginity. Remember, wearing a tampon has nothing to do with a girl or woman's sexual status, and it does not mean that she is no longer a virgin.

If you have considered your daughter's motor skills and her general menstruation management abilities, and you are comfortable with the idea of tampon use, the next step is to teach your daughter how to insert and remove a tampon successfully—something we have learned is often easier said than done! Our next case study is about a young woman for whom learning to use a tampon was quite a challenge. This is not uncommon in our experience working with mothers and their daughters, and is often closely related to girls' visual-spatial skills and motor coordination.

Case study: Jessica

Jessica is a bright, 14-year-old young woman with Asperger's Syndrome. She is a member of her school's swimming team, and when she got her period, she decided with her mother that she wanted to try using tampons so that she wouldn't have to miss swim team for a week each month. Jessica and her mother have a very comfortable, open relationship which served them well as she learned how to use tampons. Still, the process of learning how to use tampons successfully and independently took Jessica nine months. Despite being a very bright young woman, Jessica had significant difficulties with motor coordination and the visual and spatial skills necessary to visualize where in her body the tampon was to be inserted. After many unsuccessful attempts, Jessica and her mother had to work together with the aid of a mirror. Jessica was comfortable with having her mother assist her, which meant that for the first few months, her mother was able to help her guide the tampon inside her. With practice, Jessica was eventually able to insert a tampon while her mother held a mirror for her, and then finally she was able to do so herself in the bathroom without the assistance of her mother or a mirror. Jessica and her mother were fortunate; many girls are not as comfortable with having their mother intimately involved in their own personal hygiene. Jessica really wanted to be able to swim, and so she was motivated to learn how to insert and remove tampons on her own, and was willing to do whatever she needed to in order for that to happen.

If you and your daughter are comfortable doing so, have some practice sessions together with a mirror. You can also use diagrams to show where the tampon should be inserted, and at what angle (slightly backward and upward into the vagina). As you did with maxipads, buy boxes of tampons (with applicators and without) and practice unwrapping and using the plunger. Insert a tampon into a glass of water to demonstrate how it absorbs liquid. On a drawing of the body, demonstrate how the string of the tampon hangs out of the vagina for easy removal. Many girls are very nervous about using tampons for the first time. Take all the time you need with your daughter for her to feel comfortable with what tampons look and feel like, and how to insert one before actually trying to do so. Here are a few tips for making the first time easier:

- use the smallest-size tampon you can find; there are slim tampons for teens and for light flow days

- try inserting a tampon on a heavier flow day so that it glides more easily
- work with your daughter on relaxing her muscles, which will make insertion easier.

Your daughter will need to follow a menstrual hygiene schedule with tampons similar to that with pads. It is recommended that tampons be changed every four hours, more frequently as needed on heavy flow days. Because you do not feel a bulky pad, or the sensation of menstrual blood leaving your body, it can be easier to forget that you are wearing a tampon. Make sure your daughter fully understands and is able to follow her schedule for changing the tampon.

The gynecological exam

In Chapter 3 we discussed strategies for doctor's visits in general. Now we'll tackle the big visit—the gynecological examination. Most doctors recommend that girls be seen for their first examination by the time they are 18, or become sexually active. Sexual health is now seen as critical for all women, even beginning at a young age, and an early first examination is important for preventative healthcare and detection of illness and disease. If your daughter is experiencing missed or painful periods, pelvic or lower abdomen pain, unusual vaginal secretions, frequent urinary tract or yeast infections, changes in size, shape, or feel of her breasts, or any other symptoms, you should take her to see a gynecologist even sooner. We have already discussed body awareness; this is another important reason to work with your daughter on being aware of how her body feels. You will want her to be able to communicate with you immediately, with pictures, pointing, or words, if something hurts or doesn't feel right.

What do we know about sexual health in women with ASDs? In a study by Simon Baron-Cohen and colleagues that was presented at the Awares.org Autism Conference in November 2007, an online questionnaire was completed by 54 women with confirmed ASDs (average age 38.2 years), 74 mothers of children with ASDs, and 185 mothers of children without ASDs (Ingudomnukul *et al.* 2007). This questionnaire—the Testosterone-Related Medical Questionnaire—asked the participants about medical conditions associated with elevated levels of the hormone testosterone. Compared with the control group, women with ASDs reported higher rates of irregular menstrual cycles, dysmenorrhea, polycystic ovary syndrome, and family history of ovarian, uterine, and prostate cancers, tumors, or growths. Mothers of children with ASDs also reported higher rates of these concerns. Though this is only the first study to address possible hormone-related conditions associated with having an ASD, the results suggest that it may be very important to monitor sexual and menstrual health closely in young women with ASDs.

So how do you choose the right gynecologist? Depending on where you live, some general physicians do gynecological exams, whereas others are specialists. If your daughter's physician does internal exams, and your daughter is comfortable with him or her, we recommend that you stay with the same practitioner. If you need to find a gynecologist, ask your friends for recommendations, or contact your local autism society. You can also contact your state or provincial disability services organizations. Your daughter should see someone who is highly experienced in working with youth with developmental disabilities (preferably ASDs).

For any woman, the idea of having a pelvic exam is unpleasant and can create anxiety both before and during the appointment. Making your daughter feel more comfortable about going involves conveying why a visit to the gynecologist is important (to be healthy), what she can expect when she is there, and allowing her to ask questions ahead of time. There are excellent websites that provide detailed information about what happens during a gynecological examination (*see* Resources).

A standard gynecological exam comprises six parts: answering questions about reproductive history; the physical examination; the breast examination; the external vaginal examination; the internal vaginal examination; and the pap smear. For part one of the examination, role-play with your daughter to practice answering her doctor's questions. Make sure you have all the necessary information ahead of time to bring to the appointment (e.g. the first day of her last period, any abnormal symptoms). If your daughter is not able to communicate herself, you will need to answer all questions as accurately as possible. You will need to be able to describe what her periods look like, how long they last, how heavy her flow is, and what physical symptoms your daughter experiences. Another important reason for closely tracking your daughter's cycle each month! Your daughter has probably had a physical examination before, so this part of the appointment should be familiar to her. For the rest of the appointment, you can use the same strategies that you would use for a general doctor's appointment, such as those discussed in Chapter 3. Here are some additional techniques used by parents with whom we have worked to prepare their daughters for their examinations.

- Have your daughter be present in the room for one of your gynecological appointments (if you are comfortable with this). You can talk to her about what you are experiencing, and the doctor can explain what she is doing and show your daughter the instruments she is using. One of the girls with whom we worked went with her favorite aunt to her aunt's appointment then had her own examination a month later. She reported feeling much more comfortable having had the opportunity to see what it would be like. Could your daughter go to your appointment, or her aunt's, cousin's, or older sister's?

- Watch a teaching video or look at photos with your daughter ahead of time. The James Stanfield Company publishes a video entitled "The Gyn Exam" (*see* Resources) that follows a young woman through all the steps of her examination, from scheduling the appointment to the pelvic exam. With videos, you can use "pause and talk" opportunities to convey information, clear up misconceptions, and answer questions.

- Schedule a practice "run-through" appointment or an appointment during which only parts of the full examination are conducted (e.g. breast exam and external vaginal exam). At this time, your daughter can see the instruments that will be used in her next appointment and she can ask any questions she might have.

- Create a picture story to walk your daughter through the appointment. Google® Image Search is a great way to find pictures to use in social stories. Remember, there will be explicit pictures online so you should screen which images to show her.

- When you are at the appointment have your daughter's doctor communicate with her verbally, or with pictures, what will happen next in the appointment and what she will experience (e.g. "You will feel a slight pressure in your lower abdomen").

- Practice muscle relaxation and deep breathing while lying down before she has her appointment. Teach your daughter the difference between tightening her inner thigh and vaginal muscles, and letting them relax. During the examination, have your daughter do the following:
  - breathe slowly and deeply
  - relax her stomach muscles

○ relax her shoulders

○ relax the muscles between her legs and her vaginal muscles.

Aiming for independence

In this chapter we have reviewed many of the issues that arise for parents when they think about their daughter getting her first period and wonder whether she will be able to manage menstrual hygiene each month. We hope you are feeling a bit more comfortable with this time in your daughter's life, and feel that you can handle most, if not all, of what will come up during these years. Your daughter may be able to deal with her period each month quite independently. If you are able to apply what you have learned in this chapter to work toward this goal, then congratulations! Your daughter might also need more support as a result of her set of strengths and weaknesses. Remember, your overall goal is for her to be *as independent as she can be*. There is room for growth for everyone. Keep your teaching toolkit at hand, and always apply the same general principles we learned in Chapter 2:

- simple, concrete instruction
- support with visuals
- repeat, repeat, repeat
- practice, practice, practice
- reward and reinforce.

Have a happy period!

Resources

Non-fiction for parents

Ferreyra, S. and Hughes, K. (1991) *Table Manners. A Guide to the Pelvic Examination for Disabled Women and Health Care Providers*. Alameda/San Francisco, CA: Sex Education for Disabled People, Planned Parenthood.

Gillooly, J.B. (1998) *Before She Gets Her Period. Talking with your Daughter about Menstruation*. Los Angeles, CA: Perspective Publishing.

Non-fiction for girls and their parents

Feinmann, J. (2003) *Everything a Girl Needs to Know About Her Period*. Portland, ME: Ronnie Sellers Productions.

Gravelle, K. and Gravelle, J. (2006) *The Period Book: Everything You Don't Want to Ask (But Need to Know)*. New York, NY: Walker & Company.

Loulan, J. and Worthen, B. (2001) *Period. A Girl's Guide to Menstruation*. Minnetonka, MN: Book Peddlers.

Weschler, T. (2006) *Cycle Savvy. The Smart Teen's Guide to the Mysteries of Her Body*. New York, NY: HarperCollins Publishers.

Celebrating menstruation

McBride, K. (2004) *105 Ways to Celebrate Menstruation*. Vacaville, CA: Living Awareness Publications.

Morais, J. (2003) *A Time to Celebrate: A Celebration of a Girl's First Menstrual Period*. Fairfield, CA: Lua Publishing.

Smith, M.T. (2004) *First Moon: Celebration and Support for a Girl's Growing-Up Journey* (box set). Novato, CA: New World Library.

New Moon Publishing (Celebrates girls and women, has an article on celebrating your daughter's menstrual cycle) Available at www.newmooncatalog.com

Woman Wisdom (A naturalistic, healing website about empowering women and girls. Materials available for celebrating first menstruation). Available at www.womanwisdom.com

Fiction for girls

Blume, J. (1970) *Are You There God? It's Me, Margaret*. New York, NY: Yearling.

Video and teaching curriculum resources

Cooper, E. (1999) *Becoming a Woman: A Teaching Pack on Menstruation for People with Learning Disabilities*. Brighton: Pavilion Publishing Ltd.

Janet's Got Her Period[TM]. *Training in Menstrual Self-Care for Girls and Young Women with Severe Developmental Disabilities* (Video learning package). James Stanfield Company.

The Gyn Exam. Reduce Fears and Apprehension Associated with Gyn Examinations. (Video learning package). James Stanfield Company.

Resources available on the internet

Table Manners and Beyond. The Gynecological Exam for Women with Developmental Disabilities and Other Functional Limitations (May 2001) Edited by Katherine M. Simpson. Available at www.bhawd.org/sitefiles/TblMrs/cover.html

Websites related to gynaecological health

American Academy of Family Physicians: this site, operated by the American Academy of Family Physicians (AAFP), provides information on family physicians and healthcare, a directory of family physicians, and resources on health conditions. Available at http://familydoctor.org

American College of Obstetricians and Gynecologists: offers information on numerous issues and includes a women's health section. Available at www.acog.org

Estronaut. A Forum for Women's Health: Your First Gynecological Exam: available at www.estronaut.com/a/first_gynecological_exam.htm

For College Women: Health. Our Way: The First Gynecological Exam: available at www.4collegewomen.org/fact-sheets/firstgyno.html

Kids Health: Your Daughter's First Gynecological Exam: available at www.kidshealth.org/parent/system/medical/first_gyn.html

Planned Parenthood Federation of America: provides information on many areas of sexual health. Available at www.plannedparenthood.org

Chapter 5

Feeling Good Inside and Out: Self-perception and Self-confidence

My eight-year-old AS daughter today came to me and told me that when she grows up into a teenager, she is going to be a Power Ranger, and save the world. And of course, they have the healthy eating promotion segment, so she gets out the carrots and eats some, bounds up the steps, and says: "I can feel it working, I'm stronger b/c of the carrots! I flew up the steps 1–2–3!" I just find it absolutely amazing that my darling daughter who broke her fingers bowling, due to lack of coordination, is so intent on someday saving the world. If you look into her eyes, you will believe she can do it, too! (Mother of an eight-year-old girl with AS)

One of my wife's degrees is in art, and whenever we went to a display of art, she would explain the finer points of the work. I just knew I liked it. Like most parents, I want my daughter to grow up happy. I want her to be whatever she can and decides to be. They tell me she has a very high IQ, but I doubt she will ever graduate at the top of her class. Heck, I'm happy when she gets through the day without hitting or biting her teacher. Inside of that little body is a most wonderful being, and on the days when she leaves her world and visits mine, I get to share some beautiful moments. Someone once said the best tailors make the fewest cuts. I don't know, but sometimes I like to appreciate the painting instead of studying the brush strokes. (Father of a seven-year-old girl with moderate to severe autism)

Being a girl with an ASD is not easy. Every day your daughter tries to make sense of the world around her, to understand what others are thinking and feeling, to fit into a place that just might not feel quite right. As she enters adolescence she is embarking on a very important part of her journey to find her place in the world—a place in which she will feel loved and feel successful; a place in which she will be happy. The elusive state of happiness has intrigued scholars for decades, and is associated with concepts such as positive psychology, quality of life, self-esteem, wellbeing, and resilience. Happiness is related to a wide spectrum of personal traits; for example, in his book *Authentic Happiness*, psychologist Martin Seligman (2002) identified 24 personal strengths that contribute to an adolescent's happiness, including self-control, love of learning, perseverance, and enthusiasm. In this chapter, we will talk about strategies for helping your daughter to feel good about who she is, inside and out, and being as prepared as she can be to enter adulthood feeling confident, happy, and able to achieve success.

Your daughter's external sense of self

We begin with a discussion of what girls think and feel about the self they present to the world—their physical appearance and body image—and issues that may be challenging for girls with ASDs, such as eating, fitness, weight management, fashion, and personal style. Later in the chapter we will turn inward, focusing on what it means to have a positive sense of self. We will discuss fostering your daughter's self-esteem, being aware of issues with mental health and emotional regulation, and guiding your daughter toward accepting who she is—understanding her diagnosis, what it means to her, and how she can learn to advocate for herself.

Body image and physical appearance

> The biggest shock I got was when a group of girls in the library period started talking about who was the prettiest girl. It was a surprise for me to hear that, and to try to figure out how any one could notice what any one really looked like, let alone then judge a degree of looking...one of the girls said, "Well I think April's one of the pretty ones." This was even a greater shock; it felt like a physical blow, as I had no idea that people could see me, which sounds really stupid but I guess I just didn't process people well and thought that I was also invisible, or of no consequence. This then led to speculation (by me) as to how I really looked and I couldn't wait to bike home and check. When I looked in the bathroom mirror I was shocked that I was a blond girl, and not the dark-haired boy of my own real world. (April Masilamani, *Women from Another Planet?* pp.146–147)

A search for information about body image and girls, whether it be in the popular press or the academic literature, yields thousands of results. This topic has been studied in depth, and much is known as a result. Unfortunately, we know that for a variety of reasons many girls struggle with body image issues as they approach adolescence. However, very little is known about what girls with ASDs as a group think about their bodies and their appearance, and whether they experience issues with body image upon entering adolescence that are similar to those of typically developing girls.

In our practice, we have worked with girls who generally fall into one of the following four categories. Think about which one best describes your daughter:

- *No concept of her body*: complete disinterest in grooming and personal appearance; never looks in a mirror; does not have a sense if her clothing fits properly.

- *Is aware of her body and has a realistic appraisal*: generally healthy body image (likes some parts of her body, may dislike others).

- *Is aware of her body but has a less realistic appraisal*: tends to be negative about her physical appearance (dislikes most of her body).

- *Is obsessed with how she looks*: spends an inordinate amount of time devoted to personal grooming; is constantly looking in the mirror (these girls either think they look fantastic, or think they look horrible).

In our girls' groups we devote a unit to body image, and it has quickly become clear that there is wide variety in how the participants think about themselves, which may (and this is only clinical speculation) be related to their level of social understanding and awareness, and their sense of themselves in an interpersonal world. When asked to select the body that best matches their own from a set of outlines of girls' bodies (this is a standard assessment of body image), some girls are very accurate in their assessment whereas others seem to have no idea what they look like, or they see themselves as much thinner or larger than they really are. In a single group with seven participants, we had girls who fit into each of the categories described above. One girl was completely disinterested in how she looked and thought our exercise of identifying body type was, at best, strange. Three girls were aware of their physical selves and had realistic self-images: one was battling medication side effects which caused her to gain weight, while the others had fairly healthy body images. A fifth girl was also aware of her physical self but had an inaccurate self-image: she though herself to be much heavier than she actually was, and was very negative about her appearance. The final two girls were obsessed with appearance and were unable to stop looking in mirrors: one thought she had a gorgeous body and unabashedly shared this opinion with everyone, and the other couldn't stop saying how ugly and fat she looked.

What might affect body image in girls with ASDs? Research geared toward understanding how girls with ASDs think about various aspects of themselves, including their physical selves, will be very important in developing programming to address the mental health needs that tend to emerge during adolescence. Symptoms of the disorder may contribute to differences in how girls appraise (or don't) their physical appearance in a number of ways:

- Movement and coordination difficulties are common in youth with ASDs. Frustrations could lead a girl to dislike her body because it doesn't work well for her.

- Difficulties with body awareness and a sense of one's body in space could contribute to limited or inaccurate perceptions of one's body and what it looks like.

- Social impairments may make it difficult for girls with ASDs to understand the concept of comparing one's own body to a social ideal, resulting in reduced self-awareness.

Issues with eating: from complications to disorders

Hannah had her first horse show competition for the season this past weekend. She did very well. Thursday was the day the horses moved to the venue for the weekend and since I had to work, Hannah went with the trainer and the other girls to help with the horses and get set up. I went out there after work to find a very agitated, moody, emotional girl. She had a packed lunch and several water bottles that she brought with her but hadn't eaten or drank anything but a bag of Doritos. She knows the signs of hunger and thirst. She knows she gets headaches if she doesn't drink water. At home she takes very good care of making sure she drinks her water to avoid the headaches. She's pretty good at making sure she fixes herself something to eat at home when I am at work. Not 100%, she sometimes gets frustrated with her choices. Wants something we don't have or something. But she could self-advocate and say to everyone that she needed to take a break to eat or to just stop and eat or drink. This is one of my big fears about her future and trying to develop this kind of independence. I don't know how to foster this independence. I don't want to resort to having her "set an alarm" to remind her to eat because she recognizes hunger feelings. It's the part about taking care of herself when the hunger feelings come up. (Mother of a 15-year-old girl who was misdiagnosed with ADHD at the age of 8 and correctly diagnosed with Asperger's at age 11)

It is not uncommon for youth with ASDs to have eating issues, starting from a very young age, which may take a variety of forms and are often different from the sorts of issues one sees in neurotypical children. Sensory difficulties may limit the texture or smell of foods that they will eat, and resistance to novelty can also result in establishing a limited repertoire of foods. Some youth develop "food fad" restrictions related to specific characteristics of foods, such as color, or will eat one food only (e.g. will eat only ice cream for a period of time). Other youth may eat non-edible items (e.g. paper, dirt, erasers), which is known as *pica*. With appropriate intervention involving a therapist, including activities such as keeping variety in your daughter's diet, introducing new foods, and engaging her in food preparation and cooking, most concerns are typically resolved during childhood. However, a number of adolescents still present with eating issues that need to be addressed.

In her essay in *Aquamarine Blue 5. Personal Stories of College Students with Autism*, "Michelle" describes her odd eating habits that were not related to body image, the associated anxiety that she experienced, and her misdiagnosis as having anorexia nervosa. Ever since she was young, Michelle had had issues with the color, texture, and variety of foods. When she went to college and was faced with a large cafeteria, ever-changing foods, and the social scene of eating, she began to experience significant stress which further intensified the rigidity of her eating patterns. Friends began to question her eating habits and wondered if Michelle thought she was fat (which she had never considered). With the help of a male acquaintance, Michelle eventually began to have meals before the cafeteria opened, which was less stressful and allowed her to eat the food of her choice. After a while, she began to eat "pseudo-normally" and developed a better awareness of what her difficulty was—that she had formed an internal rule that she had to eat completely normally like everyone else, or not at all.

In neurotypical girls, eating issues are usually closely tied to body image and self-perceptions of weight and physical appearance. We might be tempted to assume that, because of social impairments, body image is *never* a root cause of eating disorders in girls with ASDs, but we know this to be false. In 1980, a case study was published in the *Journal of Autism and Developmental Disorders* about a 12-year-old girl with autism and significant cognitive impairments whose obsession with body image led her to develop anorexia nervosa (Stiver and Dobbins 1980). During a three-month period, the young girl began to decrease her food intake and she began to express interest in, and comment on, students' and adults' body shapes (fat or thin), stating that she herself was on a diet and that she did not want to be fat.

She developed aversive responses to foods and eating, such as refusal, gagging, and vomiting. Another example is furnished by Jessica Peers, a young woman with Asperger's Syndrome, who wrote in her memoir about her fixation with weight and beauty:

> I read my magazines. Many of these contained pictures of women I could never emulate. Supermodels were at their peak of world domination, body-fascism excluding all the regular freaks such as the short, the plump, the pimpled, the buck-toothed, those scarred with the natural stretch-marks of impending womanhood, and those pitiful creatures, the truly obese, whose waistlines overspilled a size ten. In despair, I was captivated by the preaching of those gurus of diet and beauty, standing by the mirror each night at odd angles trying to convince myself that I was "generously curvaceous" as opposed to the fashion dictation of the superwaif. Beneath the tangled rope of jewelery that hung around my neck and the deep red dye that bled little life into my hair, I would tear myself apart inside. (*Asparagus Dreams*, pp.185–186)

Research has indicated that there may be a link between eating disorders and ASDs in adolescent girls. Gillberg and Billstedt (2000) reported that 18–23% of adolescent girls with anorexia also present with signs of Asperger's Syndrome. Gillberg and Rastam (1992) suggested that, for many girls, obsessive compulsive symptoms, anorexia, paranoid symptoms, and conduct problems could in fact be symptoms of an underlying ASD. This can create a dangerous situation (possibly life-threatening) if the ASD is not diagnosed, because traditional psychotherapy is not the treatment of choice for autism. A girl with an ASD may not respond to traditional treatments, allowing the eating disorder to become highly entrenched and resistant to interventions.

Pay close attention to your daughter's eating habits, and watch for any early signs of problems, no matter what the cause may be. We have talked with many families who are very concerned about their daughter's patterns of eating; some of the specific difficulties they have reported include:

- cannot tell when she is hungry
- unaware of associated feelings when hungry (e.g. headachy, cranky)
- cannot tell when she is full
- confuses full and hungry
- confuses hunger and nausea

- forgets to eat or drink (possibly in unfamiliar settings or when her routine is disrupted)
- always feels hungry—unsure if it is "real" hunger
- eating patterns change dramatically or become more rigid when under stress
- obsessed with rules about food and food consumption
- rigid and restricted eating patterns
- eating reflexively—appears to have no volitional control.

Continued difficulty with any of the above issues may lead to eating disorders such as anorexia, bulimia, binge eating, compulsive eating, and hoarding. If your daughter is demonstrating significant difficulties with eating, make sure you meet with her physician and a dietician. It might also be critical to see a psychologist for therapy. Identifying the causes of her eating habits will be important in determining the appropriate intervention. She may need to work on awareness of internal states, anxiety management, therapy related to self-esteem and body image, developing a healthy food repertoire, or assistance with executive function and planning eating schedules.

Weight management

For many neurotypical girls, weight management becomes an issue in the pre-teen and teenage years. Girls are often comparing themselves to media images of actresses, models and teen pop stars, and to each other. As we've discussed, body image may or may not be an issue for girls with ASDs, but regardless, weight management is an important issue for parents to be aware of. For your daughter with an ASD, maintaining a healthy body weight (not too heavy and not too thin) for her age, height, and build can be affected by:

- an unhealthy diet and a restricted selection of foods
- a preference for sedentary activities—computer, video games, television
- limited awareness of internal sensations (hunger, full)
- stress eating
- medication side effects.

Medication side effects can be particularly frustrating, and at times it may seem as though the medication is creating more problems than it is solving. Weight gain and sleep difficulties are two examples of side effects that can be highly detrimental in a teenage girl's life; both contribute to feelings of not being in control or successful from day to day. One of the girls in our group is treating high levels of anxiety and mood swings with medication that, unfortunately, causes weight gain. We have been working together on diet and exercise; however, she is still struggling against the side effects of her medication. Her self-esteem suffers when her efforts to lose weight are unsuccessful. Though she realizes the medication is helpful, she wishes that it didn't come with such a high price to pay. This can be a very difficult trade-off for a teenage girl. Before trying any medication, make sure to discuss side effects with your daughter's physician; include your daughter in the discussion if she is able to participate.

Fitness and exercise

As a group, individuals with ASDs are typically thought of as sedentary and less inclined to participate in sports or physical activity. If your daughter is clumsy, awkward, has balance problems or motor planning issues, she is likely going to feel very frustrated, and possibly embarrassed, if she is required to participate in activities that emphasize her difficulties. People tend to choose to do things in life they enjoy, and the activities that youth with ASDs enjoy are often less physical in nature, such as playing computer games, searching the internet and researching favorite interests, watching movies and television programs, and collecting and trading Pokémon™ or Yu-Gi-Oh™ game cards. One of the girls in our group would spend hours each night searching the internet for information on Johnny Depp, her favorite actor. With the popularity of the *Pirates of the Caribbean* movies, the amount of information available online seemed endless to her family!

Physical activity is considered vital for maintaining a healthy lifestyle. In addition to the health and weight management benefits, exercise has been linked with improvements in sleep and mood, increased energy level, reduction in stress and anxiety, and alleviation of premenstrual symptoms—all important for adolescent girls with ASDs. Research with youth and adolescents with ASDs has found that moderate aerobic activity results in improved attention span, on-task behavior, increased correct responding on tasks, reduced aggression, and reduced repetitive behaviors (Celiberti *et al.*

1997; Rosenthal-Malek and Mitchell 1997). For girls with ASDs, the benefits of being active can also include improved self-confidence. Participating in physical activity strengthens muscles, increases flexibility, and can result in overall improvements in the motor and coordination difficulties that are experienced by many girls. Establishing an exercise routine for your daughter now will help to ensure that it becomes a regular part of her life as she gets older, so that she can continue to experience the benefits of physical activity.

Choosing the right activities: what kind of fitness is best for your daughter?

Not all activities or sports are well-suited to youth with ASDs. Think about your daughter's skill set, strengths and weaknesses, and level of motor difficulties. Some of the areas that might be more impaired, which will affect your daughter's ability to participate in certain activities, include coordination, visual tracking skills (e.g. following a ball), fine motor skills, speed of mental processing (e.g. making quick decisions in fast moving games), and attention span. It might take many attempts to find an activity that she enjoys and at which she feels successful. Keep trying—the end results will be worth it!

Some of the characteristics of activities to consider are:

- individual versus team
- simple (e.g. walking) versus complex (e.g. riding a bicycle, skiing)
- different sensory stimulation (e.g. swimming, skiing)
- takes a lot of time (e.g. travel to a ski hill) or very little (e.g. jog around the block)
- requires your assistance (e.g. transportation) or may be done independently
- structured versus informal
- highly aerobic versus calm and relaxing.

For maximum health benefits, a physical activity program should include 20–30 minutes of vigorous activity, three or four days a week. Depending on your daughter's current level of activity, you may need to work up to being more active gradually. Finding a personal trainer who has experience with youth with disabilities can be helpful in developing an individualized program that will take into account your daughter's abilities, interests, and goals. Talk to your local autism society and local recreation center. Many programs now have classes for youth and teens with special needs, and the Special Olympics program is popular all over the country.

Girls with whom we have worked have enjoyed many different activities, including gymnastics, swimming, dance classes, skiing, hiking, yoga, bowling, martial arts, and horseback riding. Dawn Prince-Hughes describes in her book, *Songs of a Gorilla Nation—My Journey Through Autism*, how dancing was the perfect fit for her life, and was a release for her:

> I had never been good at sports, not only because they required intense interaction with others but because I had always been awkward. Dancing was something different and I was good at it. For some reason, where noise and light had caused me pain before, the flashing and throbbing of the clubs pushed me deeper into myself. I knew the freedom of self-expressive movement and could dance alone all night. I was always dismayed when someone asked me to dance, because to me it was an absolutely solitary activity.

If your daughter loves animals, try to get her involved in an animal-related program that involves physical activity (which most do); this would be a perfect match both for her interests and for your goal of keeping her active. Inquire at local animal shelters; they often have volunteer programs that adolescents can participate in. Working with animals—exercising dogs, grooming, cleaning cages, and sweeping—all keep you busy and burn calories. If the volunteer program is structured and has understanding adults as facilitators, your daughter could really thrive.

Another animal-related physical activity that your daughter might enjoy is horseback riding. Horseback riding is a wonderful way to connect with animals while developing important motor skills such as balance, coordination, core strength, and flexibility. Grooming a horse, mucking out stalls, sweeping aisles, cleaning tack, and feeding are all equine-related activities that burn calories and build muscle. Horseback riding is also a fabulous social opportunity for your daughter. Many neurotypical girls love horses, and what do they all love to talk about? Horses! Many towns offer therapeutic riding programs,* including summer camps. When you are researching a program, make sure that the instructors are trained and certified, and that the program has high safety standards (e.g. approved helmets are always worn, youth are never left unattended around the horses). On the National

---

* Avoid programs that claim to treat the core symptoms of autism, or even cure autism. Therapeutic riding is a wonderful adjunctive activity with physical and social benefits, but it is never a replacement for core treatments such as behavioral and educational programming, social skills development, speech-language therapy, and counseling.

Autistic Society website, Miss Edmonds, a young woman with autism, writes about "My life with Asperger syndrome and horses". She states that she has always felt a natural empathy for animals, especially horses, and that she is never happier than when she is in their company. Girls with whom we have worked report similar feelings, and look forward to their weekly lesson. Opportunities such as these contribute greatly to girls feeling excited about having a purposeful life in which they are accomplishing goals and achieving successes.

If you're looking for an activity that involves other children, team sports can be a positive learning experience and an opportunity to practice skills and establish social connections. However, they can also be frustrating and potentially embarrassing if the coach or other team-mates don't understand your daughter's difficulties. Follow your daughter's lead. If she doesn't want to try team sports, don't push her. There are plenty of other activities she can do either independently, or with one or two other people.

Another activity that is gaining in popularity for youth with ASDs is yoga. Fitness centers have developed supported programs for youth with disabilities, and there are often opportunities for mother—daughter classes. In addition to developing core body strength and flexibility, the principles of yoga teach students to calm their bodies, quiet their minds, and control their breathing. Introductory poses tend to be simple to master, and breathing techniques promote relaxation and focusing. In our girls' groups, we often include a yoga segment when we discuss personal wellness and health. Yoga is an activity that all girls can participate in, regardless of verbal ability. With modeling, visual supports, and structured teaching, girls can gradually learn poses and work on their breathing and focusing. Yoga can be helpful for stress management, developing coping skills, and quieting an anxious mind. Yoga can be challenging—girls with ASDs will often feel uncoordinated at first and have trouble focusing. So take it slowly, and reward your daughter for trying! With gradual practice and repetition she will begin to feel successful.

What if your daughter is highly resistant to joining or participating in activities and would rather stay at home and play on the computer or play video games? The video game industry seems to have become aware that parents are concerned about their children's sedentary lifestyles—a few new games actually require you to stand up and move! The Wii™, Nintendo's fifth video game console, brings people together and makes you get off the couch to play many of its games: games such as pairs tennis, bowling, baseball, boxing, golf, and dancing require you to use a hand-held sensory bar that simulates various sports movements while playing. Parents have reported to us that not only are their children interacting with them, but they are having fun and breaking a sweat at the same time! Then there's Guitar Hero™, a rock guitar simulation game that requires participants to strap on their guitar controller (which looks like a real Gibson guitar) and learn to play rock songs by pressing the correct keys as they light up. With great music that parents will enjoy (all-time classic rock songs), a two-player mode also promotes socialization and interaction. Finally, there are dance computer games: in Dance Dance Revolution™, participants stand on a dance pad with four arrow panels, and must step on the panels in response to corresponding arrows that appear on the screen. The on-screen images are timed with the rhythm and beat of popular songs, and participants succeed if they are able to "dance" by timing their steps accordingly. So if your daughter is not yet ready to venture beyond the land of video games, you now have some options that require her to be active while playing. Try them out and see which ones she likes!

Lastly, beginning a fitness or exercise program may be so unappealing for your daughter that you will need to rely heavily on reinforcement and rewards. Just like you might not want to sign up for an advanced college calculus class, your daughter really might not want to change her routine and try something that is going to be difficult for her at first. What will motivate your daughter to begin to participate in her fitness for life program? Now is the time to really work on it.

Building a healthy self-image

Part of feeling good about oneself includes have a positive body image and feeling healthy, strong, and able to participate in physical activities. Working with your daughter now toward these goals will, we hope, result in positive lifelong beliefs and a commitment to take care of herself—eating healthy, exercising, and engaging in all the self-care and personal hygiene activities we discussed in Chapters 3 and 4. *American Girl* has a book entitled *Real Beauty. 101 Ways to Feel Great About YOU* (*see* Resources). Written for pre-teen girls and using fun activities, it discusses all the issues we have reviewed so far in this chapter—body image, healthy eating, and exercise—and it talks about how to believe yourself to be truly beautiful. If your daughter reads, or is creative and likes to draw, this might be a fun book for you and her to work on together.

First bras and beyond: the world of intimate wear

I got Angela a few of those little sports bras, along with a cute sports bra/panty set. Today before we went to the mall I brought the set to her, on the hanger, and said, "Here, Angela want to put on your new panties?" She said, "*no bras ever!!!*" when she saw the bra hanging. I said "Okay, Angela, but what are you gonna do when your breasts keep getting bigger like Mommy?" She said, "No bras!" I said okay, and turned and went down the hall, thinking I shouldn't push it under I can find a good motivator. As I walked down the hall I heard her say, "It sounds like Angela doesn't like bras at all." (Mother of an 8-year-old girl with ASD diagnosed at 23 months of age)

For our female readers, do you remember getting your first bra? How did you feel about it? For neurotypical girls, a first bra is often more than just another article of clothing to wear—it symbolizes that they are becoming a young woman. Many girls, though not all, are proud of getting a bra, and eagerly anticipate when they will be able to do so, measuring themselves weekly in the bathroom. For girls with ASDs, a bra might very well just be another article of clothing they are required to wear: one that tends to be uncomfortable, and often is perceived as unnecessary. Remember, there are social reasons for wearing a bra that your daughter might not understand. Let's address bra basics so that you and your daughter will be comfortable and ready when the time comes that she really does need one.

Getting ready for the first bra

My daughter got really silly and she said she didn't need bras yet because her boobs weren't pointy like mine. Then she lifted up my shirt to see my bra. She did try them on though and thought they were comfortable. I bought very soft Danskin ones at Target. Of course she did go and flash her little brother her new bra. I explained to her that bras are private like underwear and we don't show them to people. Anyway, I think the whole thing went pretty well. (Mother of a 9-year-old girl who was diagnosed with PDD-NOS at age 3, and then with autism at age 6)

My daughter couldn't wait to wear a bra. She is fascinated by boobs. Kylie was so excited when we told her it was time to get bras. We didn't have any problem with her wearing one, which surprised me since she has issues with clothing. Kylie always saw me in a bra and asked me when she could have one and I would tell her she would be able to wear one when she started to get breasts. One day in the shower she started yelling, "I have boobs! I have boobs!" It was very funny. (Mother of a 12-year-old girl with autism)

Remember when we talked about maxipads and practicing wearing them before your daughter's period actually starts? You can, and should, do the same thing with bras. Below is a "bra ladder" with a progression of tops and bras that you can use to prepare your daughter for wearing a full-fledged bra:

- loose tank top or camisole
- fitted tank top or camisole (e.g. with a built-in shelf bra)
- training bra
- sports bra
- soft cup bra
- under-wired bra.

Again, think about your daughter's autism and how it will affect how she feels about and responds to wearing a bra. Sensory issues can play a huge role for many girls: is she very sensitive to wearing certain clothing, especially textures and fabrics? Does she dislike wearing tight-fitting clothing? If this is the case for your daughter, you might need a longer time to practice, and she may need to eventually settle on a very comfortable, yet supportive, no-cup bra or sports bra. What about her motor skills and motor coordination? If she has difficulties in these areas, she is going to want a bra with the fewest snaps and strap adjustments; sports bras tend to be a good choice. Remember to reward your daughter for even putting the bra on! Try to think about the sensory issues from her perspective; practice your own perspective-taking skills. Maybe you do not like to wear wool, especially against your skin. What if you were told you had to wear scratchy wool right against your skin every day? You probably wouldn't be too happy about it either. Gradually work up to your daughter being able to wear her bra for longer periods of time. Eventually, it will no longer be an issue or, at worst, it will be only a minor annoyance for her to cope with.

Choosing the right bra

Hannah didn't want to wear bras. Wanted nothing to do with them, wouldn't talk about them. We had to start initially just wearing those sleeveless undershirts to get her used to wearing something under her shirts. Eventually, as she got bigger and the T-shirts weren't cutting it anymore, we managed to wear a bra. It took us a long time and lots of money spent on bras to find ones that were compatible with her unique set of sensory issues. Now Hannah has no problem wearing bras. (Mother of a 15-year-old girl with Asperger's)

If your daughter has a lot of difficulty being out in public or spending time in large department stores, it might be easier for you to make purchases and bring them home for her to try. Talk to the saleswoman; explain that your daughter is not with you because she has autism and it is hard for her to spend time in department stores. If the saleswoman is not accommodating, go somewhere else! There are plenty of malls and Walmart®, K-Mart®, and Target® stores to be found. If possible, prepare ahead of time by measuring your daughter's chest size yourself, or have her physician do it. If you don't have your daughter's measurements, the saleswoman will ask you what your daughter's breasts look like currently in order to estimate size. There seems to be an art and a science to bra fitting that takes into account your frame (the diameter around your chest under your breasts), your breast size (the diameter around your chest, over and including the largest part of your breast), and with specific mathematical calculations, your bra size, and cup size. Have you ever taken the time to determine exactly what bra you should be wearing? Many women are walking around wearing bras that are not quite the right size; results of survey studies indicate that over 70% of women are not wearing an appropriate bra for their body (Lipton 1996). Maybe you could use this opportunity to get measured together with your daughter.

Talk to the saleswoman about your daughter's sensory issues, and the comfort level of different bras. Pure cotton is often the most comfortable and many of the girls with whom we work prefer to wear cotton. Hanes™ advertises an "All Over Comfort Bra", some of which have no tags. How's that for making a bra suited for females with ASDs? What is great about women's undergarments these days is the variety of style and design. Not only will you likely be able to find bras that are quite comfortable for your daughter, but you might also find some brands that have logos or designs related to her special interests (e.g. Disney characters, Sponge Bob, Hello Kitty), or that are available in her favorite colors or patterns. No more white and beige bras—unless you want them! Similarly, underwear has been revolutionized for girls. You can now find minishorts, boxers, and briefs for girls which are more comfortable, less restrictive and often more appealing for girls who do not like tight clothing. No more tight elastic bands around your legs!

If your daughter is able to go with you to look for bras, prepare her for the trip. Write a story about it, including visuals if they are helpful for her. Tell her that a saleswoman will speak with both of you and will measure her breasts using a measuring tape. Explain that this is so the saleswoman will find the right fit for the bra that will be comfortable for her. Practice measuring at home ahead of time if you need to. Walk around the department store, feel the different textures and fabrics, and look at all the colors and patterns. Make a game of it—which bra feels the worst, is the ugliest, the silliest?

Why do women have breasts and wear bras?

If your daughter is able to understand, explain to her (using visual supports as needed) how breasts develop, what their purpose is, and why (most) women wear bras. All girls, regardless of skill level, can learn about their own body's changes from seeing a series of breast development pictures. Make sure your daughter is aware that each person's breasts are unique— many girls worry that their breasts are abnormal if they are small or large, if one is growing faster than the other, or if their nipples look different from those of their peers. Girls with ASDs may need to be told explicitly that breasts are very individual in how they develop, and what they eventually look like when they are full-grown. Refer to the typical developmental literature reviewed in Chapters 3 and 4 for books your daughter can read that explain breast development and why women have breasts. As for why women wear bras, reasons include:

- hold breasts in place
- comfort—particularly for large-breasted women, or when engaging in sports that cause bouncing
- keep breasts from touching the chest wall to avoid perspiration or skin irritation
- keep nipples from rubbing against the fabric of clothing, or from showing through clothing
- conform to modern society's dress code—your school or place of employment, certain social situations
- avoid drawing attention to your breasts in public
- …or draw attention to your breasts in public.

For a variety of reasons, some women choose not to wear a bra. However, your daughter will be going to school for many years of her adolescent and young adult life. Not wearing a bra is going to draw public attention from peers and classmates to her breasts, and it might also be in violation of her school dress code. If 90% of teens or women wear bras (Hsieh and Trichopoulos 1991) yet she does not, the extra attention might contribute to further social isolation or teasing. Perhaps your daughter will have small breasts, and wearing a camisole with built-in support will be enough. Chances are, though, that the day will come when she will need to wear a bra at school and in public, so it's best to be ready.

Fun with fashion and personal style

I took Angela and her sister to the mall this afternoon. I wanted to get some spring clothes for Angela in particular. Well, Angela has screamed for years when shopping, and it wasn't until about a year ago that she actually picked out an outfit. So, I talked it up by telling them they were going to get clothes like Hannah Montana. We walked into the store and Angela looked all around and said, "*I love this store!*" It was too cute! She immediately picked out a shirt, very overpriced denim crop pants, shoes, and a hat! I didn't want to buy some of it because of the price but how could I tell her no? Anyway, I'm going to start trying to take her shopping about once a month and maybe have a couple of buddies go with us. (Mother of an 8-year-old girl with ASD)

Many of the parents with whom we work lament that their daughters have no clue about what they look like, nor do they seem to care. Other parents are concerned about the opposite—their daughters are obsessed about appearance, their bodies, and how they cover their bodies—fashion and clothing. Before we discuss fashion, we want to start with a caveat. Our goal in working with families and girls has not, and never will be, to try to make them popular, make them more "neurotypical", or to make them conform to society's current ideas of what is fashionable for young women of their age. However, we have found that when girls dress neatly and presentably and within the loosely defined boundaries of what is considered acceptable for youth their age, they are less vulnerable to teasing and are more likely to have opportunities to develop friendships. Perhaps more importantly, learning about fashion helps girls to become more self-aware, to develop their own sense of style, and to develop confidence. We wish that girls with ASDs, and all other children who are perceived as "different", were accepted unconditionally by their peers. Although peer-awareness programs are being developed, and the general climate of acceptance within schools and youth culture is becoming more positive, youth continue to be ostracized and bullied in many areas in their lives. If fashion can assist your daughter in experiencing less teasing and in feeling more confident about herself, then let's talk about fashion!

What are other girls her age wearing?

If you do not have a neurotypical daughter, or nieces, or friends with daughters, it can really feel as if you have no idea what girls your daughter's age are wearing. If you do have access to girls your daughter's age, find out from them directly and from their parents what they like to wear, and where they shop. Parents with whom we have worked have essentially become social anthropologists, finding ways to learn about their daughter's female peers. There are a number of ways to go about this.

- Purchase magazines for girls and look at the outfits the young models are wearing—we reviewed a number of these magazines in Chapter 3.

- Look at the catalogues that arrive in the mail from department stores; what are the female models wearing in the Juniors' section of the catalogue?

- Talk to your daughter's teacher or school counselor—he or she spends time around hundreds of kids each day. Depending on how observant they are, they can probably tell you who wears what at school, and they can give you information about school dress codes.

- Watch some teen television shows and movies; what are the characters wearing? How do they dress according to their character (sporty, academic, the queen bee)? Examples of shows and movies are provided in Chapter 2.

- Take a trip to the mall. Look at the clothing in stores for teens, but also camp out on a mall bench for a while. The mall is a great location to watch adolescent girls in their natural habitat. Take note of what they are wearing—shoes, pants, skirts, belts, tops, jackets, hairstyles, hats, makeup, pocket books, purses, bags, and jewelery.

- Browse the internet. If you Google "teen fashion", you will find plenty of sites to explore.

What does your daughter like to wear?

While you are doing your anthropology experiments, think about your daughter. Do you see clothing or accessories she might be interested in? How does her autism influence what she currently wears? Many issues related to fashion are relevant for girls with ASDs, including sensory (e.g. textures, fabrics, colors, looseness, comfort), novelty (e.g. resistance to change, wanting to wear the same thing), motor skills and coordination (e.g. wrap-around clothes, zippers in the back), motivation (e.g. disinterest, difficulties with grooming in general), and social (e.g. unaware of the social components of fashion and clothing). In her memoir, *Congratulations! It's Asperger Syndrome*, Jen Birch sums up what many girls with ASDs have reported feeling about fashion and fitting in:

> Added to this was the girl students' interest in fashion hairstyles and makeup— things which still left me completely bewildered and bored. I overheard one female classmate exclaiming, "Fashion? Who *isn't* interested!" I knew that the answer to this was "Me." My lack in all these areas caused me to wonder if something was wrong with me. (p.74)

> It is usually the same with new clothes—I avoid the whole issue until someone forces me to go into a clothes shop. Well, why do I need new ones, when the old clothes I got 25 years ago are still perfectly good! In fact, people sometimes breathe the word "retro" around me in hushed tones; I didn't know what that meant, at first. The purpose of clothing is for protection from cold and sunburn. Old clothes are trusty, familiar, and soft; new ones look and feel strange and uncomfortable. Why would one, then, want to have the new ones? It's a weird-ness which *other* people have, but they try to force their peculiar notions on to me. And "fashion" and "labels!"—it's like other people are escapees from Planet Bizarre. (p.31)

Go into your daughter's closet and drawers; take an inventory of what she is currently wearing. Write down what you think are the challenges that you and your daughter will face regarding clothing selection and shopping. As you can imagine, shopping comes with its own set of difficulties, including the possibility of being overwhelmed by lighting, noises, crowds, too much selection, and narrow aisles. Even for individuals who do not typically have sensory issues, a trip to the mall can easily become too much. When you are planning a shopping trip with your daughter, you might want to avoid the holiday season.

In our teen girls groups, we have units related to fashion, accessories, make-up, grooming, and developing personal style. As a group, we do many of the activities suggested above, including looking at magazines and cat-alogs, going online, bringing clothing to group for the girls to look at, watching movie clips, and making trips to the mall or the nail salon. We recommend that parents begin to do similar activities with their daughters. If public outings are difficult for your daughter, she will need to work up to a trip to the mall. As with bras, you might need to go by yourself at first and bring home a selection for her to try on.

Girls with ASDs are not all anti-fashion or fashion-clueless; in our groups, we see a wide range of awareness and styles. Some girls come to group dressed in fashionable but somewhat inappropriate clothing (e.g. belly-baring, very tight-fitting). These girls tend to be overly conscious of their looks, and will spend excessive amounts of time examining themselves in the mirror and inspecting their bodies. Other girls dress in a casual, fashionable manner. Still other girls typically wear track pants, running shoes, baggy T-shirts, and sweatshirts. Their overall look is dishevelled, and they are often poorly groomed (e.g. hair not brushed). Does your daughter seem to fit in one of these groups? We work with all of these girls in different ways; however, one common approach is to teach the girls to be observant of others, and of what their peers are wearing. In the following quote, Liane Holliday Willey describes her experiences of attempting to notice and follow what others were doing with respect to fashion.

> Just as I took good notes on how people acted, so too did I make mental notes of how they dressed. Fashion trends have always diverted me, though I have never been able to understand them as entities deserving of a life filled with purpose. I was able to tell that my peers took their clothing choices seriously because everyone copycatted everyone else's style. I knew I was supposed to follow the rules set by fashion but try as I may, I broke them all the time. I still fought with textures and colors and patterns, like I did when I was a child and I simply could not bring myself to wear certain clothing no matter how many rules I knew I was breaking. Tight jeans that fell to the hip, shirts that were the color of clay, coarse wool jackets that wore the back of my neck raw...they were not for me. I settled for clothing a smidgen outside the lines, finding a handful of outfits that blended in well enough to avert stares, but not so well that I was miserable in them. And if those almost-trendy clothes of mine were dirty, I would wear whatever I happened to grab from my drawers even if what I had selected did not look well together. Not that I noticed. I designed myself for comfort and convenience, not trends. (*Pretending to be Normal*, p.42)

We also work with girls on selecting clothing that is going to be manageable for them. A girl might love a particular skirt, but she might not be able to manage the zipper and clasp in the back because of her motor abilities. Jen Birch talks about coordination and dressing in her memoir:

> To go back a few years, learning to dress myself was a difficulty involving not only coordination but also the understanding of which way round things went. It

seemed to take me longer than other children to grasp that looking at the front of a garment is *not* the right way round for putting it on; one must turn it around that that one is looking at the back. I would often put my clothing on the wrong way round on my first attempt, and sometimes with multiple attempts, even into my teen years. (*Congratulations! It's Asperger Syndrome*, p.87)

The nice thing about fashion today is that having a bit of a quirky or retro look is often acceptable! We work in middle and high schools doing school consultation, and when our services are needed in the lunch room, it's our turn to become youth anthropologists. No longer are there just generic plain t-shirts; cotton T-shirts have a style all of their own, with slogans, patterns and colors. Even leisurewear (e.g. track pants) has been designed so that there are fashionable styles—still cotton and comfortable, but not the baggy unisex kind that used to be the only option. It is currently fashionable for girls to wear casual cotton T-shirts and pyjama pants, often with large comfy boots (e.g. Ugg®), and with hair in a messy ponytail or bun. A teenage girl with an ASD could certainly develop a wardrobe that would fit in with this style!

Let's now discuss a few strategies for assisting your daughter in revamping her wardrobe. We'll use Maura as an example.

Case study: Maura

Maura was a 17-year-old bright young woman with Asperger's Syndrome in one of our girls' groups who, when she began coming to the group, would wear baggy jeans, running shoes, and extra large T-shirts. Her mother described her style of dressing as "dumpy". Getting Maura to wear anything else, or even to be interested in shopping, was like climbing Mount Everest. When they went to the mall, Maura would quickly become overwhelmed, look at one thing on a rack, and then say she wanted to leave. When her mother brought clothing home to look at, Maura quickly dismissed the items. We realized it was going to take time, that it was important not to rush her, and that we would need to work on developing her coping skills for handling stressful situations. After being in the group for a while and participating in the fashion units, Maura said to her mom one day, "I want to get a pair of jeans that do not make me look dumpy." Her mother was thrilled, and responded calmly and casually, saying "Sure, let's see what we can find." That was the first step. By the end of group, Maura had also developed a crush on a boy. She bought a T-shirt with a band logo on it that her crush liked in order to spark a conversation with him. She began coming to group accessorizing, wearing some jewelery, and she went to get her nails done. She also told her mother she wanted to "wear cover-up on her zits, and Nair the hair on her arms." Maura now wears jeans that fit her better and she wears fun, funky T-shirts. She sometimes wears a headband, and she has a very cool watch and bag (according to the other girls). This was a work in progress for a long time, but the end result was that Maura has become aware of how she presents to others, and she has begun to establish her own sense of style. She is now in her first year in college and has a part-time job. She is learning about appropriate clothing choices for job interviews and work.

Maura and her mother continued to work on coping skills so that she could eventually go to the mall for short periods of time (going to the mall is now one of the things Maura likes to do with her friends). Her mother's relaxed approach was critical to Maura's success; no matter how much you might want your daughter to be interested in clothing and doing mother–daughter activities, don't rush it. With the right gradual approaches, you will at the least be able to help your daughter find a wardrobe that, as Liane Holliday Willey put it, is "only a smidgen outside the lines."

Remember your teaching toolkit when working on clothing and fashion. Use visual supports—show your daughter pictures of girls who are unkempt and messy, and wearing very strange clothing, and pictures of girls who look casual and neat. Use pictures of clothing and fashion, and what teenagers wear. Put the information you provide in a social context; if your daughter is old enough, talk about job interviews and first impressions. Reward your daughter for any interest and attempt to go outside her comfort zone. Compromise and accommodate a bit—you're likely not going to get your daughter into a highly textured top and cool low-waisted corduroy jeans, even if you think the outfit would look great on her. Lower your expectations and look for clothing that is comfortable but still stylish. If your daughter has limited verbal skills, work on choice-making. Present her with two pieces of clothing to choose from and, after she tries them both on, have her select one. The more your daughter can participate in selecting her own clothing and developing skills to get dressed, the more empowered and independent she will feel.

Many families of girls and boys with ASDs report that they cannot get their child to wear jeans, which are practically the uniform of youth. Be persistent—go on a jean quest! There are many denim companies that now make soft, prewashed cotton jeans that some of the kids with whom we work have been able to wear. It doesn't always happen overnight though. Some youth begin wearing shorts for only a few minutes at a time and then are able to progress slowly to wearing long pants for a full day. Desensitizing to the way things feel needs to be done systematically and gradually, with rewards built in.

Developing a personal sense of style

> I've found brands can make a difference. The outfit she picked out last year was a Strawberry Shortcake outfit. She picked out some boots at Christmas that were Hannah Montana western boots. I think she is beginning to try and pick out trendy teen star clothing, so that's great, so long as she doesn't end up with the too skimpy stuff! I like to post our little successes in case moms are going through some of them, to give hope. I never, ever thought we'd reach a point that Angela would want to shop. One mother shared about her daughter going into the store and trying on clothes—I thought, "Yeah, like Angela would ever do that!" Now here we are. Never underestimate our kids! (Mother of an 8-year-old girl with ASD)

In our work with families and their daughters, we always encourage self-exploration and self-understanding. Even for girls with significant impairments, being able to make decisions is essential in developing a healthy self-concept. Some people have a natural "fashion sense", others don't—you do not need to have an ASD to be fashion-impaired. In our experience, most females with ASDs do not have an intuitive sense of their bodies and what might look good on them, let alone conform to current fashion trends. With guidance, though, we have seen girls who initially had no idea of what they might want to wear, or what clothing would complement their figure, begin to understand fashion and feel confident in their choices.

You, as an adult, have your own sense of style. As children grow up, parents decide what clothing they will wear until the children are old enough to begin to contribute to the decision-making process. Like parents of neurotypical teens, you will need to encourage and allow your daughter to develop her own sense of style, which will often be expressed as part of a fashion genre: she may dress sporty, casual, trendy, alternative, dressy, preppy, glam, grungy, goth, rocker, punk, urban, bohemian, chic, etc. Whether or not your daughter decides to conform and adopt her peers' style, or instead develop a style of her own, ultimately depends on what makes her feel comfortable. And remember, teens go through stages of trying on different identities. If your daughter's style changes over time, good for her! She is experiencing what neurotypical teens do—discovering who she is—and we applaud her loudly for it.

Putting it all together: fashion, grooming, hygiene, and personal style

Your daughter's goal is to be able to complete the following activities as independently as possible.

- Manage her daily and weekly hygiene routines.
- Go to a store and select clothing that is appropriate and that she likes (including bras, underwear, and outerwear).
- With assistance, can order clothing online or from a catalog if shopping at stores is too difficult for her.
- Can decide on a daily basis what she wants to wear depending on where she is going and what the weather is like.
- Can accessorize as appropriate (e.g. belt, earrings, bracelets, hats).
- When permitted, and if she wants to, learns to apply makeup appropriate for teens (e.g. lip gloss and blush).
- Takes care of her grooming routine, including making sure her hair and clothing are neat and tidy.
- Makes sure her outfit is presentable before leaving the house (e.g. checks for stains, wrinkles).
- Has a personal style that she feels comfortable with and is confident about.
- Is aware that how she presents to others is important in life (e.g. first impressions, job interviews).

Your daughter's internal sense of self

Having discussed your daughter's external image, including her body and her clothing, we now turn our attention inward and focus on helping girls with ASDs feel good about themselves. We will highlight some of the things, including mental health concerns, which can get in the way of that very important objective. The self-esteem of an adolescent girl with an ASD may be fragile for a number of reasons. She may have had difficulties making friends in the past, or she may have been teased or bullied (many of the girls in our group program experienced teasing in elementary and middle school, resulting in lasting emotions that they continue to struggle with well into late adolescence). She has also likely experienced years of feeling less successful than her peers, and may have struggled in areas such as language, thinking skills, academics, or motor abilities. She may often feel disoriented, confused, or uncertain about the world around her, and the people in it. Research has shown that, in general, neurotypical girls have lower self-esteem than boys, and many girls experience a specific decline in their self-esteem during early adolescence (American Academy of Pediatrics 1999). Does that mean that girls with ASDs are *doubly* at risk for a drop in self-esteem as they enter adolescence? We don't know the answer to this question, but self-esteem is without question an important component of your daughter's treatment program.

If you feel that your daughter has a strong sense of self, and healthy self-esteem, that is wonderful, and we hope that the following sections will guide you in helping her to continue to feel good about herself and her accomplishments in life. If, on the other hand, you feel that your daughter's self-esteem is at risk, or you have already seen significant negative changes in how she feels about herself, then your goal is going to be to help her rebuild her sense of confidence, competence, and worth as a person. You can tell her in pictures or words how wonderful she is, but if she doesn't believe it herself, her feelings will not change. An important thing to know about self-esteem is that while it develops during early childhood and becomes somewhat stable by around age 12, it is also in part dynamic and is shaped by life experiences. Positive early experiences help youth to build self-esteem and internalize feelings of self-worth. As youth grow older, new events, situations, and experiences contribute either to validate one's feelings about oneself, or cause self-doubt. For youth with ASDs, transitional periods such as entering elementary school, facing the academic challenges that begin to arise in grades three and four, becoming aware of being different from their peers, starting middle school, entering puberty, and facing adulthood, are all times when it is common to see the foundations of self-esteem become shaky. Being aware that this might occur, and being prepared to prevent or address issues as they arise, are your best strategies in assisting your daughter through tough times.

Below are what we consider to be the basics of self-esteem for any girl with an ASD, regardless of ability level. The remainder of this chapter discusses what you can do to assist your daughter in achieving these goals and feeling good about herself.

Self-esteem basics for girls with ASDs

- To be able to effectively communicate her wants and needs.
- To feel safe, loved and cared for.
- To feel a sense of agency—that she can affect her world through decision-making and assertiveness.
- To feel a sense of self-control—that she has coping skills she can rely on.
- To experience success and achieve goals.
- To develop independence and self-reliance.
- To have good self-knowledge.
- To have fun and feel happy while doing what she enjoys.

Creating success experiences

As a parent, one of your most important jobs is to always be on the lookout for possible success experiences for your daughter. Although it is important to challenge her as she grows up, it is even more important to first provide opportunities during which she is going to achieve success. Find the right balance between activities that she is familiar with, and can do well, and ones that are just outside her understanding or skill set. This can be especially important for girls with moderate to severe delays. When your daughter does something well, reward and praise her. We all thrive on positive feedback, be it praise or some other reward: it makes us feel good and motivates us to continue to try. At the same time, make sure that your feedback is accurate. If something was difficult or challenging and she was less successful, let her know that, too. But also let her know that it's not the end of the world if she did not succeed—she will have other chances to improve and do better. By giving accurate feedback, you will provide your daughter with opportunities to develop and practice coping skills, increase her self-awareness, and develop positive self-talk (i.e. telling herself that she *can* do something if she keeps trying).

You can create success experiences for your daughter by recognizing her strengths and finding ways to showcase them. If she is good at art, find local art shows for youth with disabilities. If she writes stories or poems, find somewhere they can be published, even in a school literary journal. Develop your own newsletter with some families you know. We have created an "artist's walkway" in our clinic where we hang framed artwork by youth with whom we work. It is an incredible experience to see the pride in their faces, and those of their family members, when they come back and see their work displayed. Never underestimate what it can mean to your daughter when you acknowledge what she's good at. With practice and repetition, she can internalize the dialog you use (pictorial or verbal) to praise her, which we hope she will begin to use herself. As you point out her strengths, you are also promoting self-knowledge, which is key to developing healthy self-esteem.

Developing independence, self-reliance, and responsibility

> We have a 10, almost 11-year-old daughter with autism. Thoughts about her and her future? As Ada's language and development have occurred, some of the initial "fog" of autism has lifted and allowed us to know her even more. She is a funny, loving, sensitive, vibrant person who does not give up easily and yet is confronted by the challenges of autism quite frequently now. She is more aware of these challenges, which is painful at times for both her and us, in a different way than when she was younger. My wishes for her...I want most of all for her to always be surrounded in some manner by friends and/or family who can reflect the beautiful person she is and strengthen her belief in herself. I wish also for her to have a sense of achievement and independence in whatever form they may take. (Parent of a pre-teen girl with autism)

One of the areas in which we see many girls with ASDs struggling as they enter adolescence is developing independence and self-reliance. As we discussed in Chapter 2, this is one of the biggest contributors to anxiety about growing up. If you have had an adaptive behavior assessment for your daughter, you will likely see that she is not performing at the same level as her typically developing peers. This is to be expected, as we know that girls with ASDs often developmentally lag behind their same-aged peers by a few years. It is particularly challenging, and anxiety-provoking, when the scores on adaptive measures (which assess skills to get along in day-to-day life) place her five or even ten years behind for some skills. Some of the skills that tend to be problematic have been discussed in this book—self-care and hygiene, social and communication skills, and safety skills. Others include completing chores around the house, money skills, community skills (e.g. taking a bus), and coping skills.

One of the reasons that girls (and boys) with ASDs have trouble developing these skills is that, from a young age, they have required and received more assistance than neurotypical children. For years, your daughter has been dependent on you to meet her needs, be her advocate, and take care of her—all part of being a good parent. It can be difficult to determine when she should start doing things on her own, which is ultimately what she needs to do in order to develop independence skills. Sometimes parents will continue to do things for their daughters because it seems faster and easier that way. Parents also want to keep their daughter happy; learning a new and challenging skill is certainly not always going to be enjoyable for your daughter. However, once your daughter is able to climb the initial learning curve, acquiring a new independence skill will make things easier for both of you and will improve her self-confidence. Many parents have said to us, "I wish I had been working on these skills all along," or "I wish I hadn't done so much for her myself when she was younger." The end results are worth the effort!

If you have not done so within the last year, have an adaptive behavior assessment completed for your daughter. The results will give you a good idea of how your daughter is doing compared to her typical peers and which areas you will need to work on to promote independence. You can then select specific, measurable goals to work on in the short term, and outline what you want her long-term goals to be based on your transitional planning. Try to have some of your short-term goals added to your daughter's individualized education plan at school. Remember, you want your daughter to become as independent as she possibly can, and that will depend upon her abilities in a number of areas (cognition, language and communication, motor, social). You might want to work on independent dressing as an initial goal. Or perhaps your bright 18-year-old daughter does not yet know how to do laundry herself, or she does not have a savings account—those would be wonderful goals to work on that will promote both independence and responsibility. Use your teaching toolkit for all of the adaptive skills that you target. Break tasks down into small steps, provide a model, use visual supports and written cues, practice, and reward effort and success. The more independence your daughter has, the more she is going to feel successful in her life, and the more she will experience a sense of *agency* (being able to effect change in her world). Being able to accomplish life's tasks independently reduces anxiety, helps her to feel that she can rely on herself, helps to create structure in her life, and builds self-esteem—our ultimate goal.

Promoting self-knowledge and self-awareness ("Who am I?")

Getting to know themselves is a very important task for girls as they enter adolescence. Although the focus on individuals with ASDs tends to be their limited social understanding, we have found in our work, especially with higher-functioning girls, that they also often do not understand themselves very well. If this is true of your daughter, then work on her *self-insight*: her awareness of her strengths, weaknesses, and personality traits. One concrete activity for self-exploration is to create an "All about Me" book. Help your daughter to collect pictures of things she likes and doesn't like. Take photos of her participating in some of her favorite activities. Add pictures and photos related to her accomplishments—the first book she read, the spelling test that she got a B on, riding a horse, her most recent drawing, the bed she made in the morning. Next, help her to think about things that are more challenging for her, and add these to the book as well (e.g. a math or word problem, a picture of people playing soccer, a picture of a shower).

The next step, which tends to be more difficult, is to help your daughter consider internal characteristics and develop an overall sense of herself— what *kind* of person is she? Is she funny, energetic, caring, silly, bookish, athletic, brave, artistic, hard-working, logical, polite, shy, outgoing? In our group work with younger kids and with adolescents, we complete "What would you rather do?" exercises (e.g. read a book or go skating). We also read story-books or excerpts from novels, or watch clips from movies or television programs depicting characters with a variety of traits and qualities. Our goal is to help the girls compare themselves to other people in order to develop a deeper understanding of who *they* are beyond "I'm a nice person," or "I'm good at drawing." For girls who are capable, we have them complete journal exercises, and creative activities (acting, photography, drawing, poetry) that require a lot of self-reflection. It's not easy work, and many of the girls become frustrated, but even this frustration can be beneficial. It helps the girls tap into their feelings about themselves and the world around them, and it provides them with an opportunity for developing coping skills.

Developing and expanding your daughter's interests

> When my daughter was younger she…felt more comfortable with younger kids or older ones. Same-age peers was difficult. But now that she is in high school, she's a freshman this year, she really only wants to hang out with kids her age and do "teenager stuff". She still prefers organized activities and is beginning to expand outside her preferred areas. She has been to two school dances, two school plays, and went to four football games in the fall. The latter was amazing since she *hates* football. Still it is hard to get her to want to leave the house with all her books. She *loves* her books. (Mother of a 15-year-old girl with Asperger's)

In their November 27, 2006 issue, *Newsweek* magazine highlighted adolescence as a particularly challenging time for youth with autism and their families. In the article, one mother discussed the difficulties facing her high-functioning 14-year-old daughter with Asperger's Syndrome who is still very much interested in Barbie, Pokemon, and Disney Princess, and yet knows that these interests are "not cool" for teen girls her age. As she drifts in the Peter Pan-esque land between remaining a child and growing up, secretly indulging in her juvenile interests at home, her mother walks the fine line of encouraging her daughter to develop more age-appropriate interests without pushing her too hard.

This scenario may be all too familiar to some of our readers, as it is not uncommon for pre-teens and adolescents with ASDs to remain interested in toys and activities from when they were younger. We have worked with teens who are gradually learning to play less with *Sesame Street* toys, watch fewer *Sponge Bob* shows, and talk less about *Power Puff Girls* at school. Is it a bad thing that your daughter has less mature interests? Not intrinsically; these interests may constitute for her an important sense of security, calmness, and familiarity. Allowing half an hour on the weekend to watch a *Blues Clues* tape is not going to permanently impede her development. However, it is important to distinguish between a less mature interest that can be pursued at home, and one that is all-consuming and interferes greatly with home, school, and community life. In this case it becomes important to implement strategies to reduce the amount of time spent engaging in the interest, restrict the locations in which it occurs, and introduce more age-appropriate activities. The following are approaches that families with whom we have worked have found successful.

- Using a visual schedule that includes a specified time and place for engaging in the activity.

- Using an activity schedule to introduce a selection of age-appropriate interests that their daughter can choose from.

- Rewarding age-appropriate play and activities.

- Having their daughter join a group that has typically developing peer mentors who can model activities and interests that same-aged peers enjoy.

With proper support and encouragement, your daughter's interests can progress beyond her childhood fixations and become more age-appropriate. One of the girls in our girls' group remarked to us recently that she is starting to like music and going to concerts. She thought it was really interesting that while other girls at school have already had these interests for a number of years, she was only then beginning to enjoy listening to different styles of music, wearing band T-shirts, and attending concerts. We detected a sense of pride in her voice, as if she was finally feeling that she was "catching up" with her peers and had something in common with them.

Celebrate and encourage the age-appropriate interests and talents that your daughter develops. Her interests may seem somewhat unusual (e.g. an interest in Egypt), or she may have talents in areas where her typical peers demonstrate less interest (e.g. math facts)—work hard to find a peer group that will appreciate her. Contact your local autism society. Some organizations provide peer-matching services that you can register for—if they know another family who has a same-aged daughter who also loves Egypt you might be able to get in touch with that family. Joining a social skills group with other girls who are accepting of differences and eccentricities can open up a world of possible friendships for your daughter. It might not be easy to find the right balance between encouraging age-appropriate interests and allowing your daughter to pursue her less mature or overly intense interests; bear in bind that *both* are important in the development of her self-esteem and sense of self.

Self-regulation and emotional understanding

Adolescence involves many different emotional and hormonal changes that can be frightening or confusing for your daughter, especially if she is experiencing increased fluctuations in mood and frustration with many of the daily life challenges she faces. During these years it is not uncommon for girls with ASDs to feel "out of control" in their home, school, and community environments. Girls who have the ability to verbalize these experiences often report not knowing how to control their feelings, that they never know how they are going to feel, or that they are easily set off by any little thing. Girls with limited communication skills may express their experiences through tantrums, meltdowns, and other displays of frustration. We have found that for girls, four things contribute greatly to difficulties with self-regulation and emotional expression or understanding during adolescence:

- general hormonal changes during adolescence
- premenstrual symptoms
- limited skill development in emotional understanding, self-regulation, and coping skills
- a lack of appropriate outlets and knowledge of who to talk to when these feelings arise.

The first two items are biological in nature, and apply to all adolescent girls. It is difficult to determine whether the hormonal changes and associated emotions experienced by your daughter are similar in degree and intensity to those experienced by same-aged neurotypical females, though parents of girls with ASDs have reported that their daughters do seem to have a harder time emotionally. Research in endocrinology will help shed light on this question, but it is just as likely that girls with ASDs are struggling more with hormonal changes because they lack the skills to self-regulate and cope, and do not have the same support network of peers that neurotypical girls do. Likewise, difficulties with premenstrual symptoms are commonly reported by parents of girls with ASDs, but how much can be attributed to physiological responses and sensory issues versus coping skills is up for debate.

The third and fourth items are the ones that we target when working with girls with ASDs. Developing self-regulation and emotional understanding, and having a healthy outlet for expressing feelings, are essential. For girls who long for social contact, lacking such an outlet serves to increase feelings of isolation. Self-statements such as "There is no one else out there like me" begin to eat away at whatever self-esteem a girl has left, possibly leading to further withdrawal into herself. We have found that for many girls in our group, the group is the first place they have felt accepted and understood. Even if their day has gone horribly, and they have been screaming at their mother in the car on the ride over, they know that when they walk in the doors of the clinic, no one will judge them, and they will be able to share how they have been feeling. They will also be able to learn healthy strategies for managing their emotions.

The first step to being able to *regulate* one's emotions is to *understand* emotions—both one's own and those of others. When we work on regulatory skills, we assess a girl's baseline for understanding of emotions and how emotions are connected to situations, thoughts, and behaviors. This assessment then allows us to develop an emotions program that targets her areas of weakness. A basic emotions program might include the following elements.

- Identifying basic emotions in facial expressions (happy, sad, angry, scared).
- Identifying basic emotions caused by situations (e.g. getting an ice-cream cone makes you/her feel _____).
- Identifying complex emotions in facial expressions (e.g. embarrassed, disappointed, surprised).
- Identifying complex emotions caused by situations (e.g. dropping all your books in the hallway in front of everyone makes you/her feel _____).
- Being able to identify, in the moment (using pictures or words), how she feels in certain situations.

There are a number of very good books on social skills and emotional understanding (*see* Resources at the end of this chapter and Chapter 6), and we recommend that parents make emotional understanding a teaching goal throughout adolescence. The complexities of emotional understanding and self-regulation make this an area of life-long learning for everyone, not just girls with ASDs. Strategies you can use as parents include permitting and responding calmly to your daughter's emotional expression, labeling her emotions (including using pictures) for her if she is not able to do so herself, reflecting your daughter's feelings (e.g. "You seem a bit nervous about going to the picnic"), and reflecting your daughter's experiences in her words (e.g. "You thought she liked you"). Try not to minimize your daughter's feelings, and do your best to understand her experience. For girls who enjoy reading, *American Girl* has published a book called *The Feelings Book. The Care and Keeping of your Emotions* (*see* Resources). In the following section on mental health, we are going to discuss more specific strategies related to developing coping skills and self-regulation, including connecting thoughts, feelings, and experiences.

Fostering mental health

It is now known that youth with ASDs often present with other psychiatric symptoms or disorders, specifically mood disorders (Bradley *et al.* 2004; Brereton, Tonge, and Enfield 2006; Ghaziuddin *et al.* 2002; Vickerstaff *et al.* 2007), anxiety symptoms and disorders (Gillot, Furniss, and Walter 2001; Muris *et al.* 1998), obsessive-compulsive disorders (Ghaziuddin, Tsai, and Ghaziuddin 1992; McDougle *et al.* 1995), symptoms of ADHD, and difficulties with low frustration tolerance, temper outbursts, and mood lability (Brereton *et al.* 2006; Kim *et al.* 2000). Youth with ASDs are also at greater risk for psychiatric hospitalizations than children who present with other disorders (Gallaher, Christakis, and Connel 2002), with rates of hospitalization ranging from 11% to 25% across studies (Mandell 2008; Mandell *et al.* 2005a). What does this mean for your daughter as she enters adolescence? In Chapter 2 we discussed the increased rates of depression in typically developing girls as they enter adolescence: the observed rate is twice that of boys the same age. Brereton and colleagues (2006) found that as youth with ASDs approach adolescence, increased symptoms of depression are also observed, in particular among those with IQs in the average range, and that females may be particularly vulnerable as a result of biological effects of puberty. It has also been noted that by the time they start middle school, typically developing adolescent girls are also more vulnerable to experiencing stress than boys because of greater pressures to succeed academically and socially (Cohen-Sandler 2005).

As they approach adolescence, girls with ASDs are at significant risk for developing mental health problems, or exacerbating difficulties that are already present. In the following sections we will discuss the mental health concerns we typically see in adolescent girls with ASDs. We will present approaches to reducing the chances that severe concerns will arise, as well as strategies for addressing existing problems.

Depression

Adolescent girls with ASDs can develop depressive symptomatology or serious clinical depression for a number of reasons including experiencing loneliness, failure, and frustration, an unmet desire for friendships or relationships, and neurochemical imbalances. In *The Complete Guide to Asperger's Syndrome*, Tony Attwood discusses reactive depression—a clinical depression that develops as a result of awareness of skill deficits and unsuccessful social attempts. Adolescent girls with ASDs can be at risk for reactive depression on account of a general lack of acceptance by their classmates, coming to the realization that they are different than their peers, and a greater awareness of the daily social difficulties they experience. Vickerstaff and colleagues (2007) recently reported a relationship between self-perceived social competence, depressive symptomatology, and intellectual ability in youth with ASDs. Having a higher IQ predicted a lower level of self-perceived social competence and a higher level of depressive symptomatology. Similarly, previous work found that depression is more common in individuals with autism than other young people with intellectual disability, and that it is more common in individuals with ASDs with higher IQ scores (Brereton *et al.* 2006; Sterling *et al.* 2008). These findings support the idea of reactive depression, and that a negative self-perception can contribute greatly to a young girl developing symptoms of depression and poor feeling about herself. We have also observed that depressive symptoms seem to occur much more frequently for girls around the time of menstruation.

It is very important for parents to be aware of the signs of depression, and to know that depression in youth may look different than in adults (e.g. youth tend to present as more irritable than sad). Look for changes in your daughter's baseline behavior. If she has always had troubles sleeping, insomnia might not be a sign of depression for her, but loss of interest in her favorite pastimes might be. The following are traits and symptoms of depression:

- irritability
- unhappiness, sadness
- crying
- anxiety
- loss of interest and pleasure in activities
- changes in appetite; weight loss or gain
- insomnia (can't sleep) or hypersomnia (sleeps too much)
- psychomotor agitation (restless, agitated) or slowing (can't get moving)
- fatigue or loss of energy
- difficulties concentrating
- feelings of worthlessness, hopelessness, or pessimism
- thoughts of death or suicidal ideations.

For girls who are lower-functioning, depression may manifest in the more vegetative signs, such as a regression of skills, aggressive behavior, irritability, sleep and appetite disturbance, and loss of bowel and bladder control.

Anxiety

> I have much fears off and on in the life of me, and some come and go, but most are of a permanent fear for me. My fears are triggered by logic that does not make of sense to me or things that move with unpredictability. I do not like changes, fearful of many bugs, snakes, and things with vicious sharp teeth and or things that might bite of me. Fearful of some storms, fearful of ocean storms, fearful of new changes, fearful of certain noises, fearful of police, fearful of certain voices, fearful of deep water, fearful of some toilets, fearful of certain textures if by accident touch it, fearful of stair wells, fearful of falling, fearful of hospitals and needles or testings, my list can be to go on for a long time. (45-year-old, married woman (mother and grandmother) diagnosed with an ASD in 2001; all four of her children have diagnoses of Asperger's Syndrome)

Individuals with ASDs are particularly vulnerable to experiencing stress and anxiety (Groden, Baron, and Groden 2006). Sensory issues, difficulties with communication, impaired social understanding, dislike of change, and difficulties with executive function all contribute to some individuals living life in an almost constant state of anxious arousal. Temple Grandin, one of the most prolific writers of the personal experience of an ASD, has shared that when puberty hit, she began to experience extreme anxiety that she called "nerve" or "panic" attacks. In her chapter in the edited book *Stress and Coping in Autism*, she writes:

> At puberty, fear became my main emotion because of the hormone changes associated with adolescence. My life revolved around trying to avoid a fear-inducing panic attack. Teasing from other kids was very painful, and I responded with anger. I eventually learned to control my temper, but the teasing persisted, and I would sometimes cry. Just the threat of teasing made me fearful; I was afraid to walk across the parking lot because I was afraid somebody would call me a name. Any change in my school schedule caused intense anxiety and fear of a panic attack. (p.78)

As with depression, it has been reported that having a higher IQ is associated with a greater degree of anxiety in youth with ASDs (Gadow *et al.* 2005; Sukhodolsky *et al.* 2008); however, children with greater cognitive impairments can also experience high levels of anxiety in their daily life. As your daughter enters adolescence, feelings of uncertainty are bound to increase as her life changes. Bright girls often notice the gap between their intellectual abilities and what they are able to achieve in day-to-day life. Many of the girls in our groups report that the future looks very scary and that they do not feel prepared to handle adult life.

Anxiety may manifest in many different ways in adolescents with ASDs. Girls with whom we have worked report frequent worrying, being tense and unable to relax, having difficulties sleeping and turning their minds off, having difficulty breathing or feeling their heart pounding, feeling restless and edgy, being irritable and quick to anger, being overly concerned about their abilities or performance, and fearing social situations or going to school. Some research has demonstrated a different anxiety profile for youth with IQs below 70, indicating correlations between anxiety, hyperactivity, and inappropriate speech (Sukhodolsky *et al.* 2008).

Self-injury

When I'm really upset or angry I usually just sit around and go really quiet or maybe cry. Once...I got so angry that I bit myself. I don't bite or scratch myself as often as I used to—only when I'm really, really angry. When I was about ten years old there was an incident at school where I got terribly upset because the teachers were forcing me to play with the kids at playtime and I hurt myself really badly. The teeth marks were there for weeks afterwards. (Rachel. *Asperger Syndrome, Adolescence, and Everything*, p.55)

In our clinical work, we have found that depression, overly self-critical perfectionism, and an inability to clearly and effectively express one's self and regulate one's emotions, have led many girls to engage in self-injurious behaviors (e.g. cutting, hitting, or pinching themselves, or banging their head), particularly when they do not have well-developed coping skills. In her memoir *Standing Down Falling Up, Asperger's Syndrome from the Inside Out*, Nita Jackson, an adolescent female with Asperger's Syndrome, bravely shares her struggles with mental health issues, including depression, anxiety, low self-esteem, and engaging in self-mutilation:

Now I have reached this very difficult and disturbing section of my story. This won't be to everyone's liking, but as this is an honest and open account of my experiences as an Asperger youth, I think that it is important for you to know about it. Many other Asperger youths that I am in contact with harm themselves and some are even suicidal. They have told me that they harm themselves because their life is depressing and they want to suffer—which is exactly the same as me. Depression is a horrendous thing. During these bouts of severity I am consumed with paranoia, anger, hatred and no confidence. I feel that I am a feeble, weak and incompetent failure... Then my hatred escalates and I crave to hurt more, if only to forget for a few small moments everything else in my life and just to concentrate on the physical pain that's here and now. This is why my hands and arms are tattooed with scars. (p.63)

Mental health interventions

If your daughter is struggling with depression, anxiety, or difficulties managing frustration and emotions, she could benefit from working with a psychologist to develop better self-awareness, healthy coping skills, and a greater feeling of self-control. Limited coping skills and self-awareness contribute to ongoing difficulties, so these should be a primary target of intervention. The extent to which your daughter can access some of the cognitive techniques will depend on the level of her thinking skills, however there are also a number of approaches which we have seen to be effective with girls who are more impaired, including visually-cued deep breathing and other relaxation techniques, picture rehearsal, identifying her own emotions, and using positive self-statements. The Groden Center has published a number of books and programs that are very effective in addressing stress and anxiety in youth with ASDs (*see* Resources).

Severe depression is particularly worrisome as it can sometimes lead to self-injurious behavior. If you suspect that your daughter is experiencing a depressive episode, or has begun to express thoughts of death or wanting to die, make an appointment immediately with a mental health professional who has extensive experience working with youth with ASDs and mental health difficulties. They will want to conduct a thorough assessment for depression and suicidal intent—the likelihood that your daughter is in danger of self-harm. Treatment of clinical depression often involves a combination of psychopharmacology (medication) and psychotherapy, in addition to behavioral approaches and psycho-education. Regarding medication, find a referral for a psychiatrist who is well-versed in psychopharmacology for youth with ASDs.

Before it was understood that the autism spectrum extended beyond "classic autism", it was thought that psychotherapy would not be an effective treatment for individuals with ASDs. More recent work has demonstrated that for individuals with mild cognitive impairments and average to above-average intelligence, a structured and directive approach to therapy, such as *cognitive behavioral therapy* (CBT), can be particularly effective in treating many mental health concerns in individuals with ASDs, including depression and anxiety (Attwood 2007; Chalfant, Rapee, and Carroll 2007; Gaus 2007; Ghaziuddin *et al.* 2002; Martinovich 2006; Reaven and Hepburn 2003; Reaven *et al.* in press; Sofronoff, Attwood, and Hinton 2005).

CBT is psychotherapy based on modifying everyday thoughts, assumptions, beliefs and behaviors with the goal of changing negative emotions. CBT is an evidence-based treatment that has been established as an effective treatment for typically developing children. It is founded on the premise that situations, thoughts, feelings, physiological responses, and behaviors are all connected, and that how you interpret (think about) situations will affect how you feel and act. CBT is a structured approach and the therapist and client act as a collaborative team. With adaptations to meet the learning needs of youth with ASDs (e.g. more visual supports, repetition of concepts), CBT can be an effective treatment implemented individually or in a group. CBT forms an important part of our girls' group programming. The following are some of the skills that we target when we are doing cognitive-behavioral work.

- Being able to identify situations that make them feel anxious, sad, angry.
- Being able to identify how their body responds when they are experiencing a particular emotion (e.g. sweaty when nervous, headache when angry).
- Being able to differentiate between an emotion or feeling (nervous) and an internal physiological state (racing heart, upset stomach)— back to body awareness!
- Being able to identify examples of thoughts they would have in certain situations (e.g. waiting for their math test to begin, getting to rent a movie on a Friday night).
- Skills training—relaxation (deep breathing, muscle relaxation), positive "self-talk", cognitive restructuring (challenging negative thoughts such as "I'll never pass this test"), social problem-solving, stop–think–act, and self-rewards.
- Developing healthy coping strategies—reading, taking a bath, listening to music, exercising, writing in a journal, playing with a pet, playing a video game, doing art.
- Repeated practice of skills in situations that are problematic.

Many of the techniques in your teaching toolkit can be used for CBT, in particular the more visual and concrete approaches. Some of the strategies we have used include:

- concrete mapping (using visuals) of connections between concepts
- using visual scales to rate degrees of emotion
- social autopsies—breaking situations down into their component parts to analyze what happened, how people felt, what they thought
- picture stories and picture rehearsal of coping skills
- creating a systematic, organized approach to analyzing a problem
- using power cards to support positive self-talk and as metaphors in therapy
- goal-setting, self-monitoring, and tracking progress.

Another calming activity that we have observed to be effective, particularly for girls with ASDs who love animals, is to be able to spend time with family pets. In our CBT groups, participants often say "walk my dog" or "play with my _____" when asked to generate strategies that help them feel calm and relaxed. One mother describes the soothing effect that cats have on her daughter:

> Amanda (12, PDD-NOS, OCD, ADHD) has very high anxiety levels. Our three cats are a constant source of calm and emotional release. We placed their very large scratching posts ("nap spots") right by all the busiest intersections in the house, and she never goes by without stopping to touch them and cuddle. Watching her relax instantly when she pets a cat, and smile in delight when it purrs is always amazing. (Mother of a 12-year-old girl with PDD-NOS)

"The talk": teaching your daughter about her ASD

> I wish my parents hadn't hid my diagnosis from me. I wish they hadn't been ashamed of who I am, and what I am. Ignoring autism or wishing it away doesn't make it go away, and having an answer for what makes me different would have really helped, because without anyone knowing the reason I was different there was no logic to "Why is Kassiane so strange?" No one could really deal with that and it caused more grief than anyone involved should have head to deal with. I wish my parents knew that they weren't protecting me by hiding that facet of

my identity from everyone, and I wish that the "a-word" wasn't such a taboo. (25-year-old woman with high-functioning autism)

Many parents ask us if they should tell their daughter about her diagnosis. Without exception, our response is always, yes! The decision of when and how to do so, however, depends on a number of factors, including her age, her diagnosis, her ability level, and her awareness of being different in some ways from other girls at school and in her community. Before the age of about seven to eight years, children will have difficulty understanding what a "diagnosis" is, and they are also less likely to be aware of differences between themselves and their peers. While they may realize that they don't have a lot of friends, they probably don't understand why. Explanations of diagnoses should provide age-appropriate information and present a solution—that their parents and teachers will now be able to help them with things that are difficult, like making friends. Use the strategies in your teaching toolkit, such as visual supports, using a picture book about your daughter, and power cards. With school-aged children who are receiving a diagnosis, we often work with parents to develop a plan for explaining the diagnosis. Sometimes we have a family session, during which the child is informed why they came to see us, what we learned, and how it's going to be helpful for them. From there, some children need time to think and parents will continue the process of explaining at home. Other children are full of questions and quickly realize there is a reason why they do what they do, and that they aren't "bad" or "weird". For these youth, we often offer *"all about me"* counseling.

There are a number of books and workbooks that can support your daughter's learning about her ASD, including the fact that there are more boys than girls who are diagnosed with an ASD. *Do You Understand Me? My Life, My Thoughts, My Autism Spectrum Disorder* is written by Sofie—a young, 11-year-old girl with autism. We have found girls to be very responsive to this book; they generally identify with what Sofie has to say. *A Is for Autism, F Is for Friend* is a fictional account with of an 11-year-old girl with severe autism. Other books and workbooks are included in the Resources at the end of this chapter, and are geared toward youth of different ages, from elementary school through young adulthood.

When we see older adolescents or young adults for a first diagnosis, their reactions can vary. Some of the older teens and young adults are relieved because they now finally have an explanation for the difficulties they have been experiencing. Others may deny that they have an ASD, or they may react angrily. Tasha was one such young woman who received her diagnosis of Asperger's Syndrome at the age of 18.

Case study: Tasha

Tasha was having a great deal of difficulty accepting or even talking about her diagnosis, and joined our girls' group in the hopes that spending time with the other girls would help her to better understand her strengths and weaknesses. A number of girls in the group had received their diagnoses during early adolescence, and were wonderful role models for Tasha. However, Tasha continued to angrily resist discussions about having an ASD, and frequently asserted that it wasn't fair that this was happening to her. After a few months, Tasha began weekly individual work as well; it was thought that this would be a more appropriate outlet for her negative feelings and that it would give her more of an opportunity to process what having an ASD meant to her. When the summer ended, Tasha began college and met other bright students with ASDs. She transferred into one of our young adult groups that also included female members who were in college. Tasha continues to have difficult moments, and is still quite frustrated at times, but slow as it has been, she has made progress and has connected with group members her age who will likely help her continue to grow and better understand herself in a positive way.

What having an ASD means to your daughter

After girls learn about having an ASD, they go through a process of making sense of what it means to them. How much does it define who they are? Do they see it as an impediment in their lives or as a challenge? Does it make them want to understand themselves more? Three areas of interest are relevant to your daughter's understanding of her diagnosis: self-determination and self-advocacy, disclosure, and identification.

Self-determination and self-advocacy

Self-determination comprises the skills and knowledge to engage in goal-directed, self-regulated autonomous behavior. In his book, *Promoting Self-Determination in Students with Developmental Disabilities*, Michael Wehmeyer outlines the components of self-determination and how to incorporate their teaching in the educational setting. There is remarkable overlap between the core components of self-esteem and those of self-determination. Skills such as decision-making, problem-solving, and goal-setting are highlighted, as are self-advocacy skills such as self-awareness and self-knowledge. Also included are independence, self-observation, and self-evaluation skills. An overall theme of self-regulation in problem-solving pervades one of the key theories of self-determination (Mithaug 1991). We can see that self-esteem and self-determination go hand in hand.

Case study: Jessica

Jessica was a very bright girl, but there were areas in school in which she was having some difficulty and it was hard for her to communicate this to her teachers. It was also hard for them to understand her difficulties given how bright she was. With her mother's guidance, Jessica decided to participate in and lead part of her IEP meeting. She created a Powerpoint presentation which gave an overview of who she was as a person, and also outlined her educational strengths and learning needs. At the meeting, Jessica was nervous at first but then was able to speak up and give her presentation. Her educational team was amazed, her teachers and counsellors were proud, and for many, Jessica's courage required a box of tissues to be passed around. No one was more proud, though, than Jessica herself, and her mother.

There is a growing literature in the field of developmental disabilities on self-determination and self-advocacy, and it is now becoming a standard component of the education of students with disabilities (Wehmeyer 2007, *see* Resources). Many professionals, and individuals with ASDs themselves, are strongly advocating for youth to participate in, and perhaps even lead, their own individualized education plan meetings. Starting small, your daughter could participate for the first five minutes of the meeting and introduce herself. At subsequent meetings, she could indicate (using pictures or words) her likes and dislikes, her talents, and her challenges. She could write a letter to her individualized education plan (IEP) team. Other students with whom we have worked have gone further and led their own meetings.

Disclosure

Disclosure is not an all-or-nothing proposition. In working with your daughter about disclosure, it is important to think about when, how, why, with whom, and under what context it might be helpful to disclose her diagnosis. Figuring all of this out is not easy, especially knowing whom to trust and whom to ask for help if needed. Your daughter will likely need your guidance, or that of her counsellor. In her book *Pretending to be Normal*, Liane Holliday Willey has an appendix entitled "Explaining Who You Are to Those Who Care". This section is recommended reading for all parents, and for older adolescents who are able to understand it. Your daughter's feelings about disclosure will likely change over time. She may not be ready at first, or she may be too eager and will want to share the news with everyone, regardless of what the risks might be. Assist her in decision-making and finding the right time. As professionals, we feel that disclosure of her diagnosis to the right people at the right time will be helpful for your daughter. As Liane Holliday writes in her book *Pretending to be Normal*:

> Debate rages among those in the Asperger's community whether or not people with AS should tell the world about their challenges and idiosyncracies. Those who choose to keep their AS private can often find creative ways to work through the social norms and educational systems that surround their lives. But for many, particularly those who are profoundly affected, it might be more effective to educate others about the disorder both in general terms and as it applies to your situation. (p.123)

We have found that girls with a strong sense of self, healthy self-esteem, and a desire to succeed in their lives are more open to the idea of disclosure. Having an ASD is not something they are ashamed of. These girls have integrated their disorder into their identity, and truly understand what it means to them. Being able to disclose their ASD has helped them to live a full and positive life, instead of living under the shadow of a disability.

Identification with other girls

Girls with ASDs are often alone in their ASD-ness. They may be the only girl in their class or the only girl in their social skills group. In fact, as one girl we recently saw for an evaluation said to us, "I'm the only girl with autism in my whole school!" This can be very isolating. For these reasons, it is important to find mentors for your daughter. A mentor may be an older girl with an ASD who has already gone through middle school and can relate to your daughter's experiences. She might be an older, typically developing teen who is part of a social skills group; someone who can coach your daughter on some of the social ins and outs, and who can also learn from your daughter about what it is like to have autism. There are also many successful women on the autism spectrum who have challenging and interesting careers, and who share their experiences with others by giving talks around the country. Women such as Liane Holliday Willey, Temple Grandin, Donna Williams, Dawn Prince-Hughes, Wendy Lawson, and Jen Birch might be willing to talk with your daughter at a conference, or have an email exchange with her. As younger writers begin to publish their autobiographical work, such as Jessica Peers and Nita Jackson, your daughter might have an opportunity to connect with someone closer to her age.

It is also going to be very important to find the other girls with ASDs and their parents in your community. Check in with your local autism society. If your community is small, go to the internet. There is an *Autism_in_Girls* Yahoo!® email group. Join it! Girls in our groups and their parents have stated that one of the best things about joining was feeling that they are not alone— as a parent, or as a girl. Create a girls' social group if you can, even if it's an informal once-a-month outing to a restaurant with girls at one table and moms at the other. Having a sense of community can go a long way.

Finally, have your daughters read about other girls with ASDs, whether it be fiction or nonfiction. If your daughter enjoys stories but cannot read herself, read to her. Explore how she is both similar to and different from these other girls.

Parent modeling of self-esteem

Raising an adolescent daughter with an ASD can leave any parent feeling lacking in the self-esteem department. Take care of yourself, and access the supports you need to feel healthy and good about yourself. In many ways, your daughter will learn from you. Try to demonstrate confidence and self-esteem for your daughter. Show her what it looks like on the outside. Also, model being "not perfect"—if you make a mistake at work or around the house, share this with her and use your coping statements out loud for her to hear. This is especially important if your daughter falls on the high end of the perfectionism continuum. Modeling appropriate coping techniques when you experience a failure will show her how *she* can cope when she is faced with life's difficulties. Believe, really believe, that you are a good parent for your daughter. If you need help with that, join a support group and connect with other parents—your local autism society can help you find such a group. As we all know, self-esteem comes in part from being in a loving, valued social circle. Surround yourself with friends, family, and positive experiences. If you are struggling with family issues and people in your life who cannot understand your situation, then get help, and make the important choices about who you want to spend your time with. Not only will this be the best decision for you, but it will also be the best decision for your daughter.

Resources

Books and resources for parents about exercise and physical activity

Betts, D.E. and Betts, S.W. (2006) *Yoga for Children with Autism Spectrum Disorders: A Step-by-Step Guide for Parents and Caregivers.* London: Jessica Kingsley Publishers.

North American Riding for the Handicapped Association, Inc. (NARHA): fosters safe, professional, ethical, and therapeutic equine activities through education, communication, research, and standards. The association ensures its standards are met through an accreditation process for centers and a certification process for instructors. Available at www.narha.org

Special Olympics: provides year-round sports and athletics training for individuals with developmental disabilities. Available at www.specialolympics.org

Books for parents related to developing independence

Hudson, J. and Coffin, A.B. (2007) *Out and About: Preparing Children with Autism Spectrum Disorders to Participate in Their Communities.* Shawnee Mission, KS: Autism Asperger Publishing Company.

Books for parents about self-esteem and self-determination

Martinovich, J. (2006) *Creative Expressive Activities and Asperger's Syndrome. Social and Emotional Skills and Positive Life Goals for Adolescents and Young Adults.* London: Jessica Kingsley Publishers.

Mithaug, D. (1991) *Self-Determined Kids: Raising Satisfied and Successful Children.* Lexington, MA: Lexington Books.

Wehmeyer, M. (2007) *Promoting Self-Determination in Students with Developmental Disabilities.* New York, NY: Guilford Press.

Books for youth related to having an ASD

Brøsen, S.K. (2006) *Do You Understand Me? My Life, My Thoughts, My Autism Spectrum Disorder* [written by a young girl]. London: Jessica Kingsley Publishers.

Elder, J. (2006) *Different Like Me: My Book of Autism Heroes.* London: Jessica Kingsley Publishers.

Faherty, C. (2000) *Aspergers… What Does It Mean To Me? A Workbook Explaining Self Awareness and Life Lessons to the Child or Youth with High Functioning Autism or Aspergers.* Arlington, TX: Future Horizons Publishing Company.

Keating-Velasco, J. (2007) *A Is for Autism, F Is for Friend* [fiction story involving friendships and autism]. Shawnee Mission, KS: Autism Asperger Publishing Company.

Larson, E.M. (2006) *I Am Utterly Unique: Celebrating the Strength of Children with Asperger Syndrome and High-Functioning Autism.* Shawnee Mission, KS: Autism Asperger Publishing Company.

Schnurr, R.G. (1999) *Asperger's Huh? A Child's Perspective.* Ottawa, ON: Anisor Publishing.

Vermeulen, P. (2000) *I Am Special.* London: Jessica Kingsley Publishers.

Welton, J. (2003) *Can I Tell You About Asperger Syndrome? A Guide for Friends and Family.* London: Jessica Kingsley Publishers.

Books for teens and young adults related to having an ASD

Ives, M. (2002) *What is Asperger Syndrome, and How Will It Affect Me? A Guide for Young People.* Shawnee Mission, KS: Autism Asperger Publishing Company.

James, I. (2005) *Asperger Syndrome and High Achievement: Some Very Remarkable People.* London: Jessica Kingsley Publishers.

Ledgin, N. (2002) *Asperger's and Self Esteem. Insight and Hope Through Famous Role Models.* Arlington, TX: Future Horizons Publishing Company.

Marquette, J. (2007) *Becoming Remarkably Able: Walking the Path to Talents, Interests, and Personal Growth.* Shawnee Mission, KS: Autism Asperger Publishing Company.

Prince-Hughes, D. (ed.) (2002) *Aquamarine Blue: Personal Stories of College Students with Autism.* Athens, OH: Ohio University Press.

Yoshida, Y. (2006) *How To Be Yourself in a World That's Different. An Asperger's Syndrome Study Guide for Adolescents.* London: Jessica Kingsley Publishers.

Books for teens and young adults about self-determination and disclosure of their diagnosis

Bliss, E.V. and Edmonds, G. (2007) *A Self-Determined Future with Asperger Syndrome. Solution Focused Approaches.* London: Jessica Kingsley Publishers.

Murray, D. (ed.) (2005) *Coming out Asperger. Diagnosis, Disclosure and Self-Confidence.* London: Jessica Kingsley Publishers.

Shore, S. (ed.) (2004) *Ask and Tell: Self-Advocacy and Disclosure for People on the Autism Spectrum.* Shawnee Mission, KS: Autism Asperger Publishing Company.

Books for parents about emotional development

Cardon, T. (2004) *Let's Talk Emotions: Helping Children with Social Cognitive Deficits Including AS, HFA, and NVLD, Learn to Understand and Express Empathy and Emotions.* Shawnee Mission, KS: Autism Aspergers Publishing Company.

Books for parents about identity, mental health and coping

Cautela, J.R. and Groden, J. (1978) *Relaxation: A Comprehensive Manual for Adults, Children, and Children with Special Needs.* Champaign, IL: Research Press.

Cohen-Sandler, R. (2005) *Stressed-Out Girls. Helping them Thrive in the Age of Pressure.* New York, NY: Penguin Books.

Dunn, K.B. and Curtis, M. (2004) *Incredible 5-Point Scale—Assisting Students with Autism Spectrum Disorders in Understanding Social Interactions and Controlling Their Emotional Responses.* Shawnee Mission, KS: Autism Asperger Publishing Company.

Gaus, V. (2007) *Cognitive-Behavioral Therapy for Adult Asperger Syndrome.* New York, NY: Guilford Publishers.

Groden, J., LeVasseur, P., Diller, A. and Cautela, J. (2001) *Coping with Stress through Picture Rehearsal: A How-to Manual for Working with Individuals with Autism and Developmental Disabilities.* Providence, RI: The Groden Center, Inc.

Molloy, H. and Vasil, L. (eds) (2004) *Asperger Syndrome, Adolescence, and Identity. Looking Beyond the Label.* London: Jessica Kingsley Publishers.

Paxton, K. and Estay, I. (2007) *Counseling People on the Autism Spectrum. A Practical Manual.* London: Jessica Kingsley Publishers.

Books for youth about mental health and coping

American Girl Publishers. (2001) *The Care and Keeping of Me. The Body Book Journal.*

American Girl Publishers. (2002) *The Feelings Book. The Care and Keeping of Your Emotions.*

American Girl Publishers. (2004) *Real Beauty. 101 Ways to Feel Great About YOU.*

Buron, K.D. (2006) *When My Worries Get Too Big: A Relaxation Book for Children Who Live with Anxiety.* Shawnee Mission, KS: Autism Asperger Publishing Company.

Jaffe, A. and Gardner, L. (2006) *My Book Full of Feelings: How to Control and React to the Size of Your Emotions.* Shawnee Mission, KS: Autism Asperger Publishing Company.

Novels for youth and teens with a female protagonist with an ASD

Brenna, B. (2005) *Wild Orchid.* Calgary, AB: Red Deer Press.

Hoopman, K. (2002) *Lisa and the Lacemaker. An Asperger Adventure.* Haze. London: Jessica Kingsley Publishers.

Ogaz, N. (2002) *Buster and the Amazing Daisy. Adventures with Asperger Syndrome.* London: Jessica Kingsley Publishers.

Helpful websites

My First Bra. Available at www.myfirstbra.us

The National Association of the Dually Diagnosed: an association for persons with developmental disabilities and mental health needs. Available at www.thenadd.org

CHAPTER 6

The Social Landscape of Adolescence: Friendships and Social Status

She likes boys, music, dancing, makeup, and clothes. I think this is what other girls her age like. She doesn't really socialize with typical children. (Mother of an 11-year-old girl with an ASD)

You know what, Mom? Jane, me and Lisa, have a language of our own, we understand each other. (Member of girls' social skills group referring to other members in the girls group)

The age of friendships

As typically developing girls approach adolescence, friendships become an increasingly significant part of their lives. Girls may value their friends' and peers' opinions more than their parents', or in some cases even their own! It is during these years that many young women are interested in spending most of their time with their girlfriends, and enjoy talking for hours, either on the telephone or in person, about clothes, fashion, and, yes, boys. If you have ever spent time watching typically developing pre-teens and teens during unstructured school periods (which we have done as part of our school consultation program), you have probably observed groups of girls, dressed in similar clothing and styles, huddled together giggling and sharing secrets, while talking quickly and using many emphatic gestures and emotional facial expressions.

These sorts of interactions can be both challenging and intimidating for girls with ASDs who often choose not to (or don't know how to) join the other girls. Rather, they tend to engage in solitary activities such as reading a book, doing school work, or talking to an adult. Those that want to join in might stay in close proximity to the other girls, but never really actively participate in their conversations or communicate with the same degree of expressiveness.

In this chapter we will talk about how you can help your daughter develop the skills she needs to make (and keep) friends as she enters adolescence. Much of what we will discuss applies equally well to establishing friendships with both boys and girls; later in the chapter we will review some topics that tend to be more specific to girls (talking on the telephone, possessiveness, and relational aggression). It is important to be aware of and open to the possibility that your daughter will develop male friends, both because of the sex ratio of ASDs that results in male-dominated specialized programming, and because girls with ASDs often develop interests similar to those of same-aged boys, such as video games or anime. There are, of course, a separate set of issues related to romantic interests and dating; we will return to this subject in the next chapter.

Encouraging friendships

In our clinical experience, pre-teen and adolescent girls with ASDs have expressed several different points of view about friendships in general and their desire, or lack thereof, to have one. Some girls prefer to keep to themselves and not have any friends because "it clogs up my head and distracts me from concentrating on more important things like schoolwork." Others simply enjoy spending time by themselves and don't feel the need to have these "friendships" that their parents and teachers talk about and encourage. As a parent who has tried to facilitate a friendship, you might have experienced some resistance or even protest on your daughter's part. Don't despair. Her attitude toward friendships can change with positive experiences. If you are able to find a peer with similar interests whom she enjoys spending time with, then with the proper support and encouragement you can succeed in introducing a friendship that may last for some time.

Although it is important to encourage friendships, parents should be cautious and refrain from imposing their personal definitions of friendship on their children, allowing them instead to define their own relationships (with appropriate guidance and support, of course). Based on student accounts, girls with ASDs tend to befriend other students who are also perceived as different or opinionated, and who for those reasons are more appreciative of individuality. Girls with ASDs also tend to seek out fewer friends than neurotypical girls. Rather than having several good friends and a network of peers to hang out with, many of the girls in our group sessions have expressed the desire to have a single good friend who understands them and their need to be alone sometimes. Interacting with more than one friend can be challenging owing to impairments in social information process-ing: a conversation with multiple girls means having to understand and process several people's perspectives at once, and respond in turn. In addi-tion, conversations tend to move much faster when more than two people are involved. Given the language and social processing delays that girls with ASDs tend to have, these types of interactions and conversations are especially challenging. In her book, *Pretending to be Normal*, Liane Holliday Willey states:

> I never understood group dynamics that work on giving and taking, role-playing and modeling, rule-following, and turn-taking. Somewhere along the way, I had learned to cope with the intricacies of young friendships well enough to manage one friend. Any more spelled disaster sometimes in very real forms. (p.20)

She further defines friends as "people I enjoyed passing a few minutes or a few hours with" (p.53). Similarly, the girls in our teen groups have stated that they do not necessarily want to spend a lot of time with a friend or engage in lengthy conversations about serious topics or feelings; they would prefer to spend shorter periods of time conversing about common interests (e.g. art, television shows, movies, music, books, favorite actors or actresses).

Maintaining friendships

Despite being, as a group, less interested than typically developing girls in having and maintaining friendships, many girls with ASDs do still want social contact, especially with other girls. The clients we have worked with during our social skills groups and in therapy have clearly stated that they would like to spend time with other girls who share similar interests and experiences, understand their differences, are respectful, are appreciative of their strengths, and are tolerant of their weaknesses. Several of our group members have expressed a desire to be placed in girls-only social skills groups because they feel that they have spent enough time with boys in school and other social skills groups, and because boys tend to be more immature than girls in general. In addition, they feel more comfortable dis-cussing certain topics with other girls (e.g. periods, mood lability, friend-ships, boys/flirting/crushes, hygiene). One parent wrote about our girls' group, saying:

> My daughter enjoys this group so much—it's one of the few times she ever seems really happy. She has a sense of camaraderie with these girls that she has never had before. (Mother of a 15-year-old girl with Asperger's Syndrome)

Although the girls in our groups are quite comfortable with one another, communication outside of the meetings, especially initiated by the girls themselves, is infrequent, and it is not easy to maintain the friendships that are established. This may be because of decreased motivation to do so, poor conversational skills (which would affect chatting on the phone or instant messaging), impaired *perspective-taking* skills (being able to see things from another person's point of view), and feeling overwhelmed by household and academic responsibilities. In fact, research has shown that the ability to maintain a friendship outside of a prearranged group is not as common as one would think (Howlin, Mawhood, and Rutter 2000).

In order to encourage our group members to maintain acquaintanceships and friendships outside of our prearranged meeting times, we have asked that the participants exchange contact information (e.g. phone numbers, email addresses, IM tags) within the first two or three sessions. Throughout the duration of our groups, which run for several weeks at a time, we pay close attention to which girls appear to be getting along with one another, and we convey this information to their parents so that they can arrange for the girls to communicate outside of our sessions. Parents are encouraged to plan community-based outings (e.g. pool parties, trips to the mall, bar-beques) in order to create opportunities to generalize the skills that we work on during group sessions. Several of our group members were even invited to and attended each other's Sweet 16 parties!

It is even more difficult for girls with ASDs to initiate and maintain friendships with typically developing peers. This might be because of a nar-row range of interests that are dissimilar from the interests of their typically developing peers (or are similar but unusually intense), or because during the middle and high school years, pre-teens, and teens are quite "cliquey" (have you seen the movie *Mean Girls*?), especially girls, forming an impenetrable wall to girls with ASDs. In addition, given the high ratio of boys to girls with ASDs, many young women with ASDs have been in inclusion settings or specialized programming where the majority of their classmates are boys, making it difficult for them to meet other girls at an age when same-sex friendships predominate.

Friendships for less verbal girls

Language impairments are a core feature of ASDs, and can affect any combi-nation of the *form* (articulation, phonology, morphology, and syntax), *content* (vocabulary, semantic relationships, linguistic concepts, and supralinguistics), or *use* (pragmatics) of language. Girls with greater impairments in all of these areas range from having no spoken language to being able to speak (and sometimes read) simple sentences, use basic vocabulary, answer factual and personal information questions, and possibly engage in brief (albeit limited) conversations. Many of these girls do not understand the purpose of communication or the many reasons to communicate with others, which can make friendships especially challenging.

If your daughter is moderately to severely impaired in this respect, she may have difficulty learning the social skills required to establish and maintain friendships independently. In this case we recommend that you find a small community-based social skills group to provide her with highly structured interactions with other females at or around her age. Try to choose a group that is activity-based rather than language-based, making use of group activities to promote social understanding and awareness of others. Ideally, this group would serve to complement a school-based social skills group, but in some cases your local school district might not offer one. There are a number of techniques and activities that a group might use to facilitate learning and social interaction for less verbal girls, which include:

- pictorial or written cues that outline activities and task analyses that clearly outline the sequence of desired behaviors or responses

- narratives and scripts that use simple direct language paired with pictorial cues

- a positive behavioral support plan (for both individuals and the entire group) that elicits and supports desired behavior and responses

- activities focused on common interests, basic inquiries, and responses to personal questions rather than lengthy conversations and verbal exchanges

- a visual timer that clearly indicates how long an activity will last and signals transitions from one activity to another

- multimodal strategies, including verbal, visual, and tactile cues to accommodate all learning styles

- trips to local community settings (e.g. restaurants, grocery stores, parks, bowling alleys) to practice social skills in a natural environment

- reducing the length and complexity of verbal directions; repeating them slowly to ensure comprehension.

Additional resources that address social communication and friendships for less verbal girls may be found at the end of this chapter.

Choosing a social skills group

A good social skills group can benefit girls with ASDs at any level of cognitive function. Of course, the effectiveness of a group will depend on how well it matches your daughter's specific needs and preferences. Here are some suggested questions to ask as you are researching potential groups.

- How are the group members selected to ensure a good match?
- Are there any other girls in the group?
- How often does the group meet?
- Is the group center-based or community-based? (Typically, community-based groups meet in local stores or facilities whereas center-based groups meet in a single designated location.)
- Will there be any same-aged neurotypical peer mentors (especially girls) involved in the group? If so, to what extent, and what will their role be? How are they trained to interact with students with ASDs?
- Will any topics covered in the group be specific to girls' issues?
- Does the group leader spend any time meeting with parents?
- Is there an opportunity for the group leader to communicate with other therapists who are providing treatment? If so, how often?
- What is the group leader's availability to attend team meetings to ensure generalization of newly learned skills?
- How does the group leader monitor progress toward predetermined goals?

Understanding friendships and developing friendship skills

As I approached my teenage years I began to want friends, to share my life with others. I realised that people seemed to enjoy company and appeared happier when they were not on their own. I understood friendship was valuable and I did not want to be different any more. However, I lacked social skills and the "know-how" of friendship-building. Most people felt uncomfortable with egocentric and eccentric behavior. I wanted things to go by the rules—and my rules at that! My clumsy efforts to socialize usually ended in trauma—an experience common to most Asperger's teenagers. (Wendy Lawson, *Life Behind Glass*, p.16)

Consider these definitions of a "friend" provided by teenage girls diagnosed with AS or HFA, based on responses during a standardized assessment:

- "Being nice and kind".
- "Someone you hang out with".
- "Someone you are close with and have common interests".
- "Someone you can tell everything to and can trust".
- "Someone who wouldn't betray you".
- "Someone who is always there for you; knows your faults and still accepts you".

These responses—which range from fairly superficial descriptions to definitions rooted in acceptance, respect, and loyalty—reflect a corresponding range in understanding of friendships. However, just because a person can provide a definition of friendship does not mean they necessarily know how to go about forming or cultivating one in their own life. This is a common problem for pre-teen and teenage girls diagnosed with an ASD. These girls are less likely to initiate conversations with their peers, which makes it difficult for them to get to know what another person's interests are, or to find out what they might have in common with their peers—important factors in deciding who they want to befriend. They also tend to rely upon ineffective ways of deciding whom they want to be friends with. For example, during one of our girls' groups, a member stated that she often intentionally asks someone overly personal information (e.g. age, current relationship status, weight) because it helps her to decide whether or not she is interested in pursuing a friendship with them. As you can imagine, seeking or sharing overly personal information can create a very negative first impression, decreasing the chances that the other person would want to participate in a second interaction. Girls with ASDs also have a tendency to speak their minds without an awareness of social appropriateness, inadvertently offending others with their blunt comments or observations. This makes them less likely to attract (and maintain) friends and more likely to be thought of as rude or obnoxious by their typically developing peers.

Creating a good first impression and making socially appropriate conversation are just two of the many skills involved in establishing and maintaining friendships. Other important skills include:

- appropriate facial expression and eye gaze
- body language (e.g. nodding, proximity, personal space, hand gestures or placement, posture)
- personal appearance (e.g. clothing, grooming)
- perspective-taking
- suprasegmental speech characteristics (e.g. tone of voice, volume, intonation)
- greetings and introductions
- avoiding sensitive topics (e.g. religion, weight) that can evoke a negative response from others
- finally, understanding how the above skills are affected by the social context (e.g. with close friends or acquaintances, in class or at lunch, hanging out on the weekend or at a formal dinner).

More often than not, these skills need to be taught during formal social skills instruction in much in the same way that one would teach a student a new math formula: breaking down complicated steps into simple ones, with a lot of repetition and practice. In a group setting such as a social skills group, these skills are typically taught in individual units (e.g. conversational skills, dealing with teasing, perspective-taking) to allow adequate time to practice them in isolation and to understand how they negatively or positively contribute to other people's impressions. Activities might include social behavior mapping (creating lists of expected and unexpected behaviors in social situations), social scripting (creating a script of what to say, how to say it, and the accompanying nonverbal behaviors), role-playing, review of clothing trends and how they correspond to the image you want to portray, video modeling, and constructive feedback. Social behavioral mapping was developed by Michelle Garcia Winner, a speech and language pathologist who is widely known for her work in functional social skills for pre-teens and teens with HFA or AS. It is a technique that helps students to understand the consequences of behavior: our behavior affects how other people feel, how they treat us, and ultimately how we feel about ourselves. This technique can help demystify the complexity of social thought and related behaviors.

Case study: Mandy

Mandy is a fifth-grader with HFA who is in a mainstream academic classroom with the assistance of a teaching aide. For the first time since receiving her diagnosis, Mandy developed a reciprocal relationship with a classmate that involved spending lunch, recess, gym, and other less structured periods together, and more importantly seeing each other outside of school at each other's homes. After a recent play date at Mandy's house, her classmate began avoiding her at school, refusing to play or pair up during activities, and ignoring her. Mandy did not understand what was happening or why, but apologized anyway hoping to get her friend back. With the assistance of Mandy's aide, Mandy's mother learned that the classmate no longer wanted to be friends because she thought Mandy was "weird", and felt that Mandy was overly physical during their last play date. Mandy did not recall this incident and was very sad and frustrated that her classmate no longer wanted to be friends with her (to the extent that Mandy began crying in class because "no one wanted to be friends" with her). Initially, Mandy refused to try and make friends with anyone else because she only wanted to be friends with the classmate who had rejected her. Over time, and with both counseling from an autism consultant and prompting from her aide, Mandy agreed to try and make friends with other girls in her class, but she is still faced with the task of developing a better awareness of her social behavior in order to avoid similar incidents in the future.

Social skills can be very difficult for girls with ASDs to master, so it is important for your daughter to practice in many different settings. In any well-run social skills group, weekly activities should be clearly described and presented to parents so that they can use similar strategies with their daughters at home. In addition, several parents of girls in our center-based social skills groups have shared these weekly group outlines and associated homework with counsellors, therapists, and educators so that their daughters can further develop the target skills in their school settings.

Standardized assessment of social skills

In order to help your daughter develop and maintain friendships, it is important to have a solid understanding of the specific social skills that cause her the most difficulty. To this end, there are a number of standardized measures which may be used to assess social skill development and social responsiveness. The most common measure used during diagnostic assessments is the Autism Diagnostic Observation Schedule (ADOS) (Lord *et al.* 1999). The ADOS comprises a series of semistructured tasks and elicitations for conversation which directly tap into a participant's knowledge and appreciation of friendships, emotions, social difficulties, conversational ability, and social insight. Examples of ADOS questions include: "What is your definition of friendship?" "How can you tell if someone is your friend?" "What kinds of things make you feel happy, sad, angry, nervous, etc.?" "Have you ever had any trouble with your peers?" and so on. Responses vary greatly depending on a person's verbal ability, age, and severity of autism. The ADOS is a useful tool for obtaining a functional definition of social concepts in the examinee's own words. Additional important information related to friendship skills is also acquired, such as degree of social motivation, previous success or failures with regard to friendship, and experiences of teasing (whether perceived or actually happening).

The ADOS is an interactive assessment, and is often complemented by questionnaires that contribute information from multiple sources: parents, educators, and the subjects themselves. The Social Skills Rating System (SSRS) (Gresham and Elliot 1990) is one such multirater questionnaire that assesses the acquisition and performance of multiple social skills and their importance to success in various environments. Individual subdomains include Cooperation, Assertion, Responsibility, Empathy, and Self-Control. The *Social Responsiveness Scale* (Constantino and Gruber 2005), another multirater tool (parent and teacher report), assesses Social Cognition, Social Communication, Social Awareness, Social Motivation (*see* the "Teaching tips" on the following page), and degree of Autistic Mannerisms. This questionnaire is currently the only assessment of social impairment in children with autism that quantitatively assesses social motivation in naturalistic environments.

The qualitative and quantitative social skills information imparted by these assessments is extremely helpful in determining appropriate treatment goals, therapies (e.g. cognitive behavioral therapy, psychological counseling, speech and language), and the setting in which they should be delivered (e.g. individual versus group). For example, if a student does not appear to be aware of when and how other peers might be teasing her, a specific lesson on identifying verbal and physical means of teasing might be presented across several sessions, along with teaching appropriate responses to teasing. The information from these assessments is also highly valuable to potential social skills or friendship club group leaders when organizing and pairing students to form a group. If you are seeking such a group, you should find out what role assessment plays in group formation and progress tracking. Some excellent questions to ask the instructor (in addition to those mentioned earlier in the chapter) include:

- What information do you use to select group members (e.g. age, verbal IQ, common interests, formal socialization measures, etc)?
- Do you require most recent cognitive and language testing?
- What materials do you use to assess and document progress?
- Are there group and/or individual goals for the members? If so, how are they determined, and what instrumentation is used to gather information needed to focus on target skills?

Measuring social skills

Standardized measures may be used to assess four different types of social skills:

- *Social awareness*: the ability to pick up on social cues.
- *Social cognition*: the ability to interpret social cues once they are detected.
- *Social communication*: encompasses expressive social communication (e.g. turn-taking, making friends, communicating feelings and emotions).
- *Social motivation*: the extent to which a person is generally motivated to engage in interpersonal behavior.

Stages of friendship

In his most recent book, *The Complete Guide to Asperger's Syndrome* (Attwood 2007), Dr Tony Attwood outlines four "Developmental Stages of Friendship" in typically developing individuals. Stage one involves basic sharing and turn-taking during play activities, which is the central aspect of friendship from three to six years of age, and remains important throughout the elementary years. This can be challenging for young girls with ASDs due to cognitive inflexibility (resulting in an unwillingness to end their turn), difficulty adhering to rules (specifically rules regarding sharing and turn-taking), and an inability to read their peers' body language, facial expressions, and other nonverbal behaviors (which could indicate that they want their turn).

Stage two, which occurs between the ages of six and nine years, entails the understanding that everyone involved in the activity should be experiencing pleasure and having fun. Play becomes more reciprocal; children begin to understand the thoughts and feelings of their peers and can recognize and repair basic communication breakdowns. This sort of perspective-taking and emotional understanding can be quite difficult for girls with ASDs. For example, during a classroom observation in a regular education setting, we observed a young girl with HFA appropriately and rather nicely invite a classmate to play a card game that she created. However, problems quickly arose as the young girl with HFA began to direct and correct the other child who was trying to figure out the rules, which had not been explained. The peer's facial expression dramatically changed as she became visibly frustrated and confused, while the young girl with autism continued to verbally direct her without noticing that the other girl was no longer having fun. The interaction ended abruptly, and the young girl with autism told the teacher that the other little girl was being "unfair" because she was not playing by the rules (which had never been explained). These types of interactions are quite common, and reduce the likelihood that the typically developing peer will want to play the next time they are invited to do so.

It is also during this stage that the concept of a "best friend" develops. Shared interests and experiences become important vehicles to establishing friendships. Although typically developing girls tend to select friends based on the other person's personality or demeanor, we have observed that many pre-teen and teenage girls with ASDs develop friendships based solely on shared interests (e.g. cartoon characters, anime, television programs and movies, books). This may be in part due to an inability to recognize and categorize personality traits: when we asked the girls in one of our social skills groups to describe other members' personalities, the most common response was "nice", an overly vague and nondescriptive term (one that was later banned from the group because it is so generic and was being overused). With prompting, the girls were eventually able to connect a person's actions and interests to a personality trait (e.g. an animal lover who feeds stray cats may be considered caring and nurturing).

In stage three, which occurs between the ages of 9 and 13, children become more selective in their choice of friends. Their choices are based on specific criteria and personal characteristics (including personality types). The concept of popularity and status becomes increasingly important, often resulting in the careful selection of friends for the sole purpose of elevating their own social status. As a group, pre-teens and teens become passionate about their opinions (and those of their peers), which at times might contradict the values and opinions of their parents.

These years can be quite challenging for girls with ASDs for several reasons, including the onset of puberty, self-awareness of differences in ability and desire to socialize with peers, struggles between independence and dependence on caregivers and support staff, anger and anxiety management, and an increase in social, adaptive, and academic demands. As typically-developing girls become more aware of social status, the more sensitive peers who had befriended and supported a young girl with an ASD might not associate with her any longer for fear that it might affect their own popularity. Sadly, one of the young women in our girls' group experienced just that when the mother of her long-time typically developing friend stated that they could no longer be friends anymore because the teen with AS was "holding her daughter back [socially]", which was quite hurtful to the girl with AS and her mother. Autobiographical accounts contain similar stories; Nita Jackson shares how she struggled with loss of friendships during adolescence:

> I reckon that almost everyone loses at least one friend during their lifetime... I don't know if anyone else grieves over their lost friends like I have done. I, however, struggled to accept my losses. I never took the hint that people who were once my friends now disliked me because I didn't think there was anything to dislike about me in the first place. I refused to accept the impossibility of regaining my lost friends. I'd still phone them and when they would slam the phone down on me I'd just phone them right back (this procedure could happen up to 15 times with each ex-friend)! Being the naïve, devastatingly insecure Asperger kid that I was, this all seemed perfectly natural to me. Ironically, my strategies for trying to retain friends were actually the reason I was losing them. What I really should have done was just get on with my life instead of pining over the past, and that's what I'd advise every other Asperger person who loses their friends do. So Rule No. 3: leave the past in the past, however much it might pain you. (*Freaks, Geeks and Asperger Syndrome*, pp.76–77)

Finally, Dr Attwood describes Stage Four, encompassing the ages of 13 years to adulthood, when friendships begin to deepen and friends are sought out more often than parents or caregivers. This is a crucial time for maintaining friendships, which can be difficult and emotionally challenging for girls with ASDs because of the need to read subtle social and emotional cues, the importance of conversation and negotiating skills, and the need to compromise or put another person's needs before their own. It is especially difficult for girls with ASDs at this age to accept and understand rejection, possibly causing them to second-guess their thoughts, words, and actions. They become even less tolerant of their self-perceived social faux pas. The inability to identify another person's reasons or grounds for rejection, and a decreased awareness of what might be perceived by their peers as "socially awkward" behavior, intensifies feelings of isolation, social anxiety, and possibly anger toward those people who are not accepting of them as they are.

Each of the stages of friendship has an associated set of challenges. In the following sections we will describe some of ways you can help your daughter navigate these stages and have more successful friendship experiences.

Sharing and turn-taking

Stage one comprises sharing and turn-taking, which are two of the most basic interactions in a friendship. Your daughter's personality and temperament will be a significant factor in her willingness to share preferred items or take turns during structured (or unstructured) activities. Her failure to engage in appropriate turn-taking may be attributed to a lack of motivation rather than a fundamental lack of understanding: she may *know* the turn-taking rules, but might not want to *follow* them. If that is the case, then in addition to visual cues it will be necessary to develop a positive behavioral support plan and a reward system that encourage her to share and take turns.

Therapeutic goals for turn-taking should include both verbal and non-verbal components. Activities that help to teach and develop nonverbal turn-taking skills include board and card games. Verbal turn-taking skills may be taught using activities that require verbal communication, such as arts and crafts activities in which participants must request needed items, or brief conversations. Children with ASDs have a tendency to *monologue* (talk excessively about their topic of choice or intense interest) during conversations and often fail to ask about others' opinions or experiences. If this describes your daughter, try introducing the rule of making two statements and then asking a question. Turn-taking activities should be supplemented by visual and/or written cues that clearly outline what behavior or response is expected.

Emotional understanding

A key component of stage two (which emphasizes mutually enjoyed activities) is being able to recognize and understand playmates' emotions. In our social skills groups, we have observed that girls with HFA or AS often understand the four basic primary emotions (happy, scared, sad, mad) but fail to identify or explain complex emotions, such as frustration, embarrassment, anxiousness, excitement, or confusion. In addition, they fail to understand how one emotion can change into another over time (e.g. confusion can become frustration followed by anger) or the various degrees of severity of any one emotion. Therapists (school- or home-based) should explore which emotions (and related body language or facial expressions) are clearly understood and specifically target those that are not. This can be done through direct observations during interactions with peers, parent or teacher interviews, and, if the child is capable, asking her questions about complex emotions and the context in which people experience them. At home, use your teaching toolkit to help your daughter with emotional understanding; specific tools that you can use include:

- explicitly teaching facial expressions through verbal descriptions and modeling of the position of a person's eyes, mouth and eyebrows for each emotion
- role-playing using scripts and exaggerated expressions or gestures to teach an emotion
- discussing social scenarios in specific contexts, paying attention to posture, facial expression, proximity to the other person, etc.
- modeling and video modeling of social interactions
- emotional thermometers and scales to measure intensity of a single emotion
- using brief narratives to illustrate how two people can interpret and react to each other.

Be aware of your daughter's friendships

In stage three, friendships become more social in nature. As your daughter (and her peers) get older, it may become difficult for her to maintain friendships with typically developing peers. So what can you do to help her? The first step is to be aware of who your daughter's friends are and whether or not she is having difficulties with any of them. Talk to your daughter or, if you have trouble communicating with her about this topic, write a note to her teacher or aide asking if there is anyone in her class that she enjoys spending time with, and if they have noticed any problems. Monitor your daughter for signs of difficulties: Is she acting differently (e.g. sulking, argumentative)? Do you notice a decline in how often she sees her peers outside of school?

If problems do arise, seek assistance from your school-based social worker or psychologist. Chances are that your daughter does not understand how her behavior (verbal and nonverbal) affects her ability to create or maintain friendships. She may need individual counseling or a school-based social skills group to learn appropriate prosocial behaviors. These behaviors will likely take a lot of practice to master, so keep track of the specific skills that she is working on during therapy or social skills lessons, and use your teaching toolkit to work on them with your daughter at home.

Finally, if you have not yet talked to your daughter about her diagnosis, now might be a good time to do so. As we discussed in the previous chapter, sharing this information with your daughter allows her to learn about herself: her strengths (and gifts), as well as her weaknesses and challenges. Expose her to books about autism and how it affects her ability to make and keep friends (and strategies to improve her odds of doing so). Remember that you cannot control the actions and decisions of her peers, but you can heighten your daughter's awareness of her own behavior and overall presentation to improve her chances of being accepted.

Emotional communication

Communication skills become increasingly important as friendships deepen in stage four. In a conversation between adults, communication entails not only an exchange of *information*, but also an exchange and sharing of *emotions*. This aspect of conversations can be challenging for girls with ASDs; many of the girls we have worked with have said they try so hard to pay attention to *what* is being said, that they often fail to notice *how* it is being said in order to gain information about how their communication partner is feeling. In addition, just as they have had difficulty picking up on these cues from other people, they often do not convey these cues themselves: many of these girls communicate with a flat tone of voice and a lack of facial expressions or body language to indicate their emotions. They were frequently unaware of this until we tape recorded their voices and asked them to evaluate their own intonation patterns, or videotaped a conversation and pointed out times where they could have been more animated in gesture and facial expression. This is an easy teaching technique that you can try at home with your daughter. The use of television and movies can also be very effective in teaching your daughter about subtle emotional cues, such as body language, tone of voice, gestures, and eye contact.

Popularity and social status

> Karen is doing well, although, as always, I wish she had more than one friend. But, her prior friend dumped her promptly upon starting high school last year. Her new friend, although, to my knowledge undiagnosed, has more social problems than Karen. And, her parents don't let her do hardly anything, so Karen really does little more than talk to her new friend at school. I am trying different things. It's heartbreaking to have a daughter so capable, and yet almost completely deprived of a social life with her peers. No one seems willing to allow her the time it takes her to allow her true personality and sense of humor to shine through. (Mother of a 16-year-old girl with PDD-NOS)

Many adolescent girls find it extremely important to be accepted by their peers (especially other girls) and to be considered popular. It has been our experience, based on observations during school consultations, that typically developing girls begin to become sensitive to and care about popularity around the ages of 9–10. They recognize popularity by observing the actions and attitudes of the girls around them. For example, they may begin to pay more attention to how their peers dress, wear their hair, etc. They begin to identify which girls their classmates tend to want to hang out with as well as who appears to be more outspoken and confident.

Although many of the young women we have worked with recognize that they are "different" from their peers, they are usually not as focused on popularity and social status as their peers. They may notice how other people might gravitate toward a certain individual, but they do not think about how that person dresses, looks, speaks, and acts that makes them so sought out by others. In our groups we teach girls how to analyze others' appearances, personalities, and behaviors in the context of social interactions. This helps them to understand the social underpinnings of popularity, and gives them insight into how they might be viewed by their peers. Even those who understand popularity at a conceptual level may not have the same emotional reaction as typically developing girls, as illustrated by the following case study.

Case study: Amalie

Amalie is a third-grader with high functioning autism, and a member of one of our social skills groups, whom we have observed in a private school setting. When we entered her classroom for one of our observation visits, Amalie was excited to see us and immediately began to show us around the classroom. She appropriately introduced her best friend, who shared Amalie's intense interest in fairies. After the two girls told us some stories about fairies, Amalie abruptly changed the topic and stated that several girls in the class were not speaking to them (although she wasn't sure why). She said that the other girls were popular, and that Amalie and her friend were not. Although we had not yet discussed popularity in our social skills group, Amalie was able to describe it as "when all of the girls want to talk to you and be your friend." Amalie was able to provide an appropriate definition for popularity, but she did not seem to care that she was not one of the popular girls, as she quickly returned to a monologue about her (and her friend's) shared interest in fairies.

Some higher-functioning girls with ASDs do begin to care about their social status and develop an understanding of popularity at around the same time as their typically developing peers: we have observed this both in our social skills groups and in some of the girls whom we follow as part of our school consultation program. Unfortunately, because girls with ASDs are more likely to be seen as different and to experience social isolation, this increased understanding comes at an emotional cost. They begin to feel as if nobody "chooses" to be their friend, and they become aware that the other kids around them are having get-togethers and receiving party invitations, whereas they are not. Moreoever, they do not know what they can say or do to change their situation; for this they need guidance from parents, professionals, and peer mentors.

Specific challenges for girls with ASDs

Up to this point, we have focused on issues that apply to friendships with both boys and girls. We now turn our attention to three topics that are more closely tied to female relationships: relational aggression, possessiveness, and telephone conversations.

Relational aggression

Instead of engaging in physical aggression, as their male counterparts do, pre-teen and teenage girls tend to engage in more manipulative forms of social aggression, such as telling secrets, spreading rumors, lying about another person, teasing, and isolation. This form of psychological attack is called *relational aggression* (RA) (Crick and Grotpeter 1995), and is also known as female bullying. In teen-speak, girls who engage in RA are often called "snobs", "traitors", "teasers", "gossips", and "bullies" (Shearin Karres 2004).

Relational aggression is particularly challenging for girls with ASDs because it is often not straightforward or easily observable—even to adults! A punch to the stomach, a push, or a kick in the shin sends a clear negative, confrontational message. If you have an ASD, clear messages are easier to detect, understand, and respond to. We have worked with many girls who misinterpret the behavior of mean girls as "nice", and who think the attention they are receiving signifies that they have friends, when in fact they are the subject of an elaborate joke. Your daughter will need guidance and explicit education about RA behaviors, and why they happen. Girls with ASDs need to learn to recognize nonverbal RA behaviors, such as eye-rolling, knowing glances, turning one's back, and giggling with a hand over one's mouth. The social skills of girls with ASDs are rarely sophisticated enough to detect when RA is occurring, and to know how to respond, without support and teaching. If your daughter is unable to detect RA, then she will not be able to tell you, her teachers or her counselor that it is happening to her.

The first step is teaching your daughter what RA looks like, and why girls behave this way (this will likely be difficult for your daughter to understand). The primary reasons why girls engage in RA include fear, power, control, popularity, and seeking security. Use the teaching approaches from your toolkit, including visual supports, social narratives, modeling, role-playing, social behavior mapping, watching television programs and movies, and social autopsies.

It is also helpful for your daughter to learn about the social structure of adolescent female groups, which can be quite complex. For girls who are capable of understanding the different social roles in a group setting, it may be helpful to review them with her. Roles can include the Queen Bee, the Wannabee, the Sidekick, the Gossip, the Tagalong, the Torn Bystander, and the Floater. See the list of recommended movies in Chapter 2 for examples of girl groups in action.

Unfortunately, many of the young women with whom we work have described feeling like the "odd girl out", and they often don't have friends to support them when they receive negative attention or are bullied by their peers. This makes them particularly susceptible to the emotional effects of relational aggression, which include further social withdrawal and possible avoidance, anxiety, depression, decreased self-esteem, increased mood lability, and loss of concentration on academic tasks (Crick and Grotpeter 1995). Name-calling is one of the more overt forms of RA that tends to intensify feelings of isolation; girls with whom we have worked have been called "Loner," "Teacher's Pet," "Lesbian," "Tomboy," and some girls have had to change schools in order to get a fresh start.

The website www.relationalaggression.com* provides a detailed description of relational aggression along with suggestions of what to do (and what not to do) if your child is experiencing RA. Some strategies include the following.

- Diversify your daughter's friendships by enrolling her in community-based activities.

- Encourage your daughter to keep a journal of any interactions with peers that may be forms of relational aggression. Review the journal with your daughter so that she can learn to identify RA when it occurs.

- Empathize with your daughter and give her suggestions for handling certain situations. Refrain from downplaying a situation with comments such as "It will get better."

- Closely monitor your daughter's mental health state. Seek professional counseling for your daughter if needed.

If your daughter is experiencing relational aggression, it is important to seek counseling with a trained therapist for the purpose of developing coping strategies and mechanisms (e.g. the use of positive self-statements as opposed to negative ones). You should also inform the school social worker(s) and psychologist so that they can address this issue across the grade level rather than solely with the individual who is being victimized by promoting acceptance and kindness while discouraging cattiness and exclusion.

---

* Accessed on March 23, 2008.

Possessiveness

> She wants her friends 100% of the time. She wants them to not have any other friends. In the past she'd come home from school and want to ring them up straightaway. She'd want to have sleepovers together. It's like nothing was ever enough. So if it's one friend it's just overwhelming. We've talked about it and she's getting better. The other day I said to her, "Why don't you go and play with Laien after school?" She said, "Oh, because Laien has enough of me at school. She sees me every day. I need to give Laien a break so I won't lose her." (*Asperger Syndrome, Adolescence, and Identity*, p.62)

Possessiveness occurs when a child thinks that a friend is exclusively their own and they become angry and confused when other peers are involved in their interactions. This can occur at any age ranging from early elementary years into the teenage years, and is especially difficult for young girls with autism because of their tendency toward literal interpretations: "my friend" means "*my* friend *only*." Friends who socialize and play with others may be viewed as traitors or betrayers, possibly leading to the destruction of the existing friendship if jealousy and anger do not subside or if reciprocal communication and social problem-solving do not occur (with or without prompting from parents, school-based counselors, social skill group leaders, or therapists). A young girl may also think that she and her friend no longer share the same interests if her friend develops a new interest of her own, or if her friend entertains the interests of a new addition to the group. Since girls with ASDs tend to form friendships based on common interests and may not deepen their friendship to the level of emotional needs and trust, this perceived loss of common interests can permanently damage the friendship.

It is important for your daughter to understand that just because one of her friends is spending time or talking with someone else, it does not mean that their friendship has to change in any way. Your daughter needs to know that she is still valued by her friends and that her company is desired. There may be times when your daughter is not able to attend a planned outing or get-together. At these times, your daughter might feel left out and may even think that she was excluded deliberately. Your daughter needs to know that this is a normal occurrence that happens every now and then and does not mean that her friendship is in jeopardy. Similarly, it is equally important for your daughter to understand that not all of her friends' interests will always be the same as her own. One of her friends may share a different interest with a newcomer, which does not mean that the friendship has to end. Explain that there will be times when the other girls might not be interested in her topic of discussion or suggested activity, but still want to spend time with her. Encourage your daughter to engage in a discussion or activity that the other girls have selected, even though it might not be of particular interest to her, for the sake of demonstrating flexibility and showing interest in other's viewpoints.

Case study: Talia

Brooke and Talia were two close friends in one of our girls' groups who also spent time together outside of the group. They shared a common interest in several young actors and various movies, and enjoyed talking about the actors' biographies and scenes in the movies. However, when the group conversation moved on to other topics and Brooke showed interest in what the others had to share, Talia became quite angry, vocal, and at times insulting toward Brooke for "abandoning" her and their shared interest. She was not able to understand Brooke's or the other group members' perspectives, causing visible anxiety and distress for everyone. Brooke was able to defend herself verbally and her desire to talk about another girl's interests and experiences, and she tried to explain that she did not value their friendship any less. She also told Talia that she did not appreciate being spoken to so harshly and disrespectfully. The girls were able to remain friends, but for a brief period of time did not see each other as often as they normally would.

Talking on the telephone

One social skill that can be particularly difficult for girls with ASDs, and may require extra attention, is talking on the telephone. Many typically developing teens will talk to their friends for hours on their home phone, on their cell phone, via text messaging, or via instant messaging on the internet. As a young girl, prior to the age of call-waiting and cell phones, perhaps you remember your parents yelling at you to get off the phone because you were hogging the line and preventing other calls from coming through! In contrast, most of the verbal girls with whom we have worked find the act of phoning a friend or acquaintance tedious, uncomfortable, and overwhelming. They report being at a loss for words, often not seeing a purpose in engaging in idle chatter. Problems with turn-taking skills make it difficult for them to know when to chime in, resulting in one of the two people resorting to monologuing. Caregivers report that the phone conversation skills of these girls are limited to brief questions and answers, and that they often do not know how to end a conversation, at times abruptly handing the phone to someone else while the person they were talking to is in the middle of speaking.

Despite these significant difficulties with telephone skills and the social importance of telephone conversations, virtually none of the girls in our groups have had telephone skills targeted in any therapeutic environment (counseling, speech and language therapy, school-based social skills groups, etc.). This is a social skill that develops naturally in typically developing girls, but must be taught explicitly to pre-teens and teens with ASDs. Starting at a young age (we recommend 8–9 years old) is important because girls with ASDs require much more practice and repetition than their typically developing peers.

In one of our summer girls' group programs (for girls aged 9–11), we targeted telephone skills as a goal for each girl in group. Over the course of eight weeks, we learned about *why* girls talk on the telephone (through interaction, instruction, and social narratives), we learned *how* to have a three-minute conversation (using scripts, role-playing, modeling, and video-modeling), and we *practiced* having conversations. First we practiced in the building (one room to the next). Once the girls were comfortable, for four weeks we paired them up and their homework for the week was to have a three-minute conversation with their friend from the group. A specific topic was assigned, (e.g. "What are you doing this weekend?") a script and prompts were provided, and parents were asked to be present to assist the girls as needed. Parents and girls had decided previously what their reward would be if they were successful. When the girls came to the group the following week, they shared with everyone what they had learned about their friend. It's a long process to develop telephone skills for girls who are anxious or who have difficulties with conversations, but you can be successful.

The first step toward teaching your daughter to talk on the telephone is to identify this skill as an area of need in any formal documentation, such as her IEP, so that her counselors can be accountable for teaching this skill and documenting progress. Talking on the telephone is commonly listed under the headings of social/emotional or communication goals. The clinician or provider responsible for teaching this skill can be the social worker, speech or language pathologist, or psychologist, depending on what services your child is eligible to receive as part of her IEP. Additionally, if your daughter is enrolled in a social skills group, ask the group facilitator if he or she plans to address and teach telephone conversation (and how they intend to do so).

The second step is to prepare your daughter. Don't just hand her the phone and say "Just talk to them!" Talking on the telephone without sufficient preparation may trigger a significant amount of anxiety and frustration. Explain the reasons why people talk on the phone (e.g. to inquire about specific information, to remind others about an upcoming event, to chit-chat, etc.). Use analogies to describe the reciprocal nature of communication: one of our favorites is to describe a conversation as a tennis match. In order to keep the ball in play, you must take turns hitting the ball (speaking) and waiting for your opponent to hit the ball (listening) without taking your eye off of the ball (topic maintenance). Teach your daughter to ask questions of the other person rather than talking at them. This can be done by prompting her to say two statements followed by a question about the other person's opinion, experiences, or thoughts.

Once your daughter knows what to expect and understands the rules of reciprocal conversation, the third step is to practice! Start by role-playing a telephone conversation without actually using the phone. Next, plan a phone conversation with someone she is comfortable with, such as a family member. Here are some helpful tips for your daughter's first few phone calls.

- Place a time limit on the call (you may use a standard kitchen timer or visual timer) and write out potential scripts for your daughter to use, so that she will know exactly what to say to maintain topic and have a successful conversation. Practice the scripts while pointing out and paying attention to pauses and tone of voice.

- Remember that girls with ASDs have a tendency to launch into topics without engaging in small talk. Include greetings, small talk, and appropriate ways of ending a conversation in your daughter's scripts.

- Make sure the person receiving the call knows that they are helping your daughter learn telephone skills, so that they can allow more time for your daughter to respond to their comments if necessary.

- Initially, you can let your daughter know that you will be listening on another line (while staying in her sight) so that you can provide prompts and cues for her if she needs help (either by whispering to her or by writing down prompts for her to see).

- When she is ready, encourage her to call an acquaintance or friend without having you on the call. Sticking to a script for the call can still be useful, as can be a time limit.

- After each conversation, encourage your daughter to analyze how well the conversation went from both parties' perspectives. This will help her develop the important skills of self-monitoring and self-awareness.

If having a phone conversation appears to be too overwhelming at first, your daughter might feel more comfortable using her computer to instant message (IM) with a family member or a friend. A script and a time limit can again be helpful in this setting. Of course, when using the internet and IM-ing it is important to make sure that your daughter is not talking to any potentially predatory strangers who are sometimes found in various online venues such as community gaming and chat rooms. It is important to discuss internet safety with your daughter and the dangers of giving out personal or identifying information; we will discuss online safety in more detail in Chapter 8.

Finding your daughter's social compass

For *all* individuals with ASDs, social skill development and understanding is a critical goal of programming, but for adolescent females with ASDs, navigating the interpersonal world can be even more daunting. In this chapter we have discussed issues that make friendships and socialization particularly challenging for pre-teen and teen girls with ASDs—friendships based on talking and emotional sharing rather than doing, complexities of social hierarchies and subtle forms of bullying, and the socio-cultural expectations that dictate what it means to be female. Women are considered to be the social gender, and are expected to possess an intuitive understanding of the social world. This is tough to live up to if you don't share the same needs or desires as your peers, or if you find social interactions anxiety-provoking, exhausting, or confusing. The good news is that *all* girls with ASDs can develop skills in the social domain. Some will be better at it than others; some will be more motivated to spend time with peers and make connections. Some girls will want a single friend to talk to, whereas other girls might only care to play a video game, wordlessly, beside a peer. Regardless of your daughter's initial ability and interest, with your support and teaching she can grow, develop confidence, and learn to navigate the social relationships in her life.

Resources
Books for parents

Attwood, T. (2007) *The Complete Guide to Asperger's Syndrome*. London: Jessica Kingsley Publishers.

Downey, M.K. and Downey, K.N. (2002) *The People in a Girl's Life. How to Find Them, Better Understand Them and Keep Them*. London: Jessica Kingsley Publishers.

Jackson, L. (2002) *Freaks, Geeks and Asperger Syndrome: A User Guide to Adolescence*. London: Jessica Kingsley Publishers.

Lawson, W. (2000) *Life Behind Glass. A Personal Account of Autism Spectrum Disorder*. London: Jessica Kingsley Publishers.

Lawson, W. (2006) *Friendships: The Aspie Way*. London: Jessica Kingsley Publishers.

Molloy, H. and Vasil, L. (eds) (2004) *Asperger Syndrome, Adolescence, and Identity. Looking Beyond the Label*. London: Jessica Kingsley Publishers.

Sainsbury, C. (2000) *Martian in the Playground. Understanding the Schoolchild with Asperger's Syndrome*. Bristol, UK: Lucky Duck Publishing, Ltd.

Willey, L.H. (1999) *Pretending To Be Normal*. London: Jessica Kingsley Publishers.

Books for girls

Criswell, P.K. and Martini, A. (2003) *A Smart Girl's Guide to Friendship Troubles. Dealing with Fights, Being Left Out, and the Whole Popularity Thing*. Middleton, WI: American Girls.

Koborg Brosen, S. (2006) *Do You Understand Me? My Life, My Thoughts, My Autism Spectrum Disorder*. London: Jessica Kingsley Publishers.

Curricula and programming books for parents and professionals

Baker, J. (2003) *Social Skills Training*. Shawnee Mission, KS: Autism Asperger Publishing Company.

Bellini, S. (2006) *Building Social Relationships: A Systematic Approach to Teaching Social Interaction Skills to Children and Adolescents with Autism Spectrum Disorders and Other Social Difficulties*. Shawnee Mission, KS: Autism Asperger Publishing Company.

Caldwell, P. and Horwood, J. (2007) *From Isolation to Intimacy: Making Friends without Words*. London: Jessica Kingsley Publishers.

Freeman, S. and Dake, L. (1997) *Teach Me Language: A Language Manual for Children with Autism, Asperger's Syndrome, and Related Developmental Disorders*. Langley, BC: Sfk Books.

Hodgdon, L. (2005) *Visual Strategies for Improving Communication: Practical Supports for School and Home*. Troy, MI: Quirk Roberts Publishing.

Moyes, R.A. (2001) *Incorporating Social Goals in the Classroom—A Guide for Teachers and Parents of Children with High-Functioning Autism & Asperger Syndrome*. London: Jessica Kingsley Publishers.

Nikopoulos, C. and Keenan, M. (2006) *Video Modelling and Behaviour Analysis. A Guide to Teaching Social Skills to Children with Autism*. London: Jessica Kingsley Publishers.

Quill, K.A. (2000) *Do–Watch–Listen–Say. Social and Communication Intervention for Children with Autism*. Baltimore, MD: Brookes Publishing Company.

Winner, M.G. (2002) *Thinking About You Thinking About Me: Philosophy and Strategies to Further Develop Perspective Taking and Communicative Abilities for Persons with Social Cognitive Deficits*. San Jose, CA: Think Social Publishing, Inc.

Winner, M.G. (ed.) (2007) *Social Behavior Mapping—Connecting Behavior, Emotions and Consequences Across the Day*. San Jose, CA: Think Social Publishing, Inc.

Books on female bullying and relational aggression

Dellasega, C. and Nixon, C. (2003) *Girl Wars: 12 Strategies that Will End Female Bullying*. New York, NY: Fireside.

Shearin Karres, E.V. (2004) *Mean Chicks, Cliques, and Dirty Tricks: A Real Girl's Guide to Getting Through the Day with Smarts and Style*. Cincinnati, OH: Adams Media Corporation.

Simmons, R. (2003) *Odd Girl Out: The Hidden Culture of Aggression in Girls*. San Diego, CA: Harcourt Trade Publishing.

Wiseman, R. (2002) *Queen Bees and Wannabes: Helping Your Daughter Survive Cliques, Gossip, Boyfriends, and Other Realities of Adolescence*. New York, NY: Three Rivers Press.

Video resources

My Friend Dylan [video]. Autism Ontario. Dylan is an 8-year-old girl with autism who goes to a wonderful school and has a lot of support from her friends. In this 10-minute video, which was filmed for children in grades 2–6, Dylan's classmates share how they feel about her and what they think about the friendships they share. The classmates offer tips and ideas on what was helpful for them in getting to know Dylan. It is very clear in the video that her classmates see themselves as enjoying and benefiting from their friendship with Dylan.

Chapter 7

Healthy Sexuality for Girls with ASDs

For your daughter, it is possible to be too early, but that is better than too late. Once you begin a dialog, it should be a life-long process of open communication. If you wait until it seems absolutely necessary, it is probably a bit too late... It is certainly a challenge to judge when and what to tell an autism spectrum person and depends more on their emotional and cognitive age rather than physical age. The timetable of maturing sexually, socially, and intellectually can vary a great deal. (Mary Newport, *Autism–Asperger's & Sexuality: Puberty and Beyond*, p.49)

One way I see myself is dragging my cumbersome bulk along while my friends sprint forward in romantic relationships. The majority of my friends will probably marry and have children, but somehow I don't think I will. Being in a sexual relationship right now isn't of utmost importance. I can envisage myself growing old with no partner, remaining a spinster to my dying day. It's as though my friends have all caught the express train to Lurve Central, whereas I have to settle for a bicycle (oh well, at least I'll get some exercise). (Nita Jackson, *Standing Down, Falling Up*, p.64)

Defining sexuality: finding a common meaning

One of the most significant challenges that parents face as their children enter adolescence is being able to think of their child as a sexual person. If your daughter has an ASD, it is understandably even more difficult to conceive of her sexuality; we have found this to be a significant source of concern or denial among parents. Some parents feel that adolescence and puberty sneak up on them, and that they are unprepared for emerging issues related to sexuality. Other parents allow concerns to get in the way of developing a healthy sexuality education plan for their daughter. From our work with families and their daughters, we know that the best outcomes (for teens and their parents) result from parents being able to resolve their difficulties with thinking of their daughter's sexuality, and being able to work proactively on a sexuality education plan that meets their daughter learning needs and provides her with appropriate opportunities for sexuality development.

We live in a world today that is saturated by sex. Media, music, movies, racy clothing—sexual messages are everywhere. And these messages directly influence how we tend to think about sexuality. When you hear the word *sexuality*, what comes to mind? What do you think of? When we conduct our "Girls Growing Up Parent Groups" (for parents with daughters in our girls' groups) we pose this question at the beginning of the very first session. Using a flip chart, we ask parents to generate all the words and ideas that come to mind when they hear the word *sexuality*. Invariably, most of the initial responses are related to sexual intercourse, consistent with a narrow idea of sexuality. Often, it is only with prompting that parents are able to broaden their conception of sexuality and begin to form a holistic perspective that crosses many different domains. The following are examples of what our parents have contributed, once they were able to move beyond a one-dimensional view of sexuality:

safety	identity	fantasy	need	myths
feelings	confusion	drive	intimacy	gender
love	passion	confidence	sensuality	puberty
connection	orientation	femininity	techniques	

If all you associate with your daughter and sexuality is intercourse, then it's no wonder sexuality is anxiety-provoking. Before we go any further in this chapter, we want everyone, authors and readers alike, to be able to share a similar understanding of what sexuality is. It will make a huge difference in how you understand and accept your daughter, and what you hope for her in her future. Right now, our take-home message is:

"Sexuality" is not "Sex"

A very simple message, but an incredibly important one. You might still be grappling with this idea, and that's okay. We hope that by the end of the chapter you will see why sexuality is a natural and healthy part of your daughter's life, and that it may or may not involve "sex".

So if sexuality is not sex, how are people thinking about sexuality in its broadest sense? International organizations have been working toward educating the public about integrating positive, healthy sexuality into people's lives, including individuals with disabilities. The Sexuality Information and

Education Council of the United States (SIECUS) defines human sexuality as encompassing:

> the sexual knowledge, beliefs, attitudes, values, and behaviors of individuals. Its various dimensions involve the anatomy, physiology, and biochemistry of the sexual response system; identity, orientation, roles, and personality; and thoughts, feelings, and relationships. Sexuality is influenced by ethical, spiritual, cultural, and moral concerns. (SIECUS 2005)

The World Health Organization (WHO) states that sexuality is:

> A central aspect of being human throughout life and encompasses sex, gender identities and roles, sexual orientation, eroticism, pleasure, intimacy and reproduction. Sexuality is experienced and expressed in thoughts, fantasies, desires, beliefs, attitudes, values, behaviour, practices, roles and relationships. While sexuality can include all of these dimensions, not all of them are always experienced or expressed. Sexuality is influenced by the interaction of biological, psychological, social, economic, political, cultural, ethical, legal, historical, religious and spiritual factors. (WHO 2004)

The bottom line is that sexuality is *not* sexual intercourse, or even sexual activity. Sex is part of the picture, but it is by no means all, or even most, of what sexuality is. Sexuality includes your thoughts, feelings, behavior, and values, and it is an important part of your overall health and wellbeing. The philosophy that SIECUS clearly advocates is that human sexuality is not one-dimensional; it should not be viewed within a narrow perspective. Sexuality is meant to be interpreted within a much broader context, demonstrating that all the dimensions of sexuality are a natural part of who we are, and who your daughter is, regardless of her disability or degree of impairments. As a parent, you are in an important position to be able to teach your daughter about sexuality. We'll talk about roles you will play later in the chapter, but for now, we want you to reflect on how you and your family think about sexuality.

Sexual attitudes and values

Parents are the *most important* and *best* sexuality educators for their children. You might wish that someone else could do it for you, or that her school or physician could take a bigger role. However, parents are really the only ones who are able to convey the heart of sexuality to their daughters—what lies beyond the facts, the statistics, and the biology. Your cultural, religious and family backgrounds are important components of sexual learning for your daughter. Self-exploration and understanding of your family's attitudes and values about sexuality, and sexuality in the context of disability, will lay the foundation for teaching and help prepare you for the roles you will play as your daughter grows up. Don't worry; you don't have to be alone in teaching. We will talk about developing a sexuality education plan for your daughter and who will be able to assist you, but for now, focus on your own family and community.

Take a moment to reflect on your family background and how you came to acquire your values and attitudes toward sexuality. Spend as much time as you think will be helpful for you; if you want, include others in discussions and reflection, such as your partner, your parents, or your siblings. Think about *what* you learned about sexuality when you were younger, and from *whom*? What and who have shaped your *current* values and attitudes toward sexuality, and sexuality in individuals with disabilities? How have they changed? Has having a daughter with an ASD changed how you think about sexuality? For most people, information about sexuality is received from a variety of sources, including family, the media, society, school, peers, culture, the medical profession, and religious organizations. This information, combined with your personal experiences, is ultimately integrated into a cohesive set of values, ideas, and attitudes about sexuality that are changed and shaped over time. What you thought about sexuality when you were younger may be different in some ways than how you feel now. Various sources of information also have more influence at different times; pre-teens and teenagers are often influenced more by what they hear from their peers than by their parents for a certain period of time in their lives, though we know that this may be different for girls with ASDs.

Sexual myths

The media also plays an important role in how sexuality is perceived at a broader societal level. Unfortunately, it tends to perpetuate myths about sexuality and developmental disabilities, some of which are particularly relevant to individuals with ASDs. Have you heard or been exposed to any of these myths?

- Females with developmental disabilities don't have sexual drives or interests.
- Only able-minded or able-bodied females should engage in sexual behavior.

- Females with developmental disabilities are not capable of intimate, emotional relationships.

- Sexual behavior in females with developmental disabilities is aberrant or wrong.

- If you teach about sexuality you will create more problems for your daughter.

- Females with developmental disabilities need to be protected from society.

- Females with developmental disabilities don't experience negative consequences from being abused/exploited/hurt.

In our work with families of girls with ASDs, the most common misconceptions we have come across are:

- she *doesn't have sexual interests* so you don't need to teach about sexuality

- she has an ASD so she *lacks the emotional and social understanding* to ever connect with a partner

- she has an ASD so she will *not be capable* of having a relationship

- she has an ASD so she *won't be interested* in having a relationship

- her *emotional understanding* is so limited because of her ASD that she doesn't really understand what being hurt means.

- she's a bright girl; she can easily *participate in mainstream sex education/health class* (we will discuss this issue later in the chapter).

It is disheartening for us as professionals to continue to face these misconceptions in our daily work. Through presentations and community education we do our best to correct those who continue to hold ill-informed ideas about what your daughters deserve, are capable of, or are interested in. We share your frustration when you face similar attitudes whether they come from family members, friends, strangers, or professionals and educators in your daughter's life. As a society we are moving in the right direction toward better understanding of the sexuality of individuals with disabilities. Warren Johnson wrote in the 1980s that our journey has taken us from the idea of *elimination* of sexuality, to *tolerance*, and now we are finally starting to *cultivate* sexual development and health of individuals with disabilities (Johnson and Kempton 1981). This is our goal for your daughters: cultivation of that important part of who they are which will contribute greatly to their wellbeing and to their living happy and healthy lives now and in the future.

Your roles as a parent

You will be playing a number of different roles throughout your daughter's sexual development (e.g. teacher, boundary setter, confidant, advocate), and the emphasis on each of these roles will change and shift as your daughter grows up. Overall, your role as a parent in her development is to foster and nurture her growth and life-long learning. Some of the roles listed below have been adapted from the book *Sexuality: Preparing Your Child with Special Needs* (Karakoussis, Calkins and Eggeling 1998); others are additional roles that we have found to be relevant for teaching girls with ASDs.

- *Sex educator*: provider of information and teaching materials; deciding what to teach, when, and how.

- *Confidant*: being someone your daughter can trust and come to if she has questions or wants to discuss something; being comfortable and open to discussing anything that might arise.

- *Boundary setter*: provider of clear, specific boundaries for your daughter to follow regarding personal space, touching rules, and topics of conversation.

- *Model*: demonstrating to your daughter expressions of sexuality and affection in your family and community; being a source of affection for your daughter; modeling appropriate expression of affection.

- *Demonstrator*: formally demonstrating to your daughter various skills and behaviors she will need to learn (e.g. greeting a male peer); knowing what to teach and demonstrate; being comfortable in a teaching role.

- *Social interpreter*: staying abreast of the culture of typically developing youth of your daughter's age (reading books and magazines, watching television); being able to interpret the language and behaviors of your daughter's peers for her. (Parents in our groups raise this issue frequently. They talk about trying to learn the lingo of the pre-teen crowd and how to understand the culture so that they can guide their daughters. One mother likened it to "trying to be a foreign language interpreter of a language I don't even understand!")

- *Co-problem solver*: working with your daughter as a *team* to solve life situations and social scenarios; being able to step back from the role of the adult who knows everything and trying to work *together* with your daughter to help her generate solutions and plans.

(Parents in our groups talk about this as being challenging not just because their daughter has autism, but because she is a pre-teen or teenager! We couldn't agree more!)

- *Moral guide*: teaching your daughter your family's religious and cultural beliefs with respect to sexuality and sexual behavior. Some girls with ASDs will have limited understanding in this area because of cognitive impairments or because their abstract, conceptual thought is not well-developed; learning beyond concrete concepts is very challenging for them. Understanding that your daughter will be developing her own system of values and may not incorporate all she has learned from her family; teaching your daughter about differences in values she will encounter in life and how to handle these situations. (Some of the girls with whom we have worked have had difficulties when their family values differed from those of others; girls who tend to be rigid in their interpretation of rules or guidelines may be intolerant of others' beliefs and behaviors, which can result in significant social difficulties. Work with your daughter on understanding the grey areas of morals and values, and being respectful of differences.)

- *Protector*: being aware of situations that could pose a risk to your daughter; appropriately addressing situations if they arise; preparing your daughter to protect herself. (Many parents see *Protector* as the most important role in their daughter's sexuality development. While it is clearly a very important role, parents need to be careful that they do not *overprotect*, and that they balance playing a direct role themselves with teaching their daughter skills to protect herself.)

- *Advocate*: being able to argue or present a case for your daughter when she is unable to do so for herself; this might include advocating individualized sexuality education at school; knowing when to get professional assistance in advocating for your daughter; having a clear understanding of who your daughter is and what she deserves.

- *Community educator*: when situations arise, either formally or informally, being able to teach members of the community or your family about your daughter and her sexuality rights; being comfortable speaking up when you need to, or want to; having a clear understanding of who your daughter is and what she deserves.

You may be more comfortable with some of these roles than others. Take a few minutes to think about the various roles you will assume throughout your daughter's sexual development. Are you ready for each of them? Is the rest of your family ready? As a sex educator, do you have the knowledge you need about various aspects of sexuality? If not, where can you acquire the information? Are you comfortable with any topic your child might bring up to discuss with you (e.g. homosexuality, anal sex, premarital sex, abortion)? If not, who else in your daughter's life can also act as a confidant or educator? Do you have a plan for communicating with your child's school? How about with your child's physician? Being prepared as a parent for the roles you will play can often help to alleviate some of the anxiety associated with topic. You will be much less likely to find yourself in a position where you are thinking "Oh no, what do I do now?", or "I have no idea what to say!" If you need extra help in preparing, talk to a professional who has experience in this area. Have a consultation and work together on developing a teaching plan. If you're prepared, you will feel better, and your daughter will as well.

Bill of healthy sexuality rights for girls with ASDs

Together with the girls and families with whom we have worked, we have created a bill of rights related to sexuality for daughters with ASDs. *As girls, parents, and professionals, we feel strongly that girls with ASDs deserve*:

- Knowledge about sexuality appropriate to their age, developmental level, and readiness.
- To love and be loved by others.
- Training and skill development in social–sexual behavior that will facilitate establishing friendships and intimate relationships.
- Knowledge about sexual health issues, including (as applicable) physical exams, birth control, and sexually transmitted infections (STIs).
- To have their sexuality appreciated, accepted, and understood by others.
- To express their sexuality in ways that are socially acceptable.
- As appropriate, to play an active role in their own sexual decision-making.
- To have hope for their future with regard to relationships, marriage, and children.

- To be safe from harm.

Every girl is entitled to these rights, regardless of her level of impairment. The specific role that sexuality plays in your daughter's life will, of course, depend on her cognitive and social abilities, but the most important point is that her sexuality should not be ignored. In this chapter, we will discuss what sexuality means for your daughter, and how you can help her to achieve healthy sexuality in a positive and safe manner.

Why is sexuality education important for your daughter?

You may feel awkward or somewhat embarrassed about your daughter's sexuality, but we've already begun to ease you into thinking about it—the earlier chapters on puberty and menstruation are in fact part of the sexuality package. So you've already covered some of the ground. Authors in the field of sexuality and developmental disabilities agree on a number of reasons for educating youth with disabilities about sexuality, and making sexuality an important parent of their learning and development.

- Sexuality is a *natural part* of who your daughter is; just as neurotypical girls receive information and guidance regarding their sexuality development, so too should your daughter.

- Girls with cognitive disabilities develop physically in the same way as their typical peers. We talked about this issue in Chapter 3 when reviewing puberty; you can't trick your daughter's physiology into keeping her as a six-year-old forever. Her body is going to change, and since change can be difficult for girls with ASDs, she needs to understand this physical development to the degree possible given her cognitive abilities.

- Sexuality has a strong social component and plays a role in human relationships. This is very significant for girls with ASDs as impairments in social understanding and behavior are a core feature of the disorder. It requires paying special attention to underlying social concepts when teaching about sexuality.

- Sexuality education is *essential* in reducing the risk of physical or sexual abuse and exploitation (this issue will be discussed in great detail in the next chapter). If that's not a motivator for providing sexuality education, what is?

- It is important for *all* young women to learn about sexual health issues, which can include (depending on cognitive ability and likelihood of sexual activity) gynecological examinations, proper tampon use, birth control, and sexually transmitted infections.

- Contrary to popular belief, study after study has demonstrated that the *more* education an individual has, the *less* likely they are to engage in inappropriate or dangerous behavior. By making healthy sexual development and sexuality education a priority as part of your daughter's growing up, you will be protecting her from making mistakes and uninformed decisions, and empowering her to stay safe from unwanted sexual approaches.

Sexuality education for girls with ASDs

Sexuality education for youth and adolescents with developmental disabilities has received little attention in the literature (NICHYD 1992; SIECUS 1996). Even less work has been done to understand issues related to sexuality and sexual education for children and adolescents with ASDs (Henault 2004; Koller 2000). To date, more focus has been placed on studies of sexuality in adults with ASDs. This (still relatively small) body of literature suggests that adult outcomes related to sexuality are generally poor. Self-esteem and mood are negatively affected as a result of difficulties with relationships and unmet sexual needs (Henault and Attwood 2002), and self-injurious behaviors can arise (Mortlock 1993), as may numerous sexual behavior problems which may be a result of lack of education (Van Bourgondien, Reichle and Palmer 1997). Individuals with ASDs are more vulnerable to abuse, and there is an increased risk of legal issues resulting from misinterpreted behavior (Hingsburger, Griffiths and Quinsey 1990). These studies indicate a strong need for proactive and early sexual education for youth with ASDs in order to avoid such negative outcomes later in life.

Challenges faced by girls with ASDs

In our work with girls and their families, we have learned that ASDs present unique challenges that may affect your daughter's sexuality and sexual learning, how you and your daughter's teachers will need to approach sexuality education, and how people might interpret her behavior (e.g. sensory, social, repetitive or self-stimulatory behaviors). The most common issues that arise in working with families fall within six categories: social, communication, behavior, sensory, cognition, and mental health. Note that three of the categories represent those that make up the diagnostic criteria for the disorder: impairments in the social, communication, and behavioral domains. Think again about your daughter's skills, strengths, and weaknesses. How does her autism affect *her*? Some of the specific challenges described in the following sections will be very relevant for you and your daughter; others less so. What's important is that you develop a clear understanding of how your daughter's ASD will affect her sexuality development and learning, and how best to teach her.

Social challenges

As previously mentioned, sexuality is a component of healthy social relationships. Your daughter can learn rules about privacy, boundaries, and touching; however, the underlying concepts are social, and are learned through social means. For individuals with ASDs, understanding interpersonal relationships and social rules can be difficult. With respect to sexuality in particular, difficulties in the social domain may lead to a number of issues for your daughter, including:

- deficits in the social skills needed to develop peer relationships and, eventually, romantic relationships
- varying degrees of desire to establish connections with others
- engaging in inappropriate behavior (e.g. invading personal space, touching self in public, disrobing), which can be misunderstood and misinterpreted by others
- difficulties understanding one's own emotions and the thoughts and feelings of others
- difficulty interpreting subtle and not-so-subtle body language and facial expressions (e.g. interest, non-interest, flirting).

The daughter of one mother with whom we worked was quite pretty and her mother remarked how, when they went to the mall, she could see all the boys looking at her daughter, but her daughter was "clueless". Laughingly, she expressed hope that her daughter would stay clueless for a while longer!

Youth with ASDs may also be more vulnerable to abuse and exploitation owing to difficulties reading warning signs and "red flags". As we've discussed before, girls with ASDs have difficulties listening to their "gut feeling" and the body awareness that tells them a situation is potentially dangerous. There is also the risk of your daughter engaging in harmful or inappropriate acts because of a lack of understanding of others' feelings and perspectives (e.g. stalking, inappropriate touching). We will return to these issues when we discuss abuse prevention in Chapter 8.

Communication challenges

Difficulties with communication are one of the defining characteristics of an ASD. These difficulties can affect a girl's sexuality development and learning in a number of ways:

- Impairments in communication can contribute to difficulties with expressing one's needs and indicating if a negative experience has happened.
- Frustration arising from communication difficulties can lead to inappropriate behaviors (e.g. disrobing).
- Difficulties engaging in reciprocal conversations can contribute to challenges with dating and forming intimate relationships.

Behavioral challenges

The following concerns are by no means common, but have been problems for some individuals with ASDs with whom we have worked.

- Unintentionally inappropriate behaviors are sometimes misunderstood to be "sexual" or "deviant" (e.g. a girl who climbs onto adult male's laps).
- Individuals with ASDs may become fixated on aspects of sexual drive, or develop ritualized behaviors associated with their sexuality (e.g. needing certain smells, objects or music).
- Intense fascinations and imaginary fantasies may develop about being in love with celebrities, musicians, or movie stars (e.g. Johnny Depp).
- Sexuality or sexual behavior may become a special interest for individuals with ASDs (e.g. viewing internet pornography, researching fetishes).
- Self-stimulatory behaviors related to sexual arousal may become excessive due to repetitive behavior or anxiety.

Sensory challenges

Because sexuality has a physical component, the sensory issues experienced by many girls with ASDs can be problematic. Specifically:

- *Hypo-* (undersensitive) and *hyper-* (oversensitive) sensitivity issues may affect sexuality and relationships for your daughter. She may dislike hugging and close touch, or soft touch may be uncomfortable to experience. Or, she may need intense physical contact to experience the level of sensation that you would get from a typical embrace.

- Self-stimulatory behaviors related to sexual arousal may become excessive due to hyposensitivity (e.g. difficulties achieving orgasm).

- Sensory issues may prevent your daughter from reading physiological signals in her body (e.g. menstrual cramps).

Cognitive challenges

Beyond general cognitive impairments which clearly play a role in determining what (and how) to teach about sexuality, other aspects of cognition are important when considering your daughter's sexuality:

- Inflexibility of thought can contribute to the development of rigid ideas and rules related to sexuality. To her mother's dismay, one of the girls with whom we worked developed a rule that she could not go on a date until she was exactly 22 years old. Her mother was unsure where this particular age came from, but she was adamant, and even began to chastise others if they planned on dating before they were 22.

- Literalness and black-and-white thinking can also play a role. One girl with whom we worked was told politely by the young man in whom she was interested "I don't have time for a girlfriend right now." Misunderstanding his intended meaning, she kept asking every few weeks or so if the young man had time now.

- Difficulties with *executive function* (higher-order cognitive abilities that help you navigate your day) can also be relevant. Poor inhibition and impulse control, as well as difficulties with self-reflection, self-monitoring, problem-solving, and using new strategies, can all affect your daughter's sexual development, learning, and behavior.

Mental health challenges

As we've discussed, puberty and growing up can cause significant anxiety for youth with ASDs. The anxiety and depression that may emerge during adolescence for girls with ASDs is at times tied to issues related to sexuality such as body changes, growing up, attraction and crushes, relationships, ambivalence about wanting to date, seeing other peers be successful in navigating first girlfriends or boyfriends, and rejection experiences. Some of the anxieties we have observed in pre-teen and teenage girls with ASDs include:

- fear of/concerns about menstruation or breast development
- anxiety about body changes and body image
- anxiety related to talking/thinking about sexual activity or masturbation
- anxiety about "sexual rules" (e.g. touching rules, rigid interpretation)
- sadness, depression, anger about being different from other girls of the same age
- sadness, depression about not being able to find a boyfriend
- emotional dysregulation and the effects of hormone changes during adolescence seem to be more significant for youth with ASDs, and in particular girls; this can lead to girls feeling fearful because they sense being "out of control" at times, or not themselves
- stress management and developing effective coping strategies for handling anxiety, changes in mood, and all of life's ups and downs can be hard for girls with ASDs.

You'll notice that much of what we described in this section is experienced by girls in general during adolescence—neurotypical or not. However, we have observed in our clinical work that girls with ASDs experience difficulties with mood, behavioral regulation, and anxiety during adolescence to a *greater degree* than other girls with whom we have worked. Coupled with inflexibility of thought and difficulties with problem-solving, these issues can seem insurmountable for your daughter. Developing a healthy approach to sexuality, and, more generally, working through all the issues discussed in this book, will be important in fostering your daughter's wellbeing as she enters, journeys through, and exits adolescence.

What does sexuality look like for typically developing girls?

Before considering your daughter's sexual development, it is helpful to be able to put her behavior, readiness, and learning into context. Things have changed a lot since you were young: sexuality during the pre-teen and teenage years is quite different today, and it is important for you to understand what typically developing girls are experiencing during middle and high school. Table 7.1 is adapted from the Advocates for Youth Parents' Sex Ed Centre,* and provides a good overview of typical sexual milestones for normally developing adolescents.

In contrast to this summary of sexual development, which attributes a minimal amount of actual sexual activity to younger teens, recent movies and television shows have portrayed adolescents, including girls, as being much more sexually active. In fact, studies indicate that this media portrayal of adolescent sexuality may be somewhat more accurate than that of Table 7.1. A notable change in the nature of youth sexual behaviors is the prevalence of oral sex. The National Center for Health Statistics (NCHS) reported that almost 75% of 19-year-olds have had oral sex with an opposite-gender partner, and that it has become an established part of the sexual repertoire of teens, typically preceding a first vaginal sex experience for girls (Brewster and Tillman 2008; Mosher, Chandra and Jones 2005). Girls report different reasons for engaging in oral sex than boys, including improving their relationship, pleasure, curiosity, and peer pressure (Cornell and Halpern-Felsher 2006). The sexual experience of girls is often one associated with feelings of pressure—from friends, and from potential sexual partners. What is also clear is that many teens consider oral sex less risky than vaginal sex, despite the high risk for contracting STIs. This may be because their fear of pregnancy is greater than their fear of STIs.

By 18 years of age, 70% of girls report having experienced vaginal intercourse (CDC 2005); however, studies demonstrate that most girls engage in a partner-oriented repertoire of sexual behavior that begins long before sexual intercourse happens. In their research with 12–15-year-old girls, O'Sullivan and Brooks-Gunn (2005) found that girls' sexual experiences develop from no sexual contact to hand-holding and kissing, breast-fondling, manual genital contact, oral sex, and, finally, intercourse. They also noted that girls' cognitions about sexuality, such as self-esteem, attitudes toward abstinence,

---

*   Available at www.advocatesforyouth.org/parents/index.htm.

Table 7.1 Typical adolescent sexuality development

9–12 years

- transition from childhood to adolescence
- onset of puberty
- masturbation
- increased need for personal privacy
- peer discussion about sexual behavior
- interest in the opposite sex
- early intimacy such as kissing and hugging
- first "girlfriends" and "boyfriends"
- interested in and influenced by sexual media
- curiosity and questions
- possible confusion, embarrassment, discomfort, fear

13–17 years

- completion of puberty
- body image; concerns about one's attractiveness to others
- capacity to develop healthy, mutual relationships
- influenced by peer group
- peer discussion about sexual behavior
- early intimacy such as kissing and hugging
- more frequent change in girlfriend/boyfriend
- worries about being "normal"

18 years and older

- completion of physical maturation
- establishment of body image
- formation of values; social and cultural orientation
- more serious intimate sexual and emotional relationships
- firmer sense of sexual identity, including sexual orientation
- more intense sexuality (feelings of love and passion)
- increased concern for others; empathy

and sense of approval from peers and parents, play an important reciprocal role in actual sexual behaviors. Earlier sexual behaviors such as kissing and touching were reportedly central in influencing how girls thought about themselves sexually, which then contributed to decision-making about further behaviors. Hensel, Fortenberry and Orr (2008) suggest that rather than focusing on adverse outcomes of the sexual behavior of adolescent females, we would do well to think about young women as "proactive sexual agents capable of purposeful sexual decision making" (p.174).

This increased prevalence of sexual activity in teens does not mean that your daughter will or should engage in such activities. She is, however, more likely to be exposed to sexual behavior; as a parent you need to be aware of this and be prepared to answer any questions that she has. Make sure that your daughter has the education she needs in order to make appropriate decisions for herself.

One of the defining features of adolescent sexuality for females in particular is the "sexual double standard". From a very young age, girls receive mixed messages about how to behave and feel. They are encouraged by magazines, television, and movies to be sexy and attractive to males, while being taught by their parents and educators not to engage in sexual behavior. The literature indicates that not only is this confusing for girls, but it can contribute negatively to their sexual self-concept and identity as they grow up. Now think about your daughter with an ASD. If these messages are confusing for neurotypical girls, imagine the challenges your daughter might face in trying to make sense of what's appropriate and what's not!

What does healthy sexuality look like for females with ASDs?

There is a continuum of what can and should be considered healthy sexuality for girls with ASDs. Clearly, what healthy sexuality looks like when your daughter is a pre-teen or teen could be very different from when she is a young woman or an adult. Age is just one of the many factors that contribute to where each individual girl will fall along the continuum as she grows up; others include cognitive ability, level of independence, social skills, interest, readiness, and motivation (Figure 7.1). Importantly, no matter what your daughter's abilities are, she *can* experience healthy sexuality. We want your daughter to feel loved and to be happy, healthy, and safe.

If your daughter has moderate to severe impairments, a sexual or intimate relationship with another person may not be possible. For her, healthy sexuality can be achieved through sexual health and safety, experiencing love and affection from family and friends, and being able to engage in self-pleasuring activities, such as masturbation. Opportunities for sensual experiences can fulfill sensory and emotional needs, including wanting to be touched (e.g. warm baths, therapeutic massage). Companionship with pets can also serve socio-emotional and sensual needs; many females with ASDs report a love of animals.

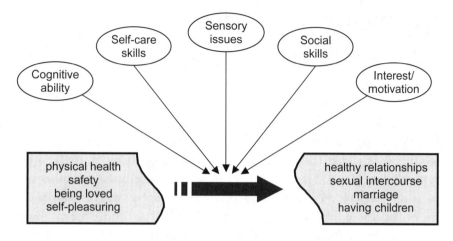

Figure 7.1 Continuum of healthy sexuality for females with ASDs.

What if your daughter has mild impairments or is of average to above-average intellect? What will healthy sexuality look like for her? Again, it will depend on a number of factors—most importantly, sensory issues, social skills, and interest—which will change over time. You may want the white dress and the reception, but does your daughter? As she enters adolescence and then young adulthood, her experiences will contribute greatly to figuring out what she wants with respect to a relationship. One of the mothers with whom we worked wanted her daughter to be able to *make the right decisions* about whether she wants a relationship or not, and to take her time so that if she does want to be with someone, she is ready when the time comes. Decision-making and insight are skills we work very hard on with older, brighter girls.

In Chapter 6, we talked about standardized measures that can aid in assessing social motivation and interest. Just because your daughter has the *capability* of being in a relationship, doesn't mean she will be *interested*. Sensory issues may contribute to ambivalence about dating and relationships: holding hands, hugging, kissing, and caressing can be very difficult for young women who have aversions to various kinds of touch. Being a few years behind socially and emotionally can also contribute to your daughter's readiness to date. What's most important for your daughter is to engage in active self-exploration in order to better understand what she wants. We have found that individual counseling or participation in a therapeutic group with same-aged girls can contribute greatly to girls' confidence in their ability to make decisions, and can help them to know when they are ready for the next step regarding dating and relationships.

Your daughter's sexual education plan

We once received a telephone call from a mother whose 12-year-old daughter had been touching herself in the classroom. This behavior had persisted for a month without being addressed, gradually becoming more frequent and obvious to her classmates. Both the school and the girl's mother were now in a panic about what to do. Another phone call we received was from a mother whose daughter was paying too much attention to a boy at school she found cute, and this young man was becoming annoyed. Yet another mother's daughter had just started her menstrual cycle, and the mother was panicking because they were not prepared. Her daughter was resisting wearing pads because they were not comfortable. All of the above are examples of "crisis responding", which is exactly what we *don't* want to do when it comes to your daughter's sexuality.

By now you have probably realized that we are strong advocates for being prepared, and in the area of sexuality this means creating a proactive plan for sexual learning and development. In *Sexuality, Preparing your Child with Special Needs* (Karakoussis *et al.* 1998), the authors give a number of reasons why it is important to develop a plan for sexuality education. They explain that by actively creating a plan with your child's educational and therapeutic team you are:

- acknowledging that your daughter is a sexual person and that this is a healthy and natural part of her growing up
- demonstrating an understanding that your daughter will need assistance with some aspects of sexuality
- setting fair and realistic goals for what your daughter's healthy sexuality will look like and how best to facilitate her sexual well-being
- preparing yourself to take advantage of and respond to life's learning opportunities and teachable moments
- preparing for crises that may arise
- developing goals which will create a starting point from which your daughter's plan will evolve
- providing a roadmap for your daughter's teaching team.

A careful individualized assessment of your daughter's current skills and knowledge, and what the next steps should be, will help to guide creation of her plan. Work with a qualified professional who has experience in sexuality assessments and developing educational plans for youth with developmental disabilities. Check with a speciality autism center in your area, and contact the American Association of Sexuality Educators, Counselors, and Therapists (AASECT).* AASECT has a sexuality and disabilities special interest group, and can guide you in locating a trained professional in your area.

General guidelines for teaching sexuality

Three of the most common questions we are asked by parents about teaching sexuality (besides "Do I really have to?") are: (1) "*What* am I supposed to teach?" (2) "*When* do I teach it?" and (3) "*How* do I teach it?" Understandably, parents tend to be apprehensive or even scared by the topic of sexuality. Addressing emotional feelings and your comfort level associated with the topic is the first step. Once we are able to move past that, teaching about sexuality is actually not much different from teaching about all the other important concepts and skills your daughter will need to learn as she grows up.

In general, teaching topics should be selected based on your daughter's chronological age (e.g. as she approaches puberty she will need to learn about her body changes), whereas teaching strategies should be selected based on her developmental age and her developmental strengths and weaknesses. That is, her chronological age assists in determining *what* she needs to learn, while her developmental age contributes to decisions about *how* she will learn best, and at what *conceptual level* she will be able to understand material. Furthermore, since not all girls with ASDs need to learn about the exact same concepts, and different girls benefit more from different learning approaches, both topics and teaching strategy will be informed by your daughter's individualized assessment.

How do girls with ASDs learn about sexuality?

As you develop your daughter's sexuality education plan, it is important to keep in mind that girls with ASDs generally learn about sexuality differently from either their neurotypical peers or boys with ASDs. Though there are biological or instinctual aspects of sexuality (genetics, hormones, sexual drive, sexual orientation), *most* of our actual sexual behavior is *learned*. We are generally taught to act in ways that are consistent with socially acceptable or culturally defined expressions of sexual behavior. Gagnon and Simon began writing in the 1970s about the *social sources* of human sexuality

---

*   Available at www.aasect.org

(Gagnon and Simon 1973). In their book, *Social Conduct. The Social Sources of Human Sexuality*, Gagnon and Simon (1973) highlight the truly social nature of human sexuality in their discussion of "sexual scripts", which provide the guidelines and context for which people understand behaviors, situations, and experiences. They explain that a sexual script assists us in:

> learning the meaning of internal states, organizing the sequences of specifically sexual acts, decoding novel situations, setting the limits on sexual responses, and linking meaning from nonsexual aspects of life to specifically sexual experience. (p.13)

The fact that much of our sexual understanding, learning, and behavior are based on socially determined sexual scripts places girls with ASDs at a significant disadvantage. Brenda Smith Myles' book, *The Hidden Curriculum*, discusses the unwritten social rules that youth with ASDs do not pick up on naturally (i.e. through naturalistic, informal, incidental learning). There are hundreds of such rules: rules of privacy; talking about what interests other people; "first date" guidelines; when to hug someone; etiquette in a movie theatre; knowing when *not* to be honest (e.g. if someone you think is unattractive asks if they are cute); and so on. Girls with ASDs need to be explicitly taught these sexual scripts that define these rules and guide our behavior, often with much repetition. Terri Couwenhoven (2007), along with others such as Griffiths, Quinsey and Hingsburger (1989), discusses "altered scripts" that individuals with developmental disabilities have because of the nature of their disability and their learning experiences. An altered script is a sexual script in "the presence of unique circumstances that affect sexual learning" (Couwenhoven 2007, p.5). The growing-up experiences of girls with ASDs are very different from those of neurotypical girls, as are the ways in which girls with ASDs learn about sexuality. There are a number of reasons for these differences:

Girls with ASDs receive less information about sexuality

- There are fewer sources for learning and fewer understandable materials available about sexuality.
- Cognitive disabilities can affect how information is processed and retained.
- Girls may be "protected" from learning.

Girls with ASDs have fewer opportunities for social contact, and the sources of sexual learning are different

- Access to appropriate peers is challenging; girls receive less information from peers.
- Male to female sex ratio of the disorder; most girls spend their social time with boys in classrooms or social skills groups.
- There are fewer natural learning situations (e.g. girls and guys hanging out).
- There are fewer opportunities for practice in applying skills and concepts learned.
- Difficulties with social reciprocity/awareness/interest can lead to a "peer void".

Girls with ASDs need to rely more on caregivers
- Girls with ASDs develop independence more slowly.
- Privacy issues are of concern when more intimate care is required.

Environmental issues are often relevant for girls with ASDs
- Girls with ASDs tend to be more closely supervised; there are often more limitations and rules.
- Girls may experience less privacy than typical peers.
- Residential or group setting environments are different than typical living arrangements.

Girls with ASDs may experience sexual side effects of medications
- Medications for mood and anxiety disorders can directly affect sexual functioning (e.g. low sex drive, difficulty achieving orgasm).

Girls with ASDs may face stereotypes or myths about their rights and others' attitudes
- Myths and stereotypes may limit the opportunities and information that individuals with ASDs receive.

Creating a basic sexuality education plan

There are three domains which form the building blocks of your daughter's sexuality education: social skill development, emotional understanding, and self-esteem. Sexuality is largely a social phenomenon, and ongoing work in social skills will help your daughter to place her sexuality education within a social context. Emotional understanding encompasses both awareness of one's own emotions and being able to interpret and respond appropriately to another person's emotions, nonverbal cues, and body language. Finally, healthy self-esteem fosters healthy sexuality development and is a critical component of sexual safety—girls with low self-esteem are more likely to engage in inappropriate sexual behaviors to feel accepted or loved. Always keep these three domains in mind, and work on them concurrently with the more specific goals that form your daughter's basic sexuality education plan.

Table 7.2 lists the content areas that are generally accepted in the literature as being central to developing healthy sexuality in youth with developmental disabilities. Previous chapters have already covered the building blocks, the body, and privacy. The following section will talk about teaching boundaries, and Chapter 8 will discuss abuse prevention in detail. Take a look at the table and think about your daughter's successes so far and what should be included next in her teaching plan.

In addition to these basic topics, a *comprehensive sexuality education curriculum* is recommended for teenage girls and young women for whom it is appropriate (depending on cognitive abilities, chronological and developmental age, interest, and motivation). A comprehensive plan includes the following more advanced topics:

- dating and relationship skills
- healthy sexual behavior (including intercourse)
- healthy relationships
- handling rejection experiences
- sexual responsibility (e.g. STIs, contraception)
- marriage
- raising a family (e.g. reproduction, giving birth, motherhood).

The Sexuality Education Council of the United States (SIECUS) (1992) and teachingsexualhealth.ca* have published documents in which they outline what they consider to be characteristics of a sexually healthy typically developing adolescent. If your daughter is of at least average intelligence it might be a helpful exercise for you to look at these documents for ideas of other areas to include in her comprehensive sexuality education curriculum. The subjects reviewed in these documents include healthy behaviors, decision-making, communication, values, self-esteem, identity, and relationship skills. By referencing these documents, some of the parents with whom we have worked have successfully advocated for the inclusion of these domains in

* Available at http://teachingsexualhealth.ca (accessed on March 22, 2008).

Table 7.2 Content of a basic sexuality education plan

Building blocks
- Social skills
- Emotional understanding
- Self-esteem

The body
- Parts and proper names
- Functions (excretion, reproduction, pleasure)
- Societal rules for body parts
- Personal hygiene
- Body image
- Doctor's examinations

Privacy
- What it means
- Private versus public places
- Private versus public behavior
- Private versus public topics
- Respecting other people's privacy

Boundaries
- Touching rules
- Appropriate expression of affection
- Able to be discriminatory (decide who will touch them and in what ways)
- Personal space rules

Abuse prevention
- Body parts (for reporting and credibility)
- Privacy and touching rules
- Body rights and ownership
- Understanding body warning signs
- Permission to say "no"
- Making choices
- Reporting offences
- Identifying appropriate and inappropriate behaviors
- Self-esteem and self-confidence

their daughter's individualized education plan (IEP) at school, thus laying the groundwork for their daughter's sexuality education.

Boundaries: personal space, touch, and affection

It was accepted when she was younger, but I wish I had had some of the information about behavior modification to teach her about appropriate physical contact before it became an issue. Now that she is 15, big, and developed, I have to remind her to shake hands and say "Hi, I'm Kayla" instead of barreling people over with her hugs. (Mother of a 15-year-old girl with autism)

Girls with ASDs often have difficulties with personal space and engaging in appropriate touch or affection based on how well they know someone (e.g. stranger versus grandparent). Importantly, "boundaries" includes both physical space and emotional or psychological space; girls with ASDs may have an easier time learning the less abstract concepts related to physical space (e.g. stand an arm's length apart when talking to someone) than learning the more psychological concepts such as why you do not discuss highly personal topics with someone you do not know well. Teaching your daughter about appropriate behavior, the importance of boundaries, and social rules around touching is essential, both for her social development and her personal safety. At minimum, your goal should be for her to learn the following skills.

- Respecting others' personal space when interacting with them or having a conversation with them.
- Demonstrating appropriate touch or affection with others depending on her relationship with them (i.e. not too close or intimate and also not too distant or detached).
- Appropriately communicating her comfort level with how others are interacting with her.
- Demonstrating appropriate conversational boundaries (e.g. types of topics, interrupting).

Below we review some techniques that we use with families to teach their daughters about personal space, touch, and affections. The techniques are organized into general strategies (e.g. visual supports), most of which should now be familiar strategies in your teaching toolkit.

Visual supports

One of the most commonly used strategies in teaching boundaries and touching rules is to use a "circles" concept to demonstrate levels of relationships, personal space, and appropriate touching (*see* Figure 7.2). Relationship circles take abstract concepts and make them concrete for learners by clearly demonstrating (in radiating circles) the level of closeness someone should have in a person's life (e.g. mailman versus grandmother). Each ring in the circle represents a specific level of intimacy (e.g. stranger, acquaintance, friend, boyfriend) and therefore corresponds to specific social behaviors that are appropriate (e.g. shake hands, hug, close hug), including topics of conversation (e.g. chat about the weather, sharing family problems). When we use circles programming, each girl is provided with her own ring of circles and a set of laminated cards representing various people, roles, topics, and social behaviors; the cards can be attached to the circles using Velcro. The girls are asked to place the names or roles of people in their life in the appropriate ring. They are then asked to add examples of appropriate social behaviors to each ring. Finally, they include examples of topics of conversations they could have with people in each ring. Moving beyond basic circles work, we talk about how people can move from one ring to another (closer

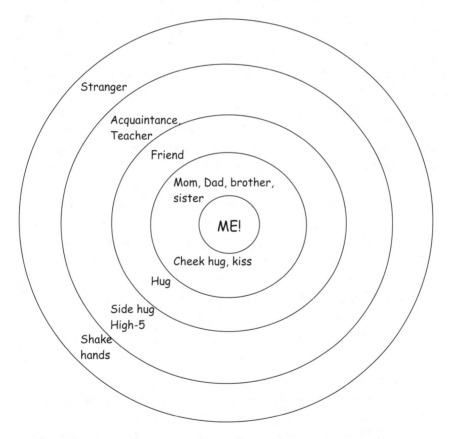

Figure 7.2 Example of a "relationship circle".

or further away) based on experiences that might happen in their lives (e.g. a friend betrays their trust, a friend becomes a boyfriend).

James Stanfield has marketed a wall-size Circles® program that may be purchased through their website (*see* Resources at the end of this chapter). You can also create your own program that best meets your daughter's needs. Involve her in creating the circles, choosing the people to include, and the behaviors that are appropriate. Use photographs of people in her life if that is going to make the concepts more meaningful and concrete for her. Using the relationship circle as a guide, role-play and practice personal space, appropriate touching, and expression of affection. When (if) she is ready, you can begin to talk about the kinds of affection reserved for girlfriends or boyfriends, husbands or wives, and life partners.

When we use this activity with girls in our groups, we sometimes have difficulty with girls who are too eager to have a boyfriend, and don't understand the concept of being friends first before starting to date. Velcro ends up flying as girls try to place close hugs and kissing beside boys they have crushes on. With repetition, role-playing, perspective-taking exercises (e.g. what would he think if you tried to kiss him at the dance but he didn't even know your name?) and further explanation, we are eventually able to come to a relationship circle that we all (mostly) agree on. Not easy, but we do get there. When girls are really struggling, we supplement group work with individual therapy in order to solidify concepts and provide girls with the privacy and trust they need to express feelings of sadness, loneliness, and confusion.

Visual aids are also effective in teaching personal space rules. One technique we use that girls tend to enjoy and understand is using hula hoops as personal-space bubbles. This can be a fun group activity—do not invade someone else's space! Visual and written cues can be provided as reminders throughout daily life to "remember the hula hoop." We also use the "one arm's length" rule to portray appropriate personal space. Remember, there are cultural variations when it comes to personal space. This is complicated for your daughter to learn, but important if she is immersed in an ethnically diverse community.

Role-playing and video modeling

Practice situations in which your daughter will be greeting, interacting with, and talking to others who are at different levels in her relationship circle. What greetings or expressions of affection are appropriate (e.g. shaking hands, high-fives, side-hugs, front-hugs, cheek-kisses)? Find out from typical peers at school what the "cool" ways are to greet someone these days. This is one of the important reasons we include typical peers in our social skills groups: they are our "inside scoop" on what is going on in schools. Also practice situations in which your daughter may need to "speak up" if her own personal space is being violated, or if someone is using inappropriate touch (*see* Chapter 8 for more information).

Video modeling is another effective way to teach your daughter how to interact appropriately with others. Video modeling involves having participants watch video clips, generally from 30 seconds to 10 minutes in length, of adults, peers, or themselves engaging appropriately in a targeted behavior (e.g. greeting someone). It has been suggested that video modeling is effective in part because attention is immediately directed to the screen; without attentional focus, learning is less likely to occur. Recent research has demonstrated that video modeling is effective in teaching a variety of skills, including social communication and social interactions (Bellini and Akullian 2007).

Prepare, redirect, and prompt

Girls who are just learning appropriate behavior may still often respond to social situations in an inappropriate manner. Prepare your daughter ahead of time by rehearsing common social situations. Provide her with portable visual and written reminders (e.g. cue cards) that she can refer to as needed. If she does respond inappropriately (e.g. if she attempts to hug a stranger), stop the interaction and redirect with the appropriate behavior (e.g. shaking hands). Sometimes people are taken aback by an overly intimate greeting and will not know how to respond. They don't want to seem rude by refusing an inappropriate hug, or physically keeping your daughter from hugging them, so it is up to you to teach your daughter that this is not acceptable behavior.

Stories and pictures

Create short stories or picture stories that illustrate the concepts of personal boundaries, personal space, and appropriate touch or affection. Take advantage of your daughter's special interests, or characters she might identify with, by using power cards to illustrate correct behavior. Be creative!

Television and movies

Take time with your daughter to watch developmentally appropriate television programs and movies. Point out violations of personal space, or inappropriate touch. Point out appropriate distance when interacting, appropriate greetings (e.g. shaking hands) and appropriate expression of affection (e.g. hugging a family member but not a stranger). *See* Chapter 2 for a list of recommended movies and strategies for teaching use film and television. In our experience, this can be a lot of fun!

Practice, practice, practice!

This strategy should by now be immersed in your repertoire. Always find opportunities for your daughter to practice her skills, and use lots of praise and reinforcement when she succeeds, or comes closer to succeeding. Life itself is full of teachable moments: they are there for you to utilize. During your day-to-day routine, when can you teach your child about boundaries, touch, and affection? How about at the grocery store, at restaurants, at the mall, at the movies, at school, while driving in the car, at family gatherings, or while watching television? Once you find yourself tuning into those perfect moments for teaching, you will be more and more likely to notice them and include them in your teaching for the day. This kind of learning is important for your daughter, and is much more valuable than what she can learn from sitting in a formal social skills class. Put on your "teachable moment" glasses, and look for opportunities. Soon they will appear more naturally than you think.

Sexual arousal and masturbation: what's normal for your daughter?

We now move from the comfort zone of boundaries and personal space to a topic that can be more difficult for parents to think about, but one that is important to your daughter's sexual wellbeing: sexual arousal and masturbation. For daughters with more limited abilities, self-pleasuring and masturbation may be the primary form of healthy sexual expression during adolescence and adulthood. Professionals in the field *all agree* that masturbation in private stems from physical sexual desire and is a natural and healthy expression of sexuality. If your culture or religion has different beliefs, speak with a senior member in your church or your cultural community for guidance and support.

Interest and curiosity in one's own private body parts starts early: infants, toddlers, and preschoolers discover that it feels nice when they touch their genitals; it can be comforting, soothing, and pleasurable (Lindblad *et al.* 1995). By the age of 9–12 years, masturbation begins to occur with greater frequency, and research indicates that by early adolescence males engage in masturbatory behaviors more frequently than same-aged females (Leitenberg, Detzer, and Srebnik 1993). General estimates are that between the ages of 15 and 16, approximately three-quarters of boys and over half of girls have masturbated. Unfortunately, here is where girls with ASDs suffer a double disadvantage: first they are female, and the sexuality of females is less understood and less accepted than that of males; second, they have an ASD, and the sexuality of youth with ASDs (whether male or female) is poorly understood.

In her award-winning book *Dilemmas of Desire. Teenage Girls talk about Sexuality*, Deborah Tolman (2002) writes that adolescent girls are currently perceived by society as interested primarily in love, relationships, and romance; as a result, their sexuality is defined *solely* as such. Little is known about sexual *desire* or *longing* in adolescent girls' experiences. She explains that girls have been desexualized, which has significant implications for how girls understand themselves, how they act in relationships, and how their sense of agency and self-esteem develops. From in-depth interviews with teenage girls about their sexual experiences and feelings, Tolman has learned that girls often do not know how to act, or what to feel. A subset of girls, she reports, are very much out of touch with their sexual feelings, and in interviews were unable to describe what sexual desire feels like, or what happens in their bodies. This problem is compounded in girls with ASDs who have trouble with body awareness to begin with, making it very difficult for them to properly understand and respond to their own sexual arousal.

Communicating with your daughter about arousal and masturbation

My daughter is 14. She is on the spectrum has OCD in varying degrees, and has a history of anxiety. She has recently discovered masturbation. I have told her that this touching is something private, appropriate for the bedroom, and that she needs to use good hygiene. I do not want to make a big deal of this or make her feel bad about it in any way, especially since she is not inappropriate with it thus far. (As an aside, I have not used the word "masturbation" with her for, though I believe mightily in educating people about their bodies, she tends to repeat certain things endlessly and to anyone and everyone... So it is "private touching" for now.) (Mother of a teenage girl on the autism spectrum)

As with sexual desire, female masturbation is rarely discussed. In our parent groups, we ask parents to think of euphemisms for male masturbation and for female masturbation. Inevitably, the list is much longer for male masturbation. If society believes that "good" girls do not experience sexual desire, why would they masturbate? The answer of course, is because they are human, and because it feels good!

You will need to be at least somewhat comfortable in order to communicate with your daughter about sexual arousal and masturbation. If self-stimulation is your daughter's primary outlet for sexual expression, you do not want her to feel as if she is doing something wrong, embarrassing, or dirty. First, make sure that she understands privacy rules: she should only masturbate in her bedroom with the door closed. Then, let her know that it is normal, natural, and that it feels good for her to touch herself in private. The general messages you should convey to your daughter about arousal and masturbation are the following.

- It feels good to touch your genitals, especially your clitoris (use visual supports as needed to show her where this is, or visit her physician).
- Touching your genitals is natural and part of being a girl.
- Touching your genitals is okay and it is something you do in *private, in your bedroom, when you are alone, and when the door is closed.*
- If you rub your genitals enough, you may have an orgasm. When this happens, the muscles in your vagina contract (squeeze) and it feels nice and warm.
- Masturbation is a private topic that you should only discuss with people you feel close to (review your relationship circle!). Talking about touching your genitals should only happen in *private* such as when you see the doctor or with your parent if you have questions or concerns.
- Sometimes girls want to touch themselves when they have romantic feelings about someone else.
- Sometimes girls think about someone when they touch themselves.

Difficulties that might arise

There are a number of common problems that you may encounter related to masturbation. If your daughter is touching herself in public, use visual supports and guidance (e.g. direct her to her room with the door closed) to show her where she needs to engage in masturbation. Narratives with visual supports can be developed about masturbation and about having special private time. If you need to, set up her daily schedule so that she has designated "private time". Be sure to inform her when private time is over and that she has other activities to do next.

Another difficulty you might come across is your daughter spending too much time masturbating. Not only can this result in physical irritation, but it can take away from the time your daughter has to engage in all the other important activities in her life. Make sure that there isn't a physical reason your daughter is engaging in frequent masturbation. A medication she is taking may make it difficult for her to achieve orgasm, which can leave her feeling frustrated. If she experiences irritation from touching herself, show her how to use a water-soluble lubricant such as KY® jelly or Astroglide®. Also, make sure that she lets any irritations heal before touching herself again. Sometimes girls with ASDs have difficulties achieving orgasm because of the motor coordination required, or because they cannot quite figure out the sequence of the movements. An excellent book and video to assist girls in learning about masturbation is *Finger Tips: A Guide for Teaching about Female Masturbation*, by Dave Hingsburger and Sandra Harr (*see* Resources). Talk with your daughter's physician if she is having difficulties achieving orgasm. Some females also use vibrators to provide sexual pleasure. A vibrator is a hand-held appliance that produces a steady, rapid rhythm which provides intense clitoral stimulation. Because motor coordination and dexterity are not necessary, vibrators can be much easier to use.

If your daughter has significant difficulty understanding the privacy concepts associated with masturbation, if she spends far too much time alone in her room, or if she has injured herself by masturbating too frequently or incorrectly, talk to your daughter's doctor. She may need more specific education and programming about masturbation.

Masturbation is not the easiest topic to discuss for anyone, especially female masturbation. If you approach the subject in a calm, clear, and accepting manner, your daughter will learn what she needs to know, and feel comfortable throughout the process. There are some very good websites that discuss female masturbation and orgasm and the functions of female sexuality anatomy. Some websites even provide instructions for females on how to masturbate if your daughter is having difficulty (*see* Resources).

Romantic feelings and being "interested" in someone

From our work with girls so far, we have observed that pre-teen and adolescent girls are generally at one of five levels with respect to awareness of and interest in dating. Table 7.3 lists these levels, which range from being completely unaware to having unhealthy obsessions. Level 4 (*Interested*) is often considered to be the goal for girls, and for many girls with ASDs this is an appropriate goal. However, some girls and women with ASDs will not be interested in dating or having a romantic partner; social demands can be perceived as too challenging, or sensory issues can make having a physical relationship difficult. For example, Temple Grandin has stated publicly that she is not, and will likely never be, interested in being in a relationship. Not wanting to date is perfectly acceptable. At her age, your daughter might not know yet how she feels. With time and social experiences, she will learn more about what she wants and what will be best for her.

Table 7.3 Levels of awareness and interest in dating

Level	Daughter's experiences	Intervention
1: Unaware	• Limited or no awareness of having romantic feelings or being attracted to someone • Often unaware that other girls are experiencing romantic feelings	• No active intervention is needed at this time • Developmentally, your daughter is a few years behind her peers • Pay attention to any emerging signs of her showing interest or becoming aware of others' interests
2: Uninterested	• Not interested in dating, but aware that other girls have romantic feelings or are interested in dating • May be adamant that they would *never* want to be in a relationship, and can't understand why anyone else would	• Work on your daughter's perspective-taking—why would others be interested in a relationship? • Without pressuring her, try to understand why she is not interested so you have a better awareness of your daughter's thoughts and feelings

3: Ambivalent	• Aware of other girls' interests, and may be starting to develop her own interests • Often nervous about dating; may say "Yes I want to date, but not now." • Often fears rejection and worries that she is not attractive or desirable • May not have the skills to tell someone she is interested in them • Self-esteem may be low	• Work on skill-building in dating and relationship skills • Work on developing self-insight, self-esteem, and confidence • A combination of group and individual work is often helpful
4: Interested	• Aware of her own and her peers' interests in dating and relationships • May be nervous and fear rejection, but is realistic, insightful, and has developed an understanding of when she is ready to date • Developing a sense of what kind of person she would be romantically interested in	• This is when active dating and relationship skill building takes place. Your daughter is ready to learn more about herself, others, and what she wants in a relationship (or in someone she would just like to date) • Group and individual work is often helpful
5: Desperate	• Experiences *heightened* awareness of other girls dating, and may present as desperate or obsessed • Often angry and jealous, fearful of rejection and never having a date, and may develop obsessions, typically with unrealistic pursuits. Coping with rejection can be particularly difficult • Self-esteem is in great jeopardy; lacks insight into her own needs and the kind of person she would like to date	• Individual work is essential as personal safety is often at risk • Mental health concerns can arise, including depression, anxiety, self-injury, and poor self-esteem • Intensive work on social understanding and skill building is needed

Case study: Maura

Maura has been involved in our Growing Up programming for many years. Two years ago, when she was 17, Maura was the only female member of a teen social skills group at our center. One of the other young men in the group was interested in Maura, but she did not reciprocate his feelings. At least, she didn't think she did. In fact, it caused her some stress because she did not feel ready to think about dating, or about being attracted to boys. A year later, Maura was attending a new school, which was a much more positive experience for her, and she developed a crush on another young man who we thought also had an autism spectrum disorder. This young man had more difficulties with social interactions and conversation than Maura did, and although she thought he might be interested in her, she was never quite sure. Though nothing happened with this young man, Maura had come to the realization that she was actually beginning to be interested in dating. Now in her first year at college, Maura has been attending weekly counseling. In a recent therapy session, Maura reported feeling lonely, and that while she still didn't want a "boyfriend" in the sense of a committed relationship, she stated that she would like for someone to be attracted to her; someone with whom she could talk and go on dates. In two years, Maura has progressed from "disinterested" to "ambivalent" to a healthy state of "interested." We are now beginning to work on how to meet people at college who share similar interests as her, and what kind of person Maura would be interested in getting to know better.

In our girls' groups, we have members who fit each of the five levels described in Table 7.3. With so many different perspectives on dating in one room, it is difficult for any of the girls to understand everyone else's perspectives. It is quite an experience to put six to eight girls with ASDs in a room, each at a different level of dating interest, and listen to them to talk to each other about why on earth they would or would not be interested in dating, or boys, or kissing, or why you should not rush, or why a certain boy should absolutely want to date you. This can be an exercise in futility without significant facilitator involvement, structured teaching activities, and a lot of group processing. But it can also be very successful, and it is an important experience for girls who are capable of dating. They need opportunities to think about whether they are aware of romantic interests, whether they feel ready to date, and, if so, what they need to know and learn in order to be able to do so successfully and safely. For girls who are clearly not ready, just listening to what others have to say is important as it gives perspectives to which they can compare their own feelings and experiences. This can be very helpful in guiding them toward a healthy interest in dating.

From romantic interest to dating

As the mother of a teenage girl, I must confess to appreciating some aspects of AS more than others. My daughter's insistence on being the "rules police" extends to her social life and dare I say burgeoning romantic life. She called me last night to tell me how upset she was with a good friend of hers because he had gotten drunk at an anime convention and lost his virginity. My daughter was horrified (A) that he was drinking, and (B) that he even considered having sex with someone to whom he wasn't married. I think I may have well exploited that rigidity! Perhaps it will better keep her safe for a while. I know that she is so emotionally immature in relationships that a sexual component would only make it worse. So I suppose I can exploit the rigidity and celebrate the fact that she just had to tell me when her boyfriend kissed her—because she is not allowed to kiss until she is 16. (Mother of a 15-year-old girl with Asperger's Syndrome)

Girls with ASDs often have difficulties understanding romantic feelings (back to body basics!), how to act on those feelings, and what constitutes healthy dating during adolescence and young adulthood. Knowledge and skills in these areas are essential for your daughter's safety and for healthy emotional development. Being able to establish a connection with someone is a wonderful experience for your daughter to work toward *if* that is something she desires. Important goals related to attraction and dating for your daughter to understand include the following.

Attraction

- Understands what it means to be attracted to or have romantic feelings for someone.
- Knows if she is attracted to someone.
- Can tell if someone is also interested in her.
- Understands what flirting means—what it is, and how to flirt appropriately and respectfully.

Communication of interest

- Understands how to express a romantic interest in someone appropriately.
- Knows when she is ready to go on a date.

- Is able to respond to being asked out on a date (by making a decision and accepting or declining).
- Is able to ask someone on a date.
- Has effective coping strategies for dealing with rejection.

Relationships

- Understands the "basics" about dating:
  - can get ready for a date (e.g. hygiene, grooming, dressing)
  - knows how to act during the date (appropriate social interaction and respectful of boundaries)
  - knows how to end the date
  - knows what to do if she does or does not want to go on a second date.
- Is able to recognize and respond to unhealthy dating situations:
  - how to end the date if she is uncomfortable
  - who to talk to if this happens
  - how she can make sure it does not happen again.
- Knows what to look for in a romantic partner ("boyfriend/girlfriend material").
- Knows characteristics of healthy and unhealthy relationships.
- Has developed self-esteem and assertiveness skills.
- Understands the progression of a relationship.

Many women have shared the difficulties that they have had with these skills. In *Women From Another Planet?*, Gail Pennington wrote about her high school experiences and her limited knowledge about how to express an interest in someone:

> I had no boyfriends in high school. If a boy liked me I had no clue. Sometimes I would hear a rumor that one did, but he would never approach me. I remember my father and stepmother being upset that I didn't have girlfriends or boyfriends, especially boyfriends. They wondered what was wrong with me. I hated *the feeling* that I was somehow defective, and statements like that I took as meaning that I was defective. I wasn't chasing boys away, but neither was I doing anything to attract them. Not that I knew how! When I liked a boy I would hope that he would somehow know. I mean, other girls got guys interested in them. I just didn't know how they did it. I asked advice a few times but never figured out the *instructions* I was given. (p.184)

In *Pretending to be Normal*, Liane Holliday Willey wrote about her inability to engage in flirting:

> I noticed how effortlessly the other girls seemed to be handling the crowd of young men. I noted too, that they were not shaking hands nor conversing very much at all. They were giggling and laughing and tossing their hair behind their shoulders, gently putting their hands on the boys' arms, looking totally lost in the limelight of the attention they are getting. I could see their formula, but I could not bring myself to follow it. (p.55)

Now is the time to determine what your daughter knows. Keep track in a notebook or journal if you need to; this information is going to form the basis of your teaching plan. Has she expressed a romantic interest in someone yet? Will she know when she is ready/comfortable to start dating? How does your daughter currently feel about dating? Anxious? Excited? Scared? Indifferent? Does your daughter understand the above important concepts? Does your daughter "speak up" when she is uncomfortable in an interaction?

There are three things that will assist you and your teaching team in working with your daughter on romantic interest and dating: (1) knowing what dating level she currently falls in; (2) knowing what concepts she clearly understands; and (3) knowing what the next steps are for her teaching. With that determined, you can begin to work on conceptual understanding and skill-building. The families with whom we have worked have reported success using the same strategies we mentioned earlier in the context of boundaries and personal space: visual supports; role-playing and video modeling; prepare, redirect, and prompt; stories and pictures; television and movies; and plenty of practice. The following are some specific visual strategies that families have found to be effective.

- Use a "body chart" to demonstrate how you might feel when you have a romantic interest in someone (e.g. heart beating, face flushed, tingling in genital area). It may be awkward to discuss sexual attraction, but it's really important!
- Use your relationship circles in as many creative ways as possible.
- Create a visual hierarchy to demonstrate appropriate behavior on dates (e.g. when would you hold someone's hand, when would you have a cheek kiss, when would you have a lip kiss?).

- Use lists of healthy and unhealthy behaviors that can occur on a date—put green checks beside healthy behaviors and red crosses beside unhealthy behaviors. Get your daughter engaged!
- Use written lists of steps for "date preparation", such as hygiene and grooming, getting dressed, making sure she has her pocket book and money, cell phone, emergency contact numbers, etc.

Family values and your daughter's age, ability level, and experience are going to play an important role in what you consider appropriate for your daughter. How do you feel about your older adolescent having her breasts touched? Think about these issues ahead of time so that you and your daughter are prepared. Many parents choose to convey the message "sex is for adults only", or "touching under clothing is for adults only." Make it very clear to your daughter what behaviors are appropriate; we will talk about "sex" in a later section of this chapter.

Safe and supported dating

So your daughter has romantic feelings for someone and would like to go out on a date. If you find this to be somewhat frightening, you are not alone! The best-case scenario (though you might not think so), is if the individual in question is also interested in your daughter. In that case we can begin to work on what we call "safe and supported dating". You may be wondering, isn't all dating supposed to be safe dating? Of course! Early dating for girls with ASDs, however, needs to be not only *safe* dating, but also *supported* dating. Safe dating incorporates everything we have been talking about so far, including knowing appropriate dating behaviors, what to do if things go wrong, and being assertive. Supported dating allows your daughter to ease into dating—it's like using training wheels, or taking the bunny slope on the ski hill. Table 7.4 outlines a progression of supported dating activities that range from adult-supported group outings to traditional dates with no adult supervision. Whether or not your daughter will ever be ready for fully independent dating, supported dating will help her develop independence and confidence, and will allow her to progress to the type of dating most appropriate for her abilities.

Some girls resist the idea of supported dating—particularly those who are at the "desperate" level of interest in dating. Often, these girls are trying to be like their neurotypical peers and want to be accepted into that peer group; supported dating is embarrassing for them because their parents are involved. Other girls respond well to supported dating: three of the girls whose parents are in our parent Growing Up groups have recently embarked on supported dating. Despite everyone being nervous, the dating events were successful, and one of the girls asked the boy she was interested in for a second date!

Table 7.4 Progressive safe and supported dating for your daughter

Activity	Description	Teaching strategies
Adult-supported group outing	• Your daughter spends time with the person she is interested in, in the company of other peers and with direct adult involvement; this could be part of a social skills group, or a group outing planned by parents • Your daughter will have opportunities to talk to and interact with the person she is interested in • Adults can facilitate interactions as needed; this can happen as part of a formal social skills group	• Work on greetings • Work on saying goodbye at the end of the event • Work on starting, maintaining, and ending conversations • Work on asking questions and showing interest in the other person • You may need to work on coping skills and anxiety management • Do lots of role-playing and video modeling!
Adult-observed group outing	• Your daughter spends time with the person she is interested in, in the company of other peers; adults play more of a peripheral role • For example, a group might go to the mall or to the movies, while the parents or group leaders hang back and only intervene as needed • May involve hand-holding or hugging	• Work on solidifying above skills • Role-playing is important in helping your daughter to develop natural social initiations • Discuss ways to express interest and how to recognize if the other person is interested in her • Work on self-monitoring and evaluation; after an outing, have her rate how it went, what she did well, and what she could improve on

Table 7.4 *cont.*

Activity	Description	Teaching strategies
Adult-supervised friendly date (non-traditional date activity)	• Parents of both youths speak together on the phone or, ideally, meet in person before the date • The date is highly structured and planned, and the activity is not "date-like"; in her book *Life and Love: Positive Strategies for Autistic Adults*, Zosia Zaks calls this an "alternative date" • Examples of alternative dates for adolescents can include going to the zoo, playing mini-golf, going for a walk, taking a computer class together, or "home-based" activities such as playing a board game or video game together and ordering pizza • Parents just hang back!	• Working on *one-to-one* conversation and interaction skills • Continue to role-play • Continue to work on self-insight, esteem, and confidence, and self-monitoring • Discuss how a date goes; if it doesn't go well, do a "social autopsy"; start from the beginning and break it down into all the steps and figure out what went wrong, and what could go differently next time
Adult-supervised date	• These dates are still highly structured and planned, but are more like traditional dates, such as movies, dinners, going for ice-cream, or going to dinner and then to a dance • Parents are present, but not involved • Depending on your daughter's skill level and comfort, you can either observe from a distance (e.g. sit in the back row of the movie theater) or just wait for her somewhere close by (e.g. in the lobby)	• This is when active dating and relationship skill-building takes place; your daughter is ready to learn more about herself, others, and what she wants in a relationship (or in someone she would just like to date) • Work on safety skills and appropriate dating behavior • This is when you will begin to discuss the next step of romantic behavior on a date, for example hugging and kissing good night; limiting physical and romantic closeness is important for setting boundaries and developing assertiveness skills • Group and individual work with a counselor can be helpful

| Traditional date | • Parents are still very involved in planning, but do not attend the date

• Make sure your daughter understands the details of the plan. Where and when will she meet her date? How will she get home, and at what time? What is her emergency contact? | • Continue to work on dating and relationship skills

• Talk with your daughter about what she liked, or did not like about her date

• Talk with her about sexual boundaries, saying "no", asserting herself |

Your daughter will also need to learn that just because she went on a date, that person is not her "lover" or "boyfriend". She may need to be taught explicitly what constitutes "having a boyfriend" and the social steps that lead up to this. Dating for teenage girls with ASDs should occur slowly and gradually, and depend on her progress with "dating etiquette", understanding safety, and her comfort level. We have recommended to many families that girls do not engage in "steady dating" until college or until after graduation. There is just too much to learn about themselves, and about dating and relationships, to rush into steady independent dating. In the next chapter, you will learn more about personal safety and keeping your daughter safe. In the Resources section at the end of this chapter, we have included some excellent websites that review dating violence and how teenage girls can keep safe when dating or in a relationship.

What about intercourse and intimate sexual activity?

At the start of this chapter we made the point that sexuality is not sex. So far we've talked about many dimensions of sexuality—from emotional understanding and body awareness to masturbation and romantic interests—and why they are all important for your daughter. Now we are ready to return to the subject of sex itself, and to tackle two questions that are probably already on your mind: Will your daughter be engaging in sexual intercourse? And, if so, what can you do to prepare her?

Whether or not your daughter will be interested in sexual intercourse or intimate sexual activity involving genital contact will depend on a number of factors, all of which we have already encountered at various points throughout this book. The first is *social motivation*: your daughter may or may not be interested in having a relationship that might involve physical sexual contact. Her thoughts and feelings about connecting with others will become more clear to her as she learns relationship skills and acquires experience throughout adolescence and young adulthood. Wendy Lawson wrote in her memoir *Life Behind Glass* about her evolution in understanding and desiring relationships:

> The ideas of "relationships", "marriage", and "family" are all-pervasive. It seems to me that people prefer the company of others, especially when they are afraid. While I have come to accept that desire, it is not one I fully understand. I am beginning to discover what it is like to enjoy the company of someone else and not feel afraid. Sometimes I am actually able to find comfort in being together with another person. This is something I have been developing over the past ten years. (p.12)

Your daughter's *social skills* will contribute greatly to her interpersonal relationships and to whether or not she engages in sexual intercourse. In her book *Asperger's Syndrome and Sexuality*, Isabelle Henault states that sexually active women with ASDs are likely to have sexual relations with many different partners, either simultaneously or sequentially. Your daughter needs to learn about boundaries and red flags in relationships, and to develop solid decision-making skills and judgment. Too frequently we have talked to girls with ASDs in our programs who say that they are ready to have sex after dating for only a few weeks! See the Resources at the end of this chapter and Chapter 8 for suggested readings related to boundaries, healthy relationships, and decision-making.

Intellectual ability is another important consideration when determining whether your daughter will be able to have a sexual relationship. In the next chapter, we will discuss consent for sexual activity, which at a minimum requires an understanding of the body and what happens during sexual contact.

Sensory factors are also particularly relevant for young women with ASDs. A number of women have written that intimate physical contact is too overwhelming to be pleasurable; smells, physical sensations, and sounds combine to create an experience that is anxiety-provoking, uncomfortable, and sometimes painful. Intercourse itself can be a challenge on its own even if other physical contact is not experienced as aversive. Liane Holliday Willey has written about sensory issues that affected her relationship with her husband:

> I knew that even though Tom recognized my differences, he was still interested in being with me. This gave me the go ahead to confess, if you will, every single sensory issue that exasperated, overran and confused me. It felt so liberating to

tell Tom my fingers felt like they were being torn apart when he interlocked his fingers with mine—that I felt bugs under my skin when he touched me lightly—that my mouth watered and my nose burned and my stomach turned when he wore certain kinds of cologne—or that when he came too near me, it took everything in me to keep from shoving him aside. (*Pretending to be Normal,* pp.83–84)

Motor coordination can affect a woman's ability to engage in a variety of sexual behaviors. If your daughter has significant difficulties with motor coordination, she may feel self-conscious and anxious when with a partner.

Finally, *communication impairments* may make it difficult for your daughter to express her desires, thoughts, or concerns (either verbally or nonverbally) regarding sexual behavior, or to be able to say "no" if she is not interested in having sex.

Parents with whom we have worked have handled discussions about "intercourse" in different ways, and the foundation of these discussions is rooted in family values ranging from waiting until marriage to engage in sexual activity, to being in a committed, monogamous relationship. Typically developing youth start to learn at school about the male and female reproductive systems in grade six. Depending on your daughter's age and intellectual ability, what you teach her about sexual intercourse will vary. You may want to discuss with your daughter's physician or with her psychologist how much information is appropriate, and when. A simple explanation that does not include details might be:

Sexual intercourse, or "making love", is when two people feel very attracted to each other and want to be as close to each other as possible in a sexual way. It feels nice and is a way for each person to express their love for the other person.

From there, explanations can become more detailed, including descriptions (and visuals) of the sexual response cycle and the act of intercourse (the man's penis goes inside the woman's vagina). As we've discussed all along, you want to put behaviors and actions in social context (e.g. why people have sex, why both people have to agree, why they do it in private, why they wear condoms and act responsibly).

For young women who will be learning about the details of sexual intercourse, they will also need to know about the following topics:

- contraception and practicing safe sex (e.g. use of condoms)
- sexually transmitted infections

- pregnancy and the reproductive cycle
- respecting others' desires and wishes (consent to sexual activity)
- abuse prevention
- responsibility and decision-making
- long-term relationships and marriage.

There are a number of books and curricula that cover basic explanations of sexual intercourse and also include more detailed information with visuals (*see* Resources). Remember to use your teaching toolkit and the strategies that are most effective for your daughter. Also, try to be prepared! Your daughter might show interest or ask you questions before you expect them. Have materials ready, and know what you want to tell her. From there, your conversations will unfold and follow a natural course as you learn more about what she needs to know, and when.

Your school's sexuality education curriculum: to participate, or not?

The *Guidelines for Comprehensive Sexuality Education*, published through SIECUS (1996), cover six key concepts that are considered important in a sexuality education curriculum. These concepts include: human development; relationships; personal skills; sexual behavior; sexual health; and society and culture. Based on the work of a large taskforce, the guidelines are a valuable resource for sexuality educators. In the guidelines, it is suggested that male and female reproductive systems, reproduction itself, and pubertal changes should be included in the curriculum for grades 6–8. The guidelines are very comprehensive, and each school in North America has its own plan for youth participating in health and sexuality education classes.

Unfortunately, no similar set of comprehensive guidelines exists for youth with developmental disabilities. However, in 2005, the Department of Education in Manitoba, Canada published a handbook entitled *Supporting Inclusive Schools: A Handbook of Developing and Implementing Programs for Students with Autism Spectrum Disorder*. One of the mothers with whom we were working in Colorado told us we really needed to take a look at this handbook. We thought, okay, maybe it will be a nicely outlined, comprehensive program for educating youth with ASDs—definitely worth a look. What we weren't expecting was an appendix entitled *Human Sexuality Education and the Student with ASD*. We were astounded, and of course thrilled. This was the first example we had seen of an education department recognizing that youth with ASDs might need sexuality education addressed with a different teaching approach.

In our work with middle and high schools, we are typically faced with three primary misconceptions: (1) she has an ASD so she does not need sexuality education; (2) yes, she has some impairments but we can probably just use the regular sexuality education curriculum we have; and (3) yes, she has an ASD but she is very bright; she will be fine in the regular sex education class. We're sure you can guess what our responses are: Yes, she needs sexuality education; and no, she likely won't be okay with the regular curriculum, even if she is very bright.

Based on their daughter's unique needs, parents with whom we have worked have made many different decisions regarding sexuality education for their daughter:

- Removed her entirely from the sexuality education curriculum and sought private services to address learning needs.

- Permitted her to participate only with active support from the teaching team; each lesson was sent home beforehand for preteaching and for review afterwards to ensure that concepts were understood.

- Requested individual sexuality education on her IEP, including the addition of sexuality education goals as part of the IEP.

- Had their daughter participate in some lessons (e.g. sexual health, factual classes) but not others (e.g. classes that addressed societal issues and abstract concepts).

Whatever your decision, it is best to make it with your educational team and, if possible, a professional in your community who has experience with sexuality issues and developmental disabilities. We have seen too many disastrous experiences that have set girls back in their learning: participation in the classes was actually harmful! Examples include girls thinking that if they have sex, a banana will be inserted into their vagina (they were unable to understand the symbolic representation of the banana), and girls being teased relentlessly for weeks or months later because they asked questions in class that their peers perceived as "stupid", "childish", or "prudish".

Making decisions about the role your daughter's school will play in her sexuality education is important. Schools and districts vary in how flexible they can be with respect to individualizing curricula. We have been invited to give workshops and training to teachers and school psychologists about educating youth with ASDs about sexuality. These situations typically have the best outcomes, as the team is informed and has a vested interest in your daughter's wellbeing and education. It can be so rewarding for school staff to see these girls attending the senior prom knowing that they are happy and safe.

Gender identity and sexual orientation

Like everyone else her age, your pre-teen or teenage daughter is developing a better understanding of who she is and what she enjoys in life. Part of this process involves developing her sexual identity, including her sexual orientation and gender identity. She will go about this in a different way than her neurotypical peers, and in particular if she is socially, emotionally, and psychologically less mature than her peers, it might happen at a slower rate. However, in the same way that your daughter's disability does not prevent her body from developing during puberty, it also won't prevent her from developing a sexual identity as she enters her later teen years and young adulthood, if not sooner.

Sexuality and ASDs is a topic that is rarely addressed to begin with; certain aspects of sexuality, such as diversity and gender identity, are discussed even less often, which has resulted in a much-neglected area of study. Even within the general developmental disabilities literature, little work has been done to understand gender and sexual identity, sexual preferences, and sexual orientation of individuals with disabilities.

If gender is socialized from a young age, and girls with ASDs are less interested or less aware of the socialization of gender, and of being female, will issues related to acceptance and understanding of one's gender arise later? Preliminary studies in the literature point to a possible link between ASDs and concerns with gender identity (Abelson 1981; Gallucci, Hackerman, and Schmidt 2005; Mukkades 2002); however, not enough work has been done to truly understand how girls with ASDs experience their gender. In her book, *Congratulations It's Asperger Syndrome*, Jen Birch discusses her early experiences with gender:

> My preference, at this time, for male company (because it was proving to be less problematic than female company) was also part of my life-long feeling of androgyny. I had never felt like a girl...so how, therefore, could I fit in with girl-only groups? Again, in hindsight, it seems to be a matter of the "secret language of in-

direct communication" which was at least one component of my deficits in all-female company—I could not decipher the code. Also, I have, for a lifetime thus far, lacked the "feminine" desires to dress prettily, use make-up, wear jewelery, follow fashion, style my hair, or have babies. When, in adulthood, I learned the word "androgyny"—that is, neither male nor female, or having equal amounts of both—I was glad to have a word to describe how I felt. (pp.120–121)

Gender identity, which is one's sense of being a male (boy) or a female (girl), develops in neurotypical children approximately between 18 and 30 months of age (Steinberg, Belsky, and Meyer 1991). Gender stability happens some-what later, and is the understanding that gender is a stable trait: girls will stay girls, and boys will stay boys. We know very little about this process in children with ASDs. There are reports in the literature and in early inter-vention treatment programs that preschoolers with ASDs have difficulties identifying boys and girls, and using "he" and "she" correctly. In fact, teach-ing programs have been developed that target these goals specifically. The socialization of gender identity may also occur very differently for males and females with ASDs. Some women with ASDs have shared their experi-ences in trying to understand their identity. In *Women From Another Planet? Our Lives in the Universe of Autism*, Mary Margaret wrote:

> My gender came in question at that time—the boys would say, "You aren't like other girls. You don't cry when you get hurt, so you are better than other girls, but you aren't a boy, so you are a Mary Margaret." Of course it was lonely being given a category to myself and it taught me to hate my gender. It would take feminist readings many years later to move me out of my male-identified posi-tion. (p.38)

In the same book, Jean Kearns Miller wrote:

> For some of us here, our lives, outlook, and behavior don't have much of a sense of gender at all. I myself live a somewhat femme life but it feels in some sense detachable, like a costume. I was an androgynous kid and most clearly perceive the world in a non-gendered way. (p.38)

We also know little about the relationship between ASDs and sexual ori-entation. To date, there is no empirical evidence of different rates of sexual orientations in individuals with ASDs (heterosexual, homosexual, bisexual). In a study of 24 high-functioning young males (verbal IQ greater than 70) living in a group home, Hellemans and colleagues (2007) reported that 17% of youth self-reported either homosexual (4%) or bisexual (13%) orienta-tions. There were no women in the study. In her book, *Asperger's Syndrome and Sexuality*, Isabelle Henault includes a chapter entitled "Sexual Diversity and Gender Identity". In it, she reviews cases of male and female youth and adults with ASDs with differing sexual orientations and their experiences of their gender. She highlights the importance of understanding what contributes to experiences of sexual orientation and gender identity for individuals with ASDs.

In the autobiographical literature there are many examples of women with ASDs with non-heterosexual orientations who have had healthy sexual experiences and lead healthy sexual lives. Jeanette Purkis, Jen Birch, Martine Stonehouse, Wendy Lawson, Zosia Zaks, and others have candidly shared their experiences through their writing and public speaking about sexual experiences growing up, both positive and negative, and their current lifestyles (*see* Resources).

How can I support my daughter?

Your daughter may be exploring her sexuality in many different ways. As a parent, your role is to support her self-understanding and provide teaching and guidance as necessary. At some point, your daughter might be wondering about her gender identity or sexual orientation, or she may have questions about how she is feeling. She may not be interested in boys as you might have expected, or she may be confused about feelings of attraction. Using the strategies in your toolkit, assist your daughter in understanding that people can be attracted to males, females, or both. Help her to explore how she might be feeling.

Our professional stance with young women is that all sexual orientations are acceptable, and that exploring one's sexual orientation and preferences is natural. However, we live in a society in which heterosexuality is still often seen as the only acceptable sexual orientation, and this can be a highly sensitive topic for many people. If you are struggling with accepting or understanding your daughter's sexual development, we recommend that you seek guidance within your cultural and religious communities, and also from professionals who work in this area. There are also many excellent books and online resources about sexual orientation and youth. *Advocates for Youth* has a wonderful set of resources for parents and their youth who are questioning gender and sexual identity and orientation. The only resource we know of that is specific to developmental disabilities is a book by John D. Allen entitled *Gay, Lesbian, Bisexual, and Transgender People with Developmental Disabilities and Mental Retardation. Stories of the Rainbow Support Group.* Don't be afraid to get the help you need in order to be supportive of your daughter—she should feel that she is accepted by her family, and that it is safe for her to express her feelings. How you respond to her is going to directly affect her self-esteem and sense of worth as a person.

Providing reading materials for your daughter

Unfortunately, there are few teaching materials available that are appropriate for youth with ASDs, particularly youth with cognitive impairments or reading difficulties. There are, however, a number of books written for typically developing teens that we have used in an instructional context to teach girls with ASDs (*see* Resources). When using such books, it is important to pre-read them and decide ahead of time which sections are appropriate for your daughter and will be effective in meeting your teaching goals. For example, *Unmasking Sexual Con Games. A Teen's Guide to Avoiding Emotional Grooming and Dating Violence*, by Kathleen McGee and Laura Buddenberg, has an excellent section on dating steps (pp.72–79) which we have found is accessible to many of the girls in our programming. It clearly walks teens through seven dating steps, and helps to teach the importance of establishing opposite-sex friendships before jumping into dating. It also has a parent's guide and a guide for facilitators who want to use the program with a group. *Boundaries. A Guide for Teens*, by Val Peter and Tom Dowd, is written in a clear, concise manner and includes exercises that may be completed as part of a group, or as individual work, or with a parent. The *American Girl* series has a book entitled *A Smart Girl's Guide to Boys; Surviving Crushes, Staying True to Yourself, and Other Stuff*, which we also like to use. It has excellent concrete information on handling rejection, turning down a date, and importantly for some girls at the "desperate" level of dating interest, determining if you are "boy crazy".

To our knowledge, there are only two books that have been written specifically for youth with ASDs. *Autism–Asperger's & Sexuality: Puberty and Beyond* was written by Jerry and Mary Newport, a married couple who both have Asperger's Syndrome. It includes excellent information for youth, but be aware that it does come with a parental guidance recommended label on the cover. *A '5' Is Against the Law! Social Boundaries: Straight Up! An Honest Guide for Teens and Young Adults*, by Kari Dunn Buron, includes important information for teens with ASDs about boundaries and boundary-crossing. The information is presented visually and logically in a manner accessible to youth with ASDs. Our own group is working on developing appropriate reading materials for teen girls and boys with ASDs, and we hope other professionals will begin to publish books and manuals that will assist girls with ASDs in navigating this difficult time.

Resources

Books for youth with ASDs

Brown, K.L. and Brown, M. (1997) *What's the Big Secret? Talking About Sex with Girls and Boys.* Boston, MA: Little, Brown, and Company.

Buron, K.D. (2007) *A '5' Is Against the Law! Social Boundaries Straight Up: An Honest Guide for Teens and Young Adults.* Shawnee Mission, KS: Autism Asperger Publishing Company.

Harris, R. (1994) *It's Perfectly Normal: Changing Bodies, Growing Up, Sex & Sexual Health.* Cambridge, MA: Candlewick Press.

Holyoke, N. (2001) *A Smart Girl's Guide to Boys, Surviving Crushes, Staying True to Yourself, and Other Stuff.* Middleton, WI: American Girl Press.

Mayle, P. (1977) *Where Did I Come From?* New York, NY: Kensington Publishing Corp.

McGee, K. and Buddenberg, L. (2003) *Unmasking Sexual Con Games—A Teen's Guide.* Boys Town, NE: Boys Town Press.

Newport, J. and Newport, M. (2002) *Autism–Asperger's & Sexuality: Puberty and Beyond.* Arlington, TX: Future Horizons Publishers.

Packer, A.J. (1997) *How Rude!: The Teenagers' Guide to Good Manners, Proper Behavior, and Not Grossing People Out.* Minneapolis, MN: Free Spirit Publishing.

Packer, A.J. (2004) *The How Rude! Handbook of Friendship & Dating Manners for Teens: Surviving the Social Scene.* Minneapolis, MN: Free Spirit Publishing.

Peter, V.J. and Dowd, T. (2000) *Boundaries: A Guide for Teens.* Boys Town, NE: Boys Town Press.

Books for parents—autism and developmental disability focus

Allen, J.D. (2003) *Gay, Lesbian, Bisexual and Transgender People with Developmental Disabilities: Stories of the Rainbow Group.* New York, NY: Harrington Park Press.

Bolick, T. (2001) 'Friendship and intimacy.' In *Asperger Syndrome and Adolescence. Helping Preteens and Teens Get Ready for the Real World.* Gloucester: Fair Winds Press.

Drury, J., Hutchinson, L. and Wright, J. (2000) *Holding On Letting Go. Sex, Sexuality, and People with Learning Disabilities.* London: Souvenir Press Limited.

Ford, A. (1987) 'Sex education for individuals with autism: Structuring information and opportunities.' In Cohen, D.J., Donnellan, A.M., Paul, R. (eds) *Handbook of Autism and Pervasive Developmental Disorders.* Maryland: Winston and Sounds.

Griffiths, D.M., Quinsey, V.L. and Hingsburger, D. (1989) *Changing Inappropriate Sexual Behavior: A Community-Based Approach for Persons with Developmental Disabilities.* Baltimore, MD: Paul H. Brookes Publishers.

Hingsburger, D. (1993) *I Openers: Parents ask Questions about Sexuality and Children with Developmental Disabilities.* Vancouver, BC: Family Support Institute Press.

Lawson, W. (2005) *Sex, Sexuality, and the Autism Spectrum.* London: Jessica Kingsley Publishers.

Maksym, D. (1990) *Shared Feelings. A Parent Guide to Sexuality Education for Children, Adolescents, and Adults Who Have a Mental Handicap.* Toronto: The G Allan Roeher Institute.

Monat-Haller, R.K. (1992) *Understanding & Expressing Sexuality: Responsible Choices for Individuals with Developmental Disabilities.* Baltimore, MD: Paul H. Brookes Publishing Co.

Schwier, K. and Hingsburger, D. (2000) *Sexuality: Your Sons and Daughters with Intellectual Disabilities.* Baltimore, MD: Paul H. Brookes Publishing Co.

Shea, V. and Gordon, B. (1991) *Growing Up: A Social and Sexual Education Picture Book for Young People with Mental Retardation.* Chapel Hill, NC: University of North Carolina at Chapel Hill.

Walker-Hirsch, L. (2007) *The Facts of Life…and More: Sexuality and Intimacy for People with Intellectual Disabilities.* Baltimore, MD: Paul H. Brookes Publishing Co.

Personal accounts by women and young women

Birch, J. (2003) *Congratulations! It's Asperger Syndrome.* London: Jessica Kingsley Publishers.

Holliday Willey, L. (1999) *Pretending to be Normal.* London: Jessica Kingsley Publishers.

Jackson, N. (2002) *Standing Down, Falling Up.* Bristol: Lucky Duck Publishing Ltd.

Miller, J.K. (ed.) (2003) *Women From Another Planet?* Bloomington, IN: 1st Books Library.

Stonehouse, M. (2002) *Stilted Rainbow: The Story of My Life on the Autistic Spectrum and a Gender Identity Conflict.* Toronto: Martine Stonehouse.

Teaching resources for parents and professionals

Adams, J.I. (1997) 'Relationships, the family and sexuality.' In *Autism-PDD: More Creative Ideas from Age Eight to Early Adulthood.* Kent Bridge, ON: Adams Publications.

Attainment Company (1996) *Learn About Life: Sexuality and Social Skills.* Syracuse, NY: Program Development Associates.

Dalrymple, N., Gray, S. and Ruble, L. (1991) *Sex Education: Issues for the Person with Autism.* Bloomington, IN: Indiana Resource Center for Autism.

Gray, S., Ruble, L. and Dalrymple, N. (1996) *Autism and Sexuality: A Guide for Instruction.* Bloomington, IN: Indiana Resource Center for Autism.

Henault, I. (2005) *Asperger's Syndrome and Sexuality: From Adolescence through Adulthood.* London: Jessica Kingsley Publishers.

Karakoussis, C., Calkins, C.F. and Eggeling, K. (1998) *Sexuality: Preparing your Child with Special Needs.* Kansas City, MO: Developmental Disabilities Resource Center on Sexuality.

Kerr-Edwards, L. and Scott, L. (2003) *Talking Together… About Sex and Relationships: A Practical Resource for Schools and Parents Working with Young People with Disabilities.* London: Family Planning Association.

McKee, L., Kempton, W. and Stiggall-Muccigrosso, L. (2001) *An Easy Guide to Loving Carefully for Women and Men.* Haverford, PA: Winifred Kempton Associates.

Scott, L. and Kerr-Edwards, L. (1999) *Talking Together… About Growing Up. A Workbook for Parents of Children with Learning Disabilities.* London: Family Planning Association.

Steege, M. and Peck, S. (2006) *Sex Education for Parents of Children with Autism.* Syracuse, NY: Program Development Associates.

Teach-a-Bodies®: Provides professionals and parents with anatomically correct, instructional dolls to help break down barriers when communicating with children. The Teach-a-Bodies® product line features a culturally sensitive full range of anatomical dolls, lifesize dolls, paper dolls, booklets, as well as an extensive collection of doll accessories. Available at www.teach-a-bodies.com

Books for parents: typical developmental resources

Engel, B. (1997) *Beyond the Birds and the Bees. Fostering Your Child's Healthy Sexual Development in Today's World.* New York, NY: Simon & Schuster.

Haffner, D. (1999) *From Diapers to Dating. A Parent's Guide to Raising Sexually Healthy Children.* New York, NY: Newmarket Press.

Haffner, D. (2002) *Beyond the Big Talk. Every Parent's Guide to Raising Sexually Healthy Teens—From Middle School to High School and Beyond.* New York, NY: Newmarket Press.

Video resources

Hingsburger, D. and Haar, S. (2000) *Finger Tips: A Guide For Teaching About Female Masturbation* [video and manual]. Newmarket, ON: Diverse City Press, Inc.

James Stanfield Company: extensive video library on topics such as sexuality and relationships, abuse prevention, social skills, and life skills. Available at www.stanfield.com

Program Development Associates (1991) *Person to Person: Sexuality Education for Persons with Developmental Disabilities* [video]. Syracuse, NY: Program Development Associates.

Program Development Associates (1999) *All of Us: Talking Together. Sex Education for People with Developmental Disabilities* [video]. Syracuse, NY: Program Development Associates.

Websites related to sexuality

American Association of Sexuality Educators, Counselors, and Therapists. Available at www. aasect.org

Sex Information and Education Council of Canada. Available at www.sieccan.org

Sex Information and Education Commission of the United States. Available at www.siecus.org

Websites related to masturbation

Corinna, H. *Is Masturbation Okay? (Yep.)* Scarleteen: Sex Ed for the Real World. This site has a lot of information on masturbation, including "how to" and what an orgasm is. www.scarleteen.com/article/pink/is_masturbation_okay_yep

How to Masturbate for Women. Cool Nurse. Provides instructions for females on how to masturbate. Available at www.coolnurse.com/masturbation_howto.htm

It's Normal, Healthy and Okay to Masturbate! Cool Nurse. Provides important information about masturbation for youth. Available at www.coolnurse.com/masturbation.htm

CHAPTER 8

Keeping Girls Safe: Promoting Personal Safety in the Real World

I worry about the potential for Kayla being abused by someone because of her autism, because she is vulnerable. I hope that I will be able to protect her in that regard. (Mother of a 15-year-old girl with autism)

When we began to develop our Growing Up on the Autism Spectrum program, we conducted focus groups with many families about their hopes and concerns as their child enters adolescence and young adulthood. For parents of girls with ASDs, the three most frequently shared fears were that their daughter would be abused, that she would get pregnant (if this was not desired or planned), and that she would not find someone who would love her. Sadly, our families' concerns are not unfounded. Females with developmental disabilities are among the most vulnerable members of society and are at great risk for experiencing high rates of physical, emotional, and sexual abuse. There are, however, things you can do to help your daughter protect herself and increase the likelihood that she will *not* experience abuse. In this chapter we will review what is known about exploitation and autism. We will discuss how to keep your daughter safe, and how to keep *her* from crossing *others'* boundaries in a way that might be interpreted as inappropriate. We will review abuse-prevention strategies for girls, and what to do if you think or know your daughter has experienced some kind of abuse. We will also spend some time focusing on specific topics that are important for your daughter's safety, such as safe dating, sexual harassment and bullying at school, consent to sexual activity, and safety on the internet.

We know that this is not an easy topic to think about. Many of the families with whom we have worked have told us that they wish they could protect their daughter forever and keep her from having to learn about abuse. We applaud you for being open to the information in this chapter, and for making the choice to embark on a journey of learning in order to keep your daughter safe. Ignoring these issues will not make them go away. Below we have outlined what we consider to be the personal safety rights for girls with ASDs. Everyone deserves to be treated respectfully; being reminded of what your daughter deserves can be empowering for yourself and for her, and feeling empowered can lead to action—even if it's difficult to do.

Personal safety rights of girls with ASDs

Girls and women with ASDs of all ages and ability levels have the right to:

- Feel safe…and *be safe*.
- Speak up…and *be heard*.
- Ask for help…and *be helped*.
- Set their own boundaries…and say "no" when appropriate.
- Listen to their feelings, what their "gut" is telling them.
- Be treated with dignity and respect.
- Make the right choices for themselves, with assistance as needed.
- Feel like they belong.
- Develop independence.
- Feel good about themselves.
- Learn how to protect themselves.

Abuse and developmental disabilities

The numbers are alarming. Although we don't want to shock or scare anyone, we do want to present the unfiltered truth, because only by confronting reality will you be fully prepared to protect your daughter. The reality is that the rate of abuse for females with developmental disabilities is startlingly high. Findings from a national study indicate that 39–83% of females and 16–32% of males with a developmental disability will be sexually abused before they reach 18 years of age (Baladerian 1991). Baladerian also reported that 97–99% of abusers are known and trusted by the victim. Dick Sobsey, one of the foremost researchers in abuse prevention and disabilities, found that more than 70% of women with developmental disabilities had been sexually assaulted, and that almost half of women with cognitive impairments have been assaulted up to ten times in their lifetime (Sobsey 1994; Sobsey and Doe 1991).

These are frightening statistics, but what is even more frightening is that society has not yet fully confronted the problem. The abuse of individuals with disabilities is a subject people tend to avoid, resulting in inaction. Admitting that abuse occurs is the critical first step toward making a difference in prevention, education, and policy.

Abuse and ASDs

Though the issues have not yet been explored in the literature, girls and women with ASDs may be at a greater disadvantage than other females with developmental disabilities because of the core difficulties they experience with social reciprocity and understanding. For these reasons, risk of exploitation may also be higher; recognizing "red flags" of dangerous situations and interpreting the thoughts, intentions, and behavior of others can be particularly challenging for girls with ASDs. Jen Birch, a woman with Asperger's Syndrome, wrote about her experiences having social vulnerabilities in her memoir, *Congratulations! It's Asperger Syndrome*:

> Other people have told me, at various times in my life, "Listen to your feelings about a situation; feel the vibes; trust your instincts—and thus be forewarned about dubious situations." But!—I did not have any feelings, vibes, or instincts in the sphere of social relating, so I had nothing inside me for guidance. Therefore, I had no "alarm bells" available to warn me of impending danger—where people were concerned, at any rate. I was also "slow on the uptake" in these matters, and unable to learn what had gone wrong from one time to the next. I usually had to make the same mistake a number of times before I could work out that it was a bad idea, which meant that I was getting into risky situations over and over again. (pp.82–83)

In her autobiographical account *Pretending to be Normal*, Liane Holliday Willey describes a similar experience during an interaction with a stranger who appeared in her classroom while she was preparing to teach a college class:

> I had yet to stop and worry about his presence in my classroom. I was more curious, more intrigued by the effect he had on my quiet room, than I was by the possible effect he could have on my safety. He told me he had been in jail, that he had just been released. A tiny bell sounded in my thoughts to alarm my suspicions, but I barely heard it. I was simply too engrossed by his moldy appearance to make much of a decision about his possible motives. Ironically, though

it was my AS that kept me from understanding this man was oddly misplaced at the best, and harmful at the worst, it was also my AS that helped me to realize I was in trouble. The tiny bell turned into a blaring alarm the moment he came within an arm's length away from me. I am disturbed anytime anyone breaks my personal space rule, but in this case, I was mortified. The instant he violated my space, I backed up... It never dawned on me to scream. It did not occur to me to run... The experience at the university pointed out to me just how little I understood about human behavior. Objectively, I was able to see how close my inability to judge a person's motive properly had brought me to personal harm, but I still could not categorize what made one person safe, another fun, another someone to build a relationship with or another someone to avoid. (pp.66–67)

Other women with ASDs have also written about abuse experiences in their books (e.g. *Life Behind Glass* by Wendy Lawson; *Songs of the Gorilla Nation* by Dawn Prince-Hughes; *Finding a Different Kind of Normal* by Jeanette Purkis), adding strong testimonials that reinforce the realities faced by young women with ASDs when they are not taught social rules and abuse-prevention skills.

Two large-scale population-based studies found no differences in rates of abuse between children with autism and other disabilities (Spencer *et al.* 2005; Sullivan and Knutson 2000); however, these studies focused primarily on very young children and vulnerability arising from intellectual impairments. What about the impact of having social-cognitive deficits? Is it possible that the risk of abuse might *increase* for young women with ASDs as they get older and are functioning more independently in the community? If girls are not taught abuse-prevention strategies when they are younger, vulnerability may increase as they grow up and spend less time with parents and other adults who had been able to watch out for them more closely when they were children.

Few published studies have examined the prevalence of abuse in autism and its psychosocial impact. Investigators at the University of Pennsylvania (Mandell *et al.* 2005b) looked at information collected from the families of 156 children with autism and found that almost one in five youth (average age 11.6 years) had been physically abused, and one in six had experienced sexual abuse (parent reports of abuse). The effect of abuse was significant in that youth were reportedly more likely to have engaged in sexual acting-out behaviors, to have run away from home, or to have made a suicide attempt. Cook and colleagues (1993) reported a case study of an adolescent male with autism who had been physically abused by a staff member at his residential school. The teen began to show signs of post-traumatic stress disorder (PTSD) and was eventually able to report to his parents that he had been hit repeatedly by a teacher. Symptoms experienced by the teen included fear, agitation and anxiety, nighttime wakening, crying spells and increased rocking, loss of interest in activities he had previously found enjoyable, and avoidance of situations related to the trauma. In individual therapy, the young man began to improve as he was able to share his feelings about his experiences and also learn that he was safe and would no longer be put in a fearful environment. *Fighting for Darla* (Brantlinger, Klein, and Guskin 1994) is a case study about a 15-year-old girl with autism and severe mental retardation. Darla had lived at a school for adolescents with autism for two months when it was discovered by staff that she was five months pregnant. Raising issues related to sexual expression of youth with disabilities, vulnerability to abuse, sterilization, sexual decision-making, and professional and community attitudes, *Fighting for Darla* is a compelling story and an important read, particularly for professionals, about the vulnerabilities of young women with disabilities and the complexities of the real world in which Darla, her family, and the professionals who worked with her found themselves.

The impact of abuse on females with ASDs is significant and can result in post-traumatic stress with long-lasting effects across all areas of a girl's life. Unfortunately, not everyone is aware that individuals with ASDs are capable of experiencing the negative effects of having been abused. We received a telephone call one day from the attorney of a family whose daughter with severe autism had been sexually assaulted in a very aggressive manner by her employer. He contacted us to inquire whether we felt this family could proceed with filing an assault claim. In his understanding of autism, individuals with ASDs would not feel hurt or exploited because they were not capable of understanding the nature of human relationships and emotions. He was very wrong! Impaired social and emotional understanding does *not* in any way affect an individual's experiences of fear, pain, anger, hurt, or confusion. The young woman in question did have limited social understanding, but she had been taught by her family and others that her body was her own, that she could say "no", and that no one was allowed to touch her against her will. Her boundaries were violated, and though she didn't understand to the same degree as others what that meant at a social or conceptual level, she knew that she had said "no", yet something painful happened anyway. Her trust and her belief in herself as an effective human being was violated. That is assault.

We can all do our part to educate others about the nature of autism, and what it does and does not mean for how girls experience harmful situations.

As stated in Chapter 7, there are still far too many myths in society's understanding of sexuality and developmental disabilities, and ASDs in particular. *Every* female with an ASD who is assaulted or abused experiences its negative effects. For girls with stronger thinking skills, their understanding of what happened may be at a deeper conceptual level than for girls with more cognitive impairments. However, a lack of conceptual understanding does *not* prevent abuse from being scary or painful. The evidence is very clear—abuse hurts.

How to keep your daughter safe: abuse-prevention strategies

Because girls with ASDs are at much greater risk for exploitation than their typically developing peers, learning skills to reduce vulnerability to victimization is essential. By teaching them the skills they need to be safe, the risk of abuse is greatly reduced. In his book *Just Say Know! Understanding and Reducing the Risk of Sexual Victimization of People with Developmental Disabilities,* Dave Hingsburger (1995) outlines what he calls the "Ring of Safety," a protective set of seven skills for keeping individuals with developmental disabilities safe: options for healthy sexuality; sex education; privacy awareness; ability to non-comply; someone who listens; understanding of personal rights; and healthy self-concept and self-confidence. Other authors in the developmental disabilities field have also outlined what they consider to be the most important components of a proactive safety plan. In the following sections we will describe the elements of our own "keeping safe" plan, which we have found to be important and successful in our work with girls and women with ASDs. This plan always starts with social skills development, which serves as the first step toward safety and supports all other components. As we have emphasized in previous chapters, it is important to think about your daughter's skill level, communication abilities, and the teaching strategies that have been most effective with her in the past. You will want to apply these approaches when working on her "keeping safe" skills.

Social skills

In the last chapter we talked about how important social skills are in the development of healthy sexuality for girls with ASDs. Naturally, the same emphasis needs to be placed on social skills in the interest of promoting personal safety. Healthy sexuality is embedded in healthy human relation- · ships. The more your daughter is able to learn, understand, and experience about people and relationships, the better she will be able to recognize *unhealthy* and *inappropriate* behaviors, situations, and relationships. Even for a girl who has limited communication skills and is cognitively impaired, if she has learned that when she has a bath *only she* uses a washcloth to clean her vaginal area, she will be able discriminate between appropriate behavior (e.g. a caretaker hands her a washcloth to use) and inappropriate behavior (e.g. a caretaker begins to clean her and touch her private body parts). Think of all the social skills and understanding that are important for personal safety. As discussed in Chapters 6 and 7, you may want to work closely with a psychologist or a speech-language pathologist who has experience with social skills and social communication development in order to assess your daughter's current skills and develop an instruction plan with personal safety in mind.

Social communication

At its most basic, *social communication* is the ability to communicate one's wants and needs and request attention from another. From there, social communication becomes endlessly complex and forms the basis for establishing multilayered intimate relationships with others. Without the ability to communicate, your daughter will not be able to assert herself, refuse, protest, say "no", communicate fear or dislike, or indicate that something has happened to her that should not have. For girls who are conversationally verbal, social communication development is essential in enabling them to stick up for themselves, clarify boundaries, ask for things to change, or end an unhealthy relationship. Regardless of your daughter's skill level, ongoing work on social communication is essential for keeping her safe.

What if your daughter is nonverbal, or has limited expressive language skills? Perhaps your daughter speaks in full sentences, but verbal communication is stressful for her and if she is overwhelmed she is not able to communicate well without the additional support of visuals. Fortunately, there are visual tools available that are related to sexuality and personal safety. *Boardmaker®* (*see* Resources at the end of this chapter), a well-known augmentative communication program published by Mayer-Johnson, has an addendum library entitled "Communicating about Sexuality", with over 400 picture communication symbols and 48 communication boards about sexuality and keeping safe. It was developed in collaboration with the "Speak Up Project" in Toronto, Canada, whose goal was to support abuse prevention for individuals using augmentative communication. More information about the Speak Up Project, including examples of communication displays and how to use them, can be found at the project website (*see* Resources). The breadth of topics covered across the communication displays is exceptional, and includes basics such as external and internal body parts, relationships and identity, and more specific visuals such as medical symptoms and examinations, reproduction, communication about abuse, and directions for assistance with sexuality.

Emotional awareness

By now you will have realized that we strongly believe in developing emotional awareness and being tuned in to what your body is telling you. You have also learned that females with ASDs often have difficulties in this area—remember what Jen Birch and Liane Holliday Willey wrote about their experiences in their books. It is very important for your daughter to be able to recognize if she is feeling nervous, uncomfortable, scared, confused, or rushed in certain situations. As we discussed in previous chapters, use all the appropriate tools in your teaching toolkit—including visual supports— to help your daughter better understand how her body responds when she feels a certain away. Help your daughter to become more aware of her feelings: help her recognize when a situation makes her uncomfortable or nervous (the idea of having a gut feeling) so that she has the opportunity to walk away. This skill obviously needs to go hand in hand with developing social understanding and awareness of appropriate and healthy interactions. Your daughter will not have a "red flag" experience (an uncomfortable feeling that something might be wrong) if she is unaware that her teacher is not supposed to hug her in a very close, sensual way.

Sexuality education

All professionals who write about abuse prevention and developmental disabilities clearly state the importance of sexuality education in keeping individuals safe. Knowledge is a very powerful protective tool in many ways. Information about body parts will enable your child to communicate about and report any inappropriate behavior: children are more likely to report molestation if they have the correct terms for their body parts, or another's. Children's testimonials in court are more likely to be believed if they use the correct terms for body parts. Teach the proper vocabulary, and teach it early! Youth with ASDs often do better with factual, rather than conceptual learning. Teach your daughter the facts about sexuality and sexual health, and help dispel the myths she might have heard. Knowledge about *healthy* sexual behavior also enables girls to discriminate between what is good and healthy, and what is wrong and bad. Greater knowledge reduces feelings of confusion and uncertainty, which can then aid in decision-making and assertiveness skills. In Chapter 7 we outlined the important components of a sexuality education curriculum, including how to develop a sexuality education plan for your daughter. By making sexuality development and sexual health an important part of her overall educational curriculum as she enters adolescence and young adulthood, you will be making great strides toward ensuring her safety, both now and in the future.

Privacy awareness

Some topics that are part of sexuality education are critical in promoting personal safety; privacy awareness is one of them. We reviewed privacy awareness in detail in Chapter 3 so we will not spend much time discussing it here. Remember that because privacy is a *social* concept, girls with ASDs often have more difficulty learning privacy rules and generalizing their skills across different situations that might not be cut and dried. You may need to practice repeatedly for privacy rules and skills to become more natural for your daughter. Girls who demonstrate an understanding of private places, behavior, and topics of conversation, and who know that their own bodies are their own and are private, will be better able to detect if someone has violated the rules.

Personal space, touching rules, and boundaries

Like privacy awareness, personal space, touching rules, and boundaries are all social concepts that are learned over time. They are also cultural concepts, and what is appropriate for one culture might not be acceptable in another. This is difficult to learn for girls with ASDs! Yet it is critical for personal safety for your daughter to demonstrate skills and awareness related to personal space. Later in the chapter we will discuss the importance of your daughter learning to respect others' boundaries (accepting "no" as an answer, not stalking or intimidating). In Chapter 7 we reviewed what and how to teach your daughter about personal space, touching rules, and boundaries (physical and emotional). Teach your daughter that if anyone touches her in a way that she does not want to be touched (e.g. rough-housing, tickling, hugging, kissing, touching private parts), she can say "no!" There are story books in the literature that have been published for children to teach them about body ownership, privacy, and saying "no" to unwanted touch, such as *My Body is Private* and *Uncle Willy's Tickles* (*see* Resources). If you are using a multimodal approach to teaching, and your daughter enjoys hearing stories or reading, you may want to supplement your teaching with books. The Circles® program from James Stanfield, which we reviewed in Chapter 7, also has a *Stop Abuse* video program with lessons designed to teach individuals that they do not have to participate in uncomfortable physical contact with others.

Case study: Zaira

Zaira is an 11-year-old girl with autism and mild cognitive impairments. She speaks in simple full sentences, yet it can be difficult at times to understand what she is trying to communicate. We saw Zaira through our clinic for her tri-ennial assessment (in the United States, students in special education programs are tested every three years on their reasoning skills, educational achievement, speech and language, and motor abilities). Zaira was a friendly, sweet, and de-lightful young girl who showed clear physical signs of approaching puberty (e.g. breast buds developing). Zaira was seen for her appointments by a female psychologist and a male psychology trainee. During her first break, Zaira stood up and approached the female psychologist stating "big hug?" while simultane-ously throwing her arms around her. Zaira's behavior was corrected and she was told to shake hands and give high-fives to doctors and teachers. The psycholo-gist put out her hand for a high five and Zaira was praised for responding ap-propriately. Within half an hour, Zaira attempted to hug the psychology trainee, and when corrected she said "blow kiss?" and blew a kiss toward him. Zaira's mother was distressed, and reported that this had been an ongoing problem for Zaira and that they had been having difficulties teaching her how to greet and express affection for teachers and other professionals in her life appropriately. She was worried that Zaira's overly affectionate and nondiscriminate behavior was going to get her into trouble in the future.

Permission and ability to say "no"

One of a parent's hopes for their daughter with an ASD is that she will continue to grow and develop new skills throughout her life. That means that from a young age (unless she has received a recent diagnosis), your daughter has probably been working with teachers, aides, psychologists, behaviorists, speech-language pathologists, and other professionals whose goal it is for her to learn new skills. They ask her to try new things that she might not be keen on doing. And we expect her to comply: eat new foods, put the video game away, say hello to a girl in her social skills group, talk about something other than Egypt, Johnny Depp, or her current favorite Broadway musical, or complete her hygiene routine. Unfortunately, this can convey the message to your daughter that she should *always* comply with a teacher or an adult, making her more vulnerable to abuse.

There is also a social aspect to this problem. Generally, it is seen as positive if a child with a developmental disability is agreeable, good-natured, and compliant. In most cases, yes, agreeableness and an easy-going temperament are good things; your daughter will learn more and have more opportunities to try new things in her life. However, being *too* agreeable or *too* easy-going is *not* good. Think about your daughter: has she been socialized to always say "yes", and go along with something that she would rather not do if an adult makes the request? It is essential to teach your daughter when and where she is allowed to say "no", and to provide her with the skills to do so effectively.

At times it can be difficult to strike the right balance between teaching your daughter safety skills and teaching her behaviors that are socially expected or acceptable. Without meaning to, we often teach our daughters that it is not okay to disagree or to say "no" to someone, especially to an adult who has responsibility over her. For example, think back to your last family gathering. Were there family members present whom your daughter rarely sees? Did any of these family members want to give your daughter a hug or kiss, or expect her to reciprocate in turn? In the interest of promoting her safety skills, we recommend that you do not make your daughter tolerate undesirable personal contact with unfamiliar family members. For neurotypical youth, an occasional "grin and bear it" kiss from Great Aunt Mabel isn't the end of the world. For youth with ASDs, it presents a confusing message, especially if your goal is to teach the message "your body is your own."

When considering abuse prevention, however, the ability to say "no" is an important skill for your daughter to develop. Which of the following have you worked on with your daughter? Which skills does she need to continue to work on?

- Provide plenty of opportunity for your daughter to *make choices* when you can.
- When presented with a choice between two options (e.g. two kinds of snack, two sweaters she could wear), can she make a decision based on her preferences? Teach decision-making as part of her curriculum.
- Give your daughter opportunities to say "no" when it is appropriate.
- Always distinguish between questions (e.g. "Do you want to _____?") and demands or requirements (e.g. "I need you to clean up your *Yu-Gi-Oh* cards"). If you ask a question, be sure to respect her choice if she says "no." By asking, not requiring, you are giving her permission to respond in the way she wishes.
- Teach your daughter that access to her body is always under her control.
- Teach your daughter that she can always decide if she wants to touch another person or to have them touch her (e.g. not forcing her to hug a relative if she doesn't want to).
- Teach your daughter how to say "No" in an assertive voice. An assertive "No" tells a potential abuser that your daughter clearly understands the rules of touching. If your daughter knows the rules, and knows when they have been broken, she will be more likely to report any abuse.
- Teach your daughter that she may need to repeat "no" before a potential abuser listens to her.
- Teach your child to use assertive body language:
  - shake her head while saying "no"
  - make fists with her hands
  - stand up tall
  - look a potential abuser in the eye
  - shout with conviction
  - fight back.
- Take your daughter to a self-defense class designed for youth with disabilities. *Kidpower* (*see* Resources) is a nonprofit organization that was founded in 1989 with the aim of developing programs

to empower youth and keep them safe. Some state chapters of *Kidpower*, like the one in Colorado Springs, CO, offer courses for youth and young adults with developmental disabilities, and private classes for youth who need extra attention.

In our teen groups for girls with ASDs, we role-play and practice assertiveness skills, using strong body language, and saying "no"; we use mirrors, videotaping, and planned scenarios. Practice and role-playing is an important part of abuse-prevention skills training. Unfortunately, the research indicates that it is not enough to teach (provide knowledge) and practice (role-play) *out of context*. Often, abuse-prevention skills learned in an unrealistic setting do not carry over to day-to-day life (Miltenberger *et al.* 1999). In most areas of skill development, girls with ASDs demonstrate difficulties transferring skills from one context to another. So how can you practice in a more "real-life" situation? We have worked with families on developing scenarios that can test their daughters' skills and decision-making out of the clinic or educational setting in which they were initially taught. Here are some examples of *in situ* scenarios we have tried with families.

- *Not getting into a car with a stranger*: have a family friend drive up while your daughter is outside and ask her if she can come and help him look for his lost dog.

- *Telling a store clerk she is lost*: go to a department store with your daughter. Tell her that you are going to go to another part of the store and that she will need to tell the clerk that she cannot find her mother. Yes, this one is scary, but it has been very successful!

- *Saying no to an offered "hug"*: have an unfamiliar confederate staff member or teacher (someone with whom you are working) greet your daughter and ask for a hug.

In his work with adult females with developmental disabilities, Miltenberger has found that skills such as resisting a lure were generalized more frequently when they were taught with a confederate staff member in an "*in situ*" situation rather than in a planned, role-play context. More work is needed on developing abuse-prevention programs that target not only skill acquisition, but also *generalization* and *maintenance* of skills over time. We know that this is essential for the safety of girls and young women with ASDs.

Safety in the curriculum

To protect your daughter...

- Teach her that her body is her own.
- Give her the power of the word NO. Then respect it. No doesn't have to be verbal.
- Girls who can take self-defense should.
- Self-bathing is a good goal. The less chance staff will ever see a vulnerable person naked the better.
- Teach your children private areas, and to tell and tell and tell some more if someone makes them uncomfortable.
- Give them the means (pics, typing, words, whatever helps).
- BELIEVE HER and keep your eyes open.

I pray every night that no more girls will be victimized, that no more autistics will be hurt, or killed or raped or mistreated. But our communities (autistics and autism families) need to work together to solve this one... We know what would help us learn. You all know how YOUR kids learn and how to implement it. (Kassiane Sibley—25-year-old woman with high-functioning autism)

Abuse prevention is such an important topic that we could write an entire book on developing personal safety skills; the preceding sections have discussed the skills that we have identified as being most relevant for the safety of girls and young women with ASDs. Other areas related to abuse prevention include teaching your child about emergency situations and what to do in an emergency (e.g. Who can you ask for help when you are lost? What do you do if someone knocks on the door or calls when you are home alone?), ensuring your daughter is familiar with and embraces her personal rights (discussed at the beginning of the chapter), and ongoing attention to self-esteem and self-confidence (discussed in Chapter 5). Continued development of self-esteem and personal talents and skills teaches your daughter that she is loved and that she is a powerful person—she has the ability to make decisions and choices, she is competent, and she can affect others. Like sexuality education, abuse-prevention skills are part of your daughter's life-long learning, and they are just as important as any other subject in her educational curriculum.

The seven components of your daughter's abuse-prevention education

- Social skills.
- Social communication.
- Emotional awareness.
- Sexuality education.
- Privacy awareness.
- Personal space, touching rules, and boundaries.
- Permission and ability to say "No".

Sexual harassment and bullying at school

This year there is "less harassment" from the other kids and fewer "meltdowns". We did talk about some harassment from the boys, which Sandi thought was flirting, but was actually mean-spirited (blowing kisses, asking for dates). One teacher has given her some advice and we have talked a little. (Mother of a girl in eighth-grade with Asperger's)

In recent years, we have learned much about the experiences of girls with ASDs being bullied and teased at school, and how this differs from the bullying experiences of boys (*see* Resources for books on bullying). Unfortunately, another form of bullying—sexual bullying—is becoming more prevalent in schools, particularly middle and high schools. The incidence of sexual bullying and harassment is alarming, and has prompted task forces to look carefully at how to put a stop to it. In 2001, the AAUW Educational Foundation reported that 81% of students will experience some form of sexual harassment during their educational career, and that 27% of students are frequent targets of sexual bullying. Moreover, most sexual harassment begins between the sixth and ninth grades. In Neil Duncan's (1999) detailed study of sexual bullying in England, he found that early maturing girls are often a target of bullying, with comments being made about girls' pubertal signs and menstruation. Girls will also engage in bullying as an expression of sexual jealousy and asserting power over other girls lower on the social ladder. Sexual bullying can take many forms, and it is important that your daughter is aware that these behaviors are not okay, and that some of them are illegal:

- name-calling
- target of sexual comment, jokes, looks, teasing
- sexual rumors
- been shown or given sexual pictures or notes
- being touched, grabbed, or pinched.

Some of the girls in our groups have experienced name-calling because they dress casually and are not aware of fashionable trends or style; they don't dress or wear make-up and have accessories that are "teenage feminine". Consistent with inaccurate stereotypes of the appearance of people of different sexual orientations, girls in our groups have been called "Lesbos", "dykes", and "queers". It is heartbreaking when they come to the group confused and hurt, sharing experiences about being called names when they don't even understand why they are being teased, or what the names themselves mean.

In her autobiographical account *Finding a Different Kind of Normal*, Jeanette Purkis, a woman with Asperger's Syndrome, recalls experiences of being sexually bullied in secondary school when she didn't understand what was happening:

> After a while, anyone who took pity on me and was friendly got picked on themselves, and, with few exceptions, usually gave up and joined in on the teasing. Older kids would make sexual jokes that I didn't really understand and ask me to hump them, screw them…knowing that I had no idea what they were talking about. (p.22)

Other examples in Ms Purkis's story include boys pulling her underwear down, lifting her skirt, or trying to reach up her skirt.

Girls in our groups have reported being groped, being sent sexual messages (with content that they haven't fully understood), having been asked out on dates as a dare (not knowing it was a dare), and having sexual comments made about their bodies. Sexual harassment and unwanted sexual contact at school are not acceptable, and the first step you can take as a parent is to identify that it is happening. If your daughter is verbal, talk with her, using the strategies in your teaching toolkit (visuals, speaking, writing), about harassment and what behaviors are not appropriate. A basic definition of harassment is *unwanted* and *unwelcome* sexual behavior. Your daughter might not be aware that some names are sexual in nature; ask her to tell you if she is being called any names at school. If your daughter is less verbal, use your visual supports to identify any instances of bullying and harassment. Pay close attention to changes in your daughter's behavior and mood. Negative changes in mood or behavior, and fear or avoidance of school, are signs that something might be happening.

If your daughter is experiencing harassment, you will need to assist her in reporting what has happened. Sexual harassment at school is widespread and it is likely that other students are experiencing what your daughter is going through. Talk to someone at school who is on your daughter's educational team with whom you having an ongoing, positive relationship. They will be able to assist you in determining what the next step should be.

Finally, be aware of your daughter's school's policies and programs. Ask to see the school's sexual harassment policy and find out how they are implementing an anti-harassment program. Ongoing programs are essential in promoting awareness and teaching girls to speak up (or point to a picture) to indicate that something is happening to them that they are not comfortable with. Without consequences for perpetrators, sexual harassment will not stop. Make sure proactive anti-harassment strategies are part of your daughter's IEP.

Harassment prevention strategies for you and your daughter

The best protection against harassment is the following powerful set of skills. None of these skills are new; we have already been reviewing them throughout this book. Keep working on them together with your daughter—practice, repetition, practice, repetition. Your daughter will come closer to becoming her own safe warrior woman.

- Knowledge of body parts and how to report.
- Knowledge of appropriate and inappropriate behaviors.
- Knowledge of privacy boundary crossings.
- Knowledge of healthy relationships.
- Ability to say "no" and not comply.
- Assertiveness skills.
- Self-esteem and self-confidence.
- Being comfortable and able to communicate with you.

What are the signs of abuse?

Youth with or without disabilities share similar indicators of abuse, though communication difficulties can impede a girl's ability to report experiences that may have happened to her. Familiarize yourself with the most common signs of abuse (*see* the box on the next page). Most of these signs on their own do not immediately point to the occurrence of abuse. Be aware of *patterns* of physical and behavioral signs, and of *changes* in your daughter's behavior and emotional state. If your child reports having been victimized, listen to her. Later in the chapter we will discuss what to do if you think, or know, that your daughter has experienced assault or abuse.

In a paper in the *Journal of Autism and Developmental Disorders*, Howlin and Clements (1995), who were at St George's Hospital Medical School in London, reported strategies to assess the effect of abuse on youth with pervasive developmental disorders. Criminal charges had been laid against the staff of a specialist day school for children with autism in England, where the families of 12 children (between the ages of 4 and 18) had sought assistance in demonstrating that their children had suffered trauma while at the school. Howlin and Clements had been asked by the families' lawyer to assess the impact of the abuse and noted that the three primary difficulties they faced in their task were the fact that few of the children had meaningful communicative language, that youth with autism demonstrated many emotional and behavioral difficulties as part of the disorder itself, and that they needed to rely on second-hand accounts by family members. After careful development of an interview schedule that was designed to assess five areas of functioning, including behavioral problems associated with stressful experiences, Howlin and Clements were able to document changes in behavior across the period of time during which it was purported that the abuses occurred. Children continued to show growth in areas where it was expected that they would continue to improve, such as in language and self-help skills, and yet demonstrated increased rates of problematic behaviors, including aggression and self-injury, fears and reluctance to go to school, tantrums and mood swings, increased activity level, and difficulties with sleeping. A number of the children also developed problem-eating. For the majority of children, problems had persisted to varying degrees for a long period of time after removal from the school. Despite not having a carefully controlled research design, Howlin and Clements concluded that the *consistency* observed in the types of behaviors the children demonstrated and the *timing* of the behavioral changes suggested that the children really did experience significant

Do you know the signs of abuse?

Physical signs
- bruises in genital areas
- genital discomfort
- torn or missing clothing
- sexually transmitted infection
- broken bones
- head injuries
- headaches

Behavioral signs
- depression
- withdrawal
- atypical attachment
- avoids certain settings
- avoids specific adults
- excessive crying spells
- regression
- sleep disturbance
- poor self-esteem
- non-compliance
- eating disorders
- resists examination by doctor
- self-destructive behavior
- sexually inappropriate behavior
- sudden drop in school achievement

distress from their experiences at the school. They also made two important conclusions: that it is possible to evaluate the effects of abuse on youth with pervasive developmental disorders, and that there are particular signs or red flags that families and professionals should be aware of that might indicate a child is suffering maltreatment of some kind.

Case study: Sarah

Sarah is a pretty 13-year-old girl with classic autism. She is usually happy, loves to read and draw, and loves the colors red and purple. She will primarily reply to questions directed to her with one-word answers, though she can read story books up to a fifth-grade level. Spontaneous speech is infrequent, and has become less so after she was raped by a teenage boy in her own home. When we saw Sarah in therapy, she was experiencing significant post-traumatic symptoms, including nightmares, difficulties being in a room alone, talking to herself about sharks with sharp teeth and monsters, and screaming frequently, which was thought to be caused by a memory she was having. Her performance at school had declined and she was beginning to aggress toward others, including her aides and teachers. After a few months in therapy, parent training, and careful attention to her educational program, Sarah's behaviors began to improve: she began to sleep through the night and was able to spend increasing periods of time completing activities by herself, such as reading and drawing. Sarah was not able to communicate to others how she felt; however, her behavior and emotions spoke loudly for her. With calm, nurturing parenting, and a regular routine, Sarah will be able to enjoy life more and more again. What the long-term consequences of her experience might be, we don't yet know.

Building a safety circle

If something should happen to your daughter that she is uncomfortable with, she will need to know what to do and who to contact depending on where she is—is she at home? At school? At a friend's house? At the mall? The first step in preparing for potential abuse is determining who will be part of your daughter's *safety circle*. Who is someone that will listen to your child, someone your daughter can turn to no matter what—whether it is five in the morning, or ten at night, or if she needs a ride from ten miles away and it's long past midnight? For girls who are verbal, who can your daughter talk to about important things that are going on in her life? Who can your daughter talk to about difficult issues such as someone acting inappropriately toward her? For less verbal girls, who understands her means of communication; how she uses pictures and expressions to share her ideas? It is not enough to have only one person as part of your daughter's safety circle. Ideally, someone in your daughter's family will fill this role, as well as someone at her school, someone in the community, and perhaps a professional that she sees for therapy. Many families with whom we have worked have been able to identify at least one trusted person at school—a favorite teacher, a guidance counselor, a school psychologist. Having someone at school be part of your daughter's safety circle is very important because this is where she will spend as much as six to eight hours of her day.

Below, we review what we consider to be the important steps in developing your daughter's safe reporting plan. Using your teaching toolkit, work with your daughter to establish skills in areas that might be more difficult for her right now.

Teaching tips: steps to safe reporting

- Choose members of your daughter's safety circle with her input. Make sure everyone knows they are part of your daughter's circle, and what their role will be.
- If she is capable, teach your daughter how to use a cell phone in an emergency. Program phone numbers for people in your daughter's safety circle into her cell phone.
- Put safety circle information on a laminated card that can go in your daughter's school bag.
- Teach your daughter how to call 911 (put this information on a card if necessary).
- Teach your daughter how to identify police officers. Work on this skill while you are out in the community. Identify police vehicles and police officers at various locations such as the mall. Approach a police officer and explain that you are working with your daughter on identifying safe people in the community she can go to if she is in danger.
- Teach your daughter about good and bad "secrets" and that she will never get in trouble for telling a "bad secret".
- Develop a script (verbal or pictorial) for what your daughter should do and say if she has been hurt by someone. Keep a shortened version of this script in her bag or pocket book so that she can refer to it if she forgets what she should do. Use pictures as needed (remember the pictures from the Speak Up Project).

- Teach your daughter when to communicate with someone in her safety circle about touching: (a) someone touches her sexually; (b) she is confused about the touching that happened; (c) someone wouldn't stop touching her when she said "no".

- Teach your daughter how to communicate in a simple, straightforward manner about touching. Whether using pictures, words, or writing, teach your daughter to report *who* touched her (name if possible), *where* she was touched (using proper vocabulary or pointing to pictures), and how she *felt*. She will also likely need to be able to report (to the extent that she is able to do so) *when* something happened, *how often* it occurred, and *where* (location). You can practice reporting touching using picture scenarios, and walking your daughter through questions such as "Who is touching the girl?", "Where on her body is he touching her?", and "Is that a good touch or a bad touch?"

Reacting to abuse

Nothing is scarier for a parent than when their child discloses information about having been touched inappropriately. How you respond will be very important in validating your daughter's feelings and ensuring that she feels safe. As hard as it might be, respond to what she says in a supportive and calm manner. Tell your daughter that you are glad she told you and that you are very sorry for what happened to her. Emphasize that whatever happened, she is never to blame. Keep your questions to a minimum as they can be confusing for her. Immediately report suspicions of or actual disclosures of abuse to child protective authorities; assume that what your daughter is telling you is true, no matter whom she is reporting about.

What happens next will be very important for your daughter. She is likely confused, scared, and may be feeling unsafe. She is experiencing something very new and unpleasant, and she will not know what to expect unless you prepare her very carefully. Work with the professionals to explain to your daughter how the situation will be handled, including who will talk to her about what happened. Make sure that you, as her parent, are very clear about what the process will be. Use picture and social stories to help your daughter understand, and make sure you check her understanding. Request that your daughter be interviewed by a professional who has experience working with youth with developmental disabilities, preferably autism. Careful interviewing techniques are needed when working with individuals with disabilities. *After You Tell* (*see* Resources) is a picture social story written by Susan E. Ludwig that outlines what happens after someone reports an abuse, right up until the end of a hearing and prosecution. In its current form, *After You Tell* is geared toward adults with a Grade 4–5 reading level. However, you may find it helpful in writing your own story for your daughter.

For too many families, their worst nightmare does come true. If you are prepared, you will be strong enough to make it through what happens next. You will be able to connect your daughter with experienced therapists, and you will be able to connect yourself with a support group. The American Association of Sex Educators, Counselors, and Therapists (AASECT; *see* Resources) is an excellent resource for therapists who have experience working with youth with developmental disabilities.

Respecting others' boundaries: Keeping your daughter, and others, safe

So far in this chapter, we have talked about girls with ASDs being at risk for being hurt, abused, or exploited. Now we need to consider the other side of the coin—what can happen if youth with ASDs do not understand and respect other people's boundaries. Unfortunately, youth with ASDs are at risk for (often unintentionally) engaging in inappropriate behavior that may be misunderstood by others and interpreted as offensive, or that is illegal and results in police involvement. In our practice we have mostly worked with teen males who have run into trouble in this respect, but your daughter is not immune to having difficulties in this area. The following are some characteristics that can lead to inappropriate behavior; think about which ones apply to your daughter, and monitor them closely while working with her to better understand boundaries and healthy relationships:

- quick to develop an intense interest or crush
- interests become all-consuming (she cannot turn them off or stop thinking about them)
- is not respectful of others' personal space
- asks personal questions of people she does not know well

- sees friendships as exclusive (a friend can be your daughter's friend *only*); becomes jealous if her friends spend time with others
- is overprotective, clingy, oppressive
- is pushy, wants everything her way; becomes angry during interactions with others
- has a difficult time accepting rejection or being told "no"
- has difficulties regulating emotion
- does not understand guidelines for expression of affection
- is physically affectionate in an indiscriminate way.

In our Girls Growing Up program, we target each of the above concerns in social skills groups and in individual therapy as needed. We role-play, video-model, use social stories, watch movie or television vignettes, use social autopsies, read storybooks, use visual and written cues, and use additional creative means to communicate the social concepts we want to teach (e.g. using hula hoops to teach about personal space). Our goal in teaching the girls is always twofold: developing skills and promoting safety. Your daughter will be less likely to get into trouble with others if she learns about boundaries and healthy relationships.

Nita Jackson recounts the intensity of her fruitless adolescent obsessions in her book, *Standing Up, Falling Down*. Celebrities such as Robin Williams, David Duchovny, and Ewan McGregor became the sole focus of her interests. Nita self-describes becoming a "maniacal stalker", and not being able to accept the fact that the men she was interested in were unattainable. She recounts leaving repeated messages on answering machines, and sending countless emails and letters. Writing with insight, Nita explains that she was not aware at the time of how severe her behavior was, and that her infatuations caused her to behave in ways she now finds humiliating when she looks back on that time of her life. Taking a proactive approach with your daughter, and carefully teaching her the nature of healthy relationships and boundaries, will help you to avoid the difficulties experienced by Nita when she was younger.

In his book, *Autism, Advocates, and Law Enforcement Professionals. Recognizing and Reducing Risk Situations for People with Autism Spectrum Disorders*, Dennis Debbaudt, a law enforcement trainer and father of a son with autism, writes for both law enforcement professionals and the community about how the behavior of individuals with ASDs may be misunderstood and how best to respond to situations as they arise. Although discussion of risky situations and interactions with the law is beyond the scope of this book, we recommend that families read Debbaudt's book, his article "Avoiding Unfortunate Situations", and visit his website (*see* Resources) for more information on how to keep your daughter safe.

On several occasions, girls in our groups have begun to develop obsessive and stalking behaviors, requiring us to intervene. In one case, a 19-year-old girl with a diagnosis of PDD-NOS developed a "crush" on one of the young men in her group, and was very vocal about how she felt about him. She persistently invaded his personal space, stating "I'm available." The young man was highly uncomfortable when she engaged in this behavior, and the facilitators needed to remind her many times that what she was doing was not appropriate.

Case study: Christie

Christie, 15, has recently "discovered boys", as her mother reports. There is a shy young man in her class who also has a developmental disability, and who has expressed some interest in getting to know Christie better. Christie has a history of being overly affectionate, being jealous of her sister's and her sister's friends' time, and developing interests that quickly become all-consuming. Her mother is concerned that her interest in "Jason" will also become "obsessive" and that even if he is interested in her, she will scare him away. Christie has begun to say things like "Let's drive by Jason's house", or "Let's call and see if Jason is home". Her mother has begun a teaching program with Christie about boundaries when you are interested in someone, and has had to develop explicit rules about how often she can call him, or go by his house. They have gone on one "safe date", which went well, so it is hoped that Christie will be able to learn to give him space and proceed appropriately slowly for a 15-year-old who is just starting to date.

Remember in Chapter 7 we reviewed *levels of awareness and interest in dating*? If your daughter is at the *desperate* level, she is at risk for violating others' boundaries, in particular those of the person she is interested in. This can be a problem whether or not the other person is also interested in her. Your daughter might stare, stand too close, follow in the hallway or outside school, or attempt to talk to them too frequently. She might not be able to read nonverbal cues that they are not interested, or are becoming upset by her intrusive behavior. She might also be at risk for jeopardizing a potential date because she is acting too forward. If your daughter is interested in a young man who also has autism, help her to understand that he may not appreciate "in your face" approaches, and that she might need to take things more slowly.

If you are concerned that your daughter does not understand healthy boundaries and how others feel, you might need to enrol her in an educational program designed specifically for teaching boundaries and healthy relationships. James Stanfield has a video program called *Becoming Date Smart 2. Avoiding Trouble and Listening for "No"*. Males and females learn what actions can unintentionally lead them into trouble. There are also some books that address these issues. If your daughter is having difficulties determining how different behaviors will make other people feel, it may help to break down behaviors into a five-point scale. Kari Dunn Buron wrote *A "5" Is Against the Law: Social Boundaries: Straight Up*, which is a social skills guide for teens with AS and HFA. It uses a concrete five-point scale to assist youth in visualizing social interactions and understanding how the people would feel who are participating in those interactions. A "5" on the rating scale indicates that a behavior is physically hurtful or threatening, whereas a rating of "1" means that the behavior is socially appropriate. Youth learn about gray areas in interactions, and how behaviors can cross from acceptable into the gray zone, and then become illegal. Another book that provides helpful guidelines for youth is *The Rules of Sex. Social and Legal Guidelines for Those Who Have Never Been Told. Written for Young Adults*, by Nora J Baladerian. Its clear, concrete text outlines the social and legal rules of sexual behavior for youth with learning disabilities.

Unfortunately, not everyone understands the behavior of someone who has an ASD, and even if they do, they are not always forgiving, or able to be forgiving, when things happen. Sometimes agency policies prevent flexibility in how they can respond to situations. We have worked with teens who have been suspended from school, expelled for stalking, charged with sexual harassment, arrested for abuse and endangerment of a child, and charged with assault of a police officer. As a parent, it is your job to work with your daughter to reduce the risk of these situations occurring, and to work together with the professionals in her lives. As professionals and educators, it is our responsibility to make sure emergency responders and law-enforcement officers understand individuals with ASDs. Raising awareness of what autism looks like, and how first responders can incorporate that information in their safety protocols, will go a long way toward creating safer schools and communities for everyone.

Consent to sexual activity

As your daughter grows up and begins exploring her own sexuality, she may want to pursue a sexual relationship with someone. As scary as that sounds, it is a natural progression during adolescence and young adulthood. Your role as a parent will vary depending on her age, and on the nature of your parental relationship. Parents are natural legal guardians of minor children until they reach 18 years of age. During this time you can assist your daughter in making decisions, set rules at home, and decide whether you would like her to go on dates or not. When she turns 18 your daughter will become a consenting adult, or the court will determine that someone will become her guardian (most often her parents). As a guardian, you would act for your daughter to make decisions about her person and her property. Decisions about guardianship are not easy and should not be entered into lightly. If you think that these issues are or will be relevant for you in the future, we recommend that you consult with a special-needs attorney in your state who has had experiences with guardianship and consent. It is never too early even to begin to think about what your daughter's future will look like with respect to her decision-making.

The American Association on Mental Retardation (AAMR) has published a very helpful guidebook entitled *A Guide to Consent* (*see* Resources) which walks parents and professionals through what informed consent means, and the role it plays in situations such as finances, health care, and sexual activity. Determining whether a person is capable of consenting to participate in sexual expression with a mutually agreeable partner is an important decision that has been influenced by historical perspectives and current societal attitudes. Today, the important elements of being able to participate in sexual contact are: knowledge (information), understanding (rationality), choice (lack of coercion), and consent (agreement). The following is a list of criteria adapted from the AAMR booklet which is essential to consider when assessing whether a young woman with an ASD is capable of consenting to participate in activities that involve another person from sexual stimulation to sexual intercourse. Which of these does your daughter understand or demonstrate? Which does she need to work on?

- understands basics of sexual activities
- demonstrates skills to participate safely in sexual activities
- demonstrates knowledge of pregnancy (physical and legal responsibilities)

- demonstrates knowledge of sexually transmitted infections and how to keep safe
- knows about inappropriate and illegal sexual behaviors
- knows what it means to cross another's boundaries
- knows that "no" means stop
- knows appropriateness of time and place for sexual activities
- understands whether or not her partner agrees to participate in the sexual activity
- can accurately report events that happen to her
- can differentiate fantasy from reality, and truth from lies
- can recognize one's own and others' feelings
- ability to recognize potentially abusive situations (reading red flags)
- is able to be assertive and reject unwanted advances
- is able to call for help.

Failure to demonstrate all of these skills does not preclude your daughter from engaging in sexual activity with a partner; however, there may be some sexual acts that she is not ready for. Remember, there is no universal definition of what *competency* means regarding sexual expression. Work with a trusted professional to assist you and your daughter in making the right decisions that will meet her needs and keep her safe and happy.

Online safety: protecting your daughter on the internet

To many parents' dismay, youth today live in an electronically connected world that can often seem like a foreign land. If you grew up with record players, eight-tracks, cassette tapes, rotary-dial telephones, and typewriters, today's online options may seem overwhelming. Even for adults who grew up with CDs, email, and computers, online technology has been changing so rapidly that it's hard to keep up. A North American survey conducted by Forrester Research in 2005 found that, on average, teens spend up to 11 hours per week online (1.57 hours per day), and one in five youth aged 12–17 spend 20 or more hours per week online (2.86 hours per day).

What do we know about how much time youth with ASDs spend online? To our knowledge, there are no official statistics about time spent online;

however, parents and teens themselves report that a significant amount of free time (time not at school, eating meals, or sleeping) is spent on the computer or playing hand-held video games, sometimes to the detriment of other aspects of life. Many parents lament that the computer presents another opportunity for self-isolation, and that they find themselves in a continual battle with their teen over limiting time online until homework is done, until they have showered or cleaned their room, until they have eaten dinner, or until they have engaged in at least a short conversation with someone in their family. Much of our work as clinicians with parents and their teens involves negotiations and plans related to "earning" computer time in exchange for completing the day-to-day activities expected of teens. Youth with ASDs who are cognitively and physically capable of spending time on the computer tend to do so for longer durations and with more intensity than typically developing teens who also enjoy spending time online. "Special interests" can blossom online as teens have access to endless amounts of information related to specific topics. Some of the girls with whom we have worked have run into difficulties with spending too much time online searching for more and more information about interests ranging from favorite animals to Broadway musicals, movie stars, and song lyrics. But there is more to do online than "browsing", and today's "teen technology" is not limited to just using the computer. We have found that with the right balance, using technology can open exciting social doors for girls with ASDs and it can promote creativity:

- Many opportunities exist online to connect with different groups of kids with shared interests; friendships can develop online between youth who would likely never connect at school.

- Fewer demands without face-to-face interactions can level the social playing field.

- There is more time to process information and respond appropriately in a social interaction.

- "Content creation" opportunities (e.g. blogging) promote creativity and sharing of artwork, writing, and other creative pursuits.

- Teachers are using information technology more frequently as part of school assignments which can be more engaging and motivating for youth with ASDs.

- Use of the internet related to special interests can promote involvement in social causes or activism (e.g. supporting endangered animals).

In the interest of becoming an informed, tech-savvy parent, take a look at the list below. What activities does your daughter currently engage in? Do you know what each of them are? If not, take time to do some research online yourself, or read some of the books that have been published about youth culture online (*see* Resources). One of the best things parents can do to keep their daughter safe online is to be informed. Which of the following forms of technology does your daughter use?

- email
- YouTube
- iPod, MP3s, and iTunes
- IM-ing
- cell phones/text messaging
- MySpace/Facebook
- chatrooms
- blogging
- googling and browsing
- gaming
- content creation.

In our experience, youth with ASDs spend the greatest amount of time engaging in the last three activities: googling and browsing, gaming, and content creation. Many of the other activities are social in nature, and thus may be less appealing to youth with ASDs; however, it is easy to stumble across chatrooms or discussion boards when browsing, and girls who are socially motivated may want to create a profile on MySpace or Facebook. This leads us to the main issue related to online safety and youth with ASDs—girls can be highly skilled at navigating the technology, yet very naïve with respect to the online social world.

Dealing with the dangers of being online

Girls with ASDs face three main dangers when spending time online: *too much time*, *too much information*, and *too few boundaries*.

Too much time is the easiest risk to manage if it is addressed promptly and clearly. Girls can spend more time online than is healthy for their development. Parents need to work together to create appropriate limits regarding the amount of time it is reasonable for their daughter to spend on the computer. Is your daughter meeting social and familial expectations? Is she getting her homework done? Is she able to complete essential day-to-day activities, such as showering and chores? Is she getting enough sleep? If you are able to answer "yes" to all of these questions, then your daughter is probably spending a reasonable amount of time pursing her online interests. If not, and you are having difficulty setting time limits with your daughter, work with a behavioral psychologist who can help you and your daughter develop a plan for earning computer time and outlining how she can earn "extra" time on the weekends. Remember, any plan will require tweaking over time!

What are the risks related to *too much information*? The first danger is sharing too much personal information with others. This can happen in many situations, such as when your daughter creates her email name, develops her MySpace profile, or chats with others about what she did on the weekend (e.g. gives the name of the mall that is just a block away from her house). The second danger associated with information is not being careful about what is shared on blogs or in other forums. Many youths, and youths with ASDs in particular, forget that information that is placed online is not private—anything that is posted enters the public domain. A final information risk related to spending time online is that youth can also have unrestricted access to too much information, some of which may be harmful (e.g. pornographic websites, pro-anorexia groups).

Case study: Paula

Paula is a 10-year-old girl diagnosed with PDD-NOS. We recently heard from her mother because of a concern that had arisen. Until recently, Paula had not been interested in learning about growing up. When her mother had tried to talk to her about sexuality and her changing body, Paula became very uncomfortable and refused to take part in the conversation. Within the last month, however, things had changed: while spending time online looking at information about growing up, Paula had stumbled across anime pornography. Unfortunately, pornography is not relegated to the password-protected realm of the internet and it is very easy for youth and teens to gain access to non-educational sexual content online, particularly if one loves anime and spends a lot of time browsing anime websites! When it was discovered that Paula was looking at pornography at home (and on the computer at her grandparents' house), she explained that she was "curious" about bodies and about sex, and did not understand that it was wrong for her to be looking at the pornography. The sad reality is that pornography is not realistic, nor is it representative of "real-life" physique or relationships. It contributes to a sexualized culture that creates confusion and conflicting messages for youth with ASDs.

What about boundaries? What risks are associated with *too few boundaries* online for girls with ASDs? We have talked in previous chapters about boundaries in the relationships your daughter has with strangers, acquaintances, close friends, romantic partners, and family. One of the online dangers that parents of all youth fear is that their child will be approached by an online predator. The likelihood of this happening is greatly increased if your child replies to communications by strangers, and if they do not understand the kinds of information you share with an acquaintance versus a friend. Youth with ASDs are particularly vulnerable to complying when being told to do something, and they may often not be aware that what they are being asked to do (e.g. by another teen online) is inappropriate. If your daughter is asked to do something by someone online—such as send a message to another person, or meet someone in person at a particular time and place— she may not be aware of the red flags associated with these requests. Lenhart (2007) reported that 32% of online teens have been contacted online by complete strangers, and that of these teens 29% responded to the contact. The danger is greatly increased for youth with ASDs for whom the social rules of online interactions tend to be less clear.

Having too few boundaries can also manifest in another way—your daughter might have difficulty respecting the boundaries of others and she may engage in what we call "over-contact". Earlier in the chapter we discussed the dangers of not respecting the boundaries of others. If your daughter has had a tendency to cross boundaries in other areas of her life, monitor her relationships carefully to ensure that she does not get herself into trouble online. Below are some scenarios where this might happen.

- Checking over and over to see if an online friend is online.
- Insisting on meeting an online friend in person even if that person expresses that they are not interested.
- Becoming possessive and upset about an online friend interacting with other friends, or not being available when your daughter wants to chat or play a game.
- Engaging in any behavior that may be perceived as harassment, stalking, or obsessive activities (e.g. repetitive emailing or text-messaging).
- Accessing a fan website for a celebrity (e.g. musician, actor) and posting inappropriate messages.
- Having difficulty understanding that celebrities do not write back to you, and are not your friend.

What you can do as a parent to keep your daughter safe

One of the first things that you can do as a parent to protect your daughter online is to *become more informed*—learn as much as you can about the technology and culture of the electronic world in which your daughter is participating. Learn about online safety by reading relevant books and visiting internet safety websites (*see* Resources). Take a computer class, or two! Perhaps even take a class with your daughter if she is interested in learning something new. Learn with her and join in on one of her interests. Does your daughter text kids at school? How about learning the text language that teens use? Do you know what PIR means?* How about BC, F2F or LMIRL?** It's a whole new language!

A second important thing you can do to promote safety online is to *share your daughter's online experiences*. Work on a school assignment together that requires internet research. Ask her to share with you and teach you about the computer and how to navigate internet sites; maybe she can show you how to set up your own MySpace or Facebook account. Send your daughter daily electronic communications such as emails or text messages. This can open up a whole new avenue for your relationship with your daughter, and you will learn more about how she communicates with others.

Using your teaching toolkit, talk to your daughter about how to stay safe online. Teach her how to judge the credibility of information received online. As we discussed above, because of their social naiveté, girls with ASDs are at risk for believing what they are told, blindly following requests made by someone online, and falling for internet scams (e.g. "You have won a new computer! Click here to enter your personal information and receive your prize!"). Your daughter will need to learn about spam, phishing, hacking, safe online gaming, and unsafe support groups (e.g. pro-suicide sites).

You can also create an *appropriate level of monitoring* of your daughter's computer time. This includes limiting the amount of time she spends online (especially late at night); keeping computers in public spaces in the house; using parentally controlled screen names, supervised email accounts, and filtering software; looking at your daughter's browser history or her online profile (with permission); and asking your daughter who her IM buddies and online friends are. Parents with whom we have worked have also set strict rules regarding online purchases and downloading of information,

---

*   Parents in room.
**   Be cool; face to face; let's meet in real life.

and have blocked certain email addresses if online bullying has become a problem.

Finally, *be aware of the potential for cyberbullying.* Unfortunately, bullying has transcended face-to-face interactions and entered the digital age. Girls with ASDs who spend time online are at risk for being the victim of online bullying, and parents have shared with us that their daughters have received unwanted or threatening emails and MSN messages. Sarah, a 12-year-old girl with Asperger's Syndrome writes about her experiences with internet harassment:

> Sometimes people can be nasty on the internet. Someone at school secretly copied down my email address when I was giving it to a friend and she must have given it to some other kids and they've been chatting to me on MSN Messenger. It was like lots of rude stuff like saying that I'm a witch and 39% angel, 50% evil...and strange things like that. In the end I had to block them so they wouldn't chat to me again. (*Asperger Syndrome, Adolescence, and Identity*, p.68)

Reported rates of cyberbullying range from 9% to above 40% depending on the kinds of bullying behavior described, and the age and sex of the youth studied. Based on a sample of 886 teens, a 2007 report by the Pew Internet and American Life Project* indicated that 32% of teens who use the internet have been targets of online harassment. Girls (38%), and older girls (41%) in particular (15–17 years), are more likely to be victims than boys (26%). Teens who share information about themselves online are also more likely to be targeted than those who keep a more anonymous online profile. Cyberbullying can take many forms, including harassment, flaming (using angry and vulgar language), gossiping or sending rumors, impersonating, stalking, exclusion, or outing someone. Recent research has also suggested that girls tend to bully others more frequently through cell phones and text messages. The impact is immediate, and the negative message can be shared instantly with many people. A recent article in the *New York Times* ("When the bullies turned faceless," December 16, 2007) underscored how dangerous online girl bullying can be. After what was described as "unrelenting" bullying through MySpace, 13-year-old Megan Meier, already vulnerable from her experiences of depression, chose to end her life rather than endure the horrible taunting any longer (being called "a liar, a fat whore and worse"). Just as you need to work with your daughter on understanding, responding

---

*   Available at www.pewinternet.org (accessed on March 21, 2008).

to, and keeping safe from offline bullying, if your daughter is spending time online, you will need to pay attention to possible instances of cyber-threats. Make sure your daughter understands that she can and should tell you about any negative online interactions, and take the time to teach your daughter about online bullies. Watch television programs where bullying is occurring and talk about it, do research online together, and role-play responding to online messages. Be creative and use teachable moments as they come up.

Resources

Books for youth with ASDs

Buron, K.D. (2007) *A '5' Is Against the Law! Social Boundaries Straight Up: An Honest Guide for Teens and Young Adults*. Shawnee Mission, KS: Autism Asperger Publishing Company.

Macavinta, C. and Pluym, A.V. (2005) *Respect: A Girl's Guide to Getting Respect and Dealing When Your Line is Crossed*. Minneapolis, MN: Free Spirit Publishing.

McGee, K. and Buddenberg, L. (2003) *Unmasking Sexual Con Games—A Teen's Guide*. Boys Town, NE: Boys Town Press.

Nunez, J. and Baladerian, N.J. (2006) *The Rules of Sex: Social and Legal Guidelines for Those Who Have Never Been Told*. Los Angeles, CA: Can Do Project.

Peter, V.J. and Dowd, T. (2000) *Boundaries: A Guide for Teens*. Boys Town, NE: Boys Town Press.

Roeher Institute (1991) *The Right To Control What Happens to Your Body*. Toronto, ON: The Roeher Institute.

Personal accounts by girls/young women

Jackson, N. (2002) *Standing Down, Falling Up*. Bristol: Lucky Duck Publishing Ltd.

Personal accounts by women

Birch, J. (2003) *Congratulations! It's Asperger Syndrome*. London: Jessica Kingsley Publishers.

Lawson, W. (2000) *Life Behind Glass. A Personal Account of Autism Spectrum Disorder*. London: Jessica Kingsley Publishers.

Prince-Hughes, D. (2004) *Songs of the Gorilla Nation. My Journey Through Autism*. New York, NY: Harmony Books.

Purkis, J. (2006) *Finding a Different Kind of Normal*. London: Jessica Kingsley Publishers.

Willey, L.H. (1999) *Pretending to be Normal*. London: Jessica Kingsley Publishers.

Storybooks for youth about touching, privacy, body ownership, and boundaries

Aboff, M. (1996) *Uncle Willy's Tickles. A Child's Right to Say "No"*. Washington, DC: Magination Press.

Freeman, L. (1984) *It's My Body*. Seattle, WA: Parenting Press.

Girard, L.W. (1984) *My Body is Private*. Morton Grove, IL: Albert Whitman & Company.

Hansen, D. (2007) *Those Are My Private Parts*. Redondo Beach, CA: Empowerment Productions.

Hindman, J. (1983) *A Very Touching Book…for Little People and for Big People*. Lincoln City, OR: Alexandria Association.

Kahn, R. (2001) *Bobby and Mandee's Too Safe for Strangers*. Arlington, TX: Future Horizons, Inc.

Kleven, S. (1998) *The Right Touch. A Read-Aloud Story to Help Prevent Child Sexual Abuse*. Bellevue, WA: Illumination Arts Publishing Company.

Maude Spelman, C. (2000) *Your Body Belongs to You*. Morton Grove, IL: Albert Whitman & Company.

Books for parents and professionals

Briggs, F. (1995) *Developing Personal Safety Skills in Children with Disabilities*. London: Jessica Kingsley Publishers.

Debbaudt, D. (2002) *Autism, Advocates, and Law Enforcement Professionals. Recognizing and Reducing Risk Situations for People with Autism Spectrum Disorders*. London: Jessica Kingsley Publishers.

Dinerstein, R.D., Herr, S.S. and O'Sullivan, J.L. (1999) *A Guide to Consent*. Washington, DC: American Association of Mental Retardation.

Dubin, N. (2007) *Asperger Syndrome and Bullying. Strategies and Solutions*. London: Jessica Kingsley Publishers.

Heinrichs, R. (2003) *Perfect Targets: Asperger Syndrome and Bullying*. Shawnee Mission, KS: Autism Asperger Publishing Company.

Herron, R. and Sorenson, K. (2003) *Unmasking Sexual Con Games—A Parent Guide*. Boys Town, NE: Boys Town Press.

Hingsburger, D. (1995) *Just Say Know! Understanding & Reducing the Risk of Sexual Victimization of People with Developmental Disabilities*. Eastman, QC, Canada: Diverse City Press.

Molloy, H. and Vasil, L. (eds) (2004) *Asperger Syndrome, Adolescence, and Identity. Looking Beyond the Label*. London: Jessica Kingsley Publishers.

Walker-Hirsch, L. (2007) *The Facts of Life…and More. Sexuality and Intimacy for People with Intellectual Disabilities*. Baltimore, MD: Paul H. Brookes Publishing Co.

Personal safety curricula

Becoming Date Smart 2. Avoiding Trouble and Listening for "No" [video program]. Santa Barbara, CA: James Stanfield Company.

Heighway, S. and Webster, S.K. (1993) *STARS 2 for Children: A Guidebook for Teaching Positive Sexuality and the Prevention of Sexual Abuse for Children with Developmental Disabilities*. Madison, WI: Wisconsin Council on Developmental Disabilities.

Walker-Hirsh, L. and Champagne, M.P. *Circles®: Stop Abuse* [video program]. Santa Barbara, CA: James Stanfield Company.

Internet safety books for parents

Goodstein, A. (2007) *Totally Wired. What Teens and Tween are Really Doing Online*. New York, NY: St Martin's Griffin.

Willard, N.E. (2007) *Cyber-Safe Kids, Cyber-Savvy Teens. Helping Young People Learn to Use the Internet Safely and Responsibly*. San Francisco, CA: Jossey-Bass Publishers.

Websites

American Association of Sex Educators, Counselors, and Therapists (AASECT). Available at www.aasect.org

Ludwig, S.E. (2005) *After You Tell*. Public Health Agency of Canada. Available at www.phac-aspc. gc.ca/ncfv-cnivf/familyviolence/html/nfntsxarevel_e.html

Debbaudt, D. *Autism Risk & Safety Management: Information & Resources for Law Enforcement, First Responders, Parents, Educators and Care Providers*. Autism Safety & Risk, Denis Debbaudt. Available at www.autismriskmanagement.com

Kidpower Teenpower Fullpower International™. Available at www.kidpower.org

Mayer-Johnson [creators of Boardmaker]. Available at www.mayer-johnson.com

Speak Up. Safeguarding People who use Augmentative and Alternative Communication (AAC) from Sexual Abuse/Victimization. Augmentative Communication Community Partnerships Canada (ACCPC). Available at www.accpc.ca/Speak_Up/index.htm

Websites about online safety

Cyberbullying.org. Bill Besley. Available at http://cyberbullying.org

i-SAFE. Available at http://isafe.org

Smartgirl. University of Michigan. Available at http://smartgirl.org

Wiredsafety.org. Wired Kids, Inc. Available at http://wiredsafety.org

CHAPTER 9

Our Journey: A Mother and her Daughter with Asperger's Syndrome

Maureen and Maura Petro

Maura is a 19-year-old young woman with Asperger's Syndrome. In this chapter Maura and her mother share with us the experience and difficulties of growing up as a girl with Asperger's Syndrome. The roman text was written by Maura's mother; Maura describes her own experiences in italics.

Friday April 13, 2001. In the secular world, another Friday the Thirteenth. On the Christian calendar, Good Friday, a holy and most solemn of days.

Sitting in my car in the parking lot of a psychiatrist, I attempt to gather my thoughts before the appointment I arranged six weeks prior. My sixth-grade, 12-year-old daughter is in the back seat quietly staring out the window. I wonder if her thoughts parallel mine.

What are we doing sitting in the parking lot of a psychiatrist? A PSYCHIATRIST??!!! How in the world did we get here? How am I going to explain to this woman the reasons for our visit? Where do I begin?

Within a few minutes, our intake interview is scheduled to start, yet I am having great difficulty trying to focus on just the "right things" to say within the short timeframe of our one-hour appointment that will adequately express my concerns regarding my daughter Maura's perplexing behaviors over the past ten years.

Characteristic of the middle school teacher that I am, I rummage through the ever-present paper pile on the passenger seat next to me that somehow never seems to get filed away successfully. I find a blank sheet and quickly scribble down random, seemingly disjointed thoughts about my daughter and her unsettling, at times rather bizarre, behaviors exhibited over the course of the last ten years:

- low frustration tolerance resulting in self-hitting/scratching
- incredible sustained attention and persistence in doing the same thing over and over as long as it is what interests her
- the ability to recount verbatim a conversation that may have taken place weeks, months, even years before
- temper fits/meltdowns when demands are made upon her
- screaming whenever someone touches, even ever so lightly, the brass banister that runs alongside of our staircase
- ignoring certain family members, looking through them as if they weren't even there
- directing conversations at me although she was actually speaking to the other person present
- use of strange "made-up" words that appear unrelated to her present situation

The list seemed a jumble of disconnected phrases that didn't make any sense yet certainly characterized Maura's main concerns. Would the psychiatrist be able to ascribe any possible meaning from this list? What would I say to her if she couldn't? Would we be given any ideas or clues as to Maura's problems? Would Maura display any of the listed attributes while in the presence of the doctor, or come across as a typical young adolescent whose mother had an overly active imagination? All I could do was walk through the office door and hope for the best.

We are called into the psychiatrist's office and, as I had observed on numerous occasions, Maura proceeds to look straight at me as she describes to the doctor, a soft-spoken, amiable woman, why she is there. Intermittently, Maura changes the course of the conversation to a totally unrelated event such as the time her math teacher jumped on the desk and started yelling. I am grateful for having at least one thing on my list verified. After 15 minutes of speaking with us both, the doctor asks to speak to Maura alone. I head off to wait in an adjoining office wondering, hoping, PRAYING that my daughter's behaviors would coincide with what I had written down so hurriedly in the car just minutes before.

I feel as though I am in a time warp as 15 minutes (or was it 15 years?) passes. The doctor, seated across from me, is ready to share her impressions of Maura. Finally, will there be some answers to my questions? Is my daughter emotionally disturbed as her teachers seem to think? Is my daughter just a difficult, defiant child whose behaviors will subside with more discipline and maturity? Is there an answer, ANY answer for me to take home and share with family, friends, and school personnel?

The moment has arrived and while I hope otherwise, I truly do not expect to hear any clear explanation, let alone diagnosis, of my daughter's reasons for functioning the way she does.

The only way to describe what I heard next is to envision being underwater in a pool and trying to understand what someone is attempting to tell you from somewhere above the water. The "jumble" of disjointed behaviors I had listed was being explained by a new "jumbled" list of words and phrases. Only later that same evening did I realize I had not even correctly comprehended some of the terms I had heard through that impenetrable "wall of water":

PDD

Pervasive Developmental Disorder

On the autism continuum

"Abspegers" (what the heck is that???!!??)

Extremely high functioning form of autism

Extremely lucky

"Extremely lucky?" Of all the phrases, "Extremely lucky" elicited the most conflicting emotions. The irony of that day, Friday, April 13, due to its significance on the secular and religious calendars did not escape me. Friday the Thirteenth was the ultimate "Bad Luck" day while Good Friday was, for Christians, essentially a day of mourning.

In retrospect, I now view that day as the ultimate "Good Luck" day—the day we received answers, albeit not all the answers, as to why our daughter behaves and experiences life in her own unique way. The blinders were removed and we could get on with the business of helping Maura navigate a world that was so foreign and so frustrating to her at times. And Good Friday? I view that day also within the religious context of that most solemn day. In Christianity, Good Friday does signify "death", but a death of life as we once knew it. It holds out the promise of salvation that comes within the next three days—Easter. We underwent our own personal Good Friday that particular Friday in April in that our old way of life was gone and, through a diagnosis of Asperger's Syndrome, we were essentially saved from a life of "not knowing", perhaps the worst kind of life. Understanding and associated resources were now accessible once we discovered the "name" for the reasons our daughter struggled so hard to cope in our world. Maura looks back on that day from her own unique vantage point.

When I was in sixth grade, my mother started taking me to a number of doctors. We went from one appointment to the next starting with a psychiatrist. I don't remember much about that appointment, but she seemed very calm and asked me questions about myself.

A few weeks later, I went to another doctor, a pediatric neurologist. She was very nice and had me do some balancing and coordination tests. We then went to see another pediatric neurologist, a male this time. I did the same type of test as before but I noticed he kept looking at his watch every five minutes and suddenly said he had to go. I thought he was very strange and rude, too. After learning about Asperger's, I thought even he might have had it!

I had never heard of Asperger's Syndrome until I saw books my mother left around the house. I always knew I was different—I had different behaviors from everyone else, nobody seemed to like me, and I was beginning to be bullied a lot. I remember asking my mother if I had Asperger's Syndrome, but at first she told me she was reading the books for school. I did really know it was about me all along. I started thinking that maybe Asperger's Syndrome was a life-threatening disease. One of my biggest fears remaining to this day is getting a disease, especially when it's currently in the news.

One evening we were driving home from an appointment when I asked my mother one more time if I had Asperger's Syndrome. She finally told me that I did and explained as just a different way my mind worked. I was so relieved that I wasn't sick and that it was something we could work on.

Our Journey—BD ("Before Diagnosis")

As with any journey, ours has a beginning. I had great difficulty getting pregnant with Maura, my second and last child that resulted in the use of fertility medication. After two courses of treatment we were thrilled when I became pregnant in April of 1988. Although I did experience difficulties with my asthma, I delivered Maura by Caesarian section. The first signs of Maura's differences may have been voiced by one of the nurses responsible for caring for the newborns. In the nursery, Maura would stare very intently around and didn't cry as often as the other babies, something I noticed throughout her infancy as well.

Over the next two years, Maura developed in a similar manner as her older sister. Developmental milestones were met within the normal timeframes and nothing seemed to be out of the ordinary. Maura was so accommodating that I would often joke that she was "taking it all in" and would someday "let it all out". Prophetic, to say the least!

Not long after, Maura's temperament started to change. She would scream if not given her way and didn't show much of a response when relatives or friends came to visit. Ignoring their arrival, Maura would go about her business as if they weren't even there. However, within her immediate family and those relatives she saw often, she was very appropriate in her interactions.

During the preschool and early elementary years, Maura continued to interact well with our family but showed increased signs of low frustration tolerance at home as well as in school. Behaviors that were preexisting tended to worsen while new unexplainable behaviors were developing. Although there were behavioral changes, they did not occur every day, but rather sporadically, especially in times of stress.

The greatest period of change happened about age three, immediately after Maura began preschool. After attending a summer day camp program at our local public school, Maura began a prekindergarten program in the same building with the same teacher for the next two years. Her teacher related that Maura had great difficulty changing activities, would want to continue with whatever she was doing that interested her, or would want to talk about her favorite topic at that time—cats. When not getting her way, Maura would scream, often having to be brought into the hallway to calm down. Her teacher felt these were maturational issues, informing me they had stopped by the end of the school year.

Maura was described as very active, running around the classroom with her arms outstretched. She would attempt to engage other children in play, but when they didn't want to play her game, she was very content to play on her own. I also had noted that Maura just didn't seem to care if she was playing alone or not. Another behavior that developed at the time was thought to be part of a game Maura was playing with the teacher. Maura would repeat, word-for-word, exactly what the teacher said to the class, in her own words, a "millisecond" after she spoke. Other different behaviors included difficulty with the noise level of the classroom, especially if the children were singing. Yelling out, "It's too loud!" Maura would place her fingers in her ears to block out the noise.

Kindergarten and first grade progressed in much the same manner. Academically, teachers would describe Maura in terms of being very bright, even brilliant! We just saw an extremely verbal, curious little girl who had a mind of her own and a will of steel to match! Again, the main problems revolved around Maura's inability to switch gears from one activity to the next, an increasingly low frustration tolerance, and greater difficulty "letting go" from discussing her favorite topic—cats. Maura's first-grade teacher related that she would talk out loud about cats at inappropriate times such as during a math lesson.

Socially, Maura was interested in pursuing friendships, but not to the same extent as others her age. However, comparing her to other children or even her perception of any such comparison would lead to extreme upset. It wasn't as if she wanted any type of praise or to be thought "better" than any other student. On the contrary, Maura hated any attention, negative or positive, directed toward her.

It was during first grade that Maura developed her first really close friendship with another girl. It was reciprocated until Maura's feelings for this relationship became very intense. She wanted this girl to be just *her* friend and was constantly talking to her. Additionally, as this girl was in Maura's class, she had first-hand knowledge of Maura's behavioral differences. Maura was absolutely heartbroken when her friend had a birthday party toward the end of the school year and didn't invite my daughter. The reason? She was told that her friend's mother didn't "want a girl who would be screaming and crying at my daughter's party." Unfortunately, it was the first sign of things to come.

I attended preschool in the same building where my mother taught. I remember not really playing with the other kids. I just wanted to be left alone. I really hated singing in class because it was too loud and very annoying to me. In kindergarten, my teacher was very sweet. She would read us many stories and then have us write our own. I liked being able to draw and write my own stories. Once I wrote a story with near-perfect spelling and my teacher was very impressed.

In first grade, I had a good friend named "Rebecca". She was my first real friend. We would talk all the time and play together. She lived around the corner from my grandmother and we would talk to each other through the fence. I don't remember anything about being invited to her party, but she stopped talking and being nice to me.

I now began to think that Maura was in need of counseling and that her problems, which were extending out into the social realm, were not due exclusively to maturational issues. With first grade over and having moved to a new neighborhood and public school, I was hoping that perhaps we would see an improvement in Maura's socialization and behaviors, but in the back of my mind was an uneasy feeling that it was not to be.

Maura started in her new school that fall and as I had suspected not only did things fail to improve, but they steadily worsened. The same issues with frustration and socialization were obvious to all. In October, Maura fell from playground equipment, fracturing her arm. This required surgery and a two-day stay at our local children's hospital. With her arm in a cast, Maura's frustration level was at an all-time high. Even before her cast came off in November, Maura started engaging in injurious self-hitting.

It was at this time that I sought professional counseling for her. Maura initially saw one psychologist who felt she was experiencing adjustment problems due to moving to a new home and school within the past year. The opinion of a second psychologist was sought and Maura continues to see him today. Although no diagnosis was immediately forthcoming, Maura developed a rapport with her new psychologist.

From second through fifth grade, Maura progressed academically with high grades and managed to maintain a small group of friends, but socially, the proverbial handwriting was on the wall. Bullying at the elementary level started in third grade with one girl singling out Maura and taunting her with remarks such as, "Everyone hates you! No one wants to be your friend!" By fifth grade, there was a boy who also harassed Maura on a daily basis. She dealt with these situations by basically trying to ignore them and only once did I have to intervene.

Because these students had difficulties with others besides Maura, I viewed them in terms of general bullying. I knew Maura was seen as different, and even odd, but I held on to the belief that having her small group of friends proved she was not socially isolated. Maura was a good friend, easygoing when deciding what to do as a group, not loud or bossy, just happy to be included.

Another new friendship grew between Maura and her friend, "Isabel". They were the best of friends, sharing secrets during sleep-overs and play dates. I would hear them from Maura's room as they wrote original plays and then, together, acted them out. I remember referring to "Isabel" as Maura's "angel", always there, looking beyond Maura's differences, not caring what other girls might think or say. Maura was a great friend in return, never arguing, teasing, or misbehaving in "Isabel's" presence. If anything, Maura always deferred to her best friend's wishes. And then middle school began.

In the beginning of second grade I attended the elementary school in my new neighbor-hood. The memories of breaking my arm are vivid. I fell off the monkey bars of the playground near my house and needed to have surgery. My arm was in a cast for about five weeks. I would pound and scratch myself on the hand of my broken arm out of frustration whenever things went wrong.

I did meet a nice girl in my class named "Isabel". We were best friends and got along very well. We would go over to each other's houses and I would be so excited to see her and spend time with her family. We were inseparable. Unlike the other kids, she never made fun of me and she gave me a friendship necklace. It was heart-shaped with the words "Best Friends" inscribed on it. Divided into two pieces, there was one part of the heart for each of us to keep. We kept our friendship throughout the years of elementary school, but then in middle school things started to change as she met new friends.

Middle school. Who better to anticipate the difficulties of middle school than I? I had my own personal experiences surviving those years pretty much unscathed and patiently parented my older daughter through varying degrees of social or emotional difficulties involving girls, boys, or both! But most of all, I was a middle school teacher who taught sixth grade. Surely, I had a tremendous advantage from having viewed this transitional year from both sides of the desk. Despite Maura's challenges, I was confident I would be able to successfully maneuver my younger daughter through the turbulent waters of middle school in much the same fashion I had done for myself and her older sister.

I actually anticipated the middle school years as a time where Maura would mature enough to not only maintain, but expand, her small group of friends. There were two other elementary schools in our district which would filter into Maura's new middle school. Perhaps there were other girls just like Maura—good students, socially awkward, different, interested in the same things, looking for a loyal friend. Maura, too, was excited to finally be able to do things with less supervision and "hand-holding", the very things she so vehemently resented in her earlier school years. Although optimistic, I had a foreboding sense about the reality of the situation. Sadly, my fears were about to be realized.

Maura started middle school in September 2000. She seemed to adjust well, and her high academic performance continued. Unfortunately, problems began with students at the lockers in the hallway. The lockers in her middle school were extremely narrow, less than five inches in width, and placed one next to the other in a straight row along the hallway walls. We were to discover later that Maura's difficulties with extreme sensitivity to touch and the invasion of her personal space by others were exacerbated by the placement of her locker in the middle of the row, causing her extreme

sensory overload. In October, the inside of her locker was vandalized, insti-
gated by one of the girls who had complained about Maura always being in
her way. The group had apparently watched Maura as she put in her locker
combination. They were able then to access it and write "Maura is an ass" on
the inside. I was sickened by the thought that now it was not just one boy
or girl, but an entire group of students who didn't even know Maura from
elementary school!

Problems continued by her locker area as a boy on the other side of her
locker would also harass Maura and keep his locker door open wide enough
that Maura was unable to get into hers. On her birthday in January, Maura's
friend decorated the inside of her locker with candy. This boy would not
allow Maura to close her locker and told her he would close it for her.
Always a strong rule-follower, she left for class so as not to be late. As a
result, when she returned, all the candy her friend had placed inside was
missing, stolen by the boy who pretended to be so "helpful".

*Starting middle school wasn't as bad as I had thought it would be. Those first few weeks
I enjoyed having my own locker, going to different classes, having my friends in the same
classes with me, and having a greater sense of independence. However, a few weeks into
the new school year it all started going downhill. It was extremely crowded in the hallways and I felt too clustered together with everyone. We were all on top of each other.
I felt a heightening of my sensory issues, especially being caught in between too many
people.*

*One day I opened up my locker to find nasty words written on the inside of the
locker door. I felt so very angry and upset that someone would do this me. I had never
caused any problems with any of the students and felt betrayed upon learning who had
done this. I didn't even know these kids!*

It was now November of Maura's sixth grade and parent–teacher conferences were scheduled. As I met with each of Maura's team teachers, they
all made the same basic observations. I was told that Maura's academics
were outstanding but her social skills were of concern to almost all her
teachers. I informed all teachers that Maura was under the care of a psychologist for low frustration tolerance and its negative impact on her social
skills development. Although they had not seen any evidence of negative,
acting-out behaviors, I politely asked to be kept informed of any difficulties Maura might be encountering and provided them with all my contact
information.

After the locker incident, I took Maura to a psychologist who conducted social skills groups. Maura was evaluated, but unfortunately, the psychologist did not have an appropriate age group that matched Maura's needs.

It was at this time, early January 2001, Maura started to express a great deal of anger about her math teacher. Even though Maura had difficulty with frustrating situations, it was always the "situation" and never any one "person", whether a friend, other student, or teacher, to which Maura responded. Now, it was different. Being an excellent student who was polite and always met academic expectations, Maura never had to deal with much criticism from any teacher. I had even received a note from this particular teacher about Maura being a wonderful student and "Great Kid!"

Maura's math teacher began berating her class, comparing her class's academic progress and behavior to that of other classes he taught. The teacher also told them that he was going to treat them differently than the other classes he taught by assigning them double homework ("You have fourth grade skills!"; "I expect low grades from this class"). Needless to say, Maura, the child who absolutely abhorred critical comparisons and unfairness in any form, was incensed. Despite the range of Maura's negative behaviors I had observed over the years, nothing compared to this!

Nightly, I would hear how unfair her teacher was acting. "He has no proof, Mom!" she would tell me. "We haven't even had any homework or tests for him to say this!" she would contend. As try as I might, Maura could not stop obsessing over these "grave" injustices. I suggested that she speak to him, but she refused.

I contacted the social worker, afraid that Maura would lose control, as the situation was getting out of hand. Each day another unfair pronouncement by this teacher was brought home. I could see Maura's anger escalating and feared she would have an outburst in school if things weren't resolved. To the best of my knowledge, Maura's frustration hadn't been exhibited in any manner during the school day. A brief conversation with the social worker resulted in her assurance that she would speak to Maura's math teacher.

Four days later, my husband received a call from the middle school while I was at work. The assistant principal related that Maura was having extreme difficulties in school and school personnel wanted to arrange a "Child Study Team" meeting with us. Needless to say, I was stunned, especially since I had asked the teachers during parent–teacher conferences, just a few short months ago, to contact me if they saw signs of possible problems. I had never received any calls from any teacher, guidance counselor, school psychologist, or administrative staff member up until this point in time.

I promptly returned the assistant principal's phone call and was informed that Maura's math teacher, the very same teacher who had caused so much anxiety in my daughter, called the meeting because of behaviors Maura had been exhibiting the past few weeks of school. All I could think about was my phone call to the school social worker just a few days prior. She had given absolutely no indication whatsoever that there had been any ongoing issues concerning Maura, or that she even knew Maura at all. During the course of my conversation with the assistant principal, it was obvious that Maura had been in great distress for some time. I heard about an incident in the crowded hallway right outside Maura's first period classroom.

Apparently, no students were permitted to enter the school building before the first bell. Rather, they were to remain outside waiting by the double-door entrance. When the first bell finally rang, all students entered the building en masse and were required to go immediately to their lockers to gather their books and proceed to their first period class. A period of five minutes was allowed for the students to accomplish all of this amid the start-of-day chaos that swirled around them. Maura had been caught up in all of this day after day and finally reacted.

Three weeks prior to the school's phone call, Maura was making her way to her locker to get what she needed for her first period class, math. As she tried to get through the throng of rushing students, Maura finally had had enough and her sensory issues were brought to a head. She stood in the hallway and started to pound herself on her forehead, crying out, "I can't take this any more!" With a sinking heart, I listened to the assistant principal's recounting of Maura's behaviors and made an appointment to meet with Maura's team teachers.

The day of the Child Study Team meeting arrived and I entered the school in a state of despair. Maura was unable to provide me with much information about what had been going on except that she was still extremely upset about her math teacher and his ongoing comments. I was ushered into a conference off the main office hallway and there before me sat the following people at the large oval conference table—Maura's four team teachers, both assistant principals, the school psychologist, the school nurse, and Maura's guidance counselor. Other school personnel who had been originally scheduled, but unable to attend due to absences, were the middle school dean of discipline and the school social worker. Imagine! A grand total of 11 people invited, nine attending and me who had no idea how many people were "lying in wait" for me!

As a sixth-grade middle school teacher, I had been on the other side of the table many times myself, but always part of a much smaller group—three team teachers and perhaps the guidance counselor and/or school psychologist in the most serious of cases. To see all these people around me to discuss my daughter was daunting to say the least. I listened first to Maura's math teacher as he described in detail what occurred in the hallway when Maura had her meltdown three weeks before. He told me pretty much what I had heard from the assistant principal during our previous telephone conversation. I did ask him what he did to help Maura during the incident. His response?

"I was too busy calming down the poor little girl who was standing next to me. She was so upset by what was happening."

I couldn't believe my ears!! Calming down another student while my daughter was in the throes of an apparent panic attack? I asked the other teachers what they did. Their response?

"We didn't see it."

This from teachers whose job it was to oversee the students as they were getting ready for class. As the teachers were adding their own comments concerning Maura's behaviors over the last few weeks, I noticed that her social studies teacher, who had Maura the last period of the day, wasn't contributing at all to the conversation. I asked her how Maura was behaving. Her response?

"She's fine with me."

I then proceeded to move my way backward through Maura's other class periods and questioned each subsequent teacher in the same manner. The English and science teachers both stated that, although Maura appeared somewhat anxious during class, she didn't have any outbursts at all. The science teacher, who taught Maura second period immediately after math, reported that Maura would come into the classroom very agitated at times. She did experience some difficulties socially but tended to settle down and do her work.

Remembering my conversations with each teacher back in November during parent–teacher conferences, I asked the social studies, science, and English teachers if I had given them my cell phone number and requested to be called in the event of any problem. Each answered, "Yes." I asked each in turn if they ever tried to call me. Each answered, "No." I turned to the math teacher and asked him directly the same questions. His response to each was the same as the other teachers only this time I also asked him, "Why not?"

He just looked at me and couldn't answer. Fortunately for him the period bell rang and he had to go to lunch duty.

The meeting continued and I continued with my questions.

"Was my daughter ever referred to you after this incident?" I asked the guidance counselor.

"No," he answered.

"Have you ever spoken with or even met my daughter?" I asked him

"No," he replied.

"Was my daughter ever referred to you after this incident?" I asked the school psychologist.

"No," she answered.

"Have you ever spoken with or even met my daughter?"

"No," she replied.

"Did you know that Maura's locker had been vandalized in October?" I asked the teachers, guidance counselor, school psychologist, and assistant principal.

"No," they collectively replied.

I was beginning to get the picture. Mother calls social worker about daughter's difficulties with her math teacher; social worker speaks to math teacher; math teacher calls team meeting regarding daughter's problem behavior to deflect attention away from him and any role he may have played in daughter's behavioral difficulties.

Did I believe that Maura was having extreme difficulties? Absolutely, a resounding "YES!"

Was I grateful to be notified? Absolutely a resounding "YES!"

Was I appalled by the lack communication and compassion exhibited by most, if not all, present? "YES, YES, YES!"

Although extremely upset after the meeting, I did realize that it was time to pursue reasons why Maura was experiencing such overt negative, out-of-control behaviors more rigorously. Other students had seen her get so very upset without understanding the reason for it which, in a middle school setting, is socially a "kiss of death." With the exception of her friend "Kristen", a physically challenged young girl, the small group of friends she had built up in elementary school was no longer a part of her social life.

I had observed on several occasions, especially during Maura's weekly Girl Scout meetings held at her local elementary school, that "Isabel" and several of the girls in the troop would play mean tricks on Maura. I watched this happen one evening while waiting for the meeting to end. While Maura was finishing up a project in the school cafeteria, the group ran into the girls' restroom. Upon completing her work, Maura went in search of her friends. When she couldn't find them right away, she was becoming upset. I was waiting to see if this was just some silly harmless joke, hoping the girls would jump out and laugh together once they realized how much their actions were upsetting their friend. It truly broke my heart to see Maura running through the hallway and into the gym while these girls laughed, peeking out the restroom door as she ran by calling their names. When they saw me standing outside the door, they stopped. I just looked at them and shook my head slowly and sadly. I realized then that peer pressure was beginning to play a prominent role in how others related to Maura.

Maura continued to invite them to her yearly birthday parties, yet there was no longer any reciprocation from her friends. "Isabel", her best friend in elementary, actively shunned Maura and never responded back to her phone calls. Maura was devastated! She just couldn't understand why this was happening. I was to find out later that it had become common knowledge that "Isabel"'s mother no longer wanted her daughter to socialize with Maura, despite the fact that they always enjoyed each other's company without any indications of problems during their friendship. Perhaps it was hearing how Maura was reacting in school, or that other girls were starting to shun Maura. Perhaps "Isabel"'s mother didn't want her own daughter to be adversely affected socially by continuing a friendship with girl who appeared "disturbed". It was so obvious that Maura was beginning to be set apart by her behaviors at a time in her life when conformity was the ultimate social rule.

I now look back upon these experiences as a pivotal moment in our lives, for it was the awareness of Maura's difficulties in school and their impact on her socialization which prompted me to contact Maura's psychiatrist and make that crucial "Good Friday", "Friday the Thirteenth" appointment seven years ago. With Maura's diagnosis of Asperger's Syndrome, we were given the answer to the question, "Why does Maura act the way she does?" and were challenged with the mandate to help her as best as we were able.

Our Journey—AD ("After Diagnosis")

After our appointment with the psychiatrist was over, I returned home and began to research all I could on Asperger's Syndrome. I still couldn't quite believe that my daughter was considered somewhere on an "autism continuum" as the psychiatrist had sought to explain to me. I immediately went to my computer to research online what this so-called "Abspegers" was all about. I remember typing in that term, yet it came up showing "no result". The only other term I could recall the psychiatrist telling me was something about PDD, and so I typed that into my computer. I laughed to myself when one result came back that PDD was some sort of parrot disease! But then I saw it, Pervasive Developmental Disorder, and realized that this was one of the phrases the doctor has used in describing Maura. When I typed that term into the computer, I realized that it was "Asperger's" that the doctor had been talking about, not "Abspegers!" Now knowing Maura's diagnosis, the first question I asked myself was, "What in the world is Asperger's Syndrome?"

Asperger's! What a strange word! Yet I knew that we had truly found our answer. Years of not knowing, not understanding, fell away with each stroke of the keyboard, each new website opened, each new article read (no, devoured!), each description so precisely characterized my daughter and the world she had inhabited for all those years. We just didn't know!

Article after article, I didn't read only my daughter's life written into each line on each page—No, I was also reading about one of my younger brothers, a young man who had always been "different", socially isolated, extremely intelligent with an IQ of 139, a true expert, knowledgeable on all aspects of the American Civil War, yet unable to continue in college after just one semester. He was one of five siblings I grew up with who struggled throughout his childhood with bullying and lack of friendships. People thought he was retarded, emotionally disturbed because he just didn't fit in. I only knew him as a gentle person, a Civil War enthusiast, with an amazing knowledge of *Star Trek* episodes who would look down at the ground, while stroking his beard, whenever he spoke to you.

That night I learned so many things which rekindled distant memories of my mother's cousin, another brilliant young man who had been diagnosed with childhood schizophrenia in the 1950s. Could he have been possibly misdiagnosed? Was it really Asperger's Syndrome? What about my mother's brother, now deceased? A very odd, private person, never married, having no social life, and who lived with his parents until they both passed away when he was in his sixties. Had he also been on the autism spectrum? My deceased mother herself, avoiding social contact unless she could be in total control, a "black-and-white" thinker with tendencies toward OCD, social phobia, and depression—had she also been exhibiting signs of Asperger's all along?

I felt as though I had unraveled some great, fantastic family mystery that night, sitting and typing on my computer. With each minute spent reading, I began to understand my daughter's intense anxiety and frustration of living in a world that is so utterly unforgiving of differences. I was relieved to find out there was a name for Maura's way for functioning. It all made so much sense now! Her aversion to crowds, her intense pain on hearing high-pitched sounds such as a hand rubbing against the brass banister along our staircase, her phenomenal memory—the very things I had listed on that piece of paper while sitting in my car waiting to see the psychiatrist!

It had been three months since meeting with the middle school staff when Maura received her diagnosis and in those three months I did get a number of phone calls expressing concerns about Maura's behavior. However, most of the behaviors were still related to Maura's difficulties with her math teacher. He continued to compare her class to his others, criticizing her class's skills.

"I don't expect you to do well on the final. I expect low grades from this class."

These incidents resulted in Maura pounding her desk and acting out in school. But now, I knew why Maura reacted so intensely to these remarks. One of the hallmarks of Asperger's is "black-and-white thinking" resulting in rigid thinking with absolutely no tolerance for anything considered "unfair". Understanding this made it that much easier to view Maura's experience through the lens of Asperger's Syndrome. Maura's difficulties with her math teacher were clarified by using this lens as well. One of the articles I came across in my exhaustive research on Asperger's Syndrome stated:

> Asperger himself realized the central importance of teacher attitude from his own work with these children. In 1944 he wrote, "These children often show a surprising sensitivity to the personality of the teacher... They can be taught, but only by those who give them true understanding and affection, people who show kindness towards them and, yes, humour... The teacher's underlying emotional attitude influences, involuntarily and unconsciously, the mood and behavior of the child." (Bauer 1996)

We now understood that a teacher who exhibited mood swings, engaged in harsh criticism of his students, and was, more importantly, unresponsive to Maura's needs was the antithesis of the type of teacher best-suited to work with a student such as Maura.

With a few short months of sixth grade remaining, we helped her cope with the situation better than we had previously. At the conclusion of sixth grade, I called a meeting with the assistant principal, the social worker, and her new guidance counselor. We spoke about an appropriate seventh-grade placement for Maura, her locker location at the end of the row, and involvement in a social skills lunch group.

Seventh grade began as sixth had, with Maura continuing her strong academic performance. I met with her main subject teachers and the guidance counselor immediately to discuss Maura's unique characteristics and her newly acquired diagnosis of Asperger's Syndrome. I was very direct in communicating Maura's social and behavioral concerns, especially her sensitivity to teacher criticism or comparisons, and her social and emotional immaturity. Additionally, I asked their help in completing paperwork for a neuropsychological evaluation Maura would be undergoing at our local children's hospital. We were anxious to clarify Maura's areas of deficit and strength, what strategies would be necessary to help ameliorate some of her difficulties, and if her needs would best be met through services that could only be accessed and implemented by an individualized education plan (IEP).

By the time of parent–teacher conferences, early November 2001, I once again met individually with Maura's teachers to discuss her progress both academically and socially. Each teacher gave his or her assessment of Maura. As with previous conferences, it was stated that she was "very bright"; "an exceptional writer, performing at the level of a high school student"; "an excellent student who knows everything"; "phenomenal memory"; "participation is a positive influence in class". However, along with such positives came the concerns—"experiences some problems with creative writing"; "students seem to be afraid to trigger an emotional reaction from her"; "doesn't seem to be here"; "can get agitated at times"; "pounds on desk when class's performance on tests is discussed". I listened carefully and took notes, anxiously anticipating Maura's upcoming neurological evaluation in December.

Results of the evaluation did confirm the psychiatrist's diagnosis of Asperger's Syndrome with associated OCD and significant symptoms of anxiety and depression. Her verbal skills were much stronger than her nonverbal skills, evidenced by her superior naming and verbal abstraction skills in the verbal domain and her weakness in perceptual organization in the nonverbal domain. The neuropsychologist made numerous recommendations for Maura which included participation in a social skills group, continued individual therapy for anxiety and depression, and participation in speech or language therapy to address weaknesses in pragmatic skills. The final and most important recommendation was to request a Committee on

Special Education (CSE) evaluation to address longstanding concerns about Maura's emotional/social/behavioral functioning in light of her Asperger's diagnosis.

Bullying—the nightmare that was middle school

The vandalism of Maura's locker at the start of sixth grade was the work of a few individuals. There were additional incidents of harassment in her classes also. While dressing for gym class, Maura was targeted by a group of girls who would laugh at her and make comments about her body. They called her "coconut girl" in reference to her developing chest. Although frustrated, Maura would tend to ignore their taunts but was more upset by their refusal to include her in their conversations, yelling her to "get the hell away" whenever she approached them. Gym was on an alternating day schedule, with Maura taking orchestra the second day of the schedule. Unfortunately, one girl in her gym class, "Donna", was in Maura's orchestra class. She continued to taunt Maura throughout the entire sixth grade. One day toward the end of the year, "Donna" was escorting a visiting fifth-grade student on a tour of the middle school. Maura was running an errand for her teacher and encountered "Donna" in the hallway. Without a word, Maura passed "Donna" and the younger student but as she did, "Donna" turned to the other girl stating that Maura was a "psycho". When I found out I spoke to the social worker but nothing was done.

Not even outside of the school building was Maura safe from bullying and harassment. On the way home from school, she was pelted with candy and coins by a group of boys on her bus, one of whom was our neighbor. This particular boy would get great pleasure from calling Maura such things as "retard", "dumb", and "f*cking pain in the ass". One day during the bus ride home, this boy started to ask Maura questions about explicit sex acts and called her a "f*cking retard". When she told me I was shocked and disgusted. I had contacted the school about the physical abuse on the bus and the boys had been issued a warning, but now the physical abuse was replaced by sexual harassment. My husband was the one to handle it and he did so quite well, well enough that our neighbor's son steered clear of Maura.

If sixth grade saw a continuation of relatively isolated incidences of bullying by an individual or a very small group of individuals, seventh and eighth grade would see bullying escalate to a frequency and intensity which we couldn't have imagined in our wildest dreams. "…wildest dreams"?? The last two words of this commonly used idiomatic expression convey a sense of something so outlandish that it is beyond comprehension within the realm of human experience. In describing Maura's experiences in seventh and eighth grade, I choose rather to restate this idiom as "in our wildest nightmares".

As I continued my research of Asperger's Syndrome, article after article, book after book made reference to the incredible amount of childhood bullying to which this population was extremely vulnerable, resulting in depression and anxiety disorders later in their lives. I couldn't help remembering the terrible bullying my younger brother, whom I suspected of having Asperger's, had been exposed to in his childhood and adolescence. One neighborhood boy relentlessly picked on my brother for 11 years, from the time they attended elementary school together to the time they attended the same high school. Intervention by my parents proved fruitless. Unfortunately, this was a time when bullying was almost considered a "rite of passage", especially for males. One day my brother had had enough. Sitting behind him in class, this bully said the wrong thing at the wrong time. With a swing of his arm, my quirky, quiet, gentle brother turned around and broke the boy's nose. The school disciplined my brother for his inappropriate physical behavior and had him attend mandatory counseling. As for the bully? I don't remember if he faced any consequence for his taunting, but I do know he never bothered my brother again.

One of my greatest fears was that Maura would someday react in a similar manner as my brother in response to someone bullying her. I was determined to get Maura classified if only for the limited amount of protection an IEP would provide her. Although there would be disciplinary measures for a display of physical aggression, the incident would be evaluated in relation to her disability.

Seventh grade began, and so, too, the bullying. Verbal abuse was now accompanied by sexual harassment. Boys would come up to Maura and discuss the unique features of their private parts or tell her what they wanted to do with her in terms of sexual acts. Physical harassment continued with Maura being forcefully pushed on the school staircase and into lockers by a boy who taunted her with name calling. "Psycho! Psycho!" he would call after her as he followed her throughout the school. Maura didn't even know this boy but apparently another boy, who bullied Maura on a regular basis, had pointed Maura out as an easy target.

But the worst was yet to come. Somehow, a boy discovered that invading Maura's personal space and yelling "SHUSH" inches from her face resulted in a volatile reaction. All the students witnessing this saw a Maura completely out of control. Other students started to emulate this boy in hope of eliciting a similar reaction for their amusement. Bullying that had occurred individually or in small groups was now school-wide, spreading like wildfire among the student body. It wasn't only her grade involved but the students from other grades as well. It became known that if you wanted to get Maura upset and see her go off, you simply had to "SHUSH" her and wait for her reaction.

Up to this point, I had intervened on Maura's behalf, appropriately going up the "chain of command" that exists in all schools when a parent has an issue. I contacted her teachers, her guidance counselor, the social worker, the school psychologist, and the assistant principal. They were all aware of what was happening but, due to a recently enacted federal law related to family privacy, were prohibited from giving me any information on the students involved or any consequences meted out.

I came home from work one February afternoon to find my daughter in bed under her covers unable to even bear the thought of going into school the next morning. I called the principal but he, as had the assistant principal, refused to provide me with any information for the same reasons. Although he tried to put me off, I insisted on meeting with him the next day. My daughter had rights, too, and I told him I had documented each incident in detail to prove how terribly she was being treated by the very students he was charged with supervising.

I spent the evening gathering all the pieces of paper on which I had written each incident. By the end of the night I had a six-page document written in a very cut and dry, almost clinical manner that included the "who, what, where, why, and how it was dealt with" for each bullying episode Maura had experienced over the year and a half she had been a middle school student. I decided to drop it off at the school two hours before our meeting so that the principal would have time to consider just how awful things were for Maura.

When I arrived for our meeting, the principal warmly greeted me and showed me into his office where the assistant principal was already waiting. Before I even had a chance to utter a single word, the principal told me in great detail the number of phone calls he had made to parents regarding their child's inappropriate behavior toward Maura. Disciplinary action had been taken against a number of students ranging from verbal warning and detentions to in-school suspensions. Under the guise of being proactive, he was trying to assure me that he was on top of things. In reality, I knew that it was only because of my phone call the day before, my insistence on a meeting, and the provision of documentation that anything was done at all. I was prepared to give him the benefit of the doubt and listened to him telling me about his three daughters and how he could empathize with me. And then it happened. As he spoke, his tone changed and what he said next stunned me.

"After speaking with some of the boys involved, Mrs Petro, it seems like Maura's behaviors are the cause of her bullying."

I stared at him, astounded by his comment. I asked him point blank, "Are you blaming the victim?"

He appeared flustered, replying that he only wanted to make me aware that Maura's behaviors were the source of the problem. I managed to ask him to give me an example of Maura's contributing to her own bullying.

"Yesterday, Maura ran past my door, screaming and pounding her hand on her chest."

I asked him if he tried to stop her and ask what happened.

"No, she was on her way to guidance to speak to the social worker."

Amazingly enough, Maura had told me about the incident the night before. While she was at the girls' bathroom during health class, a boy took her work sheet and wrote "Psycho" on it. Upon returning and seeing it, Maura became extremely upset and went to the guidance office to seek help. I told the principal exactly what Maura had related to me concerning her state of upset the previous day. Maura's reactions were due to the actions of her tormentors, not the other way around! It had become a vicious cycle of victimization that was happening on a daily basis.

I left his office with the sense that the principal would not prove an effective ally in preventing future bullying of Maura by the students in his school. For the rest of the school year, he did intervene when problems arose, but the bullying was ongoing. It had now become so widespread that Maura was not only targeted in the school environment but in our community as well. Maura dealt with harassment while we shopped in local stores and even on the soccer field.

What made the situation on the soccer field particularly upsetting was the fact that she was singled out by her own team members for teasing and name-calling. If I hadn't witnessed it myself, I would not have believed it! I saw Maura approach the older girls on her team as they were talking together before a game. There was nothing in Maura's demeanor that could have prompted their cruelty. I watched her stand quietly next to them and join in their conversation. All seemed well until I saw the inevitable eye rolling and smirks exchanged between the girls as Maura talked to them. The group went to take their positions on the field as the game was getting ready to begin. As Maura went to assume her position on the field, I heard a chorus of, "Maura is a homo", coming from the direction of the teammates with whom she had just been speaking. Maura looked back at the group in confusion but continued on to her position.

Once again I was sickened by what I had heard and seen. My only hope was that Maura did not hear what was yelled at her across the length of the soccer field. On the way home Maura made no mention of the name-calling and I thought she had been spared at least one hurtful experience. However, as I kissed her good night later that evening, she looked up at me sadly and said, "Mom, I think someone called me a homo today during soccer." What could I say? I told her that yes, I had heard it also and offered to call her coach and discuss it with him. With every incident I always gave Maura the option of having me intervene on her behalf and, as long as the situation was an isolated event, I honored her wishes. She didn't want to get kids in trouble and gave them the benefit of the doubt that it was a one-time happening. I spoke to the coach and he reprimanded the girls. Maura quit soccer shortly thereafter.

Before seventh grade ended, I began the process of having Maura classified and eligible for an IEP. I sent a letter the district's director of special education requesting a CSE multidisciplinary evaluation to address concerns about Maura's emotional, social, and behavioral functioning as well as possible communication, language, and sensory deficits. Maura's disability was having such a negative impact on her educational functioning with episodes of school avoidance, test anxiety, and overall extreme school-related stress we attributed to her history of sensory dysfunction and social difficulties. Her situation was further exacerbated by the frequency and severity of bullying occurring at the middle school.

All were in agreement that an IEP would make available to Maura services that would remediate some of her difficulties. At the meeting the school psychologist's report reflected what we believed all along, pointing out Maura's extreme sensitivities to noises and smells, crowded situations, and comments by her teachers. The report also noted strained relationships with peers. The CSE concluded with recommendations for an IEP to include speech-language services and inclusion in a social skills lunch group.

With the end of seventh grade and the principal and staff fully aware of the bullying Maura faced each day, we looked forward to her last year in the middle school. Within the first month of school, however, I documented at least eight bullying episodes and realized that the time had come to take my concerns to the district superintendent. The principal no longer could control the level of harassment that was directed toward Maura in the middle school. Applying disciplinary measures against such a large group of aggressors was like applying a band-aid to a hemorrhaging wound.

I called the district office to make an appointment to meet with the superintendent one-on-one. Later that evening, I received a message on my answering machine from the superintendent's secretary that he wanted to meet with me and the entire middle school pupil personnel staff. "Been there, done that, have the tee-shirt!" as the popular saying goes. Once again, I insisted on a one-on-one meeting with the superintendent. Once again, I received a call from his secretary that he would not meet with me but would have a phone conference with me instead. I told her exactly what I intended to say to him, "I would like to meet with you to discuss the district's 'Zero Tolerance' policy and how it affects my daughter, a middle school student, who is being subjected to severe verbal, physical and sexual harassment." She assured me she would relay my message.

On the appointed day, the superintendent promptly called me and asked how he might help me. I simply restated what I had told his secretary the day before, "I would like to meet with you to discuss the district's 'Zero Tolerance' policy and how it affects my daughter, a middle school student, who is being subjected to severe verbal, physical and sexual harassment." I was outraged by his reply, "I don't know what you expect to get out of that meeting!" I simply reiterated, "I would like to meet with you to discuss the district's 'Zero Tolerance' policy and how it affects my daughter, a middle school student, who is being subjected to severe verbal, physical and sexual harassment." He begrudgingly agreed to meet me the following week.

Another meeting, another annoyed administrator! I now had a document totaling nine pages and, as before with Maura's middle school principal, I sent it to the superintendent prior to our meeting so that he, too, might understand the difficult times my daughter was going through at the hands of some middle school students.

At first, it was a replay of what had happened when I met with the middle school principal—a warm welcome as I was ushered into his office—but it quickly became apparent that he actually intended to help. The superintendent had a copy of my document listing, in chronological order, Maura's bullying experiences, and he listened intently as I gave an overview of what life had been like for my daughter the last year and a half. After I delivered the document to his office, he had even gone to the middle school to observe Maura. We spoke at great length and finally ended our meeting on a more positive note than I had ever anticipated.

This time there were results. Not only was approval given for the hiring of a "shadow" aide, Maura was to benefit from consultation services provided by a recently opened autism center in our area. The district had already contracted with this center to address the needs of more severely affected autistic students in the district through staff development. The center's staff conducted a workshop on student diversity and antibullying for the eighth-grade students, and the more overt forms of bullying finally ceased. In their stead, though, remained shunning and isolation of Maura, especially by the girls in her classes.

Maura would attempt to join in their conversations as she had with her soccer teammates, only to be rebuffed by statements such as, "Why don't you go and talk to that group over there. They probably don't want to talk to you either!" I remember how she came home one afternoon and, crying continuously for well over two hours as she laid huddled on the floor of our living room, begged me to "fix" her. Isolation and rejection had over-whelmed her that day as Maura attempted to speak to some of the girls in her last period class during a short break from class work. All she wanted was to be included, to be given a nickname, like all the other girls had, as a crucially important symbol of social acceptance. Maura did finally get one. They called her "Maura Pester" paraphrasing her real full name, Maura Petro. There were a few students who did stand up for Maura and I greatly appreciated their bravery. Whenever this occurred, I made it a point to call not only the principal, but the student's parent to let them know how coura-geous I thought those students were.

By spring of eighth grade, I knew Maura would never be able to survive, never mind thrive, emotionally in our local public high school. The same students from the middle school were moving up with her to the high school and unfortunately, her history would accompany her, too. The thought of an additional three grades of students possibly targeting Maura with harass-ment was impossible to even fathom. As the social, emotional, and now even academic stresses of middle school became intolerable for her, I had to find a new educational environment suitable for meeting her needs.

We had hired a lawyer as our educational advocate and were able to find an out-of-district program that seemed ideal for Maura. It was an alternative high school which had just started up a specialized program for students classified as "Other Health Impaired" or OHI. The program population included quite a number of Asperger's Syndrome students, and Maura would be educated in a setting where staff members were knowledgeable about her unique needs.

In April, Maura and I went to an alternative school for an interview. We met with two of the staff psychologists and discussed the different aspects of the OHI program. Maura was very animated, discussing her Asperger's in detail and the particular challenges she faced with sensory issues, frustration control, social difficulties, and bullying. She was assured that there would be daily access to counseling, small classroom instruction, and a reduced homework load all designed to alleviate the stress Maura was feeling in her middle school.

To Maura's great relief, bullying of any sort would not be tolerated and would be immediately addressed by the principal. As we discussed the greater amount of boys than girls in the program, Maura impressed them by stating the statistics associated with gender characterized by Asperger's—anywhere from a 8:1 to a 4:1 ratio of boys to girls having the disorder.

When we arrived home, I explained to Maura how different this school would be and that it was considered a special education high school. Maura just looked at me and said. "It's the closest thing to heaven a school could be." With a high school program already in place for the following fall, the only thing left was to get through eighth grade.

At long last—Graduation Day! As my husband, older daughter, and I sat in the auditorium listening to the congratulatory speeches in honor of Maura's graduating eighth-grade class, I thought back over the last few years and felt a sense of relief that it would soon be over. Maura was bound for high school away from those who tormented her year after year. I watched Maura intently for any signs of frustration or anxiety as she sat among her classmates. She was calm and happy as she applauded each speaker, an active participant in her graduation ceremony.

With the rest of the students in her row, Maura rose to walk down the aisle and up onto the stage to receive her diploma. As she approached the steps of the stage I saw that same look of confusion and then despair on her face I had seen many times before. I knew that something was wrong, but what? Maura walked toward the principal to get her diploma, but I could see she was upset. She made an attempt to talk to the principal, but she was hurried off the stage. I knew we had to get her out of there immediately, as did a teacher who was standing nearby. Quickly exiting the auditorium, we all met in the outer hallway.

Maura was clearly very agitated, telling us how she as walked toward the stage passing the rows of her fellow graduates, a number of them yelled in unison "SHUSH" at her. Even during what should have been a wonderful memorable moment in her life, they just couldn't leave our daughter alone. And so, the nightmare that was middle school finally ended.

Most of my school life in my home school district, before I left for the alternative school, I had been socially lost. It was always hard for me to get along with my peers and I was harassed a lot. This might have been because I seemed so socially out of place compared to everyone else. I had a disability that made me not as socially literate as everyone else. Because of this I did not know how to greet people or get into conversations appropriately.

My lowest point was in middle school around seventh grade until I graduated. In middle school, all the other students seemed to be in a different world than me. I felt like an outsider looking into a strange, different place, I felt I didn't belong, and this was made apparent by the other students around me. They harassed me because I would break into conversations inappropriately, act out a lot, and get frustrated easily. Most of these problems were unintentional, as I did not know any better back then. They also vandalized my things by writing horrible sentences on my test papers and even in my locker.

Because of all this harassment, I felt like the other students did not want me around or even to exist. I was never so depressed in my life. It only got worse in eighth grade. People harassed me and I would react very badly, which was amusing to them. It seemed as the days went by, I could not bear to go to school anymore. I would dread going to my high school even more, as it would only get worse from there in terms of the work load and harassment.

The teachers didn't help the situation either. They always sided with the other students, thinking it was my fault that I was harassed. They did not understand my problems or my side of the story. And, no matter what the people who ran my middle school did to stop the harassment, it was extremely ineffective, as the students would just come back from their meaningless suspensions to bother me even more.

However, I began to get better at the end of my last year of middle school. Some students became friendly and defended me from the cruelty of others. I then found out that I would not be going to my local high school, and my parents were looking into different schools to get me out of my school district. It slowly felt like my life would change for the better.

High school: the highs, the lows, and the in-betweens

For the first time in a very long time, Maura was so excited about starting a new school year. Her acceptance into the alternative school was received and a listing of services along with it—daily counseling sessions built into her class schedule, lunch group once a week that would meet and go out to a local pizzeria for lunch on Fridays, both of which would be conducted by one of the psychologists who had interviewed Maura the previous April. She even sent Maura a welcoming note before school began! We knew that the alternative school was the right place for Maura.

The first day of school finally arrived and Maura left the house, anxious to start her day. What a vast difference from just a few months before! As I tried to get Maura out the door each morning, she would cry and beg me, "Please don't send me to hell!" I had, on occasion, allowed her to stay home if I thought she would be unable to get through her day at school, but on the advice of all the professionals, I sent her in many more days than not. As long as her stress levels were only slightly elevated, Maura was able to cope in school. We were able to get a "shadow" for her, a school aide who would stay in the background and keep an eye on her. Maura's psychiatrist had written the CSE advocating for Maura to have a one-on-one aide as a form of protection against the severe harassment she had been encountering.

But now, there was no need for an aide. Each class Maura attended actually had a teacher and an aide present for all the students. The class size was small, no more than nine students, and the teachers caring and accommodating. Homework was assigned, but kept at a minimum. Students could even choose to attend the homework club held the last period of the day and complete it.

Maura arrived home that afternoon in a great mood. I knew it was not the end of her difficulties by any means, but at least there was a place where she felt she belonged. I found the following note in her backpack:

Good things that happened today
- started new school
- bus is clean
- great morning
- great students and teachers in school
- having fun in school (finally!)

- not only girl in classes
- I know my way around
- funny people in classes
- getting an extra point on a test.

The weeks went by quickly, and Maura adjusted well. She progressed academically and made the honor roll at the end of the quarter. No longer did we receive daily phone calls about Maura's behaviors and requests that we pick her up and take her home. The first year at the alternative school had its up and downs but nothing in the way of the bullying that haunted Maura in her middle school.

There were more challenges, however. Maura began to realize just how different she was and the enormity of her struggles to fit in socially. The school's population did not entirely consist of OHI or Asperger's students, but was a mix of students with other emotional and behavioral concerns. We feared that Maura would be singled out by students who might have been the bullies in their own home school districts before they were sent to the alternative school. Our fears never materialized. These students, with their own significant emotional disabilities were, for the most part, very supportive of Maura.

I was right about my feelings about my life changing for the better after graduating middle school. I knew my life would be drastically different when I went to visit the alternative school. That September was the beginning of the rest of my life. I slowly reached my high point in my school career because I was much better accepted in the alternative school and the teachers were much friendlier. I felt like I belonged for the first time in school. Going to the alternative school was a very enjoyable experience and one of the best things to happen to me. The students faced similar problems as me, and because of this, they were more empathetic towards others than the people in my school district. Most of the students were kind and knew what it was like to be harassed. While they had their fair share of problems, they were generally better behaved than I thought they would be. For the first time, I finally belonged in school socially and the alternative school felt like home. At last I found my way in the social culture of school despite what I went through.

Maura's first year at the alternative school proceeded pretty much without any major difficulties. She did begin to show signs of a worsening in her depressive symptoms, especially between the months of November through to April. Maura was diagnosed with seasonal affective disorder (SAD) and had new medication added on to what had already been prescribed by the psychiatrist.

Despite a supportive staff and interventions by the professionals Maura saw privately, her depression deepened. During her second and third year at the alternative school, her world again began to fall apart, maybe not directly because of her bullying experiences in middle school, but they definitely were a major contributory factor in Maura's struggles with depression. She relived many of those experiences and would feel the pain of rejection again and again as she tried to make sense of her world. There were just too many stressors in Maura's life that she found overwhelming to deal with on top of daily sensory overload. The services she was receiving—social skills training, speech/language therapy, behavioral therapy—all helped her cope socially but only to a point. Depression and anxiety had a stranglehold on her life and, no matter the intervention or change in medication; Maura just couldn't break free from it. According to a report by her school psychologist, her presentation at the alternative school became extremely variable, totally dependent on her stress level at any particular moment. Often, Maura became so overwhelmed she would leave her classroom to seek out help from her psychologist with a variety of somatic complaints—headaches, dizziness—in addition to displays of agitation. Meltdowns ensued, some severe, but Maura was usually able to deescalate with the help of her psychologist. Afterwards, she would always apologize to staff.

Constant complaints about exhaustion, too much class work, high stress, and not feeling well were affecting Maura's functioning in school. As an adolescent female with Asperger's Syndrome, she had to deal with the monthly hormonal fluctuations that were part of her menstrual cycle, something her male counterparts did not have to endure. This was a major complaint of Maura's and I feel a significant difference between males and females on the spectrum. She was exquisitely sensitive to the changes her body underwent each month and the stress, anxiety, and depression Maura already felt was significantly magnified and being expressed through her inability to function appropriate in school.

In eleventh grade, I had depression. School greatly stressed me out because I would often get upset. Many things went wrong in my life that year. Another student I had an interest in wanted nothing to do with me despite my attempts to be nice to him. I also felt lonely because many of my older friends in the alternative school left for college. Another girl I knew cut me off completely from her life the year before, and I still felt the effects of it in eleventh grade.

I began to become more depressed as the year went on and it got worse over time. School also got harder for me, as I could not keep up with the school work and my social problems became worse. It felt like nobody wanted to be with me because I would get upset a lot due to my stress. Finally, my doctor gave me a new medication to try but I felt even worse. It got to the point where I could not take the anxiety anymore. I finally told my mother and school psychologist about it, and I let them admit me into the hospital to help me recover from this depression.

After a period of two weeks, Maura was discharged form the hospital into a day treatment program to help her develop coping strategies. Daily, we saw improvements in her ability to socialize and appropriate express her feelings. The stress was still present but at level where Maura was more receptive to the help we were trying to provide her. The students and staff at her school were so supportive.

While I was in the hospital, I relied on my friends and family as well as my will power to get me through. Friends would call me during phone hour. Family came to visit me, and they offered advice to help me feel less stress and stay calm. As I got more and more people to support me, I began to improve. Even the students at my high school would leave me notes, and my parents said that people there missed me. Slowly, my depression got more manageable, and my anxiety went down. The afternoon I was discharged from the hospital I was relieved. I knew that I got the help I needed, but I also knew that the support from my family and friends me through. I was now able to handle my problem better because I used the strategies I learned in the hospital. While I did not like being there, it helped me become a stronger person.

Maura's four years at the alternative school were years of tremendous growth and maturity despite her struggle with depression. She was able to gain an incredible amount of insight into her strengths and challenges, understanding for the first time in her life the impact they had not only on her but on others, too. The "cause and effect" of her behaviors became clearer to her as she matured emotionally. Maura knew that areas of her day-to-day functioning required work and was willing to do what was necessary to make life better socially for herself.

One positive event that signaled this was getting a job. Both her private speech therapist and her business teacher at school gave her an assignment to go to a place where Maura would like to work and fill out a job application. Videogames were a source of great enjoyment for Maura and being quite knowledgeable about them, she decided to make out an application to work at a local store that sold them. She handed it in, got called in for an interview and was hired!

New anxieties came into play, and we were concerned that Maura's social challenges would prove too overwhelming for her to be successful in this new endeavor. School refusal was now replaced by job refusal. Her anticipatory anxiety was so great that Maura would get extremely upset just before her shift at the store would start. She would beg me to call up the store and tell them she was quitting, but I refused. I told that it was her own responsibility and decision whether or not to quit, but that she would have to do it herself by giving proper advance notification. Every time I picked her up from work, I asked her if she had quit and each time she told me no, things were fine once she started to work. This scenario was repeated over the course of the next few months until finally it stopped. Maura was now gainfully employed and a major hurdle had been overcome.

Once I was unemployed. I felt like I had no freedom, and that I had to rely on my parents for money. I felt dependent on people to do things for me such as pay for me to buy what I wanted and needed. I had very little experience in the real world and my social skills were below average for my age because I did not deal with people often. I used to sit all day I in my room playing games on the computer and going on the internet.

Now I am working at a videogame store. At first I was extremely nervous because it was my very first time being on my own in the real world, but after a while, I got used to it and learned to deal with both nasty co-workers and customers. Slowly, I developed my social skills through helping customers with their purchases and working cooperatively with my co-workers. They became friendly to me once they got to know my personality and how hard I worked. I felt independent because I had my own money to buy things. Now I do more than sit at the computer all day.

After four years of learning and socializing alongside a majority of boys, Maura began to develop relational interests appropriate to her age. Where the boys in middle school were her main tormentors, the boys in high school were her friends, and Maura's thrived on their friendship. Where once she feared boys, she now craved their attention. As a young woman on the spectrum, Maura now had to figure out appropriate ways to initiate conversations with the opposite sex, something that came so easily to girls her age. Developmentally, I could see that she lacked the relationship skills other girls had innately, but she was on her way.

When I was younger, I absolutely hated boys! I especially disliked having to work with them in middle school because at that time everyone thought that the boy you worked with was your boyfriend. Even if you were just friendly with a boy, you were teased about liking him.

In high school it all changed. Since my school was about 90% male I had to learn to adapt to being around a lot of boys very quickly. I was one of only a few girls in my school and the only one in my grade at the beginning of high school.

As time went on, I realized boys really weren't so bad and became friendly with many of them. Since I was more mature than they and didn't cause "drama" like some of the other girls in my school, they actually considered me a friend. My interest in boys grew.

During my sophomore year of high school, I developed an interest, not quite a crush, on a boy in my English class who I though might be interested in me. I tried to be nice to him, but he just wouldn't respond. I quickly realized he was too mature for me.

Eleventh grade changed how I felt about boys forever when I met a new boy in the school. At first he seemed very nice, complimenting me on my drawings in art class and even the shirts I wore. Within a short time, however, this boy did not want anything to do with me. He was an enigma! Many times I would try to figure him out only to fail. This would depress me because he was my first crush and I wanted it to work out. Others would tell me it wasn't my fault he acted the way he did; it was just his person-ality. Still, I would blame myself as if I were doing something wrong. I see some of the Asperger's boys in and out of school wanting a relationship with a girl, but sometimes they seem to be stalking who they like. I just didn't want to come across as doing the same thing with this boy.

Since my high school had a number of students like me with social disabilities, I began to realize that perhaps he, too, had these difficulties so I stopped blaming myself. To this day, I can't figure out if he liked me or not. Maybe he did and just hid it well. I guess it could have gone either way.

What I want, though, is what I see my older sister as having—a boyfriend. I get jealous sometimes because I want that kind of relationship, too. While I don't want to be in a sexual relationship yet, or get too intimate, I do want a boy who thinks I'm special, someone whom I could really trust and to whom I could talk. I'm still thinking about my future and what I want in a relationship.

In June of 2007, Maura once again made her way on to a stage to accept a diploma, but this time it was to the cheers of her teachers, school support staff, fellow classmates, and their families. The pain and heartache we all experienced that other June four years prior was replaced with the knowledge

Maura was loved, respected and above all, accepted for the unique individual that she is.

The "here and now"

Today, Maura is a freshman at our local community college where she has been fortunate to find another group of caring and supportive educational professionals who are helping her meet the challenges of post-secondary education. Just as we had stumbled upon the OHI program at the alternative high school, we discovered a college program ideally suited to Maura's needs. Professors, counsellors, and other staff well-versed in the special needs of Asperger's students are giving our daughter the opportunity to attain her goals in life in an educational environment that mirrors that of the alternative high school—one of compassion, understanding, and support. As in every new endeavor in Maura's life, mixed emotions abound.

I was stressed about going to college. I wanted to go, but I was unsure what would happen to me. I was also nervous I would fail my classes or dislike the professors. The possibility of the idea of college falling through and dropping out got me worried. The last thing I wanted to do was leave college because I would feel like I was not good enough to go to school.

Because I have social and anxiety issues, I decided to go to a community college. I have difficulty dealing with living away from home because I can't adjust very well to changes. This would have made going away to college even worse for me. My sister went away to college, and seeing how hard it was for her to adjust, I thought I would never be able to go to school beyond high school. I did not even look at colleges when I was in high school.

I decided to go to our local community college in my senior year of high school since it was close to home and smaller than most colleges. I was not sure what was going to happen to me and nervous that I would not be able to stay in classes because I had that problem in high school. I was also afraid of getting lost in campus and being late for classes. Despite these fears, I decided to go to college anyway.

College feels so much different than high school. One of the major reasons is the amount of independence students are given. They do not need their parents to get involved in school-related business anymore. Students have to learn to advocate for themselves, get needed services on their own and must seek out support from their professors. It feels great to be independent because I don't feel like others have to do things for me. I enjoy the feeling of doing things myself. The way professors treat me and the other students in my classes makes me feel like an adult, contributing to a feeling of independence.

Most people in college are a lot more mature than students in high school. They are more tolerant of people with differences and more wiling to make friends. While I was nervous about going to college, those fears have gone away. Just like my high school, college is like home to me. Now I actually look forward to going to classes instead of feeling anxious about them. I think college is a great part of my life. I am starting to get a sense of what I want beyond it, and I think this is a great place to start!

Maura is in the middle of her second semester working toward an applied associate's degree in commercial art. She is learning to advocate for herself and manages her time on her own. Through trial and error, with a perseverance honed over the years, Maura is beginning to find her way in the world.

Thoughts on being a female adolescent with Asperger's Syndrome

I think having to deal with a monthly menstrual cycle is one of the most difficult things an Asperger's female has to endure. I was well-prepared when I started menstruating since my mother had told me about it, given me books to read, and that my older sister had already gotten hers.

At first it wasn't so bad but growing older, I became increasingly sensitive to its effects—severe premenstrual syndrome (PMS) with intense pain and extreme emotions. From the time I started to ovulate straight through to the first few days of my next cycle, I was extremely irritable, emotional, had cravings for certain foods, and experienced severe stress. These symptoms greatly affected my tolerance for frustration and the added stress impacted negatively on my schoolwork. The only strategy I found that worked well was to take a bath when I got home from school and then nap for a couple of hours.

After many years of suffering, my mother finally took me to her doctor for my first gynecological exam. She prepared me well, describing what the doctor would be doing and why.

When the gynecologist came in the room, I really wasn't all that nervous. She seemed very nice and had a good sense of humor. The doctor also explained in greater detail what the exam would be like so I would know what to expect.

I was a little nervous at first when she did my Pap smear, but the doctor told me to relax which I did. The internal exam was very painless because she used a small speculum since I have not had sexual relations. It was a quick procedure lasting only five minutes. It was done before I even knew it!

We talked in her office about various options for helping me with my severe PMS and its symptoms. The doctor decided to have me take a birth control pill which would stop my ovulation and my PMS.

Since starting the pill, I feel much better and my emotional state has improved. I don't get upset as much as I used to, especially over small frustrations. The pain and cramping are a lot more manageable. In the past I had to take medication to alleviate the pain, but now I rarely need to use it at all and when I do, the dosage is much less.

Starting menstruation also meant I was growing up. Unlike most of the neurotypical girls I knew, I did NOT want to grow up. Because I was developing earlier than most of the girls my age, they made fun of me by calling me "Coconut Girl". I was mortified and it made me not want to grow up even more! I realized they were probably jealous because what I had was what they wanted to prove to others they were maturing. At the time I was so upset, but now I can look back and laugh. Although boys with Asperger's Syndrome have other serious things to deal, they are lucky not to have to deal with periods!

Thoughts on being a mother of an adolescent daughter with Asperger's Syndrome

When Maura was born, it was one of the happiest days of my life. My husband and I had difficulty getting pregnant with her and were thrilled when we found out that we were having another girl. I remember two things so distinctly at the time of her birth: the shock of black hair on her head and the screams emanating from her lungs! We used to joke that when her older sister was born, she came out sleeping and to this day *loves* her sleep, while when Maura was born, she came out screaming and…well, you know the rest!

As frustrating as life may have been at times these past 19 (and still counting!) years, we have maintained our sense of humor through some pretty tough times. To paraphrase one of Maura's comments above, "…but now we can look back and laugh." At everything? No, but we have learned to put things in perspective—Maura, more than anyone else in our family. She is the first to give someone the benefit of the doubt and the first to forgive. I wish I could say the same about myself, but I'm learning from her and still working on it!

I am truly proud of my daughter; she is an amazingly resilient and loving young lady. I have seen the great strides Maura has made with the help of so many others we have been fortunate to meet along our journey. All of them—her psychiatrist, psychologists, language pathologist, teachers (yes, even middle school!), high school administrative and support staff, friends, family—have helped pave the road Maura journeys today with their kindness, love, patience, and compassion.

Our journey continues, but it is Maura who now leads the way to her future.

CONCLUSION:

Embracing Change

Changes in life can mean a lot of different things to different people. Change can be exciting or stressful; it can make you feel hopeful, relieved, worried, exhilarated. As we know, even the most positive of life's changes bring with them a certain degree of stress—change is never 100% easy for anyone. For your daughter with an ASD, changes, no matter how small, can be much more difficult than they are for other people.

In this book, we have talked about one of the biggest changes your daughter is going to face in her life: growing up, and everything that comes with it. Although everyone's development follows a unique course, there are certain common threads that, thankfully, can guide families and their daughters on their journey. Will you embrace this journey as an adventure that you may or may not be completely prepared for? What will you learn about your daughter and yourself along the way?

> Lesley has helped me to have a better understanding that each of us has a unique purpose in life. She has taught me about tolerance, difference and love. My hope for Lesley is that she will find success in her life—what she would de- fine as success—not that which others are measured by, relationships that are meaningful and fulfilling to her and a comfort and happiness with who she is. (Mother of an almost 14-year-old daughter with PDD-NOS)

When your daughter was younger, what did you think adolescence would look like? What has she accomplished, and what will she continue to learn as she passes through adolescence and enters young adulthood? As always there will be ups and downs; you and your daughter will struggle, but with determination you will succeed. If you welcome the changes in her life, then you can help your daughter become a healthy, safe, confident, and happy young women. Take a deep breath, and try to have some fun along the way; you know more than you realize about how to prepare your daughter, and yourself, for her future.

> KNOW that things will evolve and your daughter will grow and learn and she will amaze and delight you and make you very proud. Part of the process of growth for any of us is letting go of expectations of how things were supposed to be, to

make room for how they really are. Your life has challenges for sure, and your daughter has them and will have them and she will need you to be there for her all along the way, but you will rise to this, just you wait and see. She will not be like your other children but with love and help she will be her own unique person and you will come to see that there are many positive things about her and there are silver linings even within the diagnosis—have faith. There is more support out there than you know. Be patient with yourself and with her and with others. Avoid succumbing to the "you missed the boat" or the "it's too late now, if you'd only gotten her _____ when she was three" stuff. Individuals with autism, just like other individuals, learn and grow all their lives, with the right supports. And what is right will change over time as she changes and you change, and someday you will look back at this time of intense sadness and turmoil and you will marvel at how far you have come. (Melinda Coppola, mother of a 15-year-old girl diagnosed with ASD and OCD)

Throughout the last ten years, we have been inspired by the families and daughters with whom we have worked, and who continue to challenge us by asking the questions that do not yet have answers: difficult questions that deal with safety, independence, mental health, happiness, self-esteem, friendships, relationships, and the future ahead. We encourage our families, and others who work with them, to keep asking these questions. With time the research will be conducted, the intervention programs will be developed and evaluated, and the educational strategies will be implemented and examined. Clinicians, scientists, and educators alike are beginning to recognize the importance of understanding the unique experiences of girls growing up with ASDs. What we hope this book has provided is a much-needed resource for both families and those who work with them and their daughters, and a starting point for asking meaningful sex-related research questions in the areas of assessment, clinical presentation, diagnosis, treatment, and development. We encourage everyone to keep asking. Without the questions, there can be no answers.

About the Authors

Shana Nichols, PhD, is Clinical Director of the Fay J. Lindner Center for Autism and Developmental Disorders affiliated with AHRC Nassau, and the North Shore-LIJ Health System on Long Island, New York. She is a licensed clinical psychologist and has worked in the areas of assessment, treatment, and research related to autism spectrum and other developmental disorders for over ten years.

Gina Marie Moravcik, MA, CCC-SLP, is Coordinator of Education and Speech Language Services at the Fay J. Lindner Center for Autism and Developmental Disorders. She is a speech and language pathologist specializing in social communication and autism spectrum disorders. She is Adjunct Professor and Clinical Supervisor in the Speech Pathology program, St. John's University, USA, and also runs a private speech-language therapy practice.

Samara Pulver Tetenbaum, MA, is a doctoral candidate in clinical psychology at the State University of New York at Stony Brook. She has been working in the field of autism and related developmental disabilities for the past five years and is currently employed as an applied behavior specialist at the Fay J. Lindner Center for Autism and Developmental Disorders.

REFERENCES

Abelson, A.G. (1981) 'The development of gender identity in the autistic child.' *Child: Care Health and Development 7*, 343–356.

American Academy of Pediatrics (1999) *Caring for Your School-Age Child: Ages 5 to 12*. New York, NY: Bantam Books.

American Association of University Women Educational Foundation Sexual Harassment Task Force. (2001) *Harassment-Free Hallways. How to Stop Sexual Harassment in School. A Guide for Students, Parents, and Schools*. AAUW Educational Foundation: Washington, DC.

American Psychiatric Association (1994) *Diagnostic and Statistical Manual of Mental Disorders* (4th edition). Washington, DC: American Psychiatric Association.

Attwood, T. (1998) *Asperger Syndrome. A Guide for Parents and Professionals*. London: Jessica Kingsley Publishers.

Attwood, T. (2007) *The Complete Guide to Asperger Syndrome*. London: Jessica Kingsley Publishers.

Bacon, A.L., Fein, D., Morris, R., Waterhouse, L. and Allen, D. (1998) 'The responses of autistic children to the distress of others.' *Journal of Autism and Developmental Disorders 28*, 129–142.

Baladerian, N. (1991) 'Sexual abuse of people with developmental disabilities.' *Sexuality and Disability 9*, 4, 323–335.

Baron-Cohen, S. (2003) *The Essential Difference: Male and Female Brains and the Truth about Autism*. New York, NY: Basic Books.

Baron-Cohen, S. and Hammer, J. (1997) 'Is autism an extreme form of the male brain?' *Advances in Infancy Research 11*, 193–217.

Baron-Cohen, S., Tager-Flusberg, H. and Cohen, D.J. (2000) *Understanding Other Minds: Perspective from Autism* (2nd edition.). Oxford: Oxford University Press.

Bauer, S. (1996) *Asperger Syndrome*. Online Asperger Syndrome information and support website. Accessed March 26, 2008 at www.udel.edu/bkirby/asperger/as_thru_years.html

Bellini, S. and Akullian, J. (2007) 'A meta-analysis of video modeling and video self-modeling interventions for children and adolescents with autism spectrum disorders.' *Exceptional Children 73*, 261–284.

Berndt, T. (2002) 'Friendship quality and social development.' *Current Directions in Psychological Science 11*, 7–10.

Bettelheim, B. (1967) *The Empty Fortress: Infantile Autism and the Birth of the Self*. New York, NY: The Free Press.

Bloss, C.S. and Courchesnem, E. (2007) 'MRI neuroanatomy in young girls with autism: a preliminary study.' *Journal of the American Academy of Child and Adolescent Psychiatry 46*, 515–523.

Bradley, E., Summers, J., Wood, H. and Bryson, S. (2004) 'Comparing rates of psychiatric and behavior disorders in adolescents and young adults with severe intellectual disability with and without autism.' *Journal of Autism and Developmental Disorders 34*, 151–161.

Brantlinger, E.A., Klein, S.M. and Guskin, S.L. (1994) *Fighting for Darla. The Case Study of a Pregnant Adolescent with Autism. Challenges for Family Care and Professional Responsibility.* New York, NY: Teachers College Press.

Brereton, A., Tonge, B.J. and Einfeld, S.L. (2006) 'Psychopathology in children and adolescents with autism compared to young people with intellectual disability.' *Journal of Autism and Developmental Disorders 36*, 863–870.

Brewster, K.L. and Tillman, K.H. (2008) 'Who's doing it? Patterns and predictors of youths' oral sexual experiences.' *Journal of Adolescent Health 42*, 73–80.

Brizendine, L. (2006) *The Female Brain.* New York, NY: Morgan Road Books.

Cantino, R. (2007) 'Epilepsy in autism spectrum disorders.' *European Journal of Child and Adolescent Psychiatry 16*, 61–66.

Carr, E.G., Horner, R.H., Turnbull, A.P. *et al.* (1999) *Positive Behavior Support for People with Developmental Disabilities: A Research Synthesis.* Washington, DC: American Association on Mental Retardation.

Carr, E.G., Newsom, C.D. and Binkoff, J.A. (1980) 'Escape as a factor in the aggressive behavior of two retarded children.' *Journal of Applied Behavior Analysis 13*, 101–117.

Carter, A.S., Black, D.O., Tewani, S., Connolly, C.E., Kadlec, M.B. and Tager-Flusberg, T. (2007) 'Sex differences in toddlers with autism spectrum disorders'. *Journal of Autism and Developmental Disorders 37*, 86–97.

Centers for Disease Control (CDC) (2005) *Advanced Data 362. Sexual Behavior and Selected Health Measures: Men and Women 15–44 Years of Age, United States, 2002.* 56 pp. National Center for Health Statistics.

Celiberti, D.A., Bobo, H.E., Kelly, K.S., Harris, S.L. and Handleman, J.L. (1997) 'The differential and temporal effects of antecedent exercise on the self-stimulatory behavior of a child with autism.' *Research in Developmental Disabilities 18*, 139–150.

Chalfant, A.M., Rapee, R. and Carroll, L. (2007) 'Treating anxiety disorders in children with high functioning autism spectrum disorders: a controlled trial.' *Journal of Autism and Developmental Disorders 37*, 1842–1857.

Charlop-Christy, M.H., Le, L. and Freeman, K (2000) 'A comparison of video modeling with in vivo modeling for children with autism.' *Journal of Autism and Developmental Disorders 30*, 6, 537–552.

Cobb, N.J. (1996) *Adolescence: Continuity, Change and Diversity.* Mountainview, CA: Mayfield Publishing.

Cohen-Sandler, R. (2005) *Stressed-Out Girls. Helping Them Thrive in the Age of Pressure.* New York, NY: Penguin Books.

Constantino, J.N. and Gruber, C.F. (2005) *Social Responsiveness Scale.* Los Angeles, CA: Western Psychological Services.

Constantino, J.N., Przybeck, T., Friesen, D. and Todd, R.D. (2000) 'Reciprocal social behavior in children with and without pervasive developmental disorders.' *Journal of Developmental and Behavioral Pediatrics 21*, 2–11.

Cook, E.H., Kieffer, J.M., Charak, D.A. and Leventhal, B.L. (1993) 'Autistic disorder and posttraumatic stress disorder.' *Journal of American Academy of Child and Adolescent Psychiatry 32*, 1292–1294.

Cornell, J.L. and Halpern-Felsher, B.L. (2006) 'Adolescents tell us why teens have oral sex.' *Journal of Adolescent Health 38*, 299–301.

Couwenhoven, T. (2007) *Teaching Children with Down Syndrome about their Bodies, Boundaries, and Sexuality. A Guide for Parents and Professionals.* Bethesda, MD: Woodbine House.

Crick, N.R. and Grotpeter, J.K. (1995) 'Relational aggression, gender, and social-psychological adjustment.' *Child Development 66*, 710–722.

Didden, R., Duker, P. and Korzilius, H. (1997) 'Meta-analytic study on treatment effectiveness for problem behaviors with individuals who have mental retardation.' *American Journal on Mental Retardation 101*, 387–399.

Didden, R., Korzilius, H., Oorsouw, W. and Sturmey, P. (2006) 'Behavioral treatment of challenging behaviors in individuals with mild mental retardation: Meta-analysis of single-subject research.' *American Journal on Mental Retardation 111*, 290–298.

Duncan, N. (1999) *Sexual Bullying. Gender Conflict and Pupil Culture in Secondary Schools.* New York, NY: Routledge.

Durand, V.M. and Crimmins, D.B. (1988) 'Identifying the variables maintaining self-injurious behavior.' *Journal of Autism and Developmental Disorders 18*, 99–117.

Durand, V.M., Crimmins, D.B., Caulfield, M. and Taylor, J. (1989) 'Reinforcer assessment: I. Using problem behavior to select reinforcers.' *Journal of the Association for Persons with Severe Handicaps 14*, 113–126.

Ehlers, S. and Gillberg, C. (1993) 'The epidemiology of Asperger syndrome. A total population study.' *Journal of Child Psychology and Psychiatry 34*, 1327–1350.

Erikson, E.H. (1950) *Childhood and Society.* New York, NY: WW Norton.

Erikson, E.H. (1968) *Identity: Youth and Crisis.* New York, NY: WW Norton.

Field, A., Camargo, C., Taylor, B., *et al.* (1999) 'Overweight, weight concerns, and bulimic behaviors among girls and boys.' *Journal of the American Academy of Child and Adolescent Psychiatry 38*, 754–760.

Fombonne, E. (1999) 'Epidemiological surveys of autism: a review.' *Psychological Medicine 29*, 769–786.

Fombonne, E. (2001) 'Prevalence of pervasive developmental disorders in the British Nationwide Survey of Child Mental Health.' *Journal of the American Academy of Child and Adolescent Psychiatry 40*, 820–827.

Gadow, K.D., Devincent, C.J., Pomeroy, J. and Azizian, A. (2005) 'Comparison of DSM-IV symptoms in elementary school-age children with PDD versus clinic and community symptoms.' *Autism 9*, 392–415.

Gagnon, J.H. and Simon, W. (1973; 2005) *Sexual Conduct. The Social Sources of Human Sexuality.* (2nd edition). London: Transaction Publishers.

Gallaher, M., Christakis, D. and Connell, F. (2002) 'Health care use by children diagnosed as having developmental delay.' *Archives of Pediatrics & Adolescent Medicine 156*, 246–251.

Gallucci, G., Hackerman, F. and Schmidt, W. (2005) 'Gender identity disorder in an adult male with Asperger's Syndrome.' *Sexuality and Disability 23*, 35–40.

Gaub, M. and Carlson, C.L. (1997) 'Gender differences in ADHD: a meta-analysis and critical review.' *Journal of the American Academy of Child and Adolescent Psychiatry 36*, 1036–1045.

Gaus, V.L. (2007) *Cognitive-Behavioral Therapy for Adult Asperger Syndrome.* New York, NY: The Guilford Press.

Ge, X., Conger, R.D and Elder, G.H. (1996) 'Coming of age too early: pubertal influences on girls' vulnerability to psychological distress.' *Child Development 67*, 3386–3400.

Ghazziudin, M. (2002) 'Asperger syndrome: associated psychiatric and medical conditions.' *Focus on Autism and Developmental Disabilities 17*, 138–144.

Ghaziuddin, M., Ghaziuddin, N. and Greden, J. (2002) 'Depression in persons with autism: Implications for research and clinical care.' *Journal of Autism and Developmental Disorders 32*, 299–306.

Ghaziuddin, M., Tsai, L. and Ghaziuddin, N. (1992) 'Comorbidity of autistic disorder in children and adolescents.' *European Child & Adolescent Psychiatry 1*, 209–213.

Gillberg, C. and Billstedt, E. (2000) 'Autism and Asperger syndrome: coexistence with other clinical disorders.' *Acta Psychiatrica Scandinavica 102*, 321–330.

Gillberg, C. and Rastam, M. (1992) 'Do some cases of anorexia nervosa reflect underlying autistic-like conditions?' *Behavioural Neurology 5*, 27–32.

Gillot, A., Furniss, F. and Walter, A. (2001) 'Anxiety in high-functioning children with autism.' *Autism 4*, 117–132.

Grandin, T. (1995) *Thinking in Pictures*. New York, NY: Doubleday.

Grandin, T. (2006) 'Foreword.' In C. Sicile-Kira, *Adolescents on the Autism Spectrum: A Parent's Guide to the Cognitive, Social, Physical, and Transition Needs of Teenagers with Autism Spectrum Disorders*. New York, NY: Berkley Publishing Group.

Gray, J. (1992) *Men Are From Mars, Women Are From Venus*. New York, NY: HarperCollins Publishers.

Gresham, F.M. and Elliot, S.N. (1990) *Social Skills Rating System*. Bloomington, MN: Pearson Assessments.

Griffiths, D., Quinsey, V.L. and Hingsburger, D. (1989) *Changing Inappropriate Sexual Behavior*. Baltimore, MD: Paul H Brookes.

Groden, J., Baron, M.G. and Groden, G. (2006) 'Assessment and Coping Strategies.' In M. G. Baron, J. Groden, G. Groden and L. P. Lipsitt (eds), *Stress and Coping in Autism*. New York. NY: Oxford University Press.

Hall, A.V., Abramson, R.K., Ravan, S.A., Wright, H.H. *et al.* (2006) 'ADHD Symptoms as a Function of Speech, Race, and Gender in Individuals with Autistic Disorders.' Poster presented at the International Meeting for Autism Research, Montreal, Canada. June 1–3 2006.

Hall, G.S. (1904) *Adolescence* (vols. 1 & 2). Englewood Cliffs, NJ: Prentice Hall.

Havinghurst, R.J. (1971) *Developmental Tasks and Education*, (3rd edition). New York, NY: Longman.

Hellemans, H., Colson, K., Verbraeken, C., Vermeiren, R. and Deboutte, D. (2007) 'Sexual behavior in high-functioning male adolescents and young adults with autism spectrum disorder.' *Journal of Autism and Developmental Disorders 37*, 260–269.

Henault, I. (2004) 'The sexuality of adolescents with Asperger Syndrome.' In L.H. Willey (ed.)., *Asperger Syndrome in Adolescence. Living with the Ups, the Downs, and Things in Between*. London: Jessica Kingsley Publishers.

Henault, I. and Attwood, T. (2002) The Sexual Profile of Adults with Asperger's Syndrome: The Need for Understanding, Support, and Sex Education. Paper presented at the Inaugural World Autism Congress, Melbourne Australia, November 10–14, 2002.

Hensel, D.J., Dennis Fortenberry, J. and Orr, D.P. (2008) 'Variations in coital and noncoital sexual repertoire among adolescent women.' *Journal of Adolescent Health 42*, 170–176.

Hingsburger, D. (1995) *Just Say Know! Understanding & Reducing the Risk of Sexual Victimization of People with Developmental Disabilities*. Edmonton: Alberta Tourism Education Council.

Hingsburger, D., Griffiths, D. and Quinsey, V. (1991) 'Detecting counterfeit deviance.' *The Habilitative Mental Healthcare Newsletter 10*, 51–54.

Howlin, P. and Clements, J. (1995) 'Is it possible to assess the impact of abuse on children with pervasive developmental disorders?' *Journal of Autism and Developmental Disorders 25*, 337–354.

Howlin, P., Mawhood, L. and Rutter M. (2000) 'Autism and developmental receptive language disorder—a follow-up comparison in early adult life II: Social behavioral and psychiatric outcomes.' *Journal of Child Psychology and Psychiatry and Allied Disciplines 41*, 561–578.

Hsieh C.C. and Trichopoulos D. (1991) 'Breast size, handedness and breast cancer risk.' *European Journal of Cancer 27*, 131–135.

Ingudomnukul, E., Baron-Cohen, S., Wheelwright, S. and Knickmeyer, R.C. (2007) 'Elevated rates of testosterone-related disorders in women with autism spectrum conditions.' *Hormones and Behavior 51*, 597–604.

Johnson, W. and Kempton, W. (1981) *Sex Education and Counseling for Special Groups.* Springfield, IL: Charles Thomas.

Karakoussis, C., Calkins, C.F. and Eggeling, K. (1998) *Sexuality: Preparing your Child with Special Needs.* Kansas City, MO: Developmental Disabilities Resource Center on Sexuality.

Kim, J., Szatmari, P., Bryson, S., Streiner, D. and Wilson, F. (2000) 'The prevalence of mood problems among children with autism and Asperger syndrome.' *Autism 4*, 117–132.

Koegel, L.K., Koegel, R.L. and Dunlap, G. (1996) *Positive Behavioral Support: Including People with Difficult Behavior in the Community.* Baltimore, MD: Paul H Brookes.

Koenig, K. and Tsatsanis. K. (2005) 'Pervasive developmental disorders in girls. In D. Bell-Dolan, S.L. Foster and E.J. Mash, (eds). *Behavioral and Emotional Problems in Girls.* New York, NY: Kluwer Academic/Plenum Press.

Koller, R. (2000) 'Sexuality and adolescents with autism.' *Sexuality and Disability 18*, 125–135.

Kopp, S. and Gillberg, C. (1992) 'Girls with social deficits and learning problems: autism, atypical Asperger Syndrome or a variant of these conditions.' *European Child and Adolescent Psychiatry 1*, 89–99.

Lainhart, J.E., Piven, J., Wzorek, M., *et al.* (1997) 'Macrocephaly in children and adults with autism.' *Journal of the American Academy of Child and Adolescent Psychiatry 36*, 282–290.

Leitenberg, H., Detzer, M. and Srebnik, D. (1993) 'Gender differences in masturbation and the relation of masturbation experience in preadolescence and/or early adolescence to sexual behavior and sexual adjustment in young adulthood.' *Archives of Sexual Behavior 22*, 87–98.

Lenhart, A. (2007) 'American Teens & Online Safety: What the research is telling us...' The First Family Online Safety Institute Conference and Exhibition. Washington, DC, December 6.

Linblad, F., Gustafsson, P., Larsson, I. and Lundin, B. (1995) 'Preschoolers' sexual behavior at daycare centers: an epidemiological study.' *Child Abuse and Neglect 19*, 569–577.

Lipton, B. (1996) 'Are you wearing the wrong size bra?' *Ladies Home Journal, March*, p.46.

Lord, C., Rutter, M., DiLavore, P. and Risi, S. (1999) *Autism Diagnostic Observation Schedule— WPS Edition.* Los Angeles, CA: Western Psychological Services.

Lord, C., Rutter, M. and LeCouteur, A. (1994) 'Autism Diagnostic Interview-Revised: a revised version of a diagnostic interview for caregivers of individuals with possible pervasive developmental disorders.' *Journal of Autism and Developmental Disorders 24*, 659–685.

Lord, C., Schopler, E. and Revicki, D. (1982). 'Sex differences in autism.' *Journal of Autism and Developmental Disorders 12*, 317–329.

Lotter, V. (1966) 'Epidemiology of autistic conditions in young children: I. Prevalence.' *Social Psychiatry 1*, 124–137.

Lucyshyn, J.M., Horner, R.H., Dunlap, G., Albin, R.W. and Ben, K.R. (2002) 'Positive behavior support with families.' In J.M. Lucyshyn, G. Dunlap and R.W. Albin (eds). *Families and Positive Behavior Support: Addressing Problem Behavior in Family Contexts.* Baltimore, MD: Paul H Brookes.

Mandell, D.S. (2008) 'Psychiatric hospitalizations among children with autism spectrum disorders.' *Journal of Autism and Developmental Disorders 36*, 6, 1059–1065.

Mandell, D.S., Walrath, C.M., Manteuffel, B., Sgro, G. and Pinto-Martin, J.A. (2005a) 'Characteristics of children with autistic spectrum disorders served in comprehensive community-based mental health settings.' *Journal of Autism and Developmental Disorders 36*, 475–485.

Mandell, D.S., Walrath, C.M., Manteuffel, B., Sgro, G. and Pinto-Martin, J.A. (2005b) 'The prevalence and correlates of abuse among children with autism served in comprehensive community-based mental health settings.' *Child Abuse and Neglect 29*, 1359–1372.

Marcia, J.E. (1980) 'Ego Identity Development.' In J. Adelson (ed.), *Handbook of Adolescent Psychology.* New York, NY: Wiley.

Marcia, J.E. (1994) 'The Empirical Study of Ego Identity.' In H.A. Bosma, T.L.G. Graadsma, H.D. Grotevant, and D.J. De Levita (eds), *Identity and Development.* Newbury Park, CA: Sage.

Marshall, W.A. and Tanner, J.M. (1969) 'Variations in pattern of pubertal changes in girls.' *Archives of Disease in Childhood 44*, 291–303.

Martin, A. Koenig, K., Anderson, G. and Scahill, L. (2003) 'Low dose fluvoxamine treatment of children and adolescents with pervasive developmental disorders: a prospective, open-label study.' *Journal of Autism and Developmental Disorders 33*, 77–85.

Martinovich, J. (2006) *Creative Expressive Activities and Asperger's Syndrome. Social and Emotional Skills and Positive Life Goals for Adolescents and Young Adults.* London: Jessica Kingsley Publishers.

McDougle, C.J., Kresch, L.E., Goodman, W.K., *et al.* (1995) 'A case-controlled study of repetitive thoughts and behaviour in adults with autistic disorder and obsessive-compulsive disorder.' *American Journal of Psychiatry 152*, 772–777.

McLennan, J.D., Lord, C. and Schopler, E. (1993) 'Sex differences in higher functioning people with autism.' *Journal of Autism and Developmental Disorders 23*, 217–227.

McClure, E. (2000) 'A meta-analytic review of sex differences in facial expression processing and their development in infants, children, and adolescents.' *Psychological Bulletin 126*, 424–453.

Mendle, J. Turkheimer, E. and Emery, R.E. (2007) 'Detrimental psychological outcomes associated with early pubertal timing in adolescent girls.' *Developmental Review 27*, 151–171.

Mesibov, G. (1982). Sex Education for People with Autism: Matching Programs to Levels of Functioning. University of North Carolina, Chapel Hill. Paper presented to the National Society for Children and Adults with Autism.

Miltenberger, R.G., Roberts, J.A., Ellingson, S., *et al.* (1999) 'Training and generalization of sexual abuse prevention skills for women with mental retardation.' *Journal of Applied Behavior Analysis 32*, 385–388.

Mithaug, D. (1991) *Self-Determined Kids: Raising Satisfied and Successful Children.* Lexington, MA: Lexington Books.

Mortlock, J. (1993) The Socio-Sexual Development of People with Autism and Related Learning Disabilities. Paper presented at the Inge Wakehurst Trust study weekend, UK. Accessed on July 8, 2008 at www.nas.org.uk/nas/jsp/polopoly.jsp?d=364&a=2187

Mosher, W.D., Chandra, A. and Jones, J. (2005) 'Sexual behaviors and selected health measures: men and women 15–44 years of age.' *Advance Data from Vital and Health Statistics 362.* Hyattsville, MD: National Center for Health Statistics. Accessed on March 26, 2008 at http://www.cdc.gov/nchs/data/ad/ad362.pdf

Mukkades, N.M. (2002) 'Gender identity problems in autistic children.' *Child: Care, Health and Development 28,* 529–532.

Muris, P., Steerneman, P., Merckelbach, H., Holdrinet, I. and Meesters, C. (1998) 'Comorbid anxiety symptoms in children with pervasive developmental disorder.' *Journal of Anxiety Disorders 12,* 387–393.

Murphy, N.A. and Elias, E.R. (2006) 'Sexuality of children and adolescents with developmental disabilities.' *Pediatrics 118,* 398–403.

National Information Center for Children and Youth with Disabilities (NICHCY) (1992) 'Sexuality education for children and youth with disabilities.' *NICHCY News Digest 17,* 1–37.

New York Times. (2007) 'When the bullies turned faceless.' 16 December.

Newsweek. (2006) 'Growing up with autism.' 27 November.

Nyden, A., Hjelmquist, E. and Gillberg, C. (2000) 'Autism spectrum and attention disorders in girls.' *European Child and Adolescent Psychiatry 9,* 180–185.

O'Sullivan, L.F. and Brooks-Gunn, J. (2005) 'The timing of changes in girls' sexual cognitions and behaviors in early adolescence: a prospective, cohort study.' *Journal of Adolescent Health 37,* 211–219.

Penn, H.E., Perry, A., McMullen, T., Freeman, N.L. and Dunn Geier, J. (2007) 'Differences in Autism Symptoms and Adaptive Functioning in Preschool Girls and Boys with Autism Spectrum Disorders.' Poster presentation at the Society for Research in Child Development Biennial Meeting, Boston, MA, March 29–April 1.

Perkins, D.F. (2001) *Adolescence: Developmental Tasks. Fact Sheet FCS 2118.* Gainsville, FL: University of Florida IFAS Extension.

Pickles, A., Bolton, P., MacDonald, H., Bailey, A., Le Couteur, A. and Sim, C.H. (1995) 'Latent-class analysis of recurrence risk for complex phenotypes with selection and measurement error: a twin and family history study of autism.' *American Journal of Human Genetics 57,* 717–726.

Piran, N. and Ross, E. (2006) 'From Girlhood to Womanhood: Multiple Transitions in Context.' In J. Worell and C.D. Goodheart (eds) *Handbook of Girls' and Women's Psychological Health: Gender and Wellbeing Across the Lifespan.* New York, NY: Oxford University Press.

Reaven, J.A., Blakeley-Smith, A., Nichols, S., Flanigan, E. and Hepburn, S. (in press) 'Cognitive-behavioral group treatment for anxiety symptoms in children with high-functioning autism spectrum disorders.' *Focus on Autism and Other Developmental Disabilities.*

Reaven, J. and Hepburn, S. (2003) 'Cognitive-behavioral treatment of obsessive-compulsive disorder in a child with Asperger's Syndrome: a case report.' *Autism: International Journal of Research and Practice 7,* 145–164.

Reese, R., Richman, D., Belmont, J. and Morse, P. (2005) 'Functional characteristics of disruptive behavior in developmentally disabled children with and without autism.' *Journal of Autism and Developmental Disorders 35*, 419–428.

Rice, F.P. and Dolgin, K.G. (2005) *The Adolescent: Development, Relationships, and Culture* (11th edition). New York, NY: Allyn & Bacon.

Rosen, D.S. (2003) 'Eating disorders in children and young adolescents: etiology, classification, clinical features, and treatment.' *Adolescent Medicine 14*, 49–59.

Rosenthal-Malek, A. and Mitchell, S. (1997) 'Brief report: The effects of exercise on the self-stimulating behaviors and positive responding of adolescents with autism.' *Journal of Autism and Developmental Disorders 27*, 193–202.

Rossi, G., Posar, A. and Parmaggiani, A. (2006) 'Epilepsy in adolescents and young adults with autistic disorder.' *Brain Development 22*, 102–106.

Santrock, J. W. (2007) *Adolescence* (11th edition). New York, NY: McGraw Hill.

Schellenberg, G.D., Dawson, G., Sung, Y.J. *et al.* (2006) 'Evidence for multiple loci from a genome scan of autism kindreds'. *Molecular Psychiatry 11*, 1049–1060.

Schreck, K.A. and Williams, K. (2006) 'Food preferences and factors influencing food selectivity for children with autism spectrum disorders.' *Research in Developmental Disabilities 27*, 353–363.

Seligman, M.E.P. (2002) *Authentic Happiness*. New York, NY: Free Press.

Shearin Karres, E.V. (2004) *Mean Chicks, Cliques, and Dirty Tricks: A Real Girl's Guide to Getting Through the Day with Smarts and Style*. Cincinnati, OH: Adams Media Corporation.

Sicile-Kira, C. (2006) *Adolescents on the Autism Spectrum*. New York, NY: Berkley Publishing Group.

Sexuality Information and Education Council of the United States (SIECUS). (1992) *Sexually Healthy Adolescents*. SIECUS Report, 21:29, December 1992/January 1993.

SIECUS (1996) *Guidelines for Comprehensive Sexuality Education. Kindergarten through Grade 12.* (2nd edition). Accessed on October 9, 2008 at wwww.siecus.org/_data/global/images/guidelines.pdf

SIECUS (2005) *Position Statements*. Accessed on March 23, 2008 at www.siecus.org/about/abou0001.html

Smith, T. (1997) 'Sexual differences in pervasive developmental disorders.' *Medscape Psychiatry and Mental Health e-Journal 2*.

Smolak, (2006) 'Body Image.' In J. Worell and C.D. Goodheart (eds) *Handbook of Girls' and Women's Psychological Health: Gender and Wellbeing Across the Lifespan*. New York, NY: Oxford University Press.

Sobsey, D. (1994) *Violence and Abuse in the Lives of People with Disabilities: The End of Silent Acceptance?* Baltimore, MD: Paul H Brookes.

Sobsey, D. and Doe, T. (1991) 'Patterns of sexual abuse and assault.' *Sexuality and Disability 9*, 243–259.

Sofronoff, K., Attwood, T. and Hinton, S. (2005) 'A randomized controlled trial of a CBT intervention for anxiety in children with Asperger syndrome.' *Journal of Child Psychology and Psychiatry 46*, 1152–1160.

Sparrow, S.S., Balla, D.A. and Cicchetti, D.V. (1984) *Vineland Adaptive Behavior Scales*. Circle Pines, MN: American Guidance Service, Inc.

Spencer, N., Devereux, E., Wallace, A., *et al.* (2005) 'Disabling conditions and registration for child abuse and neglect: A population-based study.' *Pediatrics 116*, 609–613.

Steinberg, L., Belsky, J. and Meyer, R. (1991) *Infancy, Childhood, and Adolescence: Development in Context.* New York, NY: McGraw Hill.

Sterling, L., Dawson, G., Estes, A. and Greenson, J. (2008) 'Characteristics associated with presence of depressive symptoms in adults with autism spectrum disorder.' *Journal of Autism and Developmental Disorders 38*, 6, 1011–1018.

Stiver, R.L. and Dobbins, J.P. (1980) 'Treatment of atypical anorexia nervosa in the public school: an autistic girl.' *Journal of Autism and Developmental Disorders 10*, 67–73.

Sukhodolsky, D.G., Scahill, L., Gadow, G.D., *et al.* (2008) 'Parent-rated anxiety symptoms in children with pervasive developmental disorders: Frequency and association with core autism symptoms and cognitive functioning.' *Journal of Abnormal Child Psychology 36*, 117–128.

Sullivan, H.S. (1953) *The Interpersonal Theory of Psychiatry.* New York, NY: WW Norton.

Sullivan, P. and Knutson, J. (2000) 'Maltreatment and disabilities: a population-based epidemiological study.' *Child Abuse & Neglect 24*, 1257–1273.

Szatmari, P., MacLean, J.E., Jones, M., Bryson, S.E., Zwaigenbaum, L. and Bartolucci, G. (2000) 'The familial aggregation of the lesser variant in biological and nonbiological relatives of PDD probands: a family history study.' *Journal of Child Psychology and Psychiatry 41*, 579–586.

Tolman, D. (2002) *Dilemmas of Desire. Teenage Girls talk about Sexuality.* Cambridge, MA: Harvard University Press.

Tsai, L.Y. and Beisler, J.M. (1983) 'The development of sex differences in infantile autism.' *British Journal of Psychiatry 142*, 373–378.

Tsai, L., Stewart, M.A. and August, G. (1981) 'Implication of sex differences in the familial transmission of infantile autism.' *Journal of Autism and Developmental Disorders 11*, 165–173.

Twenge, J.M. and Nolen-Hoeksema, S. (2002) 'Age, gender, race, socioeconomic status, and birth cohort differences on the Children's Depression Inventory: a meta-analysis.' *Journal of Abnormal Psychology 111*, 578–588.

Van Bourgondien, M.E., Reichle, N.C. and Palmer, A. (1997) 'Sexual behavior in adults with autism.' *Journal of Autism and Developmental Disorders 27*, 113–125.

Varley, J.A., Estes, A. and Dawson, G. (2007) 'Sex Differences in Autism Endophenotypes.' Poster presented at the International Meeting for Autism Research, Seattle, WA, May 3–5.

Verbalis, A.D., Sutera, S., Boorstein, H.C., *et al.* (2006) 'Sex Differences in Toddlers with Autism Spectrum Disorders.' Poster presented at the International Meeting for Autism Research, Montreal, Canada, June 1–3.

Vickerstaff, S., Heriot, S., Wong, M., Lopes, A. and Dossetor, D. (2007) 'Intellectual ability, self-perceived social competence, and depressive symptomatology in children with high-functioning autistic spectrum disorders.' *Journal of Autism and Developmental Disorders 37*, 1647–1664.

Volkmar, F.R., Szatmari, P. and Sparrow, S.S. (1993) 'Sex differences in pervasive developmental disorders.' *Journal of Autism and Developmental Disorders 23*, 579–591.

Waschbusch, D.A., King, S. and Northern Partners in Action for Children and Youth. (2006) 'Should sex-specific norms be used to assess attention-deficit hyperactivity disorder (ADHD) or oppositional defiant disorder (ODD)?' *Journal of Consulting and Clinical Psychology 74*, 179–185.

Wing, L. (1981) 'Sex ratios in early childhood autism and related conditions.' *Psychiatry Research* 5, 129–37.

World Health Organization. (2004) 'Sexual health—a new focus for WHO.' *Progress in Reproductive Health Research 67.* Accessed on March 26, 2008 at www.who.int/reproductive-health/hrp/progress/67.pdf

Zucker, N.L. LaBar, K.S., Losh, M., Bulik, C.M., Piven, J. and Pelphry, K.A. (2007) 'Anorexia nervosa and autism spectrum disorders: guided investigation of social cognitive endophenotypes.' *Psychological Bulletin 33*, 976–1006.

Subject Index

Author Index